A TEXT BOOK OF

ENGINEERING GEOLOGY

FOR

SEMESTER - II

SECOND YEAR DEGREE COURSE IN CIVIL ENGINEERING

AS PER NEW REVISED SYLLABUS OF NORTH MAHARASHTRA UNIVERSITY

(EFFECTIVE FROM ACADEMIC YEAR : 2013-2014)

Dr. PRAKASH RAO
Ph. D.
Consultant Geologist
Most Experienced & Eminent Professor,
Pune.

RAVIRAJ R. SORATE
B.E. (Civil), M. Tech (Geotech)
Assistant Professor (Civil Deptt.)
Singhad Academy of Engineering,
Kondhwa, Pune

N3081

ENGINEERING GEOLOGY (S.E. CIVIL, NMU)　　　　　　　　　ISBN 978-93-83971-09-1
First Edition : January 2014
© : Authors

　　The text of this publication, or any part thereof, should not be reproduced or transmitted in any form or stored in any computer storage system or device for distribution including photocopy, recording, taping or information retrieval system or reproduced on any disc, tape, perforated media or other information storage device etc., without the written permission of Authors with whom the rights are reserved. Breach of this condition is liable for legal action.

　　Every effort has been made to avoid errors or omissions in this publication. In spite of this, errors may have crept in. Any mistake, error or discrepancy so noted and shall be brought to our notice shall be taken care of in the next edition. It is notified that neither the publisher nor the authors or seller shall be responsible for any damage or loss of action to any one, of any kind, in any manner, therefrom.

Published By :　　　　　　　　　　　　　　　　　　　　　　　　　　　**Printed at**
NIRALI PRAKASHAN　　　　　　　　　　　　　　　　　　　**Repro Knowledgecast Limited**
Abhyudaya Pragati, 1312, Shivaji Nagar,　　　　　　　　　　　　　　　　　　　**India**
Off J.M. Road, PUNE – 411005
Tel - (020) 25512336/37/39, Fax - (020) 25511379
Email : niralipune@pragationline.com

DISTRIBUTION CENTRES
PUNE

Nirali Prakashan　　　　　　　　　　　　　　　　　*Nirali Prakashan*
119, Budhwar Peth, Jogeshwari Mandir Lane　　　　　S. No. 28/25, Dhyari,
Pune 411002, Maharashtra　　　　　　　　　　　　Near Pari Company, Pune 411041
Tel : (020) 2445 2044, 66022708, Fax : (020) 2445 1538　　Tel : (020) 24690204 Fax : (020) 24690316
Email : bookorder@pragationline.com　　　　　　　　Email : dhyari@pragationline.com
　　　　　　　　　　　　　　　　　　　　　　　　　　　　　　bookorder@pragationline.com

MUMBAI
Nirali Prakashan
385, S.V.P. Road, Rasdhara Co-op. Hsg. Society Ltd.,
Girgaum, Mumbai 400004, Maharashtra
Tel : (022) 2385 6339 / 2386 9976, Fax : (022) 2386 9976
Email : niralimumbai@pragationline.com

DISTRIBUTION BRANCHES

NAGPUR　　　　　　　　　　　　　　　　　　　**JALGAON**
Pratibha Book Distributors　　　　　　　　　　　　*Nirali Prakashan*
Above Maratha Mandir, Shop No. 3, First Floor,　　　34, V. V. Golani Market, Navi Peth, Jalgaon 425001,
Rani Jhanshi Square, Sitabuldi, Nagpur 440012,　　　Maharashtra, Tel : (0257) 222 0395
Maharashtra, Tel : (0712) 254 7129　　　　　　　　Mob : 94234 91860

BENGALURU　　　　　　　　　　　　　　　　　**KOLHAPUR**
Pragati Book House　　　　　　　　　　　　　　　*Nirali Prakashan*
House No. 1, Sanjeevappa Lane, Avenue Road Cross,　New Mahadvar Road,
Opp. Rice Church, Bengaluru – 560002.　　　　　　Kedar Plaza, 1st Floor Opp. IDBI Bank
Tel : (080) 64513344, 64513355,　　　　　　　　　Kolhapur 416 012, Maharashtra. Mob : 9855046155
Mob : 9880582331, 9845021552
Email:bharatsavla@yahoo.com

CHENNAI
Pragati Books
9/1, Montieth Road, Behind Taas Mahal, Egmore,
Chennai 600008 Tamil Nadu, Tel : (044) 6518 3535,
Mob : 94440 01782 / 98450 21552 / 98805 82331, Email : bharatsavla@yahoo.com

RETAIL OUTLETS
PUNE

Pragati Book Centre　　　　　　　　　　　　　　*Pragati Book Centre*
157, Budhwar Peth, Opp. Ratan Talkies,　　　　　　676/B, Budhwar Peth, Opp. Jogeshwari Mandir,
Pune 411002, Maharashtra　　　　　　　　　　　Pune 411002, Maharashtra
Tel : (020) 2445 8887 / 6602 2707, Fax : (020) 2445 8887　Tel : (020) 6601 7784 / 6602 0855

Pragati Book Centre　　　　　　　　　　　　　　*PBC Book Sellers & Stationers*
Amber Chamber, 28/A, Budhwar Peth,　　　　　　152, Budhwar Peth, Pune 411002, Maharashtra
Appa Balwant Chowk, Pune : 411002, Maharashtra,　Tel : (020) 2445 2254 / 6609 2463
Tel : (020) 20240335 / 66281669
Email : pbcpune@pragationline.com

MUMBAI
Pragati Book Corner
Indira Niwas, 111 - A, Bhavani Shankar Road, Dadar (W), Mumbai 400028, Maharashtra
Tel : (022) 2422 3526 / 6662 5254, Email : pbcmumbai@pragationline.com

PREFACE

It gives us immense pleasure to present this book on **Engineering Geology** to the students of second year (S.E. Civil) degree course in Engineering of North Maharashtra Univeristy, Jalgaon.

The book is concerned with the different aspects and principles of geological science and also with the systematic description of various applications primarily related to civil engineering projects. It gives an introduction to geology and especially the properties and behaviour of the rocks. The book is intended essentially for advanced undergraduates or graduate students.

A large number of excellent books have been written on engineering geology, some of which are listed in bibliography. Thus, the authors do not claim any originality. The book is divided into two sections. The first section attempts to introduce engineering students to general geology including mineralogy, petrology, surface processes, structural geology and historic geology. The second section is a compilation of several topics on the interlink between geology and engineering. It includes information on site investigation, dams, tunnels, soils and engineering properties of geologic material. It is estimated that civilization receives a great set back every year from the geologic hazards. This book incorporates useful information on earthquakes, landslides, volcanoes and induced hazards.

Geology is a fascinating science in which emphasis is always given on field investigations. However, it is difficult to predict precisely how a given set of geologic material will behave in a specific engineering problem. Therefore, in this field the most important requisites are experience, analytical ability and wisdom.

The authors are very much greatful to Shri. Dineshbhai Furia & Jigneshbhai Furia of Nirali Prakashan and Shri. M. P. Munde whose efforts are responsible for publication of this text. Our special thanks to Mr. Santosh, Mrs. Roshan Khan, Mrs. Prachi Sawant, Shri. Pandya and other staff for their tireless efforts. Last but not least authors are greatful to family members and Well wishers.

Despite of our best efforts, it is possible that some errors have escaped our attention. We would gratefully acknowledge if only of these is pointed out. Also any suggestions and comments for further improvement of the book would be greatefully received and acknowledge.

1st January 2014   **AUTHORS**

SYLLABUS

UNIT 1 : MINERALOGY AND PETROLOGY (7 Hours, 16 Marks)

1. Introduction to the subject : Objects, scope, rock forming minerals, primary and secondary minerals.

2. Silicate and non-silicate minerals, felsic and mafic minerals, essential and accessories minerals.

3. Origin, texture, structure, classification of igneous rocks, secondary rocks, metamorphic rocks and their engineering applications.

4. Study of common rock types prescribed in practical work.

UNIT – II : STRUCTURAL GEOLOGY, PLATE TECTONICS AND GROUND WAETR (8 Hours, 16 Marks)

(a) Structural geology : Outcrop, dip and strike, conformeable series, unconformity and overlap.

(b) Faults and their types, folds and their types, inliers and outliers.

(c) Structural features resulted due to igneous intrusions, concordant and discordant igneous intrusions.

(d) Joints and their types and introduction to plate tectonics.

(e) Water table and depth zones, relation between surface relief and water table, perched water table.

(d) Natural springs and seepages, contact, springs, hot springs and geysers, artesian wells.

UNIT III : GEOMORPHOLOGY, HISTORICAL GEOLOGY AND BUILDING STONES (8 Hours, 16 Marks)

(a) Geomorphology : geological action of river, rejuvenation, land forms resulted due to river erosion, deposition and rejuvenation.

(b) Physiographic divisions of India and their characteristics, geological history of peninsula, study of formations in peninsula and the significance of their structural characters in major civil engineering activities.

(c) Requirements of good building stones, engineering properties of rocks, availability of blocks of suitable size and appearance on mineral composition, textures, structures.

(d) Earthquake and its causes, classification, seismic zones of India and geological consideration for construction of building.

UNIT IV : PRELIMINARY GEOLOGICAL STUDIES, REMOTE FUNCTION, GEO PHYSICAL EXPLORATION (8 Hours, 16 Marks)

(a) Verification of surface data by subsurface exploration, drill holes, test pits, trenches, exploratory tunnels, shafts, adits, drifts etc.

(b) Compilation and interpretation of information obtained from these, correlation of surface data with results of subsurface exploration.

(c) Limitations of drilling, comparative reliability of data obtained by drilling and excavation.

(d) Engineering significance of geological structures such as stratification, dips, folds, faults, joints, crush zones, fault zones, dykes etc.

(e) Landslides and its causes, preventive measures and case studies.

(f) Principles of geo physical exploration methods for sub surface survey.

UNIT V : ROLE OF ENGINEERING GEOLOGY IN DAMS AND TUNNELING (8 Hours, 16 Marks)

(a) Preliminary geological investigation form tunnels, important geological consideration while choosing alignment.

(b) Role of groundwater, geological conditions likely to be troublesome, suitability of common rock type for tunneling, unlined tunnels, case studies.

(c) Geological requirements for construction of dams and geological structures influence of geological condition on the choice of type and design of dam.

(d) Preliminary geological work on dam sites, favourable and unsuitable geological conditions for locating a dam, precaution to be taken to counteract unsuitable condition.

(e) Treatment of leaky rocks, faults, dykes, crush zones, joints, fractures, unfavorable dips etc. and case studies.

•••

CONTENTS

Unit – I : Mineralogy and Petrology 1.1 – 1.62

Unit – II : Structural Geology, Plate Tectonics and Ground Water 2.1 – 2.66

Unit – III : Geomorphology, Historical Geology and Building Stones 3.1 – 3.106

Unit – IV : Preliminary Geological Studies, Remote Function, Geophysical Exploration 4.1 – 4.64

Unit – V : Role of Engineering Geology in Dams and Tunneling 5.1 – 5.22

•••

Unit 1
MINERALOGY AND PETROLOGY

PART (A) : GENERAL GEOLOGY

1.1 THE PLANET EARTH

The planet earth is a dynamic planet, only of its kind in the solar system. It shows presence of four-fold envelope : atmosphere, hydrosphere, lithosphere and biosphere.

Atmosphere : It consists of gases predominantly nitrogen, oxygen, carbon dioxide and water vapour. The planet earth is unique in this sense because no other planet has such an atmosphere.

Hydrosphere : In the earth's atmosphere are white clouds of condensed water vapours. The clouds are formed due to evaporation of water from hydrosphere, which consists of oceans, streams, lakes, ground water, ice sheets, glaciers etc. Other planets have hydrosphere, but the planet earth has a hydrosphere consisting of water, ice and water vapour.

Lithosphere : It is the uppermost 100 kilometres layer from the earth. It exhibits presence of varieties of rocks of different origin which have been subjected to weathering and erosion due to their exposure to the atmosphere, hydrosphere and biosphere. As a result, the surface of the earth displays numerous topographic expressions. Lithosphere behaves in a dynamic manner and its behaviour is heterogeneous in nature. Thus, at some places, lithosphere is prone to volcanic eruptions and earthquakes. The study of these factors is a very fascinating subject.

Biosphere : The earth is the only planet on which life has flourished. The biosphere includes innumerable large and small living beings, grouped into million of species.

1.2 INTERNAL STRUCTURE OF THE EARTH

Planet earth contains three compositional layers (Fig. 1.1). At the centre is the dense most of these three layers, the *core*. The core is a spherical mass, composed mainly of metallic iron, with minor amounts of nickel and other elements.

The thick shell that surrounds the core is called the *mantle*. It is less dense than the core, but denser than the outermost layer. Above the mantle lies the thinnest and outermost layer, the *crust*.

It is seen from Fig. 1.1 that the core and mantle have almost uniform thickness. However, the crust differs in thickness from place to place. The crust beneaths the oceans, the oceanic crust, has an average thickness of 8 kilometres, while the continental crust has an average thickness of 45 kilometres. It shows variation in thickness from 30 to 70 kilometres [Fig. 1.1 (b)]. Details of internal structure of the earth are discussed in section 6.10.

In addition to compositional layering, other changes including changes in physical properties also occur within the earth. These are largely controlled by temperature and pressure, rather than rock composition. The places where changes in physical properties do not coincide with the compositional boundaries, are shown in Fig. 1.1.

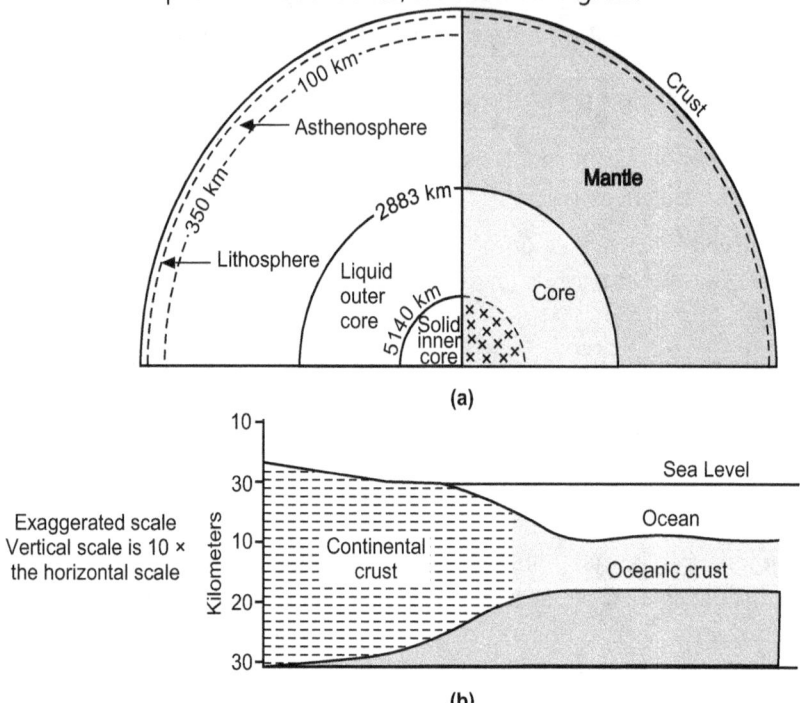

Fig. 1.1 : The structure of earth (a) Section through the earth showing compositional and physical stratification, (b) Detail of the crust.

Within the core exists an inner region where iron is interpreted to be in solid state despite of very high temperature. This solid centre of the earth is called *inner core*. It is believed that the solid state of the iron is due to presence of very high pressure. Surrounding inner core is a zone of outer core where temperature and pressure are balanced in such a way that iron is molten and behaves like a liquid.

Similarly, difference in temperature and pressure divides the mantle and crust into three distinct regions : the mesosphere, the asthenosphere and the lithosphere. (Fig. 1.1 (a)).

In the lower part of the mantle, the rock has a considerable strength despite of very high temperature (from 2883 km to 350 km). This solid region of high strength and temperature is called the *mesosphere* (intermediate or middle sphere).

Within the upper mantle i.e. from 350 km to about 100 km, is a region called the *asthenosphere* (weak sphere). Here the rocks are weak and easily deformed like butter.

Above the asthenosphere, i.e. the uppermost region of 100 km, is called the *lithosphere* (rock sphere) where rocks are cooler, stronger and rigid than plastic asthenosphere. The lithosphere is not a homogeneous continuous layer. Instead it is broken into a number of larger or smaller plates.

1.3 MAJOR FEATURES OF THE EARTH'S SURFACE

The earth's surface is made of diversified features of limitless sizes and shapes which are classified into several orders on the basis of their scales. Features of the highest order are seen only with the help of satellite images or may be identified on the world map. These cover an area of several million square kilometres and are the products of internal earth processes, for example, continents, oceans, major mountain chains, rift valleys etc. Features of intermediate order cover an area of several hundred square kilometres. They are formed due to earth's external processes controlled by climatic conditions and also originated due to earth's internal processes, for example, San Andreas fault, river terraces, tectonic landforms etc. Features of the lower order can be easily recognised on aerial photographs or on topo sheets having a scale 1 : 25,000, for example, a meandering steam, soil horizons etc. The features of different orders are summarised in Table 1.1

Table 1.1 : Major features of the Earth's surface

Order	Area	Landforms
(1) Highest Order :		
I	100×10^6 km^2	Continents and oceans.
II	10^6 km^2	Plate boundaries, ocean ridges, trenches, fold mountain chains.
III	10^2 to 10^4 km^2	Rift valleys.
(2) Intermediate Order :		
IV	10 km^2	San Andreas fault, large folds, river basins.
V	10^2 m^2	River deposits, alluvium.
(3) Lowest Order :		
VI	1 to 10^2 m^2	Meandering stream.
VII	10 cm^2	Soil horizons, weathering.

From the above table, it can be said that the features are prominently formed due to the earth's internal and external processes. The external processes can be visualised by considering weathering erosion and deposition caused by the work of natural agencies including running water, wind, glaciers and sea. The internal processes may be explained with the concept of plate tectonics, the most important discovery in the 20th century.

The major features of the earth show that about 71% of the earth's surface is covered by oceans and their average depth is 3800 metres. The depth is extremely variable and maximum depth, 11035 metres, is recorded at **Mariana Trench**, in the **western Pacific**. (Fig. 1.2).

The remaining 29% of the earth's surface is occupied by land. It has an average elevation of 800 metres above mean sea level. The surface of continents is constantly modified by weathering and erosion. Thus, the surface morphology is dissected in a very complicated manner. The maximum elevation, 8848 metres, is recorded at Mount Everest, Nepal. (Fig. 1.2)

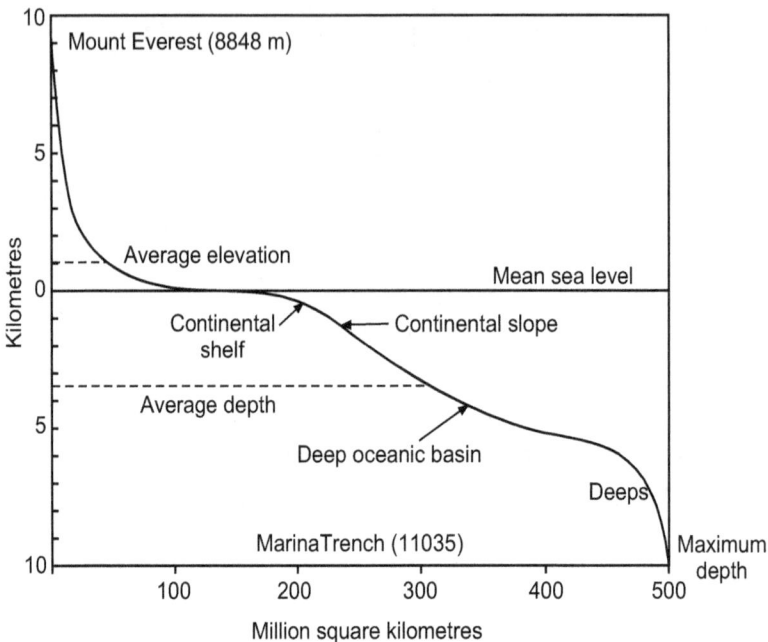

Fig. 1.2 : Hypsographic curve

Modern coastal lines do not coincide exactly with the boundaries between continental and oceanic crust. The boundaries are covered by oceanic water and the present day boundaries are actually all the continents. Thus, each continent is surrounded by a gently dipping continental shelf. With the changes in slope, continental shelf passes into continental slope, which may be considered as a bottom of continental surface. If we take this as a boundary of the continents, then it is estimated that about 60% of the earth's surface is occupied by the oceanic basins while the remaining 40% is covered by continents. Thus, 10% of the continental crust is occupied by oceanic water.

The continental rise lies at the base of continental slope. It is a region of gently changing slope where the floor of oceanic basin meets the margin of the continents. The rise is actually a part of oceanic basin and is generally covered by a thick pile of erosional debris derived from adjacent continent.

Beyond the continental slope and rise, lies the deep oceanic floor which exhibit two prominent features i.e. oceanic ridges (mid – oceanic ridges), and long narrow trenches.

Most important topographic expression of oceanic basins is the large flat areas known as *abyssal plains*. They generally are found at depths of 3 to 6 km below the sea level and range in width from 200 to 2000 km.

1.4 INTERNAL AND EXTERNAL PROCESSES

Energy from the sun reaches the earth as heat rays. Approximately 60% of the sun's heat is absorbed by the land, the sea or the atmosphere. The heat absorbed by the sea increases temperature of water and promote evaporation which forms clouds and ultimately rain, snow or hails. Similarly, the heat absorbed by the land increases temperature of the exposed rocks and soil. The above two initiate the process of weathering and erosion. Warm seawater, warm rocks and soils heat the air. Warmed air expands, becomes less dense and rises. On the other hand, cool air flows into and occupies the place of the rising air. Flowing air is wind, and as wind blows over the sea, it produces waves. Thus, it can be said that the surface processes are produced by the energy received from the sun.

Some parts of the earth are prone to earthquakes and volcanic eruptions. Origin of these is related to interior of the earth. Similarly, in the case of deeper mines, temperature increases with increase in depth. Careful measurements made in deeper mines and bore holes around the world suggest that temperature increases with depth, known as *geothermal gradient* which varies from 15°C/km to 75°C/km from place to place (Fig. 1.28), average geothermal gradient is 30°C/km.

1.5 CHEMICAL COMPOSITION OF THE CRUST

The upper surface of the earth is known as *crust*. The composition of crust is given in Table 1.2. It is seen that out of 80 stable elements, more than 99% of the crust is composed of only eight major elements.

Table 1.2 : Major elements in the continental crust

Element	Symbol	Volume per cent	Weight per cent
Oxygen	O	94.27	46.40
Silicon	Si	0.88	28.15
Aluminium	Al	0.47	8.23
Iron	Fe	0.48	5.63
Magneisum	Mg	0.58	4.15
Calcium	Ca	0.68	2.36
Potassium	K	1.65	2.33
Sodium	Na	0.99	2.09
		100.00	99.34

1.6 THE ROCK CYCLE

Based on their origin, three major divisions of rock are recognised :

(1) **Igneous Rocks :** (igneous meaning fire) Igneous rocks are the product of consolidation of magma.

(2) **Sedimentary Rocks :** Sedimentary rocks are the weathering products of pre-existing rocks deposited near the earth's surface by wind, water, ice and biological activities.

(3) **Metamorphic Rocks :** (Meta meaning change, and morphe meaning form, thus change of form). Metamorphic rocks are those rocks of which original form has been changed as a result of rise in temperature, pressure or both.

Much of geology is concerned with the interactions among the forces that produce these three rock types. The relationship can be explained with the help of rock cycle. (Fig. 1.3)

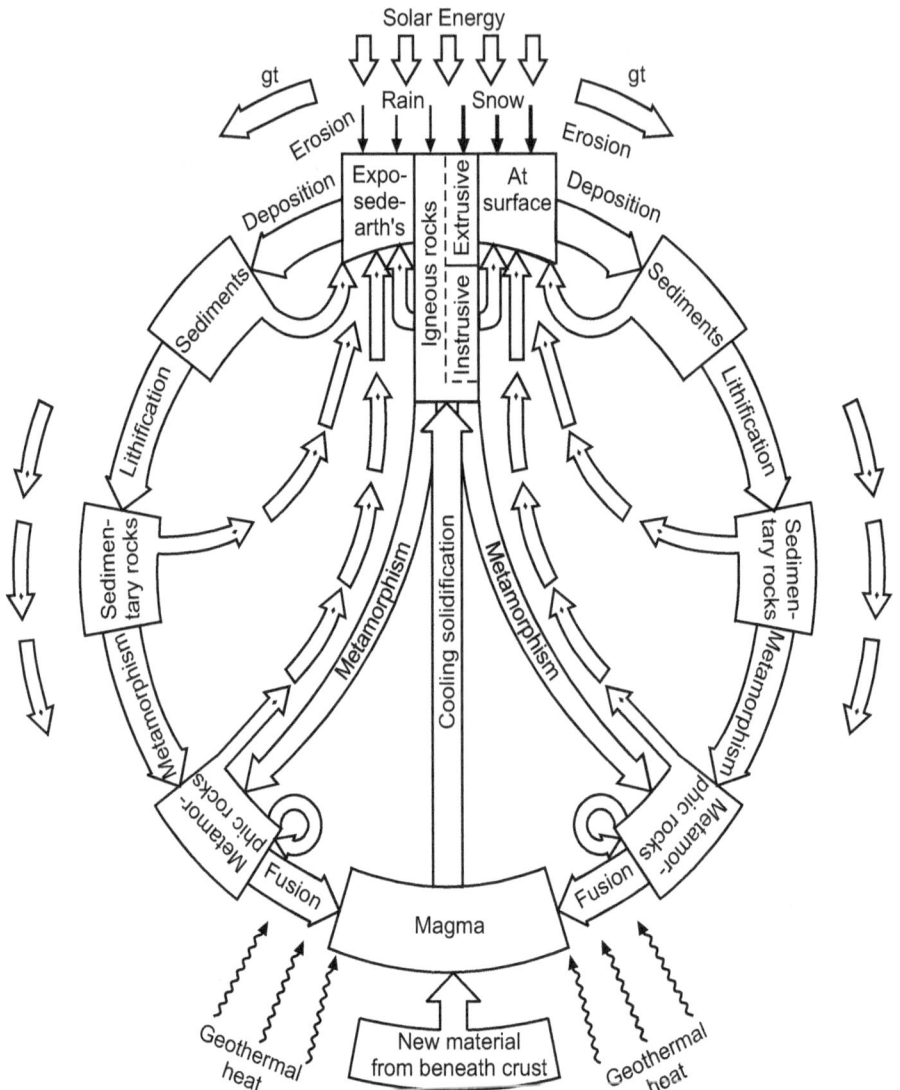

Fig. 1.3 : The rock cycle

In simple terms, igneous rocks are eroded, forming sediment and solution load which are deposited and become sedimentary rocks. Burial may lead to change in temperature and pressure forming metamorphic rocks. Eventually, temperature and pressure may rise so high that rock melts and forms new magma. The magma rises, forms new igneous rocks and the cycle is completed. Thus, any new type of rock may be formed from parent igneous, sedimentary and metamorphic rocks.

1.7 CATASTROPHISM

The new idea of catastrophism is based on the fact that geologic and geomorphic features were the result of cumulative and slow change by natural processes operating at relatively constant rates. The term natural implies that the processes are related to the internal and external surfaces of the earth and they are bounded by the laws of nature. The type and rate of processes active today have remained active throughout geological time. For example, occurrence of earthquakes /volcanic erruptions etc.

The term 'catastrophism' indicates large magnitude or sudden events that modify the pre-existing landscapes. It can be divided into two parts. The first implies a rare event or frequent events of large magnitude (for example, a coastal storm), while the second concept implies some sudden change that will not easily revert back to the pre-catastrophic state, for example, an earthquake of high magnitude like, Tokyo earthquake, 1923.

1.8 BRANCHES OF GEOLOGY

The 'Geological Science' can be studied from different view points. Each aspect is considered as an arm of geology and thus geology is divided into different arms/branches. :

(1) **Petrology :** An important branch of geology that deals with the occurrence, origin and history of rocks is known as *petrology*. The knowledge of basic properties of rocks and minerals constituting the earth's crust is necessary in geotechnical studies.

(2) **Geomorphology/Physical Geology :** This is a study of the processes that activate at or beneath the surface of the earth and the material on which those processes operate. The aspects of geomorphology are discussed in Unit-3.

(3) **Structural Geology :** This is a branch of geology devoted to the study of rock deformation and geometry of rocks (Unit-2).

(4) **Historical Geology :** Study of the chronology of the earth's past events, both biological and physical (Unit-3 (b)) is covered in this branch.

(5) **Hydrogeology :** This is the geological aspect of surface and subsurface water. This aspect is very important in deciding stability of many civil engineering operations (Unit-6 (b)).

(6) **Geophysics :** This branch deals with the study of the application of the methods of physics to the properties of rocks and soils. (Partly discussed in Unit – 4).

(7) **Pedology :** It is also known as soil science which is a study of the uppermost layers of the earth's crust.

(8) **Engineering Geology :** This branch is concerned with the application of geology to various engineering operations.

PART (B) : PETROLOGY

Petrology is the science of rocks, (petros - rock, logos - science). It deals with the mode of occurrence, composition, classification and origin of rocks and their relation to the geological processes and history of the earth.

1.9 DEFINITION OF ROCK

A rock is an aggregate of minerals. It may be made up of one mineral i.e. monomineralic, or it may consist of different minerals i.e. polymineralic.

Rocks, on the basis of their origin, are broadly divided into three major classes viz., Igneous, Sedimentary and Metamorphic Rocks.

(1) Igneous Rocks : Rocks crystallised from hot magmatic material (lava) are called *igneous* or *primary rocks*.

(2) Sedimentary Rocks : Rocks exposed to surface are attacked by weathering agents. The disintegrated and decomposed material is transported into lakes, oceans by running water, wind, glaciers. The accumulated material on compaction and cementation turns into secondary rocks. These are also called as *sedimentary rocks*.

(3) Metamorphic Rocks : Rocks which are deeply buried may be subjected to high temperature and pressure under the influence of chemically active fluids. This new environment brings out a change in the mineralogical and structural characters of the parent rocks. These altered rocks are called *metamorphic rocks*.

It is estimated that the lithosphere is prominently composed of igneous and metamorphic rocks (95%) and only a small portion (5%) of the entire bulk is made up of sedimentary rocks. On the other hand, about 75% of the earth's surface is covered by sedimentary rocks and only 25% is occupied by igneous and metamorphic rocks. (Fig. 1.4)

1.9.1 Percentage of Rock Types in the Crust

Relative proportion of three major types of rocks may be measured by considering either weight percentage [Fig. 1.4 (a)] or volume percentage i.e. area occupied [Fig. 1.4 (b)].

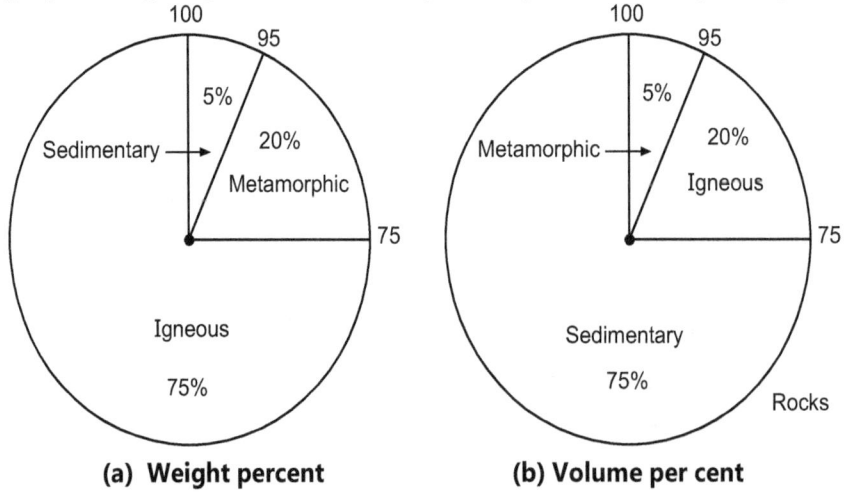

(a) Weight percent (b) Volume per cent

Fig. 1.4 : Relative proportion of rocks

From the above Fig. 1.4, it is seen that major bulk of the crust is occupied by igneous (75%) and metamorphic (20%) rocks, while sedimentary rock (5%) forms a thin cover at or near the surface. On the contrary, the sedimentary rocks cover 75% of the surface, while igneous (20%) and metamorphic (5%) rocks occupy very less area.

When the rocks are studied in the laboratory, as handspecimens, with a view to analyse and discuss their texture, mineral composition, chemical composition etc., the study is called as **petrography**, while **petrogenesis** includes the study of origin and processes of formation of different rocks. Petrology is a broad term that includes both petrography and petrogenesis.

1.10 MINERALOGY

Rocks are made up of different minerals that are arranged in various ways. Before going into the details of the rocks, we must, therefore, know something about rock forming minerals.

Definition of a mineral : A mineral is a naturally formed inorganic solid substance which possesses a definite chemical composition or a definite range of chemical composition and a definite atomic structure. (Fig. 1.5)

The last statement indicates that the atoms are arranged in a definite three dimensional pattern, characteristic of individual mineral group. Similarly, atoms of several elements of similar size may be able to replace one another in the pattern. This may be well illustrated by the example of Graphite and Diamond, they both are made of carbon. But their properties are quite different due to their arrangement of carbon atoms. Bonding between the carbon atoms is weaker in graphite than in diamond. The structure of graphite is leaf like, made up of flat hexagonal nets, so that mineral easily splits into parallel flakes. On the other hand, diamond crystallizes in cubic system and thus bonding in the structure is very strong.

	Arrangement of silica tetrahedra	Formulae of the complex anions	Typical mineral	
			Name	Composition
Isolated tetrahedra		$(SiO_4)^{-4}$	The Olivine family	$(Mg, Fe)_2SiO_4$
Isolated Polymerized groups		$(Si_2O_7)^{-6}$	Lawsonite	$CaAl_2Si_2O_7(OH)_2H_2O$
		$(Si_3O_9)^{-6}$	Wollastonite	$Ca_3Si_3O_9$
		$(Si_6O_{18})^{-12}$	Beryl	$Be_3Al_2Si_6O_{18}$

Continuous chains	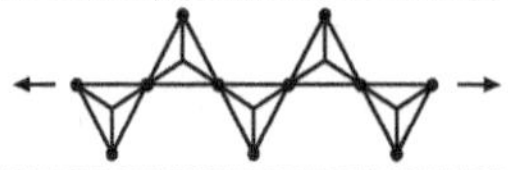	$(SiO_3)_n^{-2}$	The pyroxene family	$(Fe, Mg)Si_3$
	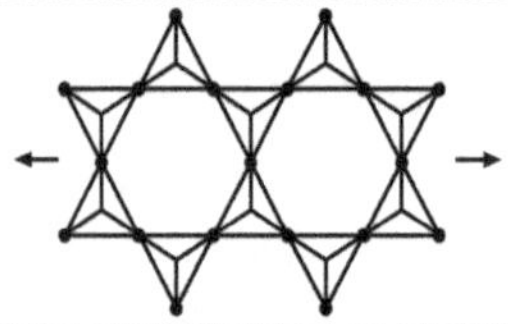	$(Si_4O_{11})_n^{-6}$	The amphibole family	$Ca_2Mg_5(Si_4O_{11})_2(OH)_2$
Continuous sheets	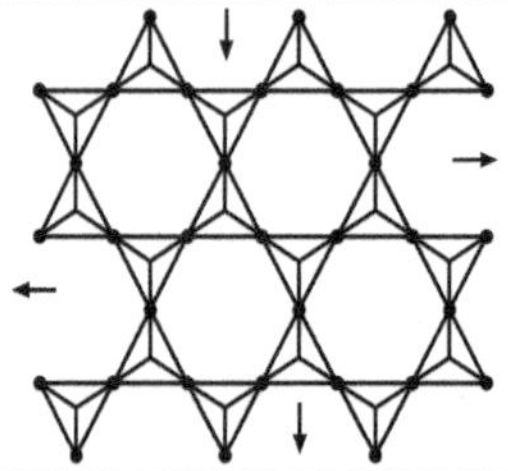	$(Si_4O_{10})_n^{-4}$	The mica family	$KAl_2(Si_3Al)_{10}(OH)_2$
Three dimensional networks	Too complex to be shown by a simple two dimensional drawing	SiO_2	Quartz	SiO_2

Fig. 1.5 : Sharing of oxygen produces different classes and composition of silicate minerals

1.10.1 Identification of Minerals

The definition of a mineral suggests that minerals can be identified in several ways.

Minerals have fixed chemical compositions which means that ordinary methods of chemical analysis can be used to identify minerals. But certain minerals, though possess identical chemical compositions, have very different internal structures, e.g. graphite and diamond. The problem of identification may be solved by using simpler techniques or with the help of certain visual observations, called as *physical properties*, supplemented by spot chemical tests, if required.

The physical properties include colour, lustre, crystal form, hardness, the act of spliting, fracture, fluorescence, specific gravity etc.

Colour : The term colour indicates colour of a fresh, unaltered surface. It is often useful and most diagnostic character. However, many a times the same mineral may show a wide colour variation e.g. Quartz. Quartz commonly occurs colourless when it has a composition SiO_2, but the presence of certain impurities substantially change the colour of quartz. For example, titanium gives violet colour for amathyst, manganese produces rose quartz, iron gives deep red jaspar. Similarly, Corundum, Al_2O_3 is white to colourless, but presence of a small amount of chromium produces deep red colour of ruby, while a little titanium and iron give cornflower blue of sapphire. Thus, a pure mineral possesses its own inherent colour but presence of impurities changes its colour.

Streak : Streak is the colour of the powdered mineral, and may be obtained by rubbing the mineral on a streak plate or any piece of unglazed porcelain. The streak may be of a very different colour from the mineral colour. For example, brass-yellow chalcopyrite gives a greenish-black streak, the minerals magnetite, limonite and haematite are reddish-black in colour, while the streak of haematite is cherry-red; magnetite has a brown-black streak and limonite has a yellow-brown streak.

Lustre : Lustre is the way, a mineral reflects light, and it depends on the quantity and quality of the reflected light. Lustre is independent of the colour of the mineral. The intensity of lustre is influenced by transparency, reflectivity and surface structure of the mineral. Thus, a clear distinction in lustre shown by quartz and that of opaque mineral like galena may easily be made.

Following are the kinds of lustre recognised :

(1) **Metallic :** These minerals are opaque as no light is transmitted through the substance, e.g. Galena.

(2) **Sub-metallic :** Lustre shown by semi-opaque metal oxides e.g. Rutile, Chromite etc.

(3) **Vitreous :** Lustre shown by broken glass, commonly exhibited by silicate minerals e.g. Quartz, Feldspar.

(4) **Resinous :** Similar to lustre seen in resin, e.g. sphalerite.

(5) **Pearly :** Play of colours e.g. Talc.

(6) **Silky :** A lustre shown by fibrous minerals, e.g. Gypsum, Asbestos.

(7) **Almandine :** Brilliant surface e.g. Diamond.

(8) **Dull :** No lustre, surface is very dull and thus a complete lack of reflection e.g. Magnesite.

Cleavage : Cleavage is a naturally occurring weak plane along which splitting is most easy. The cleavage plane is the one in which the atoms are closely packed and which is separated from its parallel neighbours. Note that cleavage is a direction, therefore, one cleavage direction will, in general, produce two cleavage surfaces. A mineral may show one, two, three or four sets of weak plane.

e.g. : Mica   - One set - basal cleavage.

Feldspar - Two sets – roughly at 90°.

Calcite   - Three sets - at 60° or 120°.

Fluorite - Four sets.

Form : All crystalline substances crystallize in one of six crystal systems. The solid forms bounded by plane surfaces arranged in symmetrical and regular manner are called *crystals*. These crystal faces are parallel to planes in the atomic structure in which the atoms are closely packed. The arrangement of the faces in a crystal is an expression of the internal atomic structure and its uniformity gives symmetry to the crystal.

However, minerals seldom develop a perfect shape bounded by equally developed plane faces. Minerals showing good form are known as idiomorphic or euhedral, e.g. calcite. On the other hand, a majority of the minerals occur in aggregates of many kinds and they are known as *allotriomorphic* or *anhedral*.

Three major groups are recognised which may further show different types of aggregates as follows :

(1) Aggregates in which crystal growth is prominent along one direction compared to other directions. Some of the types of such aggregates are listed below :

(a) **Accicular :** Development of long needle like crystals, e.g. Asbestos, Zeolites.

(b) **Bladed :** Elongation along one direction and a flattening along a second, platy appearance, e.g. Kyanite.

(c) **Columnar :** Appearance like a slender column, e.g. Beryl.

(d) **Fibrous :** Columns are long and hair like, e.g. Gypsum and Asbestos.

(e) **Foliaceous :** Excessive development parallel to a particular crystal face associated with the appearance of a strong cleavage e.g. Mica.

(f) **Radiating :** Radial growth from a centre e.g. Stilbite.

(g) **Reticulate :** Honeycomb appearance.

(2) Aggregates in which crystal growth is more in two directions and less in third direction. Such a form is known as **tabular**, e.g. Orthoclase, dolomite.

(3) Crystal growth is **equidimensional**, a few common forms are as below :

(a) **Cubic :** e.g. Galena.

(b) **Rhombohedral :** e.g. Calcite.

(c) **Reniform :** Kidney shaped masses, e.g. Haematite.

(d) **Botryoidal :** Aggregate of spheroidal units like a bunch of grapes, e.g. Chalcedony.

(e) **Concretionary :** Spheroidal aggregate, e.g. Limonite.

Besides these, few other terms are used to describe the form of a mineral.

(f) **Massive :** An irregular mass, devoid of any shape, e.g. Magnesite, Baryte.

(g) **Amygdaloidal :** Presence of cavities.

Hardness : The hardness of a mineral is its resistance to abrasion, which is a measure of its molecular cohesion. It is a difficult property to measure because the amount of force, the shape of the scratches and the relation of the surface tested to the crystal structure will affect the measured hardness.

However, it is usual to make comparative estimates in terms of an arbitrary scale known as Moh's scale of hardness which is as below :

(1) Talc — $Mg_3[Si_4O_{10}](OH)_2$
(2) Gypsum — $CaSO_4 \cdot 2H_2O$
(3) Calcite — $CaCO_3$
(4) Fluorite — CaF_2
(5) Apatite — $Ca_5[PO_4](F, Cl)$
(6) Orthoclase — $KAlSi_3O_8$
(7) Quartz — SiO_2
(8) Topaz — $Al_2[SiO_4](F, OH)_2$
(9) Corundum — Al_2O_3
(10) Diamond — C

The intervals in this scale are not of equal value and that between corundum and diamond is greater than those between other minerals lower in the scale.

A rough estimate of the hardness of minerals that are not included in Moh's scale, may be made in the following way :

(1) The minerals that could be scratched by a finger nail will have hardness between 2 and 3.
(2) The minerals that could be scratched by a copper coin have hardness between 3 and 4.
(3) The minerals that could be scratched by a pen knife have hardness between 5 and 6.

Fracture : Any irregular break, other than cleavage, is called *fracture*. When a mineral has a perfect cleavage, it is difficult to ascertain the character of fractured surface, e.g. Calcite. A number of terms are used to describe fracture.

Even fracture : Smooth surface.

Uneven fracture : A rough irregular surface.

Conchoidal fracture : Surface of a broken glass, e.g. quartz.

Hackley fracture : Surface being covered with sharp points and depressions.

Diaphaneity : Diaphaneity is the relative capacity of substances to absorb or transmit light. Three terms are used to describe this property.

(1) Transparency : An object is seen clearly and distinctly through the crystal, e.g. Iceland Spar (calcite).

(2) Translucency : An object may be seen through the crystal, but the outlines are indistinct, e.g. Rock crystal.

(3) Opaque : Minerals that absorb most of the light and transmit a minimum, e.g. Galena.

Specific Gravity : It is the ratio of the mass of a substance to the mass of an equal volume of water.

$$\text{Specific gravity} = \frac{\text{Weight of sample in air}}{\text{Weight of sample in air} - \text{Weight of sample in water}}$$

In minerals, specific gravity depends on the kind of atomic structure, for example, Diamond, dense packing 3.52, Graphite, loose packing 2.3 (both C).

Calcite, hexagonal, 2.71, Aragonite, orthorhombic, 2.94 (both $CaCO_3$).

The light coloured minerals show lesser specific gravity than the dark coloured minerals.

Other Properties : Besides these, other properties like luminescence, magnetism, electricity, radioactivity, piezoelectricity and tenacity are also used for the identification of minerals elaborated on these.

Table 1.3 : Tenacities of Minerals

Sr. No.	Type of Tenacity	Mineral showing tenacity	Remark
1.	Elastic	Mica	Regains its original position as beding force is removed.
2.	Brittle	Natrolite, Magnesite, Calcite	Crumbles to powder easily.
3.	Malleable	Gold, Silver	Flattens easily in to a sheet, when hammered.
4.	Sectile	Talc graphite	Mineral can be cut with knife easily.

1.10.2 Important Rock Forming Minerals

Out of 2000 minerals recorded, it is estimated that seven families of these minerals make up 99% of the igneous rocks.

The common minerals in sedimentary rocks are quartz, feldspar and a number of new minerals like the clays and the carbonates. Under special conditions, halite and gypsum may be deposited from saline water.

The metamorphic rocks show presence of members of the same families as those of the igneous rocks. In addition, new silicate minerals like garnet, talc, kyanite, chlorite are also formed. The carbonates are the major constituents of metamorphosed limestones.

The major rock forming minerals are as below :

(1) **Silicate minerals :** Quartz, feldspars, micas, amphibole, pyroxene, olivine, clays etc.

(2) **Carbonates :** Calcite, dolomite, aragonite.

(i) **Feldspars :**

Feldspars are the most abundant rock forming minerals. Two major varieties recognised, are plagioclase and orthoclase.

Plagioclase feldspars are formed over a wide range of temperature. The high temperature plagioclase is calcic ($CaAl_2Si_2O_8$) i.e. Anorthite and at lower temperature, sodic plagioclase (Albite) is formed ($NaAlSi_3O_8$). Thus, it forms a continuous mineral series. In Basalts, Labradorite plagioclase (Ab.50.An.50) is formed.

Orthoclase feldspar ($KAlSi_3O_3$) is the second important type of feldspar. It is commonly associated with quartz. The high temperature potash feldspar is called *sanidine*.

Feldspars are recognised by their hardness, (6) two cleavages nearly at right angles and light colour. Plagioclase may show striations on the cleavage surface.

(ii) Quartz :

Quartz is the second most abundant mineral group after feldspar. It has the composition SiO_2. The most common crystals appear as six sided prisms associated with six sided pyramids above and below.

Pure quartz is colourless, vitreous and translucent. The transparent variety is known as *rock-crystal*. Like many other minerals; the colour of quartz is also influenced by small impurities; amethyst is violet rose quartz, pale pink red jaspar quartz etc. Quartz has no cleavage and breaks along a conchoidal fracture. Its specific gravity is 2.65 and hardness is 7.

Quartz is common in igneous and metamorphic rocks. Crystals of quartz are often seen in veins or in cavities.

Quartz is chemically very stable. It is main constituent of sand. Quartz is used as an abrasive.

Amorphous hydrated form of silica is called *opal* ($SiO_2 \cdot nH_2O$). Cryptocrystalline varieties of silica are chalcedony, flint and jaspars.

One of the most important properties of quartz is its piezoelectricity.

(iii) Micas :

The micas are easily recognised by their colour and perfect basal cleavage along which thin elastic flakes can be easily removed. Two major varieties of mica are recognized as follows :

(a) **Muscovite :** White mica, potassium aluminium silicate with hydroxyl.
   $KAl_2[(AlSi_3)O_{10}](OH)_2$.

(b) **Biotite :** Black mica, magnesium iron potassium aluminium silicate with hydroxyl,
   $K(MgFe)_3[(AlSi_3)O_{10}](OH)_2$.

Muscovite is a lighter mineral with hardness 2 to 2.5 and specific gravity 2.75 to 3.00. It is associated with light coloured minerals. Biotite is a heavier mineral, the average hardness being 2.5 to 3.0 and specific gravity 2.7 to 3.1.

The micas are abundant in igneous and metamorphic rocks.

(iv) Amphibole :

Amphibole is a name of a very large family and complex group of minerals, common most among them being the hornblende. It is a silicate of aluminium, calcium, magnesium and iron $(Ca\ Na\ Mg\ Fe\ Al)_{7-8}[(Al\ Si)_4\ O_{10}].(OH)_2$. Hornblende is black in colour. It has a hardness of 5 to 6, and two cleavages that meet at 56° or 124°. Its specific gravity is between 3 to 3.47.

Hornblende is common in many igneous and metamorphic rocks.

(v) Pyroxene :

Pyroxene forms a number of species, similar to those of the amphiboles, and augite is most common variety.

Augite is a hydrous silicate of calcium, magnesium, iron and aluminium $(CaMgFeAl)_2 (AlSi)_2 O_6$. It is black in colour with hardness of 5 to 6, specific gravity is 3.2 to 3.5 and it shows presence of 2 cleavage planes at nearly 90°.

Augite occurs prominently in basic igneous rocks and other pyroxenes are common in metamorphosed limestones.

(vi) Olivine :

Olivine is an iron magnesium silicate. $(MgFe)_2 SiO_4$ may be the simplest of the ferromagnesium minerals. The magnesium rich variety forms at a higher temperature than the iron rich olivine.

Olivine is recognised by its peculiar olive green colour. Its hardness is 6 to 7, and specific gravity is 3.2 to 4.3, increasing with the iron content.

Olivine occurs in ultra-basic igneous rocks and in metamorphosed impure limestones. Alteration of olivine gives serpentine.

(vii) Carbonates :

Many carbonate minerals are known. Some of them are known as *economic minerals*. However, only two minerals viz., calcite and dolomite are considered as real rock forming minerals. The other carbonate minerals are magnesite, $MgCO_3$, aragonite, $CaCO_3$ and siderite $FeCO_3$.

Both, calcite and dolomite are recognised by their easy reactivity with acidic water. Dolomite is less soluble than calcite. Both have a typical rhombohedral cleavage and both develop twin lamellae when subjected to stress. On the Moh's scale, calcite has a hardness number 3.

Calcite is a chief constituent of limestone and marble, while dolomite is an important mineral in dolomite limestones and dolomitic marble. Calcite often occurs as a secondary cavity mineral in volcanic rocks. When subjected to higher temperature and pressure condition, under a confined system calcite undergoes the process of recrystallization, while dolomite along with other impurities gives rise to different types of marbles.

(viii) Clay Minerals :

Clay minerals are perhaps the most important naturally occurring earth material from civil engineering point of view. In many cases, stability of man-made structures is decided by the behaviour of clay materials.

The term clay is applied to those earth materials who fulfil the following categories :

(a) Grain size is less than 0.016 mm.
(b) Essentially hydrous aluminium silicate in composition.

Clay minerals are formed in varied physico-chemical and biological conditions. They are either detrital or authigenic in origin. Being a fine grained aggregate, identification and analysis of the clay minerals is carried out with the help of sophisticated techniques like X-ray Diffraction, Scanning Electron Microscopy, X-Radiography etc.

Based on their structure and chemical composition, the clay minerals are classified into different groups :

(a) Kaoline : It is primarily an alteration product. It is residual as well as transported clay deposit.

(b) Illite : It is a common mineral in indurated shales. It is formed by the weathering from feldspar, mica or ferromagnesium minerals or it may form from smectite upon diagenesis in an alkaline environment. At low temperature metamorphism, illite is normally converted to mica.

(c) Smectite : It is a family of large number of clay minerals which commonly show swelling characteristics. **Montomorillonite** is the most important mineral in the smectite family. These clay minerals are formed from basic igneous rocks. Another important characteristics of these minerals is their base exchange capacity (80 to 150 millieqn./100 gm). Normally, in case of smectite, there exists a linear relationship between base exchange capacity and plasticity index.

It is seen that most clays are mixed layer clays, for example, smectite-illite. In such cases, physico-chemical properties of the clay minerals are influenced by the predominant mineral available in mixed layered clays.

1.11 IGNEOUS ROCKS

1.11.1 Introduction

Igneous rocks are formed from crystallization of molten material called *magma* which usually consists of a solution of the Earth's most abundant elements, oxygen and silicon, with smaller amounts of aluminium, calcium, magnesium, iron, sodium and potassium. The major elements of common magmas combine, on cooling, to produce different rock forming minerals and other minor constituents.

The history of igneous rock begins with the formation of magma. When sufficient melt has created and coalesced, buoyancy causes it to rise. The magma may rise to the surface and extrude as lava or if it contains volatile, may explode onto the surface to be widely distributed as volcanic ash. Most field evidence indicates that igneous rocks have formed from upward moving bodies of either magma, mixture of magma and crystals, magma and gas bubbles or even solid rock. The rate, at which magma flows, depends on the pressure gradient, magma viscosity and the shape of the conduit.

Magmas usually consist of many components. In order to study the solidification of magma, it is necessary to understand the process of simultaneous crystallization of different minerals. In magmas composed of several constituents, the special properties of each constituent are modified by the presence of others. Magma may undergo the process of crystallization at different cooling conditions at different depths. If cooling is rapid, the process of crystallization is also rapid and thus the final product is in the form of natural glass. On the other hand, if the cooling condition is slow, proportionally crystallization is also a slow process. As a result, the product is coarse grained.

1.11.2 Crystallization of Rock Forming Minerals

Above discussion leads to the conclusion that once formed, a mineral as a part of eutectic system, it no longer remain in equilibrium. Its composition cannot be further changed. On the other hand, a mineral of a mix crystal series is in continual reaction with the liquid from which it is formed and its composition is continually being modified. This is called *continuous reaction series* (Fig. 1.6).

In another type of reaction, an early formed mineral reacts at a certain temperature with the liquid to form a mineral of different composition. The two minerals thus related by reaction are called *reaction-pair*. Thus, a reaction relation of the same character may exist between three or more minerals which when arranged in the proper succession is called a discontinuous reaction series.

In the Fig. 1.6, the left hand is discontinuous reaction series and the right hand is the continuous reaction series of plagioclase. They converge into a single discontinuous series, of which quartz is the final product. This is particularly true for basaltic rocks.

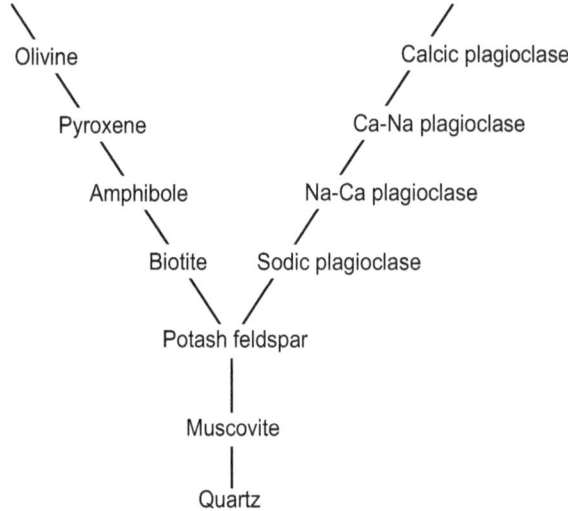

Fig. 1.6 : The reaction relation (Bowen's reaction series)

The first mineral to crystallize from the melt is olivine. May be at the same time or little later, calcic plagioclase begins to form. With the falling temperature, olivine reacts with the melt to form pyroxene which at the same time also starts to crystallize directly from the melt i.e. the minerals on the left side reacts with the melt to form the next lower member (Fig. 1.6), while the plagioclase continuously reacts with the melt to form more sodic plagioclase. This process ends when all the ferromagnesium minerals and plagioclase are formed. Then the orthoclase – muscovite – quartz are formed. The evidence for the reaction series may be observed under the microscope, when pyroxene crystals are seen with rims of amphibole.

1.11.3 Textures and Structures of Igneous Rocks

Texture is the intimate mutual relation of the mineral constituents and glassy matter in a rock made up of aggregate of minerals. Structures of igneous rocks, on the other hand, include certain field features such as ropy surface of lava, pillow, amygdaloidal structures, flow banding and spheratites.

(a) Structures :

Vesicular and amygdaloidal structure : Most lavas contain gases which escapes as soon as pressure is reduced by their erruption at the surface. The escape of gases creates the molten material with the development of vesicles, cavities or pores which may be elliptical, spherical or cylindrical in shape. The cavities are often isolated or poorly interconnected. Amygdales are the fillings of vesicles by silica, carbonate and zeolitic minerals and so called because of their resemblance to almonds. Lavas containing amygdales are said to possess amygdaloidal structure and the rocks are called *amygdaloids*. They are commonly encountered in Maharashtra.

Ropy and Blocky lava : Very mobile lava often solidify with very smooth surfaces that exhibit wrinkled, or ropy forms. This is called *ropy lava* or *pahoehoe lava*. In this, cavities are smaller in size and mostly spherical in shape.

Sometimes the, surface is covered with a mass of rough, jugged angular blocks of uneven dimensions. In this, the cavities are larger in size compared to ropy lava and irregular in shape. The lava form is called *blocky* or *as lava*.

Pillow structure : Pillow structure is found in basalts that errupted below water. They are formed when lava is chilled rapidly by water. A chilled rind (outer surface/covering) forms on the surface which is sufficiently flexible to move with the flow which remains molten inside. As lava pressure increases, the rind breaks, causing formation of a tubular lobe. The pillows may vary from a few centimetres to several metres. They may be spheroidal, ellipsoidal or even flattened. The pillows have thin skins composed of tachylite which in some cases has been altered by oxidation and absorption of water into yellowish brown waxy looking substances called *palagonite*. The interstices narrow space between the pillows are often filled with the fragments of broken glassy lava skins. Many pillows have a radiating column structure and may show concentric zonation of vesicular zones. Ancient pillows have been found in many localities of India e.g. Mumbai – Bangaluru highway cuttings near Chitradurga.

Flow structure : Layers and patches in lava differ slightly in composition, gas content, viscosity and degree of crystallization. In the process of flow, these patches are drawn into parallel lenticles, bands and lines, which may be characterised by development in various proportions of vesicles, glass and crystals of slightly different composition shown by change in colour and texture.

In addition to these structures, jointing and columnar structures are seen prominently in many igneous rocks. These are further discussed in Unit-2.

(b) Textures :

An accurate description of texture requires consideration of following points : Degree of crystallization (crystallinity), Grain size (granularity), Shape of crystals and Mutual relations of crystals and glass. The two factors together are considered as fabric. The texture of igneous rocks is a function of crystallinity, granularity and fabric.

Crystallinity : Crystallinity is a ratio of crystallized and non-crystallized matter. A rock composed entirely of crystals is called **holocrystalline**. When it consists completely of glass, it is called **holohyaline**, and when the rock is composed partly of crystals and partly of glass, it is called **mesocrystalline**. The holocrystalline texture is typical of plutonic igneous rocks and the holohyaline is characteristic of lava flows or volcanic rocks. The mesocrystalline texture is indicative of intermediate rocks.

Crystallinity is a measure of degree of cooling. Thus, holocrystalline is a product of slow cooling and holohyaline occurs due to fast cooling.

Granularity : Granularity is the absolute grain size of crystals in igneous rocks. If crystals are visible in handspecimen, the rock is said to be phaneric. On the other hand, the term aphinitic is used when the crystals cannot be recognised to the naked eyes.

Aphinitic rocks may be cryptocrystalline i.e. individual crystals are too small to be separately recognised even under the microscope or they may be microcrystalline i.e. the individual crystals are distinguishable only under the microscope.

Phaneric rocks may be coarse grained when the average grain size is more than 5 mm, medium grained when it is between 5 mm and 1 mm and fine grained when it is less than 1 mm.

Like crystallinity, granularity also depends on the rate of cooling. Thus, coarse grained nature is indicative of slow cooling and fine grained is suggestive of fast cooling.

Shapes of crystals : Crystal forms are described with reference to the development of crystals.

Euhedral is the one where the crystal is completely bounded by faces. Anhedral crystals, on the other hand are of irregular shapes and anhedral term is used when crystal faces are completely absent.

Crystal shapes may also be described with reference to their growth in three dimensions.

Equidimensional crystals are those in which crystal growth is more or less uniform in all directions. Crystals better developed in two directions than the third is referred as tabular. They form plates, flakes and tablets in the micas and some feldspars. Crystals developed essentially in one direction are called *prismatic*. They form columns, rods and needles e.g. hornblende.

Mutual relations of crystals : Mutual relations of crystals are described by taking into consideration crystallinity, granularity and shape of crystals. Based on these parameters, two broad terms are recognised; equigranular and inequigranular texture.

Equigranular texture is the one in which the mineral constituents are approximately of same size, so that the rock has uniform appearance, both in hand specimen and thin section (Fig. 1.7).

Equigranular texture is typical of plutonic rocks. It is also called *granitic texture*.

Inequigranular texture is produced when the differences of size in the constituent minerals of igneous rock becomes so prominent that they control the aspect of the rock megascopically and also microscopically. Two major varieties of inequigranular texture are observed; porphyritic and poikilitic. In porphyritic texture, the large crystals (phenocrysts) are embedded in a fine grained groundmass. It is confined mostly to volcanic and hypabyssal rocks. The phenocrysts are usually alkali feldspar and the outer zones of which enclose small crystals of biotite, plagioclase or magnetite.

Poikilitic texture is opposite of porphyritic texture. In this, smaller crystals are enclosed in the larger ones.

In many rocks like gabbros, dolerites and basalts etc. laths of plagioclase may lie in a matrix of coarse subhedral augite (pyroxene). Such intergrowth is called **ophitic texture**.

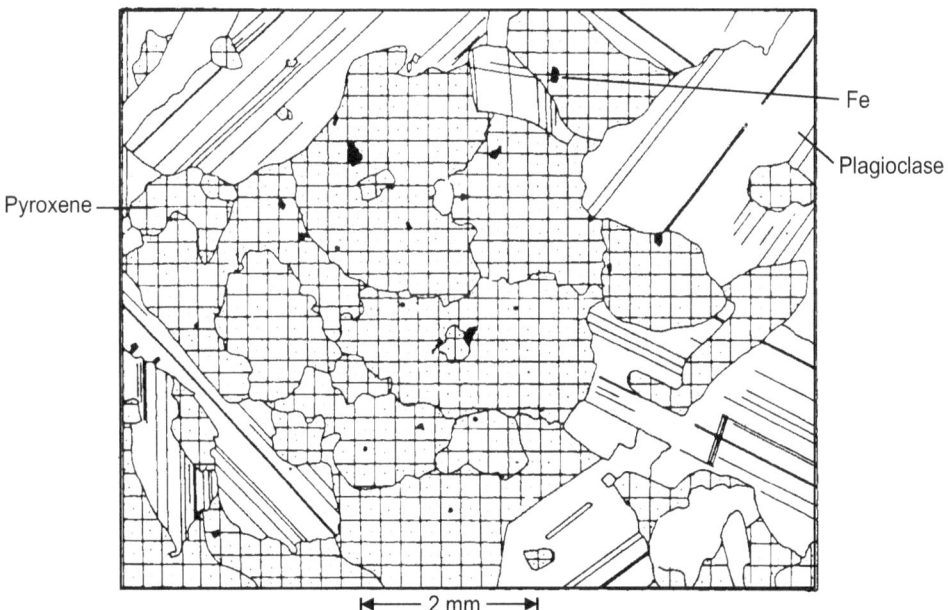

Fig. 1.7 : Photomicrograph and interpretative drawing of a thin section of gabbro. The texture is equigranular. The main minerals are pyroxene (pyx), plagiclase (plag) and iron oxide (Fe)

1.11.4 Classification of Igneous Rocks

The igneous rocks are classified on the basis of their chemical composition, texture, mineral composition and mode of occurrence. A simplified classification of igneous rocks is given in Table 1.4.

Chemical Composition : The chemical composition of rocks depends on the composition of their parent magma. It is observed that the total bulk is made up of only eight elements (refer Table 1.3) namely, oxygen, silicon, aluminium, iron, sodium, calcium, potassium and magnesium. In terms of oxides, SiO_2 is most abundant. Thus, the silica percentage is the criteria for the classification of igneous rocks. Four divisions are recognised on the basis of silica percentage.

Table 1.4 : Classification based on silica percentage

Over 66%	Acidic Igneous Rock
52% – 66%	Intermediate
45% and 52%	Basic Igneous Rocks
Less than 45%	Ultrabasic Igneous Rocks

Mineral Composition : It is seen that olivine is abundant in ultrabasic and basic rocks but absent in acid rocks (Fig. 1.8). Similarly, quartz and orthoclase are abundant in acid rocks but absent in ultrabasic rocks. These are the essential minerals for that rock type. Other accessory minerals are also present but they are in minor proportions. The prominent minerals in igneous rocks often decide its general appearance, colour and density. Acid rocks are usually light in colour while basic rocks are darker in shade.

According to their colour and composition, the minerals may further be grouped into the felsic minerals (light coloured) and the mafic minerals (dark coloured).

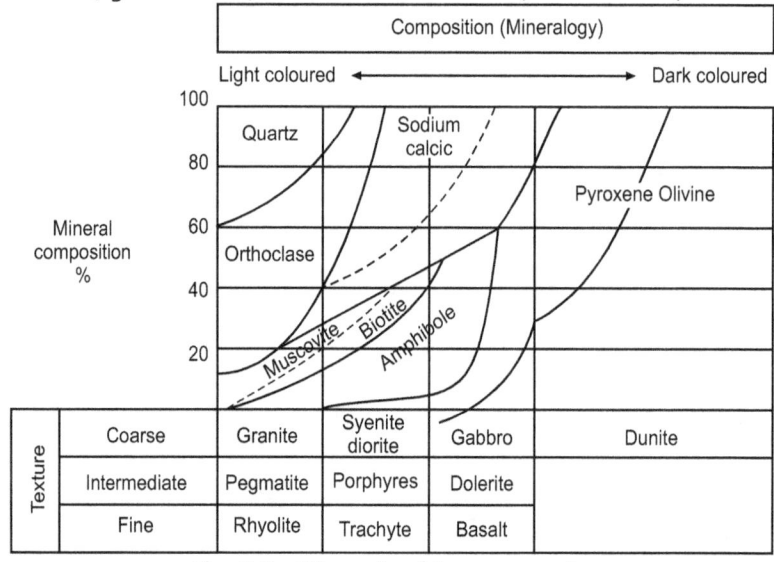

Fig. 1.8 : Minerals of igneous rocks

Colour Index : Based on the proportion of felsic and mafic minerals, colour index is used to describe various igneous rocks.

Table 1.5

Description	Colour Index (% of mafic materials)
Leucocratic (light coloured)	0 – 30
Mesocratic (medium coloured)	30 – 60
Melanocratic (dark coloured)	60 – 90
Hypermelanic (very dark)	90 – 100

Thus, on the basis of these criteria, igneous rocks are classified into different varieties.

1.11.5 Description of Common Igneous Rocks

As seen earlier, igneous rocks on the basis of mode of occurrence are divided into two types extrusive and intrusive igneous rocks. Extrusive igneous rocks are volcanic rocks formed due to erruption of molten material followed by rapid cooling. Intrusive igneous rocks are divided into plutonic and hypabyssal rocks depending upon at the depth at which they were formed.

	Plutonic	Hypabyssal	Volcanic
Acidic	Granite	Aplite, Pegmatite	Rhyolite
Intermediate	Syenite Diorite	Porphyres	Trachyte Andesite
Basic	Gabbro	Dolerite	Basalt
Ultrabasic		—— Dunite ——	

Fig. 1.9 : Common Igneous Rocks

Individual group of rocks (e.g. plutonic / hypabyssal / volcanic) are further classified on the basis of SiO_2 content and mineral composition (Fig. 1.8 and 1.9). It is seen that granite, pegmatite, aplite and rhyolite have more or less identical chemical composition but due to change in their cooling condition they exhibit different texture. Thus, Aplite is hypabyssal equivalent of granite and rhyolite is volcanic equivalent of granite. A definite change in the physical properties of these rocks is commonly observed due to significant change in the texture. Similar conclusions could be derived in case of intermediate and basic igneous rocks. Aim of this discussion is to describe similar rock types and not their physical properties. Therefore, they are described together on the basis of mineral composition.

(a) Acid igneous rocks : Acid igneous rocks are characterised by high SiO_2 content (above 66%), low percentage of mafic minerals (3 to 12%), light colour and low density (2.7 g/cm^3 approximately).

Essential minerals present in these rocks are quartz (25 to 35%), K – feldspar (35 to 40%), plagioclase (15 to 25%) and biotite (5 to 15%). Accessory minerals are muscovite and hornblende.

Granite is an intrusive holocrystalline rock. Many varieties of granite are recognised. Colour of granite varies with composition and proportion of K – feldspar. Granite, because of its texture, is a very strong and durable stone. It is often traversed by sheet joints owing to which porosity of the rock increases. They usually weather to a mixture of clay, silt and sand. Alteration of orthoclase, plagioclase and mica to clay minerals is common.

Pegmatite (Pegma : very large) and Aplite are other equivalents of granite which usually occurs as dykes and veins.

(b) Intermediate rocks : Intermediate rocks process a silica content varying between 52% to 66%; a high proportion of feldspars. Their density lies between 2.7 and 2.9.

Diorities are grey or greenish grey intrusive rocks consisting chiefly of plagioclase, hornblende and pyroxene. **Porphyrites** are similar in composition but these show a typical porphyritic texture.

Syenites (from Syene, Egypt) are deep seated holocrystalline rocks. K-Feldspar constitute 50 to 70% acid plagioclase (10 to 30%), biotite and hornblende upto 10%. Quartz is absent or if present, occurs in small proportion.

Trachytes (rough stone) are volcanic equivalents of syenites. They are rough to feel. These occur as flows or dykes.

(c) Basic rocks : Basic rocks contain 45% to 52% SiO_2 and are characterised by higher proportion of mafic minerals (45% to 50%) and plagioclase (10 to 15%). These are mesocratic rocks and their density varies from 2.8 to 3.27.

Gabbro is a holocrystalline mesocratic rock. They occur as large intrusive bodies. Anorthosite is a type of Gabbro which consists almost completely of basic plagioclase (50% to 70%).

Basalts (Basal-boiled stone) are most common of volcanic rocks; that represent volcanic equivalent of gabbro. They consist of augite, basic plagioclase and glass. Details of basalt are dealt in Unit 2. Dolerite or Diabase is hypabyssal equivalent of Gabbro.

1.12 SEDIMENTARY ROCKS

Sedimentary rocks are formed at or near the surface by the accumulation and consolidation of the products of weathering derived from older rock masses and by the accumulation of organic debris. Most of them are deposited as beds or layers. They comprise only 5% volume of the earth but they cover 75% of the exposed land surface. As they are formed due to weathering, let us in brief study about weathering.

1.12.1 Processes of Formation of Sedimentary Rocks

Sedimentary rocks are formed due to number of complex processes including weathering, erosion, transportation, accumulation, lithification and cementation (Fig. 1.10). As a result, the nature of sedimentary material is very varied in origin, size, shape and composition.

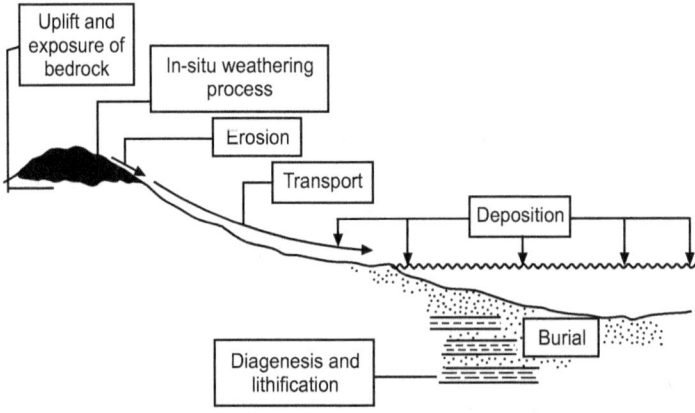

(a) Processes involved in the formation of sedimentary rocks

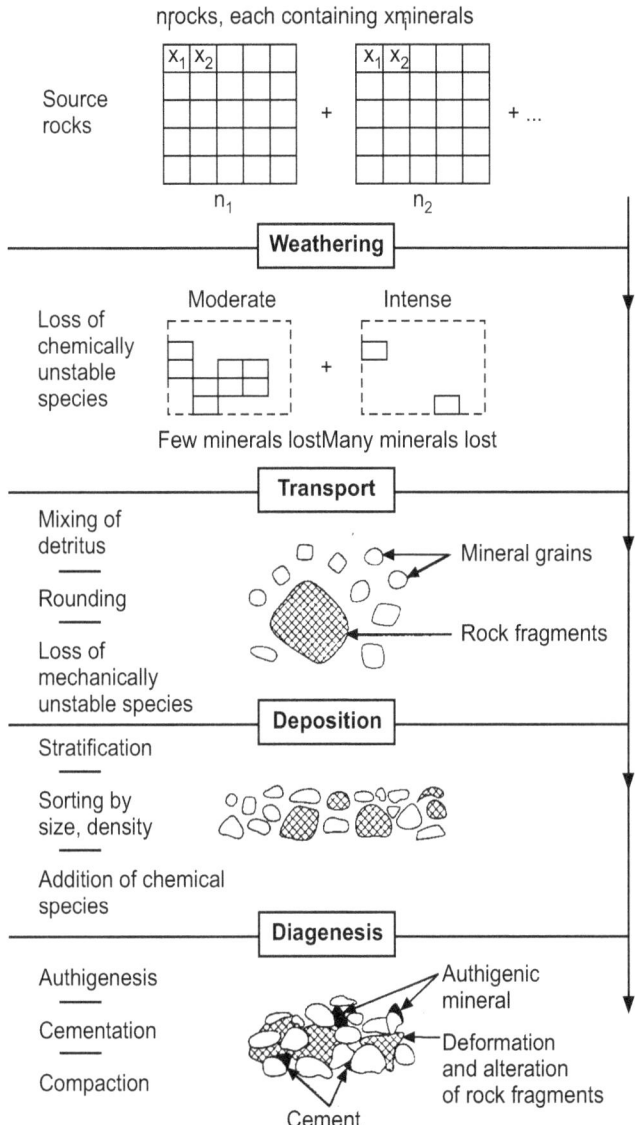

(b) The sedimentary cycle of clastic sedimentary rocks
Fig. 1.10

(A) Weathering is the in-situ process of disintegration and decomposition of pre-existing rocks (for details, refer section 2.1). The mechanical or physical weathering is progressive break down of parent material due to frost action, differential thermal expansion, pressure relief, collapse of air bubbles in water and abrasion. The chemical weathering is alteration, or dissolution of sensitive parent material due to oxidation-reduction, carbonation, hydration, hydrolysis and solution. In this, the role played by growing roots, burrowing animals, and other biotic agent is very crucial.

(B) The weathered material is removed from in-situ by water, wind and glaciers. This process of excavation of weathered debris is called *erosion*. (For details, refer sections 2.2, 2.3, 2.4, 2.5). In addition to the product of weathering, unconsolidated sediments and soil are also subject to erosion. The interrelated factors of relief, climate and vegetation the control the rates of erosion in an area along with the nature of the bedrock.

Slope is an important factor in determining the rates of erosion and all the physical processes of removal of material are in some way gravity driven. Rock falls and landslides are more frequent on steep slopes than in areas of subdued topography (for details, refer Unit-5). Erosive power of water is always more effective across steeper gradients.

Climate plays an important role in determining both, the amount of erosion which occurs and the processes which cause erosion. Erosion by wind is most effective in the absence of water. Similarly, rainfall events in desert regions may be catastrophic in terms of amount of erosion that occurs.

A dense vegetation cover is very effective for protecting the bedrock and overlying weathered debris (regolith) from erosion. Only where plant cover is absent or very thin then the regolith is likely to be removed by erosion.

In a given topographic and climatic conditions the type of bedrock is a fundamental control on the rates and styles of erosion. Where physical processes of weathering are more important, the fracture characteristics of bedrock largely control the rate of breakdown. Similarly, in humid climates where chemical weathering processes are dominant because different rocks are broken down and eroded at widely different rates.

(C) Transportation of weathered debris takes place by different transport media including gravity, water, air and ice through suspension and bedload transport.

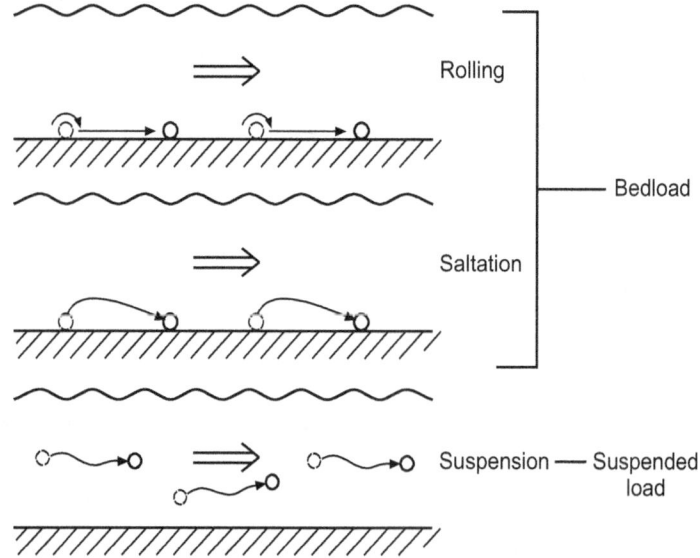

**Fig. 1.11 : Mechanisms of transport of particles in a flow :
rolling and saltation (bedload), and suspension (suspended load)**

Particles of any size are moved in a fluid by any of three mechanisms. First, they can move by *rolling* (Fig. 1.11) along the bottom of the air or water flow without loosing contact with the bed surface. Secondly, they can move in a series of jumps, periodically leaving the bed surface and being carried over short distances within the body of the fluid before returning to the bed again. This is known as *saltation* (Fig. 1.11). These two together give rise to bedload transport. Third, turbulence within the flow can produce sufficient upward motion to keep particles in the moving fluid more or less continually. This is known as *suspension* (Fig. 1.11).

At low current velocities, only fine particles (clays) and low density particles are kept in suspension while sand-size particles move by rolling and saltation. At higher flow rates, all silt and sand may be kept in suspension, with granules and fine pebbles in salting and coarser material may be kept in rolling.

Fig. 1.12 shows the relationship between water flow velocity and grain size. In this, two curved lines are seen. The lower line indicates the relationship between flow velocity and particles in motion. It is noted that a pebble will come to rest at about 20-30 cm/sec, a medium sand at 2-3 cm/sec and a clay particle almost at zero flow velocity.

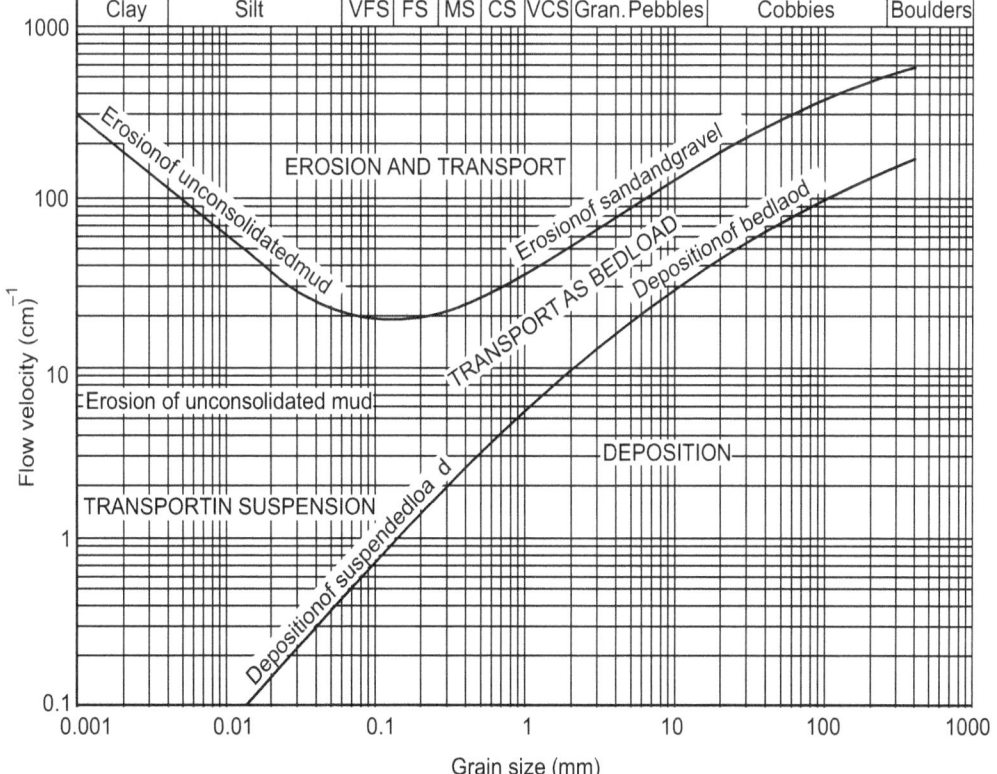

Fig. 1.12 : The Hjulstrom diagram showing the relationship between the velocity of a water flow and the transport of loose particles

The upper curved line shows the flow velocity required to move a particle from rest. The finer silt and clay particles require a high velocity to move them than sand. Once the clay particles have undergone deposition, they tend to stick together because of their cohesive nature, making them more difficult to entrain in a flow than sand grains. Thus, the plastic behaviour of muddy particles have important consequences for deposition in natural depositional environment.

The particles under motion moves down the slope by the action of water and ice. Their physical properties like size and shape modifies during transportation. Longer the distance of transportation, more is the rounding attained by the particles.

(D) Deposition : The particles undergo the process of accumulation when the stream enters the lake, shallow seas and areas of no relief. Depositional systems are highly variable. The process acting in particular depositional systems (environments) give rise to a suite of relatively small scale characteristics of resultant sedimentary deposits. On the earth, following major kinds of depositional environments are recognised. (see Table 1.6)

Table 1.6 : Major Depositional Environments

Environment	Common Sedimentary Rocks
1. Continental	
(a) Fluvial	Conglomerate, sandstone, shale.
(b) Lacustrine	Sandstone, shale, limestone.
(c) Glacial	Tillite.
(d) Eolien	Sandstone, shale.
2. Transitional	
(a) Deltas	Sandstone, shale.
(b) Esturine, lagoon	Sandstone, shale.
3. Marine	
(a) Shallow seas	
Littoral (beaches, sandbanks, tidal flats)	Conglomerate, sandstone, shale
Neritic	Orthoquartzite, current bedded sandstone, shale, Organic and chemical limestones.
(b) Deep seas	Black shale, bitumens, greywacke, limestones.
(c) Abyssal seas	Calcareous ooze, siliceous ooze. Red clay.

(E) Lithification and Cementation : Most sediments are soft, unconsolidated material at the time of deposition and are in the form of loose sediments or accumulations of the parts of dead organisms. The sediments are transformed into cohesive sedimentary rocks by means of lithification and cementation. These processes are both physical and chemical that may take place at any time after deposition.

The accumulation of sediments results in development of thick sedimentary sequence. This overburden acts vertically on a body of sediments which increases with increase in thickness of sediment mass. Loose unconsolidated material respond to overburden by changing the packing of the particles, thus reducing volume of sediment body as a whole. This process of compaction converts the loose material into semiconsolidated mass. Lateral change in sediment type results in differential compaction. Generally, when the sediment is deposited in aqueous environment the pore spaces between the grains will be occupied by pore water. As compaction occurs, this water is expelled out of sediment.

The degree of compaction in an aggregate may be determined by carefully checking the nature of grain contacts. If the sediment has been subjected to very little overburden the clasts show grain contacts. Reduction in porosity by changes in packing produces long contacts. In some cases, material may locally go into solution giving rise to convex-concave contacts. Under very high overburden pressure, the boundaries between grains become sutured.

The transported material also contains dissolved load which may be carried by fluids through the sediments to places favourable for precipitation. For example, a decrease in acidity may favour the precipitation of calcium carbonate from solution in the pore waters.

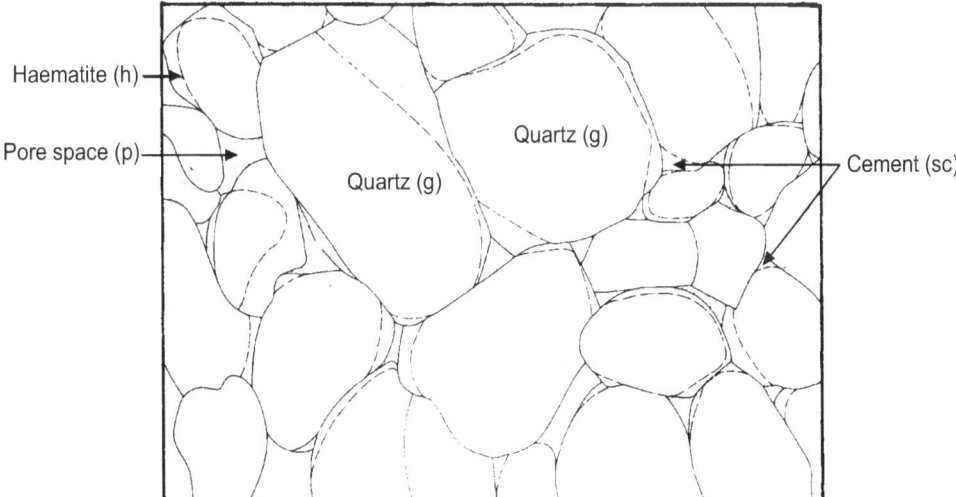

Fig. 1.13 : Sketch of a photomicrograph of a thin section of sandstone showing the interlocking of grains caused by dissolution of silica at grain boundaries between quartz grains during compaction. The dissolved material has been precipitated as silica overgrowths around the former grains, marked by dashed lines

The nucleation and growth of crystals within pore spaces in sediments is called **cementation**. Minerals precipitated within pore spaces during diagenesis are cements which are to be distinguished from matrix, the fine material deposited with the coarser material.

The commonly encountered cementing material is calcium carbonate and silica. If the cement and the adjacent grains are of same chemical composition the cement may form an overgrowth extending the mineral grain into the pore space (Fig. 1.13). Overgrowths are common in silica cemented quartz sands.

Cementation lithifies the sediment into a cohesive rock and 'in doing so, it reduces the porosity and permeability. Cements form around the edges of the grains and grow out into the pore spaces. Pore spaces can be completely filled by cement resulting into complete lithification where a rock has a moderate porosity but a very low permeability.

1.12.2 Sedimentary Structures

The interaction of the sedimentary material with the transporting medium results in the development of sedimentary structures some of which are purely depositional while others are erosional. These sedimentary structures are preserved in rocks and provide a record of processes occurring at the time of deposition. They occur on the upper and lower surfaces of the bed as well as within the bed.

Four categories of sedimentary structures are recognized namely; depositional, post-depositional, erosional and biogenic structures.

(a) Depositional Structures :

Depositional structures occur on the upper surface of beds and also within them. They are common in clastic sedimentary rocks and also in carbonates.

Bedding and Lamination : Bedding and lamination define stratification. Bedding is thicker than 1 cm and lamination is thinner than 1 cm.

Bedding is produced by change in the pattern of sedimentation. The bedding planes can represent short or long breaks in sedimentation. Flat bedding surfaces are most common in sand and sandstones of fine-medium grain size (also called as parallel lamination). Though they owe their origin to different processes but the two basic types are : those formed due to deposition of strong currents i.e. upper plane-bed phase lamination and those formed through deposition from suspension, low density turbidity currents or from weak traction currents i.e. lower plane bed-phase lamination.

Upper plane-bed phase lamination occurs in sandstones and forms through subaqueous deposition at high flow velocities in the upper flow regimes. This type of lamination is characterised by primary current lineation on lamina surfaces. The lineation is formed parallel to flow direction, and thus its orientation will indicate trend of paleo current. Lower plane-bed phase lamination occurs in sediments with grain size coarser than 0.6 mm. It forms through the movement of sediment as bedload by traction at low flow velocity in the lower flow regime. It also lacks the parting lineation. (Fig. 1.14)

Lamination occurs in a wide range of rocks, but especially in mudstones and limestones.

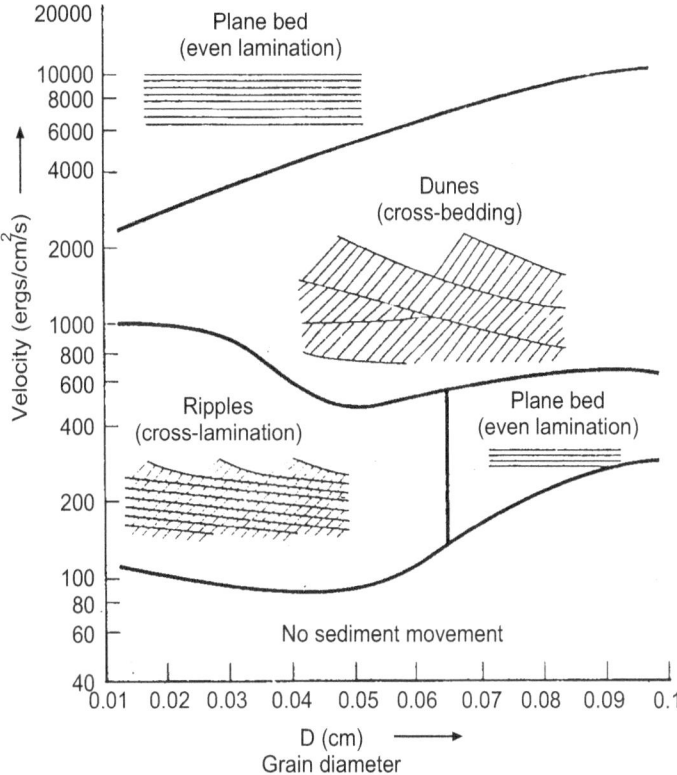

Fig. 1.14 : Bedform in relation to velocity of natural agency and bedload material

Ripple Marks : Ripples are more or less regularly spaced undulations on a sand surface or a bedding surface of sandstone. Their spacing (wavelength) is generally less than 50 cm and width is not more than 3 cm. If size of undulations exceed these limits, undulations are referred as *dunes* or *sandwaves*.

Ripples are described both in terms of their appearance in profile and plan view (Fig. 1.15). Ripple index is *'the ratio of wavelength to amplitude when measured in profile'* (Fig. 1.15). It is useful in the recognition of wind, wave formed and current ripples.

Wave formed ripples are formed by the action of waves on non-cohesive material and are symmetrical in shape. The crests of wave ripples are generally straight. In profile, the troughs are more rounded than crests. The ripple index of wave formed ripples is generally between 6 and 7. If there is a change in the direction of movement over an area of ripples then a second set of ripples can be developed.

Current ripples are developed due to unidirection currents. As a result, they are asymmetrical in shape with a steep lee and gentle stoss side. The ripple index of current tipples is between 8 and 15. These ripples do not form in sediment coarser than 0.6 mm in size (coarse sand).

Megaripples (subaqueous dunes) and bars (sand waves) are larger structures similar to ripples. Dunes are generally from a few metres to more than 10 metres in length and upto 0.5 m high. Megaripples vary in shape from straight crested to sinuous to lunate with increasing flow velocity. Sand waves are larger than dunes, almost hundreds of metre in length and several metres in height. Sand waves are present in river and also on shallow marine shelves.

Wind ripples and dunes are asymmetric like current ripples. Wind ripples are rarely preserved but cross-stratification developed due to their migration is of common occurrence in ancient sandstones.

Cross-stratification : Cross-stratification is an internal structure that consists of a stratification at an angle to principal bedding direction. Cross-stratification in many cases is formed from ripples, dunes and sand waves. In sandy sediments, it is formed through the infilling of erosional hollows and scours, lateral migration of point bars in a channel and deposition on a beach foreshore.

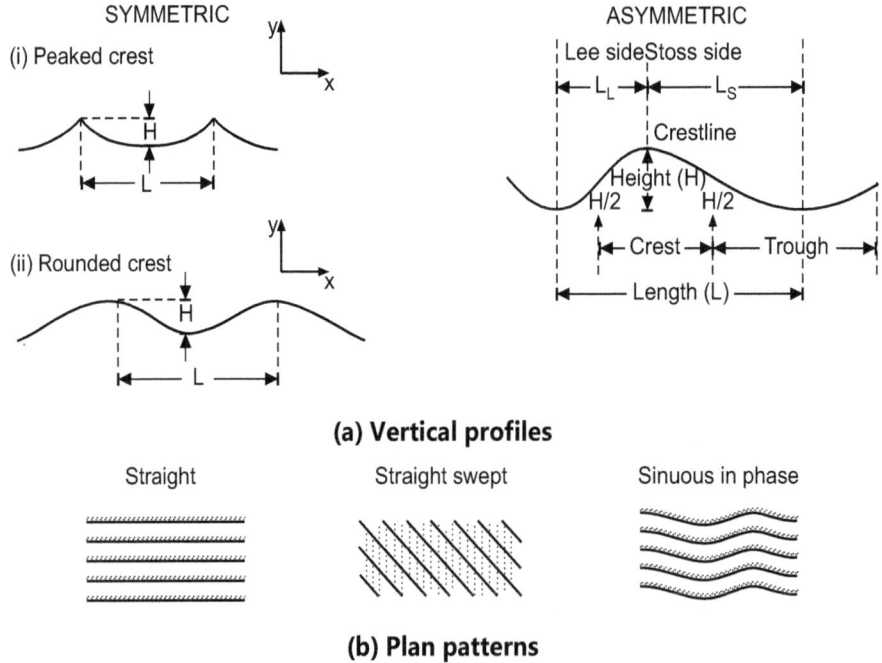

Fig. 1.15 : Different ripple patterns in profile and plan view

Cross-stratification forms either a single set or many sets (cosets) within one bed (Fig. 1.15). These may be called *cross-lamination* if the set height is less than 6 cm and thickness of the cross laminate is only a few mm and cross-bedding where the height is more than 6 cm and thickness to a centimetre or more.

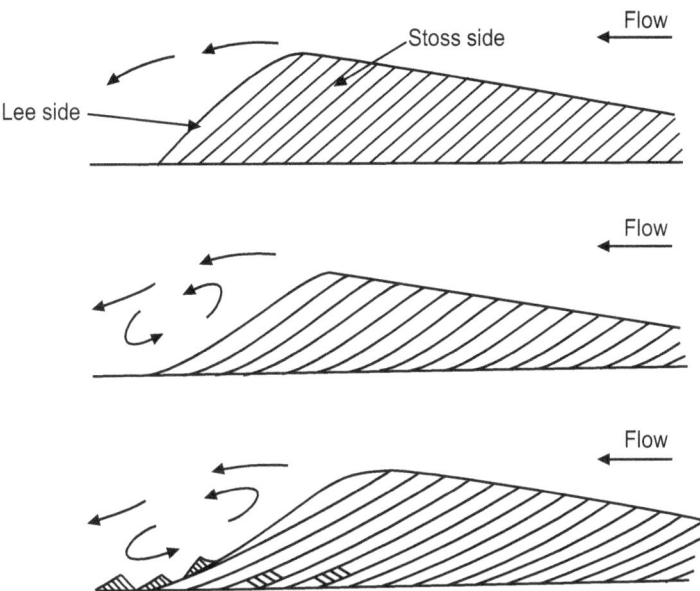

Fig. 1.16 : Tangential toe at the bottom of a set of cross beds

Cross-stratification forms due to downstream migration of ripples, dunes and sand waves when the sediment is moved up the stoss side and then roll down the lee side (Fig. 1.16). The steep dipping parts of the cross-stratification are called foresets which can have angular or tangential contact with the horizontal (Fig. 1.16). The lower gently dipping parts are called *bottom sets*. The upper bounding surface of a cross bed is generally an erosional surface.

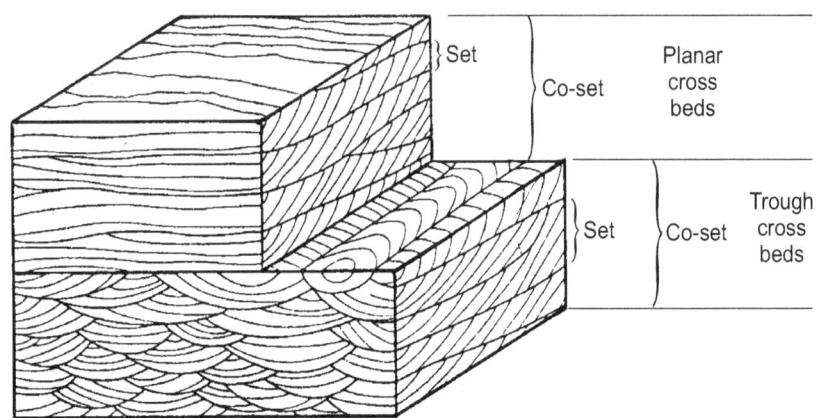

Fig. 1.17 : Sets and co-sets of cross stratification

The three dimensional shape of cross-stratification exhibits two kinds of set; trough cross bedding where the inner set boundaries are trough shaped and tabular cross sets where inter set boundaries are planar (Fig. 1.17). Both types consist of planar beds which tends to possess angular contact with the basal surface.

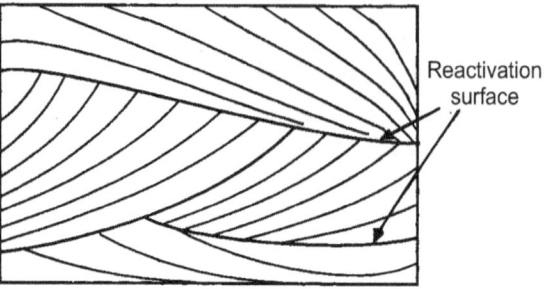

Fig. 1.18 : Erosional surfaces in cross bedding

Many a times, some cross beds show certain erosional surfaces within them, cutting across the cross strata (Fig. 1.18). These are the reactivation surfaces that represent short term changes in flow direction responsible in modifying shape of the subunit.

Graded Beds :

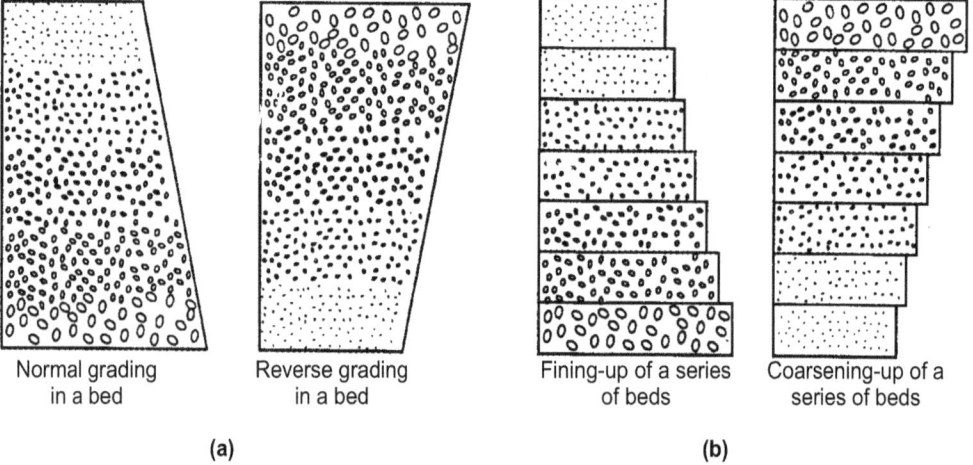

Fig. 1.19 : Normal and reverse grading in single beds; fining upward and coarsening upward patterns in a series of beds

A bed which shows a progressive reduction in grain size from bottom to top is said to be graded or normally graded [Fig. 1.19 (a)]. The decrease in grain size is shown by all particles in the bed. In a few cases, inverse grading is observed where the grain size increases upwards throughout a bed [Fig. 1.19 (b)]. Normal graded bedding is typical of deposition from waning flow, while reverse grading forms from an increasing strength of flow during the process of deposition. Generally, laminae deposited on beaches by backwash are reversely graded. Often composite or multiple graded bedding is seen where several graded units occur in one bed.

Shrinkage Cracks (Mud Cracks)

Clay rich sediment is generally cohesive in nature. As a result, the individual particles tend to stick each other as the sediment dries out. As water is lost, the volume reduces and clay minerals undergo shrinkage developing cracks in the surface. Thus, under subaerial condition a polygonal pattern of cracks develops, known as mud cracks or desiccation cracks. Generally, spacing of mud cracks is controlled by thickness of wet mud with a broader spacing occurring in, thicker deposits.

Synaeresis cracks are shrinkage cracks in clay sediments which form under water. These cracks are simple, straight or slightly curved and of tapering in nature.

Both desiccation and synaeresis cracks are often filled with coarser sediments.

(b) Post-Depositional Structures :

A variety of structures are formed after deposition may be through mass movement of sediments and reorganisation by dewatering and loading. These are seen in the form of localised disturbances and also soft sediment deformation.

For a sediment to undergo deformation immediately after deposition, its shear strength must be decreased or the applied shear stress increased. This is achieved by loss of cohesion either by rearrangement of packing or by increasing pore water pressure. It is believed that a shock applied to waterlogged loosely packed sediment can change the packing and in the process, increase the pore fluid pressure. As a result the sediment and water behaves like a fluid, undergoing *temporary liquefaction*. Often liquefaction of a sediment may be total, so that all grain contact is broken and the mass of sediment and water flows freely. In such cases, original lamination is destroyed producing 'slurried' bedding. In other instances, where liquefaction is partial, original lamination is distorted. A mass of liquefied sediment will remain mobile until the excess pore-fluid pressure is dissipated either by general intergranular flow of pore water in upward direction or along restricted path ways. Often the upward escape of fluid may lead to fluidisation of sediment along escaped pathways. The relative movement of grains and fluid during fluidisation allows some grain sorting usually by upward movement of fines. In a liquefied sediment, fluid and grains move together giving almost no escape for sorting.

Slumps : A slumped mass typically shows folding; recumbent folding, asymmetric anticlines and synclines, and thrust folding. Fold axes are parallel to the strike of the slope and the direction of overturning is down slope. They are usually bounded above and below by undisturbed sediment (Fig. 1.20).

Slumps are caused as unconsolidated sediments resting on a slope and become unstable due to increase in pore water pressure in a sensitive layer in the sediment sequence. The mass then move along the slope under gravity as a coherent mass. These may be triggered by earthquake waves.

It is noted that in this process, the down slope end is subjected to compressive stress regime and the up slope to tensional stress regime.

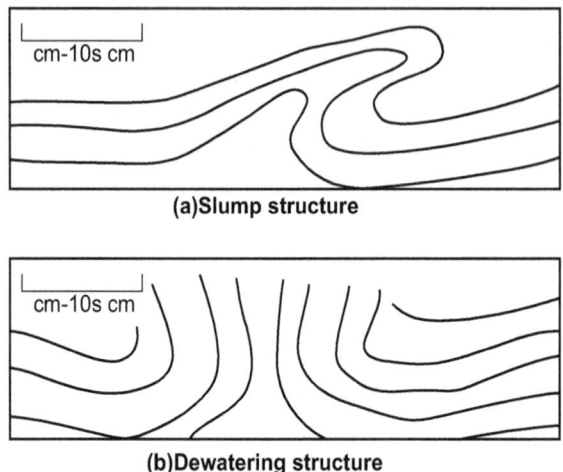

Fig. 1.20 : Post depositional structures

Deformed bedding : Deformed bedding include distorted, convoluted and contorted bedding without any large lateral movement of the sediment.

Convolute bedding occurs in cross laminated sediments with lamination deformed into asymmetric or overturned folds. Contorted and disrupted bedding applies to deformation within a bed but without any preferred orientation. In a few cases, local brecciation do occur.

Deformed bedding can arise from various processes including frictional drag produced by moving sand, shearing by currents on a sediment surface and also due to fluidisation and liquefaction.

Dish and Pillar Structure :

Dish and Pillar structure consist of the concave up laminae (dishes) separated by structureless zone of sand pillars. These are formed due to upward and lateral passage of water through a sediment. Dish structure require a significant amount of clay for their formation. In profile, the dishes appear as thin horizontal zone of a few mm in thickness and the pillars extent vertically for several centimetres which may pass through several horizontal dishes. They have a core of cleaner sand with dark clay rich fringes.

(c) Erosional structures :

Erosional structures are preserved only if the sediment mass is cohesive and strong to maintain the erosional relief. These may be easily recognised in vertical section by truncation of sediment or lamination below the erosional surface. There are two processes to consider in search of erosional structure.

(1) Erosion by scour creating a feature elongated in the direction of fluid movement i.e. channels, and

(2) Erosion by mass movement down a slope forming a slump scar.

The erosional structures occur over a wide range of scales upto kilometres wide and hundreds of metres deep.

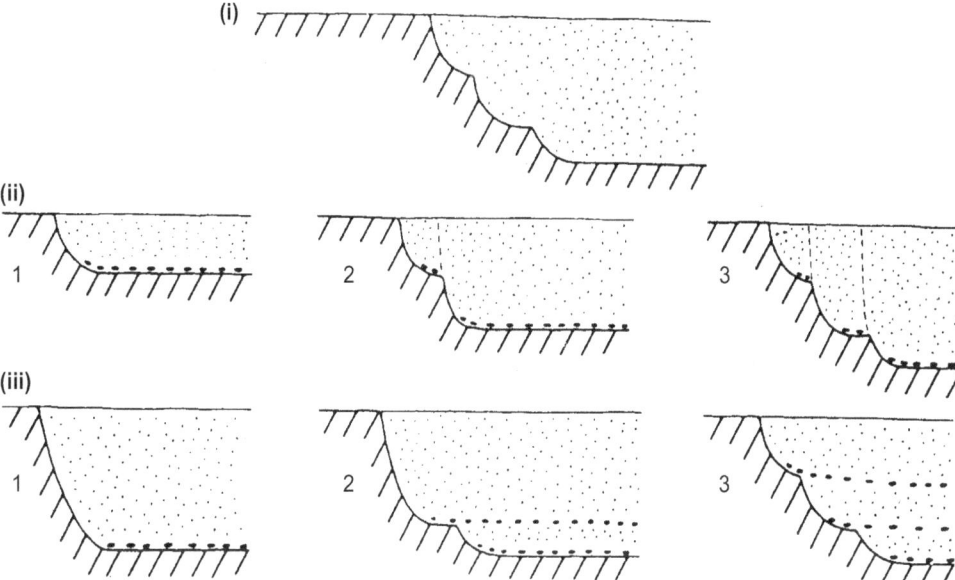

Fig. 1.21 (a) : Possible stages in the erosion of a stepped channel margin by repeated episodes of cut and fill. (i) shows the final channel shape. (ii) and (iii) show different stages by which this form could be achieved. The ability to recognise erosion surfaces within the channel fill may be vital in understanding the full history of development of the channel

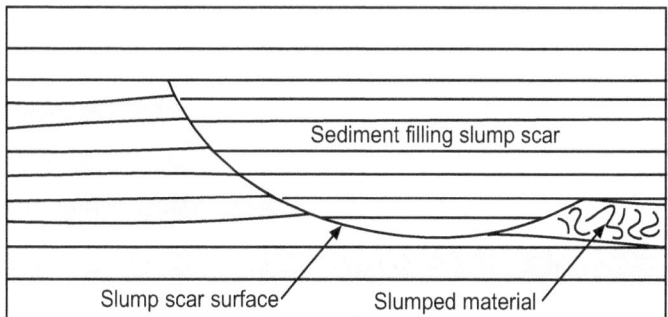

Fig. 1.21 (b) : Slump scars produced by movement of material on a failure surface

Channels are generally sites of sediment transport over long period of time. They are concave up in cross-section and their fills form elongate sediment bodies when seen in plan [Fig. 1.21 (a)]. Channels are filled with coarser sediment, often by a basal conglomerate layer.

Slump scars commonly have their maximum horizontal extent perpendicular to their down slope direction. In vertical section, they are smoothly curving, concave upward surfaces whose inclination may vary from near vertical to near horizontal [Fig. 1.21 (b)]. Sediments below the surface may show small normal faults due to local horizontal extension.

1.12.3 Textures

(a) Grain Morphology :

The morphology of grains is explained by their shape, i.e. sphericity and roundness.

Sphericity is a measure of how closely the grain shape approaches that of a sphere. Roundness refers to the degree of angularity of the edges and corners of the particles and is a function of the degree of abrasion suffered by the particle during transport. These terms are applied to grains in a clastic sedimentary rocks and are less useful for limestones.

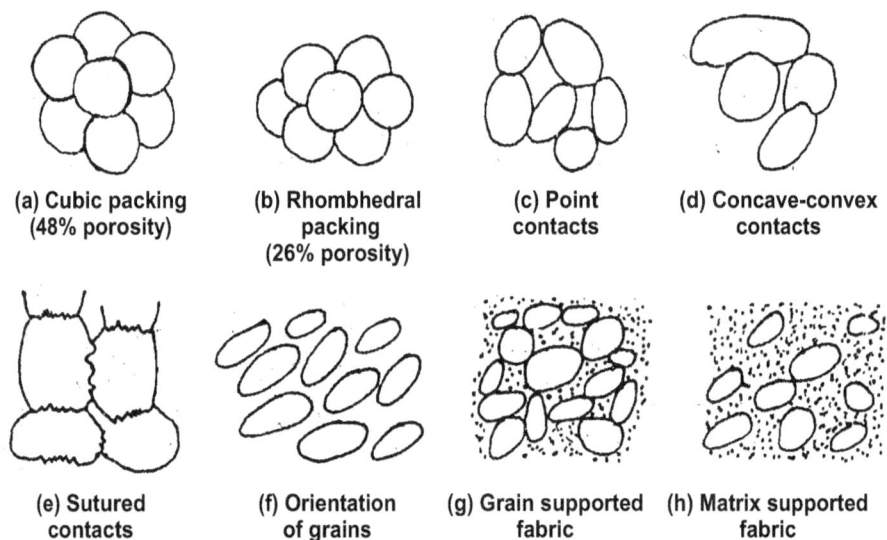

(a) Cubic packing (48% porosity) (b) Rhombhedral packing (26% porosity) (c) Point contacts (d) Concave-convex contacts

(e) Sutured contacts (f) Orientation of grains (g) Grain supported fabric (h) Matrix supported fabric

Fig. 1.22 : Grain fabric in sediments, packing, contacts, grain orientation and grain-matrix fabric

(b) Sediment Fabric :

Fabric includes the grain orientation and their packing [Fig. 1.22 (a) and (b)]. It refers to the mutual arrangement of grains in a sediment.

In many cases, a preferred orientation of elongated particles can be observed, e.g. pebbles in a conglomerate, fossils in limestone, elongated grains in sandstone seen under microscope. Preferred orientations of particles develop from interaction with the depositional medium (water, ice, wind) and may be parallel and normal to flow directions. These can be used to deduce the flow direction of the paleo currents by which they were transported and deposited.

The packing of grain has a marked effect on the porosity of a rock. The lesser the packing, lower is the porosity. Similarly, as the closeness of the packing increases, the density per unit volume of the deposit increases, and the potential volume available for occupation by the cement decreases. Thus, where grains in a sediment are in contact, the sediment is grain supported. Matrix can occur between the grains as can cement. When the grains are not in contact, packing is less and the sediment is matrix-supported.

(c) Texture Maturity :

Maturity can be measured in terms of texture and composition.

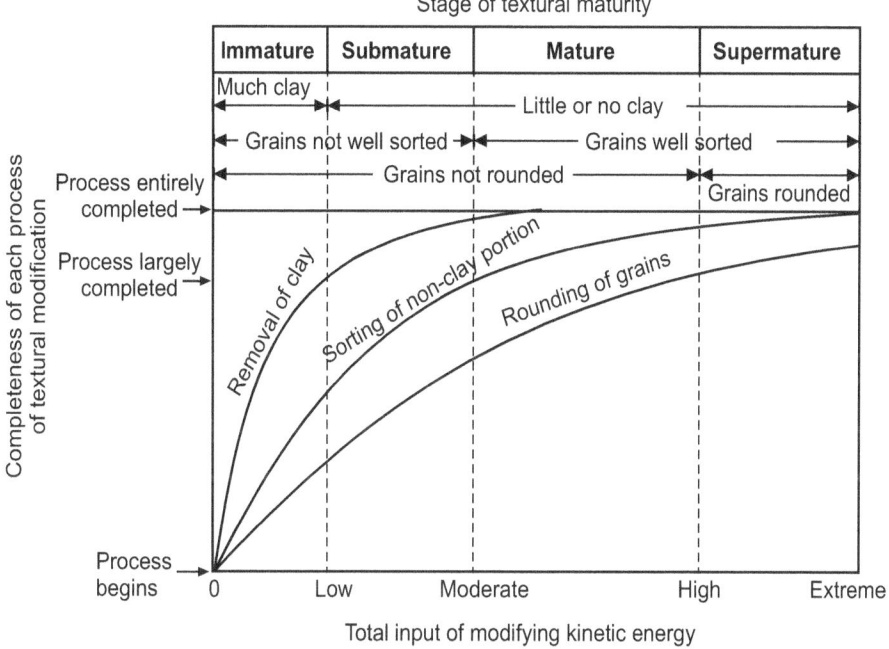

Fig. 1.23 : Textural maturity of clastic sedimentary rocks

Textural maturity can be studied by clay content, sorting and grain shape. It is an indication towards understanding the knowledge of erosion, transport and depositional history. Presence of large proportion of clay, large variation in grain size and angularity of grains together suggestive of textural immaturity of clastic sedimentary rocks (Fig. 1.23). Decreasing clay content, minor variation in grain size and presence of rounded grains tend to indicate supermaturity of clastic sedimentary rocks. Primary porosity and permeability increases with increasing textural maturity, since more mature the sediment is, the less matrix and more pore space it possesses. Examples of texturally immature sediments include braided, and glacial deposits, supermatured sediments are shown by desert, beach and shallow marine sediments.

1.12.4 Colour in Sedimentary Rocks

Colour can give information about the nature of rocks, depositional environments and diagenesis.

The colour of a rock may be controlled by :

(1) Presence of minerals and rock fragments,

(2) Colour of matrix and / or cement,

(3) Coating on the clastic grains,

(4) Presence of organic matter,

(5) Presence of iron compounds etc.

1.12.5 Classification of Sedimentary Rocks

Four major categories of sedimentary rocks are recognised on the basis of their composition and origin.

(a) Sedimentary rocks (Clastic)

(b) Chemical deposits

(c) Organic deposits

(d) Residual deposits.

Description of sedimentary rocks include an assessment of the mineralogy and / or biogenic origin of the constituents as well as quantitative analysis of size, shape and distribution of the particles present. Sedimentary origin of rocks is indicated by the following features :

(a) Presence of stratification

(b) Sedimentary structures

(c) Fossils

(d) Presence of fragments which have been transported (size and shape)

(e) Presence of minerals of sedimentary origin.

(A) Sedimentary Rocks (Clastic) :

Clastic sedimentary rocks are composed of clasts (sediments) of pre-existing rocks and minerals. Most of them are rich in quartz and other silicate minerals. They are also referred as detrital. A three fold classification on the basis of grain size is recognised. (see Table 1.7)

Table 1.7 : Terms for grain size classes and clastic sedimentary rocks

Size	Sediment	Clastic rocks
More than 256 mm	Boulder	**Rudaceous :** Conglomerate : rounded fragments, sandy matrix. Breccia : angular fragements..
64 mm – 256 mm	Cobbles	
4 mm – 64 mm	Pebbles	
2 mm – 4 mm	Granules	
1 mm	Very Coarse Sand	**Arenaceous :** Sandstone : gritty feel, Subdivided into various types.
0.5 mm	Coarse Sand	
0.25 mm	Medium Sand	
0.125 mm	Fine Sand	
0.06 mm	Very Fine Sand	
0.032 mm	Silt	**Argillaceous :** Siltstone : Mudstone. Shales : Fissile.
less than 0.016	Clay	

Rudaceous rocks : Two major rocks are included. **Conglomerate** is a lithified gravel made up of rounded to subrounded clasts of more than 2 mm in diameter. Breccia is a lithified rubble made up of angular sharp clasts coarser than 2 mm. They are best studied in field.

Most clasts in **conglomerate** and breccia are fragments of rocks and minerals which occur as coarse grained framework and fine grained matrix. Clasts are held together by **calcareous**, **siliceous** and **ferruginous** cement. Three major types of clasts are seen namely; mineral fragments, rock fragments and minor minerals.

Texture : Two varieties of conglomerate are defined on the basis of texture. *Orthoconglomerate* consists of gravel size framework grains with proportion of matrix less than or equal to 15%. Thus, the conglomerate have an intact grain supported framework i.e. individual grains are in tangential contact with each other.

Paraconglomerate have a matrix more than 15% and thus have a matrix supported framework.

These rocks are either unimodal i.e. they contain single size clasts, or bimodal i.e. grain size of clasts varies prominently. Grain surface features are important microrelief features seen on the surface of clasts. These include narrow straight scratches (striations), irregular pits, surface polish and crescent shaped percussion marks. The surface features are indicative of transportation history of the clasts.

In some modern stream gravels, the long axes of clasts are aligned parallel and dip upstream. This systematic orientation is called *pebble imbrication*.

Table 1.8 : Descriptive classification of Conglomerate and Breccia

Framework grain to matrix ratio	Fabric	Framework clast composition
Orthobreccia, Orthoconglomerate; 4 : 1 or greater i.e. (matrix < 20%)	Intact or grain supported, framework grains in tangential contact, removal of matrix does not collapse framework.	Oligomict : Most of the clasts composed of quartzite.
Parabreccia, Paraconglomerate, < 4 : 1 Laminated and unlaminated matrix	Typically unstable or matrix supported, frame-work grains float in the matrix, removal of matrix collapse framework.	Petromict : (Polymict), more than 10% of the clasts of various types of unstable rocks and minerals.

Conglomerate are also classified on the basis of clast composition. **Oligomict conglomerate** is the one where more than 90% of the clasts consist of fragments of a few varieties of resistant rocks. **Polymict conglomerate** comprises of fragments of different types of unstable rocks. Oligomict conglomerate imply decomposition and disintegration of immense volume of most resistant rock. They are thinner in nature occupying base of a sequence. Polymict conglomerate are much more abundant than oligomict conglomerate and occur in sequences thousands of metre thick. Although they are alluvium eroded from high relief sources, the polymict conglomerate are recorded in different environment. **Tillite** is an ill sorted glacier derived conglomerate. Clasts in these conglomerates are angular and heterogeneous in composition. Grains often exhibit prominent surface striations.

Arenaceous rocks : Arenaceous rocks are made up of sand size particles (diameter from 2 mm to 0.0625 mm) and sandstone is the indurated equivalent of unconsolidated sand. They constitute between 10 and 20% of the Earth's sedimentary rock record. Sandstones are major reservoirs of groundwater and petroleum.

Sandstone generally comprises of quartz (> 60%), feldspar (10-15%), micas and clay minerals in siliceous, calcareous and ferruginous cement. The texture of sandstone includes grain size, shape, fabric, surface features and size variation.

Grain size and size variation can be measured with a petrological microscope and sieve size analysis. For sieve analysis, the cohesive sandstone is needed to be disaggregated. The analysis measures grain diameter by allowing sand to settle through a number of sieves of fixed aperture (2 mm, 1 mm, 0.5 mm, 0.25 mm, 0.125 mm and 0.0625 mm). Thus, a percentage of sand retained in each sieve is calculated and presented in two ways : graphs of grain size distribution are plotted and compared, and statistical measures such as mean grain size and sorting are calculated arithmatically by taking values from the graphs and standard formula. Both methods use grain size diameter in millimeter or phi (φ) units which express grain size as the negative logarithm of grain diameter in millimeters to the base 2.

i.e. Grain size diameter in phi units

$$= -\log_2 \text{ of grain size diameter in mm.}$$

i.e.
$$2 \text{ mm} = -1\phi$$
$$\frac{1}{4} \text{ mm} = -2\phi$$

All the statistical formulae described here (Table 1.9) express grain size diameter in phi units and not in millimeters.

Generally four diagrams are prepared (Fig. 1.24).

Simple histogram is a bar diagram of proportion of grain in each size (weight percentage from sieve analysis, number of grains out of total count in thin section) against single grain size [Fig. 1.24 (a)]. This helps in isolating the most abundant grain size in the analysis.

A frequency curve [Fig. 1.24 (b)] is a smooth curve which can be superimposed directly on a histogram by joining mid-points of each size bar. The curve is a measure of grain size variation.

A cumulative curve [Fig. 1.24 (c)] is drawn by plotting graph of cumulative percentage against grain size. The probability curve is plotted on log probability paper [Fig. 1.24 (d)]. It is observed that the slope of grain size distribution on a probability curve steepens with improved sorting.

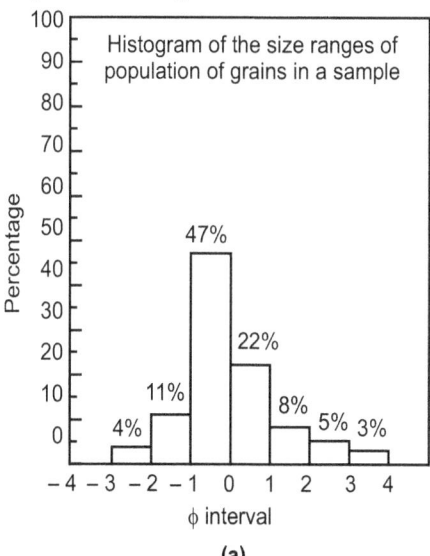
(a)

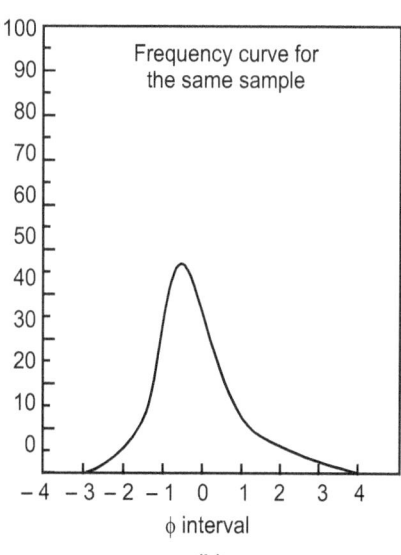
(b)

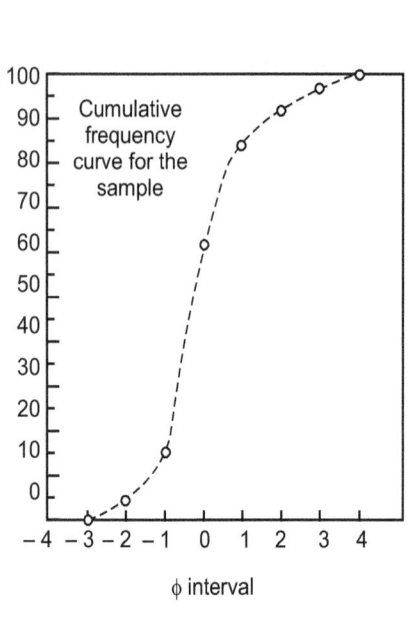
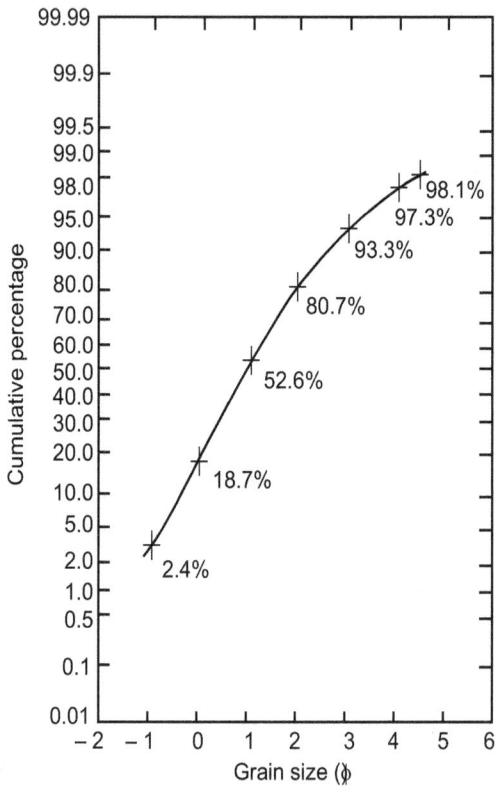

Fig. 1.24 : Histogram, frequency distribution, cumulative frequency and probability curves of grain size distribution data

The probability curve is used to find out mean size, standard deviation (size sorting), symmetry (skewness) and peakedness (kurtosis) (Table 1.9). The curves are also useful to indicate whether the deposit is unimodal or bimodal in terms of grain size.

Table 1.9 : Formulae for calculating statistical measures using ϕ scale from probability graph

1. Mean = $\dfrac{\phi_{16} + \phi_{50} + \phi_{85}}{3}$

   Median = ϕ_{50}

2. Sorting (standard deviation)

   $= \dfrac{\phi_{86} + \phi_{16}}{4} + \dfrac{\phi_{95} - \phi_5}{6.6}$

< 0.35 ϕ	very well sorted
0.35 to 0.50 ϕ	well sorted
0.50 to 0.71 ϕ	moderately well sorted
0.71 to 1.00 ϕ	moderately sorted
1.00 to 2.00 ϕ	poorly sorted
> 2.00 ϕ	very poorly sorted.

3. Symmetry (skewness)

$$= \frac{\phi_{84} + \phi_{16} + 2\phi_{50}}{2(\phi_{84} - \phi_{16})} + \frac{\phi_{95} + \phi_{5} - 2\phi_{50}}{2(\phi_{95} - \phi_{5})}$$

< + 0.30	strongly fine skewed
+ 0.30 to + 0.10	fine skewed
+ 0.10 to − 0.10	evenly skewed
− 0.10 to − 0.30	coarse skewed
< − 0.30	strongly coarse skewed

4. Kurtosis

$$= \frac{\phi_{95} - \phi_{5}}{2.44(\phi_{75} - \phi_{25})}$$

> 1.0	leptokurtic
1.0	mesokurtic
< 1.30	platykurtic

Sorting is representative of number of significant clast sizes in a population. Skewness is a statistical measure of the symmetry of a distribution. In asymmetrical distribution, the median and mean shift from central peak towards coarse or fine size. Negative skewness indicates that coarser grains are less well sorted than finer grains; and with positive skewness, finer grains are more poorly sorted than coarser grains. This is well illustrated in Fig. 1.25.

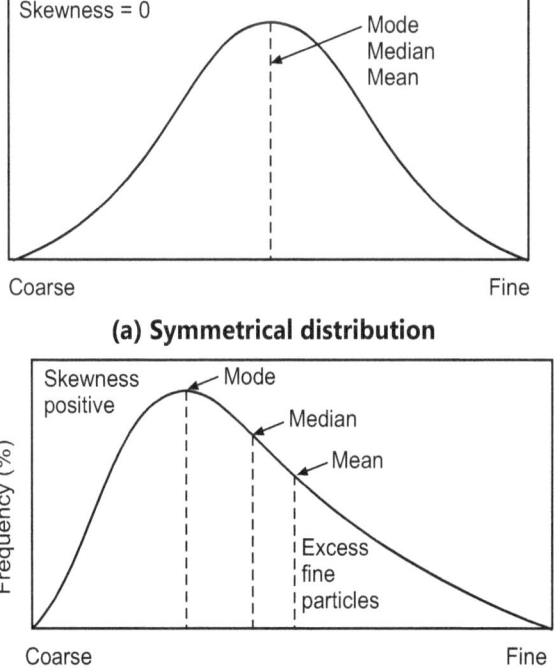

(a) Symmetrical distribution

(b) Positive skewness, better sorting in coarse grained

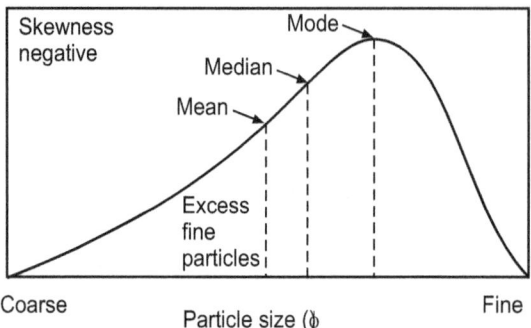

(c) Negative skewness, finer grains are better sorted

Fig. 1.25: Size frequency curves of three sediments having an identical sorting but different skewness.

Skewness is significant as the transporting agent differ in their ability to entrain transport and deposit coarse verses finer material.

Kurtosis compares sorting in the central portion of a population with that of fine and coarse fractions.

Grain shape and roundness is indicative of distance and mode of transportation. Shape may be described by using the terms : equant, tabular, bladed and prolate. Similarly, many surface features are developed on particles during rolling and transportation. Fabric of **arenaceous** rocks is either **isotropic** (random) or oriented. An oriented fabric is produced by parallel arrangement of elongate or disk shaped grains by strong directional uniform currents. In random fabric, no clast imbrication is seen.

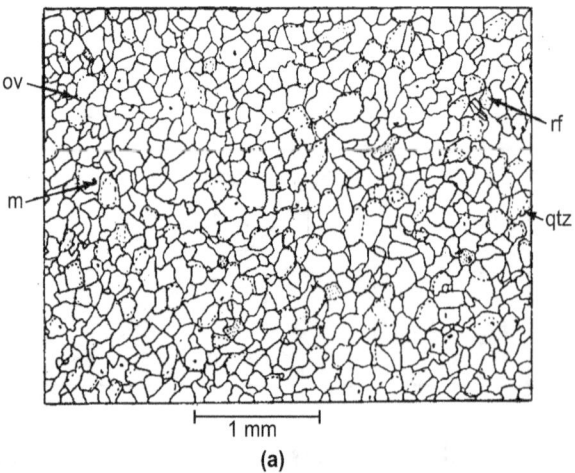

(a)

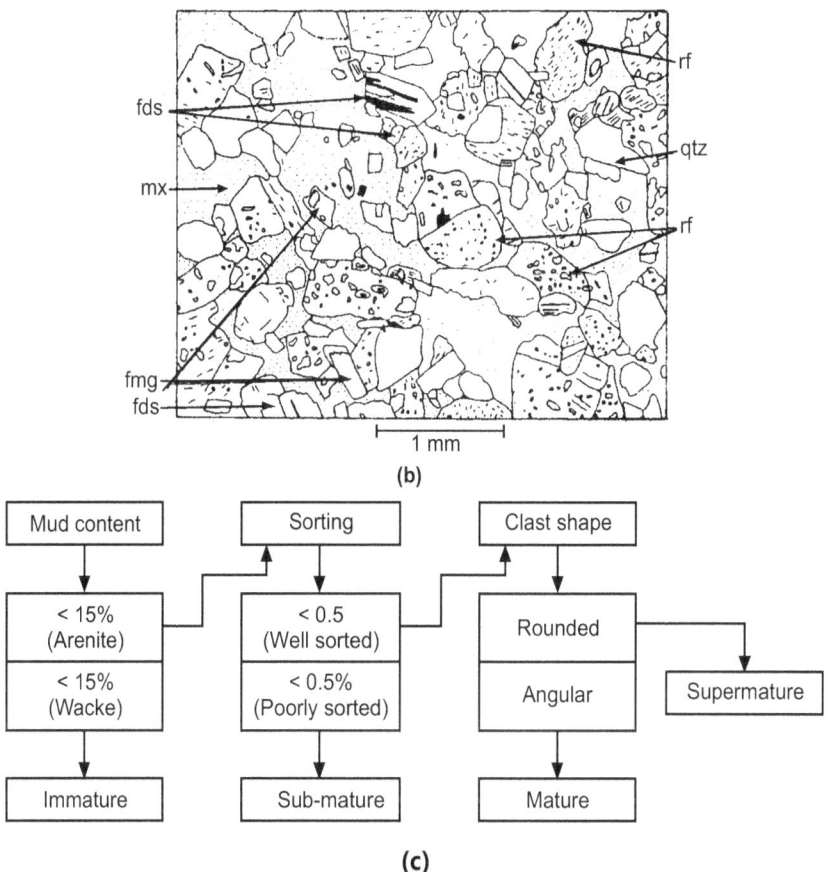

(a) Interpretive thin section sketch of a matured sandstone, well rounded quartz (qtz) cemented by overgrowths (ov) of secondary quartz, m – muscovite, rf – rock fragments, (b) Interpretive thin section sketch of an immature greywacke. Poorly sorted angular quartz (qtz) in clayey matrix (mx). fd – feldspar, rf – rock fragments, mg – ferromagnesian minerals (c) Flow chart for textural maturity of sandstone.

Fig. 1.26 : Textural maturity of sandstones.

Textural maturity of sandstone is based on three criterias : (1) the proportion of clay size fractions, (2) sorting of sand framework, and (3) roundness of sand grains (Fig. 1.26). A sandstone is texturally immature if the proportion of clay fraction exceeds 5% irrespective of degree of rounding and sorting. Immature sandstone also exhibit high proportion of feldspar and rock fragments. Texturally mature sandstones have less than 5% of clay sized fractions and the sand particles are well sorted, rounded in shape.

The above discussion leads to the conclusion that two parameters are used to subdivide the arenaceous rocks.

1. The composition of sand framework grains that include quartz, feldspar and rock fragments.
2. The percentage of matrix.

Based on these parameters, two distinct groups of sandstone are recognised : **arenites** and **wackes** (grey wackes). A third variety is also observed on the relative proportion of rock fragments and feldspar, called **arkose**.

Arenites are matrix free clean sandstone. They consist almost entirely of monocrystalline quartz, well bedded and can exhibit ripple marks, lamination, cross bedding. They occur as regionally extensive tabular bodies with the thickness of individual sheets which varies from a few metres to several hundred metres. Most quartz are shallow marine sands typical of shoreline beach zone.

Arkose or feldspathic sandstone consists of monocrystalline quartz and feldspar (even upto 50%). They are coarse grained, and ill sorted in nature. High proportion of feldspar indicates that they have been derived from feldspar rich rocks like granite and gneiss. They form as sheet flow and debris flow sediments and accumulate on the surface of alluvial fans, within river channels, point bars and also along shorelines.

Wackes consist of clasts of monocrystalline quartz (25–50%), K feldspar, plagioclase and a few rock fragments in a pulverised feldspar matrix. Grains are poorly sorted and angular to sub-angular in shape. They are typical of turbidity currents and routinely display graded bedding.

Argillaceous rocks : Argillaceous rocks are the most abundant group of sedimentary rocks covering about 65% of earth's total sedimentary cover. Following major varieties of argillaceous rocks are recognised.

(a) **Mudstones** consist predominantly of silt and clay size particles (33-65%). Two major types are seen; siltstone with 50% or more silt size particles and claystone with 50% or more of clay size material.

(b) **Shale** is composed of clay size particles with planes of fissility, lamination or both.

Argillaceous rocks rich in calcite and dolomite is, called **Marl**. Organic matter in shale can take the form of coal partings and lenses or the insoluble residual petroleum products called *kerogen*. Bituminous and kerogenous shale, known as oil shale, give off a petroleum or gas odour when struck with a hammer. Some argillaceous rocks are massive in nature without any obvious sedimentary structures.

A brief but the most common approach of identification of sedimentary rocks is given in Table 1.10.

Table 1.10 : Features to note in the description of argillaceous rocks

Attribute	Description
Colour	Grey, green, red, brown, variegated
Degree of fissility	Fissile, non-fissile, blocky, earthy.
Sedimentary structures	Bedded, laminated, slumped, massive, biogenic structures.
Mineral content	Clay minerals, quartz, mica, carbonate minerals, gypsum.
Organic content and Fossil bearings.	Organic rich, bituminous carbonaceous.

From an engineering point of view, the argillaceous rocks are divided into two classes. The first are true rocks, more deformable than other rocks but no tendency to deteriorate except after long exposure to the atmosphere. In these rocks, diagenesis has lithified the rock and recrystallization of clays into micas. This group is called *cemented shales*.

The second group is called *compaction shale or clay shales* which behaves more like soil as these rocks tend to deteriorate on exposure to atmosphere. They contain certain clay constituents which create serious engineering problems in major civil works. It is observed that the compaction shales have relatively large amount of moisture when saturated.

Mineral Composition : A typical argillaceous rock contains very large proportion of clay minerals (50 – 100%) in addition to quartz, feldspar and cement. As a result, behaviour of these rocks is controlled to a large extent by clay minerals. Two types of clay minerals are observed based on their internal atomic structure and ion-exchange capacity viz. expandable and non-expandable clays. Expandable clay minerals have a complex arrangement.

(B) Chemical and Organic Deposits :

Chemical and organic deposits constitute one of the important groups of sedimentary rocks formed due to precipitation, evaporation and biogenic activities. Important members of chemical and organic deposits are listed in table 1.11.

Table 1.11 : Important rocks of chemical and organic deposits

Name	Chemical Composition	Origin
Limestone	$CaCO_3$	Organic and chemical
Dolomite	$CaMg(CO_3)_2$	Organic and chemical
Iron deposite	Iron oxides, silicates, sulphides and carbonates	Chemical
Maganese deposits	Oxides and carbonates	Chemical
Diatomite	Silica	Organic
Radiolarite	Silica	Organic
Chert and flint	Silica	Organic and chemical
Peat, lignite and coal	Carbon, oxygen, hydrogen, nitrogen, sulphur	Organic
Rock salt	NaCl	Chemical

Carbonate rocks : Carbonate rocks include limestone and dolomite which constitute an important group of sedimentary rocks. Dissolved ions carried from source to depositional site in solution eventually precipitate when saturated and form solid minerals. In organic deposits, organisms extract dissolved components from sea water to manufacture shell or skeletons that are later converted to sedimentary rocks.

Carbonates have an economic importance as about 50% of world's petroleum is recovered from carbonate reservoir rocks. High porosity also makes limestone excellent store house for ore bearing solutions. Similarly, because of their highly porous nature, severe engineering problems like leakage, ground collapse, and foundation treatments are of common occurrence.

The main constituents of limestones are shells, crystals or fragments with the composition of mineral calcite. Dolomite is also observed due to post depositional changes from calcite particularly in older rocks. Silica, in the form of chert is also a common secondary constituent of limestones. Other common accessories are clay, silica, iron oxide and aluminium oxide.

Ground water saturated in calcium carbonate precipitates crystals of calcite or aragonite when it comes into the contact with atmosphere and loses carbon dioxide. In many instances, stream deposits, hard grounds often exhibit limy thick to thick coating. Deposits of calcite by springs and river water are called *calc-tufa* and travertine respectively. Caliche is name given to secondary calcite deposited by evaporating water at the surface in arid and semi-arid regions. Calc-tufa is a porous material and travertine is a banded dense material.

The term *dolomite* is used for limestone composed of more than 90% of the mineral dolomite. *Dolomitic limestone* is a name given to rock that is composed of dolomite (upto 90%) and calcite (10% or more). Dolomite is less soluble than calcite. It has a uniform grey or mottled colour and crystalline (sugary) texture of uniform grain size. The process of dolomitisation tends to obscure the textures and structures of original limestone rock and thus are not usually subdivided into detrital and chemical types.

Detrital limestone consist of sand or gravel size particles of older limestone or reworked fragments of shells of different grade size. It is also called as fossiliferous limestone.

Karst topography : Dissolution of carbonate rocks are of two kinds : long term and short term. For the geologically older limestones and dolomites that are denser in nature, the rate of dissolution is very slow and is unnoticed. Here the solution effects are to be visualised considering the factor of geologic time. On the other hand, in geologically recent carbonate rocks, removal of rock by water of uneven pH is a rapid process which may prove to be a threat for engineering projects.

Continued removal of carbonate rocks by water over a significant period of time results in the development of caves and passageways. Streams often disappear and reappear suddenly. The surface is seen with large and small depression. This morphology, called as *Karst topography*, is typical of carbonate rocks.

Generally, the surface of Karst exhibits many internally drained depressions, called **sinkholes**, tens to hundreds of metre across. These may be formed because of subsidence or collapse. Often the receiving openings could simply be solution of enlarged joints called *Karrens*. The styles and dimensions of these effects depend on the composition, texture and structure of the rock. Following are the observations in the Karst topography :

- Limestones and dolomites of variable proportion with shaly partings tend to develop small but persistent openings along discontinuities and bedding planes.
- Dolomites may form tiny holes, called vugs. In calcareous sandstones, narrow cavities grow along joints.
- Marbles can form large caverns elongated along foliation direction.

- Inactive (fossil) karst may occur below the surface or even below older erosional surface.
- Young porous limestones may develop friable, spongy appearance near the surface rather than cavities.

The soil developed on limestone in Karst regions is an accumulation of insoluble residues and can contain iron rich impurities. The soil is generally red in colour and thus the name **terra rossa**. In the humid regions, terra rossa soils are rich in clays, haematite and limonite. Dolomite weathers similarly, but the magnesium may find its way into clay minerals particularly **montmorillonite**. The manganese and iron often appear as manganese oxide and iron oxide. This manganiferous soil, known as **Wad**, is a highly compressible soil with very high natural water. This residual soil often create several settlement problems.

Limestone diagenesis : Diagenetic changes are more common in limestones than clastic sedimentary rocks due to their higher soluble nature. The most common diagenetic changes in the form of dissolution and replacement are seen in limestone.

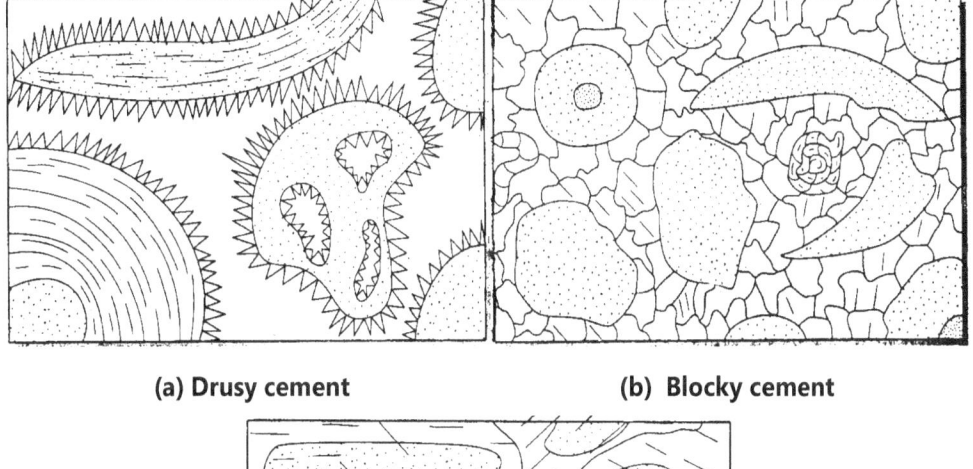

(a) Drusy cement   (b) Blocky cement

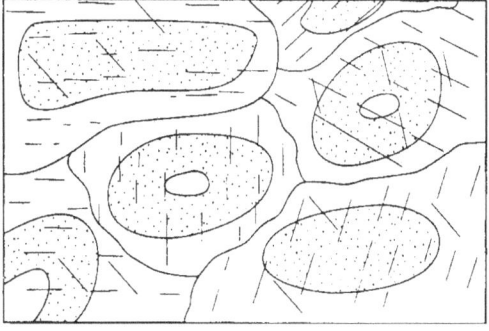

(c) Rim cement

Fig. 1.27 : Cement types in limestones

Dissolution produces pore space by dissolving pre-existing minerals. This results in development of additional porosity in the rock (secondary porosity). A typical product of dissolution is growth of **stylolite** seams [Fig. 1.27(a)]. Stylolites are formed by pressure solution. Generally, they are thin seams of clay and insoluble material which mostly run parallel to bedding in a limestone. They are frequently sutured [Fig. 1.27 (a)] and are known to be formed as a result of overburden or tectonic pressure.

Cementation occurs when carbonate is precipitated into a pre-existing void space; and often a sequence of cementing events are seen (Fig. 1.27). Initially, the cement often forms needle like crystals that radiate away from rim of the voids and towards the centre, known as *drusy cement* [Fig. 1.27 (a)]. Block cement is the one that shows larger irregular equant patches and mosaic of sparry calcite [Fig. 1.27 (b)]. This cement fills the remaining void spaces and may thus be considered as second generation cement. In a few instances, cements forms overgrowth around framework grains, giving rise to rim cement [Fig. 1.27 (c)].

Replacement involves the simultaneous dissolution of original matter and precipitation of a new mineral while preserving the original form e.g. occurrence of chert and chalcedony in carbonate as replacement minerals.

Iron-rich sedimentary rocks : Most iron dissolved in water is derived from the chemical decomposition of iron bearing minerals like pyroxene and biotite. Ionic iron occurs in two forms : insoluble ferric iron (Fe^{3+}) and relatively soluble ferrous iron (Fe^{2+}). In the presence of oxygen, ferrous ion oxidizes to ferric state. Whenever the dissolved ferric ion enters the sea, the increased salinity of sea water and presence of organic matter causes small particles of iron rich material to undergo flocculation. These particles adhere each other and settle to the sea floor. Flocculated iron particles are incorporated into sedimentary rocks mainly as components of silicate minerals.

Iron-rich sedimentary rocks are of two types where iron content exceeds 15% : **Precambrian** banded iron formation and **Proterozoic ironstones**. Most of the iron is derived from these rocks. Precambrian banded iron formations (popularly known as BIF) consist of centimetre thick, interlayered alternating bands of iron rich minerals and chert. The proterozoic ironstone is essentially a mudstone in which high concentration of iron is noted.

Modern bog iron deposits are another important iron rich rocks. They consist mainly of iron minerals geothite and siderite and manganese minerals psilomelane and pyrolusite. They are developed only in lacustrine condition.

Chert and Siliceous Sediments :

Chert is a fine grained hard sedimentary rock composed of cryptocrystalline fibrous chalcedony, minor amount of microcrystalline and cryptocrystalline quartz and amorphous silica. Most chert is formed when siliceous organic oozes deposited on the deep sea floor are crystallised. Two types are recognised : bedding or primary chert, replacement or nodular chert.

Bedded cherts occur as individual bands that shows variation in thickness from a few millimetres upto several metres. However thickness of individual layers is often uniform both laterally and vertically.

Nodular or replacement chert occurs as spherical, avoidal and flat shaped bodies of quartz, opal and chalcedony mainly in limestones and dolomites. Variations in colour from black to white to dull grey are seen due to presence of impurities. Individual nodules vary in size from a few millimetres to a few centimetres. They are often linked together forming planar bands.

Coal : Coal consists of humus organic material and undecayed plant material. Coal seams are interbedded with other sedimentary rocks and are widespread in carboniferous times.

Coals are classified on the basis of coal rank and coal lithotype. Coal rank is a measure of the degree of coalification or carbonification. Peat contains 60% carbon along with abundant volatiles and moisture. Lignite (brown coal) is the lowest rank of coal with 70% carbon and significant amount of moisture and volatile content. Bituminous coal contains 80-90% carbon and anthracite has 90 – 100% carbon with very little moisture. Higher ranked coals are more useful fuels as they generate more heat per mass consumed.

In the classification of coal by lithotype, the proportion of individual macerals (microscopic scale remains of plant matter) are taken into consideration. Based on these, four major lithotypes are recognised : vitrin, fusain, durain and clarain. Vitrinite or vitrin layers are shiny black, brittle and exhibit conchoidal fracture. Fusain occurs as soft-charcoal like layers. Durain coals display a dull lustre and irregular fracture, and clarain coal exhibit a silky lustre, smooth fracture and internal lamination.

Evaporites : Evaporites are bedded sedimentary rocks that crystallizes from hypersaline solutions known as *brines*. The most common evaporite minerals are carbonates (calcite, aragonite, magnesite and dolomite), sulphates (gypsum and anhydrite), halides (halite, sylvite and carnallite) and a few borates, silicates, nitrates and sulphocarbonates. Crystallization of evaporite minerals begin only after seawater of normal salinity (35000 ppm) has been reduced to 20 % of its original volume. The least soluble constituents crystallise first. Calcium and sulphate ions form gypsum and anhydrite. When the volume of seawater is reduced to 10% of the original volume, more soluble components such as potassium, sodium and chlorine solidify as the mineral halite and sylvite. Finally, the most soluble minerals (bitter borates and nitrates) solidify from the remaining droplets of briny fluids.

(c) Residual Deposits :

Residual deposits are insoluble products of rock weathering that have escape distribution by transporting agencies. These have two components :

(a) Unaltered minerals from the parent rocks, normally these are resistant minerals. For example, quartz.

(b) Insoluble residue, for example, hydrous-aluminium silicates, hydrous-magnesium silicates, various hydrated oxides of iron, aluminium and colloidal silica.

Residual deposits are unsorted, sharply angular in shape and heterogeneous in grain size. The major residual deposits are as follows :

(1) Laterite and Bauxite : Laterite is a reddish, brick coloured, porous concretionary material which covers large covers in tropical and sub-tropical areas. It is particularly seen in capping iron and aluminium rich rocks.

Laterite consists of a mixture of hydrated ferric oxide with hydroxide of aluminium in unequal proportion, frequently also with manganese oxide, titanium dioxide and free silica. When aluminium constituent dominates, the colour changes to yellow or white and the rock becomes dull and earthy, the rock is known as *bauxite*.

Both these rocks form due to intense weathering under highly oxidising condition in tropical climate characterised by alternating wet and dry seasons. Under normal weathering condition, the silicates of the alkalies, lime and aluminium (e.g., the feldspars) lose their bases and gain water, forming hydrous aluminium silicates of the composition $Al_2O_3; 2SiO_2, nH_2O$. The iron present is normally converted to soluble ferrous salts which are then carried away in solution. As a result under this condition the residue is poor in iron but rich in silica. However, under tropical condition, silicates lose their silica and also bases leaving behind hydroxide of aluminium. Furthermore, under strongly oxidising conditions, the iron in the rock produces, insoluble ferric salts which are then very easily oxidised to ferric oxides and hydrates.

(2) Soil : Soil is perhaps the most important residual deposit. Normally, it grades downward into the unaltered parent rock or bed rock. Soil is either residual or transported.

1.13 METAMORPHIC ROCKS

Metamorphism involves partial or complete recrystallization of the parent material that takes place at temperature less than melting temperature. The word 'metamorphism' is used here to include the responses in solid rocks to marked changes in physico-chemical environment, the changes taking place below the zones of weathering. The changes observed are typically mineralogical as well as textural. Thus, a rock that is formed originally in an igneous or sedimentary environment, recrystallizes in response to new conditions to form metamorphic rocks. Most of the metamorphic rocks retain some of the characteristics of their parent material, such as bulk chemical composition or major features like bedding, while developing new textures and minerals.

1.13.1 Types of Metamorphic Change

Two major changes are visualised during metamorphism : creation of new metamorphic minerals due to chemical reactions and recrystallization of minerals to produce new textures e.g. progressive transformation of limestone to marble.

The metamorphic processes take place essentially in solid state.

1.13.2 The Controlling Factors of Metamorphism

(a) **Temperature :** Temperature invariably increases with depth in the earth. The rate of increase in temperature with increasing depth is known as *geothermal gradient*, which is in the range of 15 – 30°C/km. However, extremes from 50 – 60°C/km do occur. A detailed study of existing data indicates that the heat flow in continental crust is higher than in the older oceanic basins (Fig. 1.28); but the younger oceanic crust lives higher heat flow values. The regional variations in heat flow are due to three major processes which contribute to surface heat flow, such as (1) heat flow into the base of crust from mantle, (2) heat generated by radioactive decay within the crust (higher in continental crust) and (3) volcanic erruptions. Furthermore, the role played by rapid uplift and erosion in bringing hot rocks near the surface without much loss of heat is crucial and thus geothermal gradient varies with temperature 30°C/km.

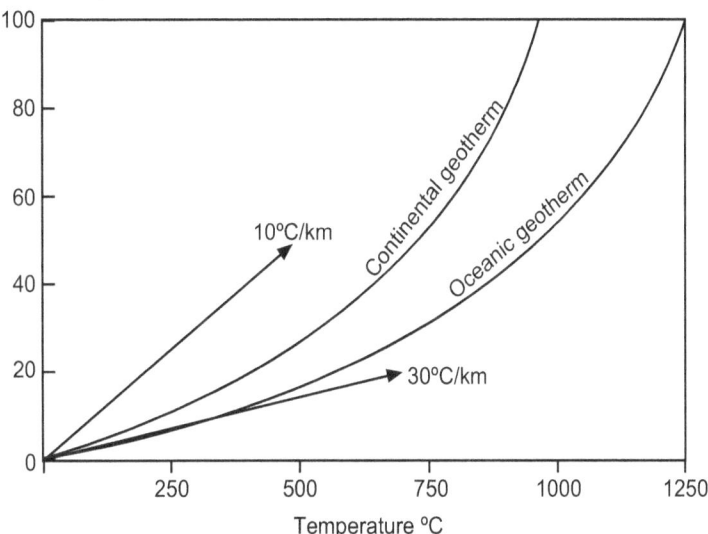

Fig. 1.28 : Effects of rise in temperature and oceanic regions

(b) **Pressure :** Pressure is a measure of force per unit area to which a rock is subjected depending on the weight of overlying rock and depth. The total pressure exerted at a point in the crust due to the weight of overlying rocks is known as the *lithostatic pressure*. In most metamorphic environment, it is believed that, the pressure acting at a point is approximately uniform in all directions and is equal to lithostatic pressure. However, in reality, deformation is also a result of (deviatoric) differential stress acting on a rock which plays a crucial role in determining the textural characteristics of rocks but may not change the mineral assemblage.

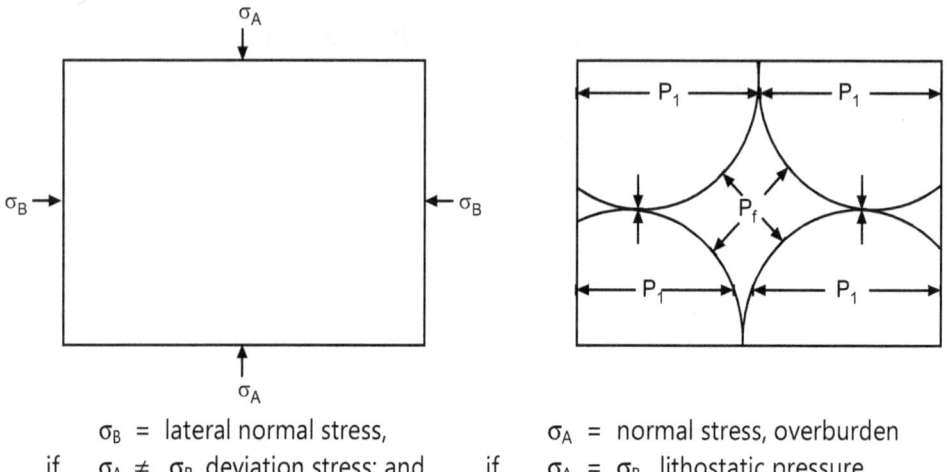

σ_B = lateral normal stress, σ_A = normal stress, overburden
if $\sigma_A \neq \sigma_B$, deviation stress; and   if $\sigma_A = \sigma_B$, lithostatic pressure

Fig. 1.29 : Schematic summery of stresses acting on rocks during metamorphism

Another important factor in the pressure variable is fluid pressure i.e. pressure exerted by fluids available in porous spaces and along grain boundaries. In case the rock is dry, fluid pressure is almost zero and the lithostatic pressure acts across grain boundaries, binding the grain together and making failure difficult. On the other hand, if a rock is wet, the fluid pressure tends to act in opposite directions, reducing the effective pressure acting along grain boundaries and thus cracking is most likely.

(c) Chemically active fluids : The role played by metamorphic fluids is also very important in some rocks; e.g. presence of talc, tremolite, micas etc. owe their origin to fluid reactions. Water is probably the most important liquid and carbon dioxide an important gas in this connection. Other gases like chlorine and boron may occur and other liquids are hydrochloric and hydrofloric acid. A significant proportion of water in voids may promote recrystallization or deformation at an earlier temperature-pressure condition.

1.13.3 Types of Metamorphism

(a) **Contact or thermal metamorphism** results from the rise in temperature in the surrounding country near major igneous intrusions. These contact rocks are known as *aureole rocks*, which undergo recrystallization to form an inter-locking grain growth.

(b) **Dynamic or cataclastic metamorphism** takes place along fault planes / fault zones as a result of intense crushing and granulation of rocks in the immediate zone of movement. The process is often accompanied by recrystallization.

(c) **Dynamothermal or regional metamorphism** gives rise to large areas of metamorphic rocks, diagnostic of orogenic belts or large mountain chains. In this, metamorphism is accompanied by deformation and folding to form a foliated rock.

The above mentioned major types of metamorphism often exhibit similarity in mineral composition, texture and the metamorphic rock produced. For example, the regional metamorphic rocks are often traversed by faults or shears. Similarly, both the contact and regional metamorphic rocks may exhibit the presence of similar mineral assemblage.

1.13.4 Metamorphic Minerals

The prominent metamorphic minerals are the same as those of igneous rocks, as for example, micas (biotite, muscovite), chlorite, feldspars, quartz and hornblende.

Some minerals are characteristic of metamorphic rocks as like tourmaline, garnet, staurolite, kyanite, talc etc.

In general, two major groups of metamorphic minerals are recognised.

(1) Stress minerals : These are formed under variable stress conditions; as for example, micas, kyanite, staurolite, garnet, talc etc.

(2) Anti-stress minerals : These occur in the absence of stress like pyroxene, olivine etc.

The typical mineralogical assemblage of metamorphic rocks with increasing pressure and temperature is given in Fig. 1.30.

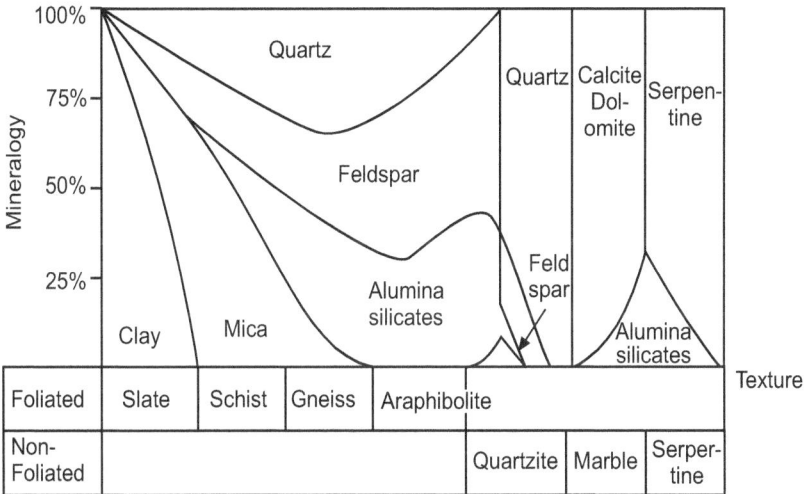

Fig. 1.30 : Classification of metamorphic rocks based on texture and mineralogy

1.13.5 Metamorphic Textures and Structures

The metamorphic textures and structures are divisible into two groups :
(1) Foliated, having a directional or layered appearance;
(2) Non-foliated, homogeneous or massive rocks.

(1) Foliated : In many regional metamorphic rocks or dynamic metamorphic rocks, micas develop a preferred orientation aligned normal to the maximum compression direction giving rise to a planar pervasive fabric called *foliation*. The folia may be planar, undulatory or lenticular which is either megascopic or microscopic. Three major types are recognized :

(a) Slaty cleavage : A planar surface along which the rocks split into thin parallel sheets. The individual grains are very fine grained and the rock has a dull appearance on fresh surfaces. This texture is the result of directed pressure on fine grained rocks accompanied by partial recrystallization.

(b) Schistose texture : Schistosity is a planar structure defined by the alignment of minerals such as micas and amphiboles where individual minerals are easily recognized in hand specimen. Rocks showing this structure are called *schists*; which are common in regional metamorphic rocks. [Fig. 1.31 (a)].

(c) Gneissose banding : Gneissose banding is defined by alternate light coloured and dark coloured bands. Foliation is imparted due to compositional layering or schistosity. Typically quartz and feldspar rich layers segregate out from more micaceous or mafic layers. The term paragneiss is used for metasedimentary gneisses and orthognessies for igneous gneisses.

(d) Mylonite : A term used for fine grained rocks produced in zones of intense ductile deformation where the pre-existing minerals are deformed and recrystallized into fine grains.

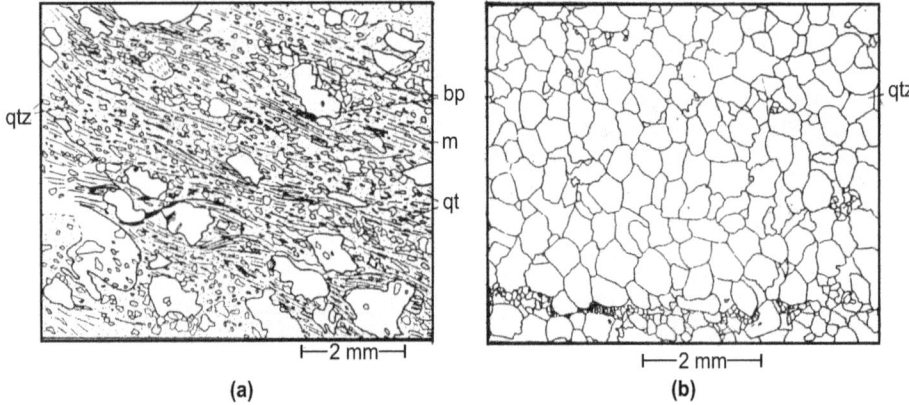

Fig. 1.31 : Photomicrograph and interpretative drawing of (a) thin section of schistose texture developed due to preferred orientation of mica (m), quartz (qtz), and large porphyroblasts of biotite; granulose (b) thin section of grancilose texture shown by quartzite. The mosaic of interlocking grains caused by recrystallization, quartz – qtz.

(2) **Non-foliated :** As the name implies, these do not show any conspicuous schistosity or any planar pervasive cleavage. The texture is characteristic of thermal metamorphism or the product of lithostatic pressure, and is formed due to recrystallization of pre-existing minerals, called as granulose texture. [Fig. 1.31 (b)]

1.13.6 Metamorphic Rock Names

Two features of metamorphic rocks are very important in the discussion of identification of metamorphic rocks; mineral assemblage, textures and structures. For rocks like quartzite and marble first feature is more important and for slate second feature is vital. Table 1.12 divides the metamorphic rocks into broad compositional classes which are further subdivided on the basis of grain size.

The metamorphic rock names in table 1.12 may be prefixed by one or more names if it is necessary to emphasis presence of certain minerals e.g. quartz mica schist, serpentine marble, talc schist. Specific textural features of a metamorphic rock may also be emphasized by appropriate adjectives e.g. augen gneiss, saccharoidal marble.

Table 1.12 : Proposed scheme of classification of metamorphic rocks in the field

Parent rock	Mineral composition	Fine grained < 0.1 mm	Medium grained (0.1 mm to 1 mm)	Coarse grained (> 1 mm)	
1. Shale	Clay and quartz	Slate	Phyllite	Schist	Gneiss
2. Sandstone	Quartz	←———	Quartzite	———→	Banded Quartize
3. Limestone	Calcite Dolomite	←———	Marble	———→	Banded Marble
4. Basalt Gabbro	Plagioclase amphibole	Green schist	Amphibolite	———→	Gneiss
5. Rhyolite Granite	K-feldspar quartz mica	–	←———	Granite	Gneiss
6. Dunite	Talc olivine Serpentine amphibole	Serpentinite	Serpentinite ←———	Talc schist ———→	Gneiss

1.13.7 Description of Metamorphic Rocks based on Parent Compositional Groups

The metamorphic rocks show a great variation in their composition controlled by several factors including composition of parent rock. Generally, the most widely derived metamorphic rocks are from sandstones, shales, limestones and basalts.

(a) Metamorphism of argillaceous rocks :

Clay rich sediments undergo extensive changes during metamorphism. The sequence produced in the metamorphism of a shale is as given in Table 1.13.

It is often observed that metamorphosed argillaceous rocks could be divided into a series of metamorphic zones, each characterised by the appearance of a new mineral form as the metamorphism became more intense. The mineralogical changes are associated with a coarsening of grain size as the progressive metamorphism from fine slate to coarse schist (Table 1.13).

Table 1.13 : Metamorphism of shale increasing temperature and pressure conditions

Shale	Slate	Schist	Gneiss
Sedimentary rock	Low-grade Metamorphism	Medium grade Metamorphism	High grade Metamorphism
Clay ———→	Clay begins ← to → transform into mica. Mica crystals are very fine, but impart a cleavage of rock, called slaty cleavage. May also be formed by mechanical rearrangement alone.	Mica grains being → coarser, the rock develops a conspicuous folidation.	Mica is altered to feldspar, giving the rock a banded or layered appearance.

The name phyllite is applied to rocks of pelitic composition with a cleavage and a grain size intermediate between slate and schist. In slate, the individual crystals are very fine to be seen under a hand lens, whereas in phyllites, grains can be seen.

(b) Metamorphism of basic igneous rocks :

The mineral composition in basalt is olivine, pyroxene and plagioclase, each of which is hydrous. When a basalt is subjected to metamorphism under conditions where fluids can enter the rock and form hydrous minerals, distinctive mineral assemblage develop (Table 1.14).

Table 1.14 : Progressive metamorphism of balsalt

Parent rock	Low grade	Intermediate	High grade
Basalt + $H_2O \longrightarrow$	Green schist $\longrightarrow$	Amphibolite $\longrightarrow$	Granulite
Pyroxene Plagioclase	Fine grained chlorite, epidote amphibole, quartz, calcite	Coarse amphibole, feldspar, quartz, mica	Quartzo-feldspathic And amphibole pyroxene.
No mica	Fine grained mica Foliated	Coarse mica Foliated	Large mica Non-foliated

At low grades of metamorphism chlorite + plagioclase + epidote + calcite form. The resultant rock has a distinct foliation, and due to abundance of green chlorite, it is termed as greenstone.

When a greenstone is subjected to higher grade of metamorphism, chlorite is replaced by amphibole; the resultant rock is rich in coarse amphibole and is called *an amphibolite*. At still higher grade of metamorphism, amphibole is replaced by pyroxene and an indistinctly foliated rock *a granulite* develops.

(c) Metamorphism of carbonate rocks :

Carbonate rocks are mainly composed of calcite, dolomite and a few impurities. The mineral assemblages produced during metamorphism are controlled by temperature, pressure, bulk rock composition and chemically active fluids.

When $CaCO_3$ is heated in unconfined system, it is dissociated with the formation of quicklime.

$$CaCO_3 \rightarrow CaO + CO_2 \uparrow$$

But when $CaCO_3$ (calcite) is heated in confined system, dissociation is hindered, the CO_2 is retained and the calcite merely recrystallizes to produce saccharoidal marble e.g. Makrana marble.

Many limestones contain dolomite which when subjected to higher temperature and pressure, give rise to talc, tremolite and pyroxene (diopside). The metamorphism may be considered as progressive and is summarised as below :

$$3\text{ Dolomite} + 4\text{ Quartz} + H_2O \rightarrow \text{Talc} + 3\text{ Calcite} + 3CO_2 \uparrow$$

The contact metamorphism of dolomite rocks under low pressure results in dissociation of $MgCO_3$, with the crystallization of calcite.

$$CaMg(CO_3)_2 \rightarrow CaCO_3 + MgO + CO_2 \uparrow$$
Dolomite   Calcite Periclase

The destruction of dolomite and crystallization of calcite is called *dedolomitization*. This process is also facilitated by the presence of siliceous or argillaceous impurities and a variety of minerals are formed. With a small amount of silica, magnesium olivine is formed.

$$2CaMg(CO_3)_2 + SiO_2 \rightarrow 2CaCO_3 + Mg_2SiO_4 + 2CO_2 \uparrow$$
Dolomite   Silica   Calcite   Mg olivine

But hydration of Mg olivine gives rise to various shades of serpentine resulting into production of banded or serpentine marble.

With somewhat larger amount of silica, pyroxene is formed instead of magnesium olivine.

$$CaMg(CO_3)_2 + 2SiO_2 \rightarrow CaMg(SiO_3)_2 + 2CO_2 \uparrow$$
Dolomite   Silica   Pyroxene

On the basis of these mineral reactions different types of marbles are observed.

(d) Metamorphism of arenaceous rocks :

Pure quartz and feldspar sandstone when subjected to higher grade of metamorphism, are recrystallized into granoblastic aggregates of those minerals with the complete obliteration of clastic structure. The new rock is called quartzite.

$$CaMg(CO_3)_2 + 2SiO_2 \rightarrow CaMg(SiO_3)_2 + 2CO_2$$
Dolomite   Silica   Pyroxene

On the basis of these mineral reactions different types of marbles are observed.

(d) Metamorphism of arenaceous rocks :

Pure quartz and feldspar sandstone when subjected to higher grade of metamorphism, are recrystallized into granoblastic aggregates of those minerals with the complete obliteration of clastic structure. The new rock is called quartzite.

EXERCISE

1. Describe with neat Fig.s various textures shown by metamorphic rocks ?
2. Give in detail, the classification of sedimentary rocks. Describe one rock from each group / sub-group.
3. Give schemes of classification of igneous rocks and describe at least one rock from each group.
4. Describe conditions of cooling and textures of volcanic rocks.
5. What is metamorphism ? What are agents and types of metamorphism ? Describe the dynamothermal metamorphism of argillaceous rock impure limestones.

6. Discuss with suitable example 'Igneous rocks', show a very wide variety of textures and this textural variation is a direct outcome of their mode of origin.
7. Write notes on : (i) Arenaceous rocks, (ii) Rock forming mineral groups, (iii) Clastic texture, concordant and discordant intrusions, (iv) Residual deposits, (v) Compaction and cementation of rocks, (vi) Textures and structures in metamorphic rocks, (vii) Physical properties of minerals.
8. Explain the process of formation of laterite and Bauxite.
9. Describe 'any two' physical properties of minerals.
10. Explain various textures of igneous rocks with neat sketches and examples.
11. Write notes on :
    (a) Modes of weathering.
    (b) Agents and types of metamorphism.
    (c) Primary and secondary minerals.
12. Describe 'Hardness' as a physical property of mineral.
13. Distinguish between 'Plutonic and volcanic rocks' and describe any two rocks from each category.
14. Explain the process of 'decomposition' of rocks in details.
15. How parallel structures in Metamorphic rocks are developed ? Explain the process in detail.
16. How variation in length of transportation leads to development of different sedimentary rocks ?

❏❏❏

Unit 2

STRUCTURAL GEOLOGY, PLATE TECTONICS AND GROUND WATER

PART (A) : STRUCTURAL GEOLOGY

The word 'structure' means something that is built or constructed. Structural geologists use the word to signify something which is produced by deformation, i.e. by the action of forces acting on and within the earth's crust. Structure consists of a geometrical arrangement of planes, lines, surfaces etc. Attitude of this orientation suggests the interaction between the deforming forces and the pre-existing rock mass.

2.1 (A) DEFORMATION

This is the process which changes the shape or form of a rock mass. i.e. the process responsible for the development of geologic structures.

2.1 (B) BRITTLE AND DUCTILE DEFORMATION

When a rock mass is subjected to deviatoric stress, often elastic deformation leads to failure, and the deforming mass losses cohesion by the development of a fracture or fractures across which the continuity of the material is broken. This kind of deformation is called brittle deformation and is responsible in the development of faults and fractures. On the other hand, ductile deformation produces a permanent strain to form structures like folds.

2.1 (C) MECHANISM OF ROCK DEFORMATION

A rock is an aggregate of minerals and the deformation of rocks depend on the properties of individual minerals and also on the texture of the rock as a whole. An igneous rock with an interlocking texture is certainly stronger and durable than a sandstone with a calcareous cement. Similarly, the igneous rock is stronger than a discontinuous rock.

In general, the rock composition has two aspects : (1) the presence of mineral composition, i.e. some minerals like quartz are brittle, while minerals like clay, mica are ductile, and (2) the presence of water in a rock which reduces brittleness and enhances ductile properties like flow.

Rock deformation is controlled by many other factors including temperature, confining or lithostatic pressure, strain rate etc.

2.1 (D) OUTCROP

The word is synonymous to exposure i.e. a place where rocks are seen in-situ. An outcrop may range in size from a few metres to several kilometres. It may show presence of one rock throughout or in association of many rocks with or without discontinuities.

2.1 (E) FUNDAMENTAL STRUCTURES

(1) **Fractures** : These are discontinuities across which the cohesion of the material is lost. Two major types are recognised.

(a) **Faults** : Faults are fractures that accommodate appreciable displacement/slip parallel to the discontinuity surface.

(b) **Joints** : Joints are discontinuities along which there is negligible or no movement parallel to the plane of the fractures. Joints are also formed in igneous rocks, called as **cooling joints**.

(2) **Folds** : A fold is a structure formed when an original planar surface becomes curved as a result of deformation. Folds are best developed in sedimentary rocks.

(3) **Cleavage, foliation and lineation** : These are formed under increased temperature, and pressure conditions through deformation and recrystallization during ductile flow in igneous or metamorphic environment.

2.1 (F) QUANTITATIVE ANALYSIS

Quantitative analysis of these structures is essential in deciding the stability of engineering structures constructed on them. The methods employed in studying them are observational. The data concerning the attitude of these structures are gathered in the field and presented in maps, sections and projections. The information collected must be sufficient to interpret the kinematic movements and the earth's forces responsible for the development of these structures. The observed structures may vary in size from microscopic to macroscopic with the magnitude of several kilometres. But, as the terminology is geometric, there is hardly any difference in the description of small and large structures.

A majority of the rocks show a planar surface along which splitting is very easily represented in sedimentary rocks by bedding planes, stratification etc. Similarly, metamorphic rocks may show schistosity and gneissosity. In igneous rocks, planar surfaces are seldom recorded; for example, flow structure.

In many cases, sedimentary beds and lava flows with horizontal disposition are observed. These, if subjected to tectonic forces, may become inclined or vertical. Thus, form/geometry of these rocks can be described considering their orientation, which is determined by measuring their trend on a horizontal surface and their inclination. These measurements are to be made by using clinometer, Brunton compass, prismatic compass etc. Attitude of a rock is described by its strike and dip.

Strike : The strike of a bed is its direction measured along a horizontal line on the bedding plane.

Dip : The dip of a bed is the angle that it makes with the horizontal plane measured in a vertical plane.

It can be seen from the above Fig.s that in Fig. 2.1 (a), beds are vertical so that $\theta = 90°$ i.e. dip of a bed and strike is N-S in direction.

In the case of Fig. 2.1 (b), beds are inclined, $\theta = 45°$ i.e. dip which is towards east and in this case also strike is N-S in orientation.

In the case of Fig. 2.1 (c), beds are horizontal. Thus, dip i.e. inclination is zero and no strike measures are possible.

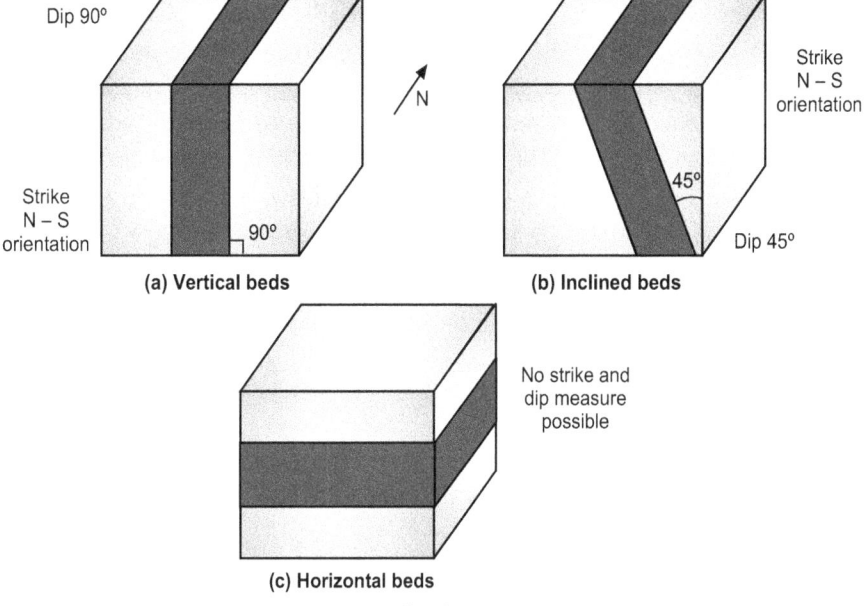

Fig. 2.1

It must be remembered that dip of a rock and slope of the ground are the two different features. Slope of the ground is an inclination of the topographic surface; on the other hand, dip is an inclination of the rock mass.

Apparent Dip :

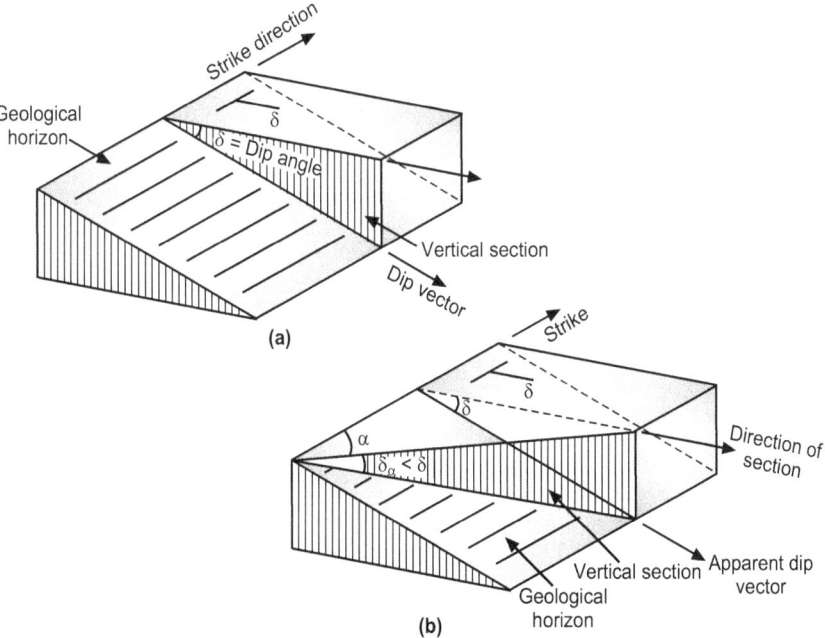

Fig. 2.2 (a) Description of the dip vector, the strike vector, and the amount and direction of dip for an inclined horizon. (b) Block diagram showing apparent dip (δ_a) in relation to true dip (δ)

At many outcrops where dipping beds are exposed, the bedding planes are not visible as surfaces. Natural cuttings, quarries and road sections may provide sub-vertical outcrop surfaces which make an arbitrary angle with the strike of the beds [Fig. 2.2 (a)] when such sections are not perpendicular to the strike [Fig. 2.2 (b)], the beds will appear to dip at a gentler angle than the true dip. This inclination which is measured in any angle than perpendicular in reference to strike, is called **apparent dip**. It is always possible to find true dip amount from two non-parallel vertical surfaces oriented at some angle to strike.

The true dip can be calculated by constructing a scaled diagram or by trignometric equation. Here a simple method proposed by Ragan (1985) is discussed. He showed that the tangent of the apparent dip can be treated as a vector and that the true dip may be calculated as follows.

Given the apparent dip (25°) in the direction N 240° and the apparent dip (20°) in the direction N 170°. Calculate the true dip and amount.

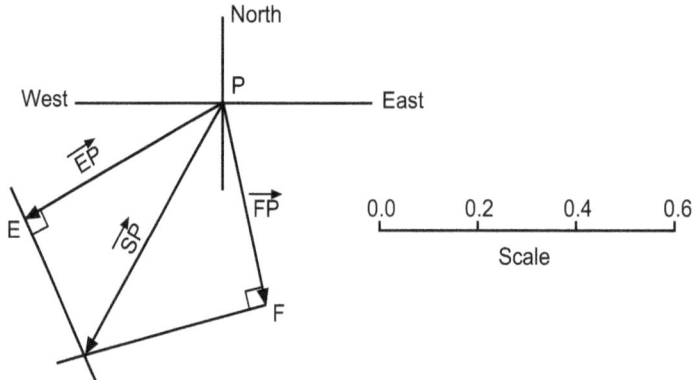

Fig. 2.3 : Tangent vector method

Draw N–S and E–W co-ordinate axes to intersect at P. (Fig. 2.3). Define an arbitrary scale. Draw vector EP in the direction of N 240°.

    length of EP = tan 25° = 0.47 units.

Similarly, draw FP in the direction N 170°.

    length of FP = tan 20° = 0.34 units.

Draw perpendicular to both vectors to meet at S. Vector SP indicates the direction of the true dip.

    length of SP = 0.51 units

    true dip = arc tan (SP) = arc tan (0.51) = 27

This method is accurate than other method.

V-shaped Outcrop Patterns :

A dipping surface which crops out in a valley or on a ridge will give rise to a V-shaped outcrop (Fig. 2.4) which depends on the dip of the geological surface relative to topography.

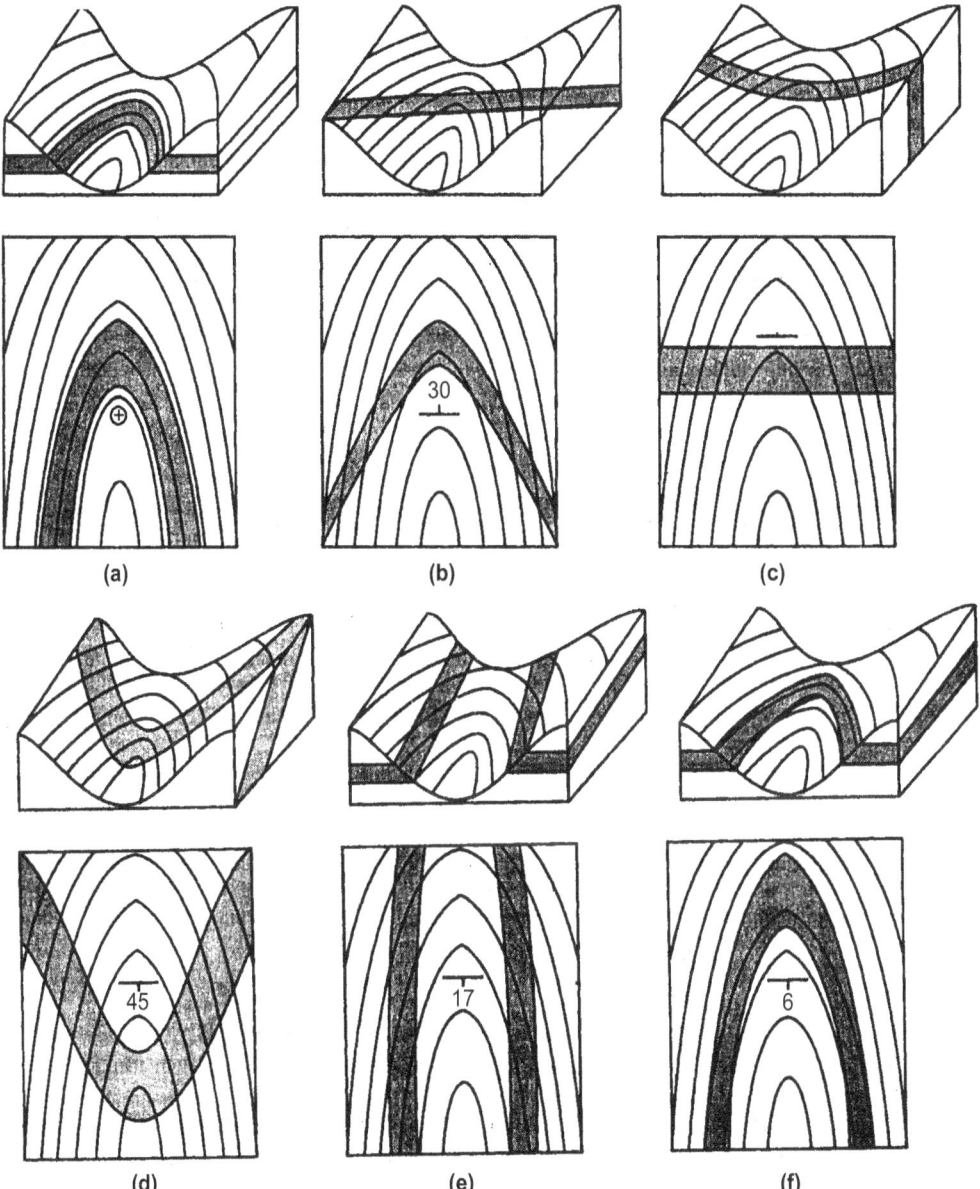

Fig. 2.4 : Outcrop patterns illustrating the rule of V's : (a) Horizontal layer, (b) Layer dipping upstream, (c) Vertical layer, (d) Layer dipping downstream, (e) Layer and valley with equal inclinations, (f) Layer dipping downstream at an angle at less than valley gradient

Horizontal planes : Horizontal planes yield outcrop pattern parallel to the topographic contours [Fig. 2.4 (a)]. Such patterns are completely controlled by topography. Therefore, the outcrop pattern 'V's upstream is similar to contour lines.

As the attitude departs from horizontal, with the dip direction upstream the horizontal plane is progressively modified into blunter 'V' still pointing upstream [Fig. 2.4 (b)]. In case of vertical dip the outcrop trace is straight and parallel to the strike irrespective of the topography. There is no 'V' and thus there is no topographic control on the map pattern [Fig. 2.4 (c)].

In case beds are inclined in downstream direction, three conditions are visualised depending upon relationship between dip and ground slope.

(a) With dip greater than ground slope, the pattern 'V's downstream [Fig. 2.4 (d)].
(b) If dip and ground slope are equal, the outcrop trace does not cross the valley and there is no 'V' [Fig. 2.4 (e)].
(c) If dip is greater than ground slope but still in a downstream direction, the pattern V will be upstream [Fig. 2.4 (f)].

Stratigraphic Thickness :

The true or stratigraphic thickness of a bed is the perpendicular distance between its bounding surfaces (T, Fig. 2.5). The vertical thickness (t) is the elevation difference between top and bottom of a bed at any point. It is the vertical 'drilled' thickness which is obtained by subtracting the height of the base from height of the top. It is seen that vertical thickness is always more than true thickness.

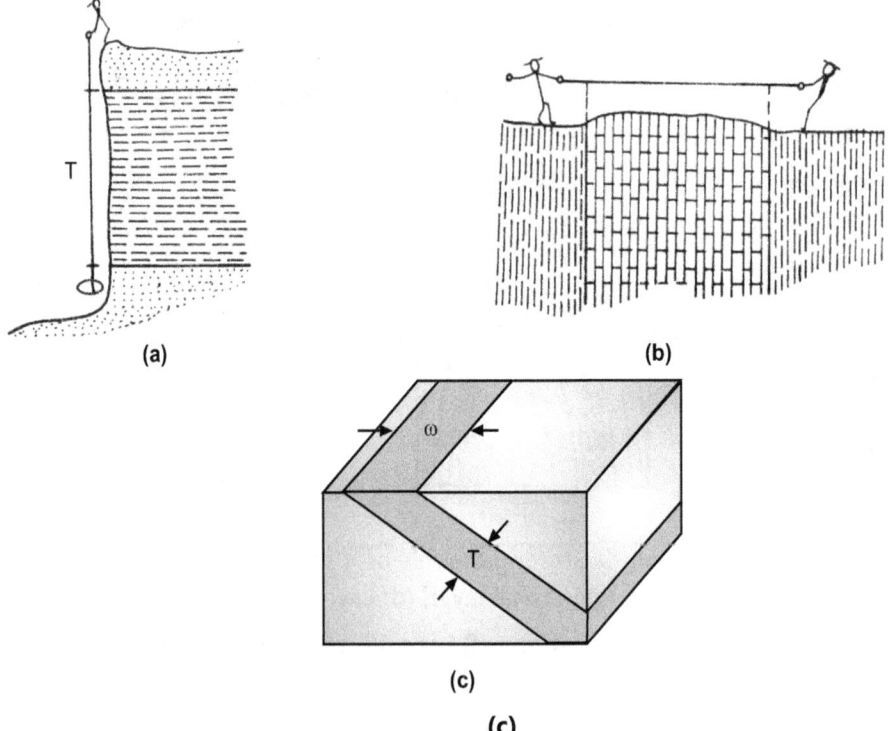

Fig. 2.5 : Thickness measurements (a) direct measurement of the thickness of a horizontal layer (b) direct measurement of the thickness of a vertical layer (c) block diagram showing outcrop width w

In the simplest case, of a horizontal layer exposed on a vertical cliff face, the thickness may be obtained by hanging a tape over the edge of the cliff [Fig. 2.5 (a)]. In this case, stratigraphic thickness is equivalent to vertical thickness. Another special case is the exposure of a vertical bed on a surface of no relief; a measuring tape extended perpendicular to the strike gives the thickness [Fig. 2.5 (b)].

When direct measurement of thickness is not possible, it is necessary to find width of outcrop (w) [Fig. 2.5 (c)] perpendicular to strike on a horizontal surface. From the width of outcrop (w) and the angle of dip (δ), the thickness 'T' can be calculated by the following equation

$$T = w \cdot \sin \delta$$

Essentially, the same method may be used when 'w' is measured on sloping ground. Here, the thickness 'T' is a function of dip angle, δ as well as ground slope, σ.

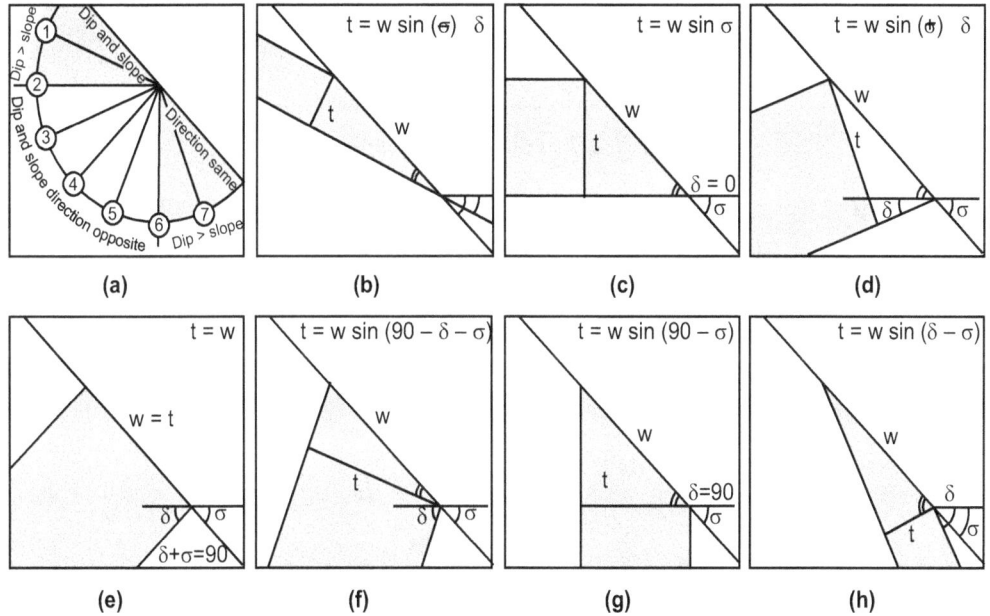

Fig. 2.6 : **Determination of thickness from outcrop width measured on a slope**

As three separate measurements (w, δ, σ) are to be made, seven subcases may be visualised (Fig. 2.6). They are shown diagrammatically in Fig. 2.6 (a) and the individual cases together with the appropriate equations are given in Fig. 2.6 (b)–(h).

2.2 FOLDS

A fold is an undulation or bending produced in stratified rocks. In simple terms, it is a curvature in a geologic surface or in a set of stacked geological surfaces. Folding results when the original planar surface is curved due to forces acting parallel to the bedding plane. It is certainly one of the most spectacular of earth's structures. Fold size varies from microscopic to regional covering a few tens of kilometres.

2.2.1 Fold Morphology

Folded surfaces tremendously vary in size and form. The geometric configuration of any folded surface is explained by various terms.

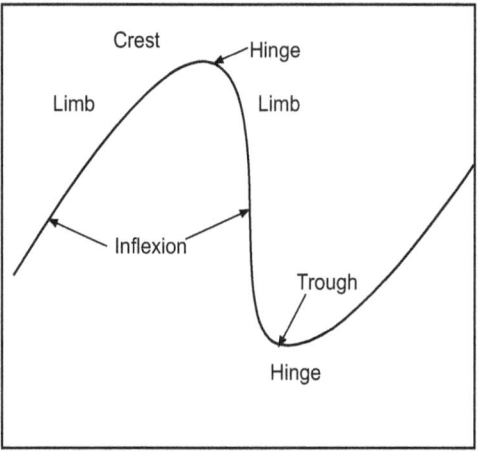

Fig. 2.7 : Fold morphology

(a) **Hinge :** It is a point of maximum curvature in the folded surface; more commonly, the hinge is a zone, called as **hinge zone**. If all the points of maximum curvature are joined, it is known as a **hinge line**. Limbs are flanks of fold and each fold has two limbs (synonyms for limbs are sides, branches, legs.) Inflexion point is the one where the individual limb has attained minimum curvature. In other words, curved limb segments of opposing convexity joins at inflexion point.

(b) **Axial Surfaces and Axial Planes : (Fig. 2.8)**

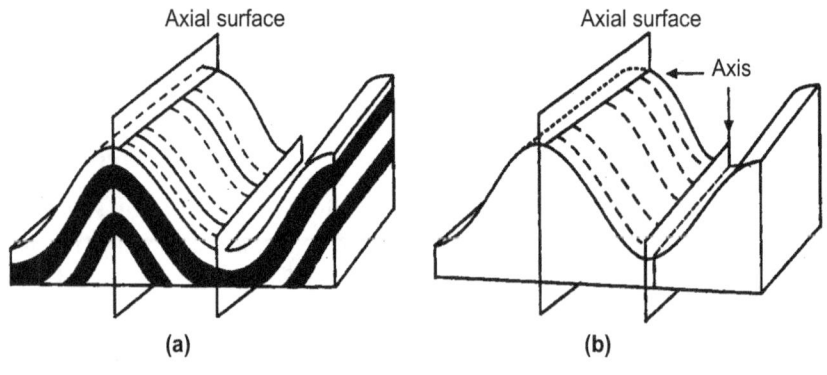

Fig. 2.8

The orientation of a folded surface can be specified by measuring its axial plane i.e. an imaginary plane which divides the fold into two parts, symmetrical or asymmetrical. [Fig. 2.8 (a)].

When a fold is made of various undulatory surfaces, it is possible to define a common surface by joining successive hing lines in a staking of folded surfaces. Such a surface which is not planar is known as **axial surface**. [Fig. 2.8 (a)].

(c) Plunge of a fold : Plunge is an inclination of the fold axis measured with respect to reference horizontal plane (Fig. 2.9).

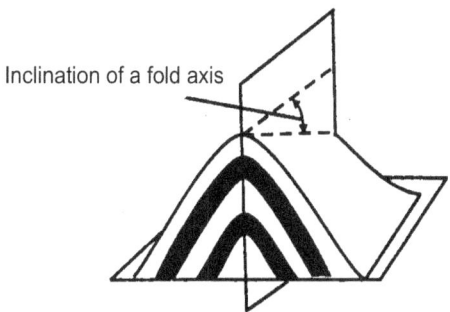

Fig. 2.9 : Plunge of a fold

(d) Inter-limb Angle : Fold tightness is described in terms of inter-limb angle i.e. an internal angle between the limbs of a folded surface.

(e) Amplitude and Wavelength : (Fig. 2.10)

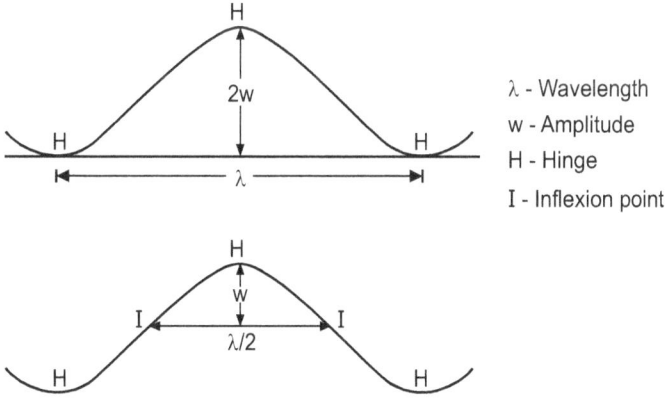

Fig. 2.10 : Size of a fold

Fold 'size' is described by two terms. Wavelength is the distance between the hinges on either side of the fold.

In many instances, the entire fold is not visible. In such cases, distance between two inflexion points on either side of the fold is measured and it is known as **half wavelength**.

Amplitude or 'height' of a fold is half the perpendicular distance from hinge to the line between the two inflexion points.

(f) Crest and Trough : When the axial plane is inclined, the points of the highest elevation and lowest elevation in a fold may not coincide with the hinge points (Fig. 2.11). Thus, the point of the highest elevation is known as **crest** and an imaginary plane formed by joining different crestal points in a folded surface is called **crestal plane**. Similarly, the lowest point in the folded surface is a *trough point* and the imaginary plane is **trough plane**.

(g) Anticline and Syncline : Two major types are recognised on the basis of fold geometry. An **'anticline'** is a fold that is convex in the direction of the youngest bed in the folded sequence [Fig. 2.11(a)]. The beds in the sequence are opposite inclined and older beds are seen in the core.

A **syncline** is a fold that is convex in the direction of the oldest beds in the folded sequence [Fig. 2.11(b)]. The beds are together inclined and the younger beds are in the core.

Anticline : Beds opposite inclined, oldest in the core.

Syncline : Beds together inclined and youngest in the core.

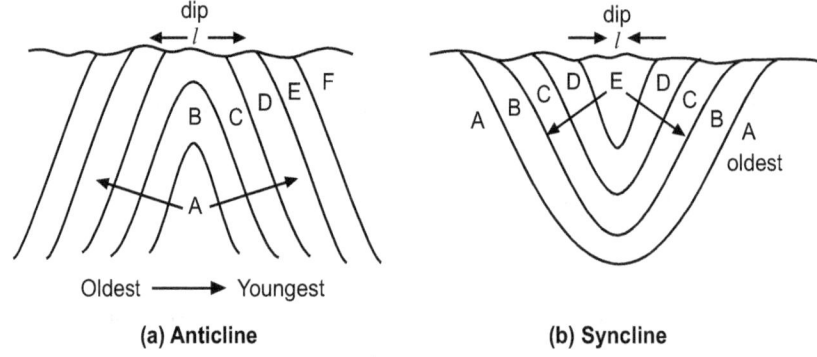

(a) Anticline   (b) Syncline

Fig. 2.11 : Types of fold

2.2.2 Fold Classification

(A) Geometric classification is based entirely on geometric configuration of folds. In this, the origin of a fold is not discussed.

(B) Genetic classification is based on the 'origin' of the fold.

(A) Geometric classification : The classification is purely descriptive and involves description based on geometric elements. For classification three modes are used :

(1) Classification based on the attitude of axial plane : Four major types of folds are recognised on the basis of dip of axial plane seen in profile.

  (i) **Symmetrical fold :** Axial surface is essentially vertical and it bisects the fold into two symmetrical halves, also known as upright fold [Fig. 2.12 (a (i)).

  (ii) **Asymmetrical fold :** Axial surface is gently or steeply inclined dividing the fold into two asymmetrical parts, also called as inclined or reclined folds [Fig. 2.12 (a) (ii), (iii) and (iv)].

  (iii) **Recumbent fold :** Axial surface is horizontal or sub-horizontal [Fig. 2.12 (a)(iv)].

(iv) Overturned fold : Axial plane is inclined and dip of both limbs of a fold remains in one direction [Fig. 2.12 (a) (iii)]. One limb is gentle and the other limb is inverted i.e. the limb is rotated beyond vertical in such a way that the facing direction of the limb points downward at steeper angle towards the same direction of the other limb.

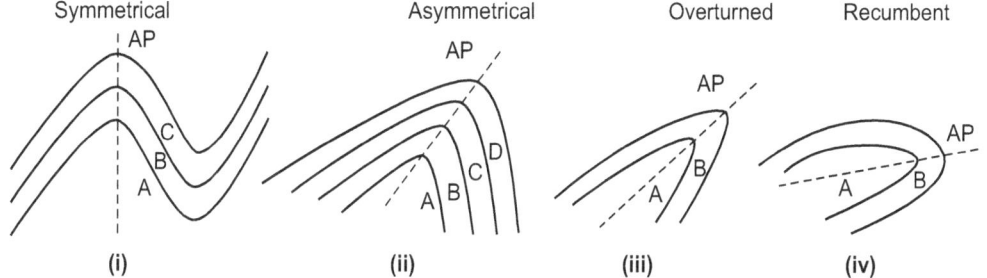

Fig. 2.12 (a) : Classification of folds based on attitude of axial plane seen in profile

(2) Classification based on inter-limb angle [Fig. 2.12 (b)] : The inter-limb angle is measured by drawing tangents to the fold curves at the point of inflexion. The angle is made by two tangents. Five types are recognised. (1) Gentle folds have inter-limb angle varying from 120° - 180°, (2) Open folds are marked by inter-limb angle between 70° and 120°, (3) Closed folds are those if the inter-limb angle is in between 30° and 70°, (4) Tight fold : Inter-limb angle is between 10° and 30°. (5) Isoclinal : Inter-limb angle is less than 10, both limbs of a fold are parallel.

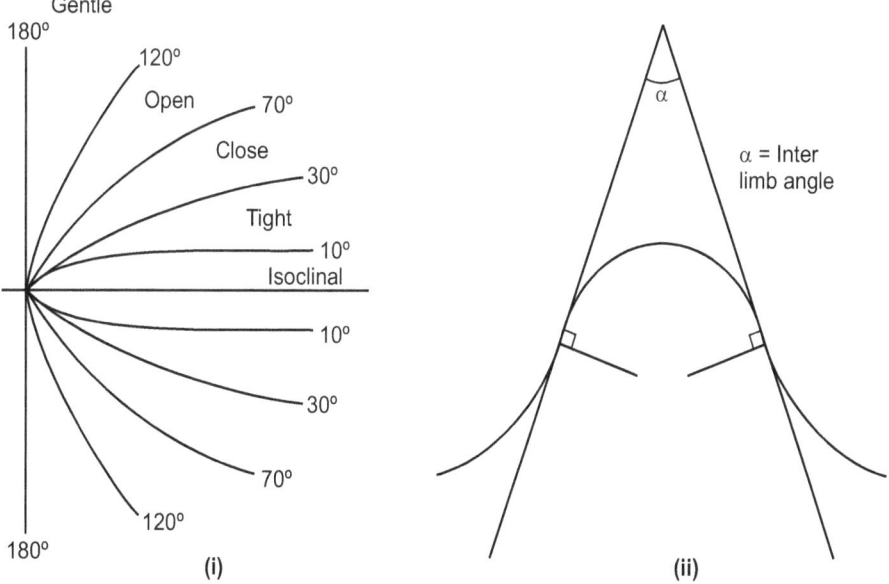

Fig. 2.12 (b) : Classification of folds based on the inter-limb angle measurement of inter-limb angle α in folds. Tangents are drawn to the fold surface at inflexion points

(3) Classification based on folds seen in profile (Fig. 2.13) : The fold 'profile' is the shape of a fold-seen in the plane perpendicular to the fold axis. Two major types are recognised :

(i) Parallel folds : In the case of parallel folds, thickness of the layer measured perpendicular to the fold surface remains constant. When seen in the profile the form is circular or elliptical. Parallel folds are also called **concentric folds**. Strictly speaking, 'Concentric' folds are those where adjacent fold surfaces are arcs of a circle with a common centre called the centre of curvature of the fold.

(ii) Similar folds : Individual folded layers which display significant thickening in the hinge and thinning on the limbs are known as **similar folds**. In other words, orthogonal thickness of the folded layers changes in a definite way so that thickness of the fold remains constant when measured parallel to axial surface.

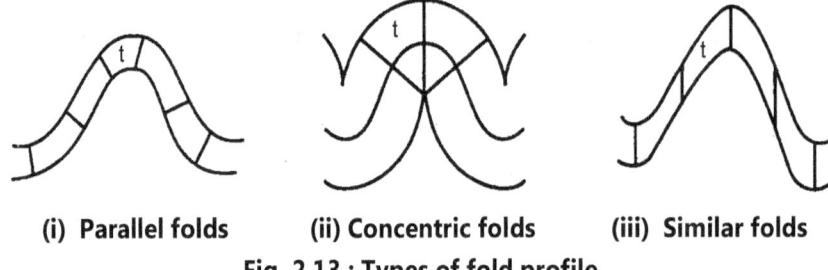

(i) Parallel folds   (ii) Concentric folds   (iii) Similar folds

Fig. 2.13 : Types of fold profile

Parallel fold : Constant thickness when measured perpendicular to fold surface.
Concentric fold : Thickness is radii of a circle.
Similar fold : Constant thickness parallel to axial surface.

(B) Genetic classification : Two principal types of foldings such as,
(1) Flexure folding, (2) Shear-slip folding are recognised.

(1) Flexure folding : It involves bending or buckling of harder material under compressional forces. This is similar to bending a sheet due to compressive forces acting parallel to the layers [Fig. 2.14 (a)]. Thus, convex side is subjected to tension, whereas the concave side is subjected to compression.

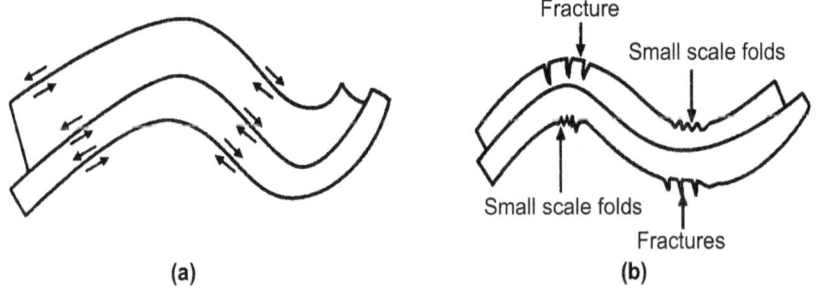

(a)   (b)

Fig. 2.14 : Flexure folding

In between, the surface is neutral i.e. there is no strain (flexural folding is similar to the bending of a dictionary) and in this, very important factor is the sliding of beds past one another [Fig. 2.14 (b)].

(2) Shear-slip folding : These folds result from minute displacement along closely spaced fractures [Fig. 2.15 (a)].

Each fracture is a tiny fault [Fig. 2.15 (b)]. Due to parallel movements of beds along fracture planes, the resulting structure is a major fold which is called shear-slip fold [Fig. 2.15(c)].

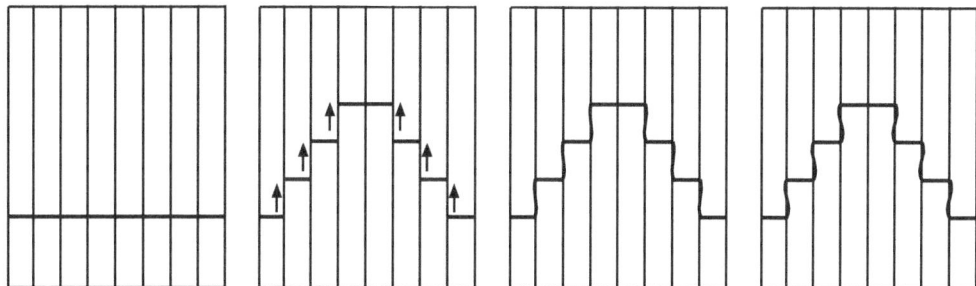

(a) Multilayered sequence   (b) Joints act as a fault   (c) Development of a fold

Fig. 2.15 : Schematic sketch showing development of a shear-slip fold

2.2.3 Other Types of Folds

(1) **Monocline :** When the bedding is flat or horizontal, the strata may locally exhibit sudden steepening of beds. This folding is called as **monocline** (Fig. 2.16).

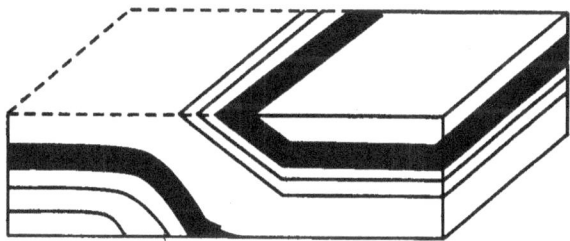

Fig. 2.16 : Monocline

(2) **Anticlinoria and Synclinoria :** A major anticline that is flanked or associated with many smaller folds is called **antichnorium** [Fig 2.17 (a)]. Whereas a major syncline associated with great magnitude [Fig. 2.17 (b)] is called **synclinorium**.

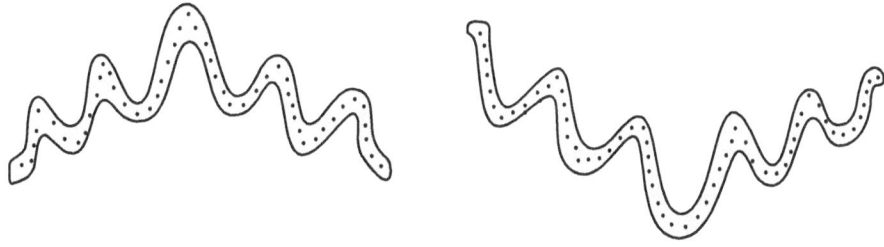

Fig. 2.17 : Regional fold structure

2.3 FRACTURES

A fracture is a **surface of discontinuity across which the cohesion is lost**. The knowledge of fractures is important in many kinds of geologic structures. Quantitative analysis of fractures or discontinuities is essential in the construction of tunnels, dams, and allied civil engineering projects. Their presence appreciably affect resistance of rock mass. Landsliding, slumping and other processes of mass wasting, in areas of high relief, are enhanced by discontinuity in the surfaces.

Quantitative analysis of fractures include orientation, persistence, surface roughness, aperture or width, number of sets, block size etc.

2.4 FAULTS

Faults are ruptures or fractures in the earth's crust along which the opposite walls move past each other. Faults may develop from a smaller distance upto thousands of kilometres. e.g. San Andreas Fault.

2.4.1 Elements of a Fault Plane

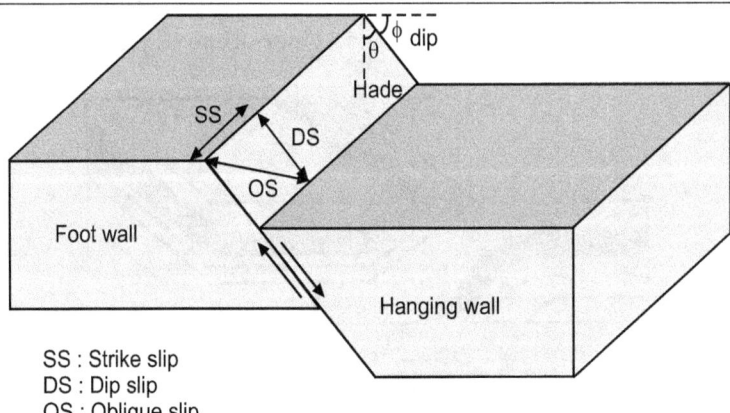

SS : Strike slip
DS : Dip slip
OS : Oblique slip

Fig. 2.18 : Elements of a fault plane

Attitude of the fault plane is measured from its strike and dip. The strike of a fault is the trend of a line in the plane of the fault and the dip is an angle between the horizontal surface and the plane of the fault. When the fault is non-vertical, the wall above the fault is called as **hanging wall** and the wall below the fault is called **footwall**. Hade is an angle between the fault and the vertical plane that strikes parallel to the fault. The term 'slip' is used to indicate the relative movement. Displacement parallel to the strike of the fault plane is known as **'strike-slip'** where dip-slip component is zero. Similarly, with a displacement parallel to the dip of the fault plane is the dip-slip and in this, strike-slip component is zero. If the movement is oblique, then the fault possesses both strike as well as dip-slip components. The measurements of movement on the inclined fault planes may be made by considering vertical and horizontal components of displacement termed as the *heave* and the *throw* respectively (Fig. 2.19).

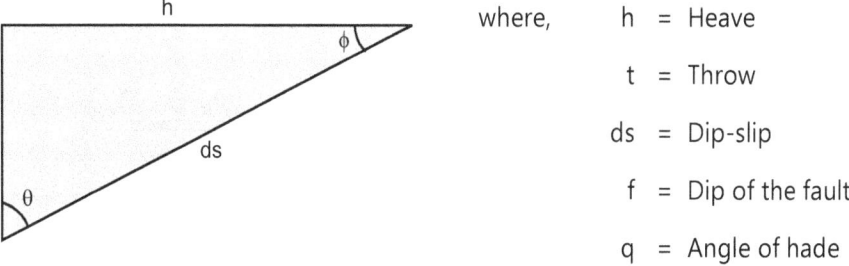

where, h = Heave
t = Throw
ds = Dip-slip
f = Dip of the fault
q = Angle of hade

Fig. 2.19 : Components of an inclined fault

Thus, if the above Fig. is considered, then it can be said that $\tan \phi = h/t$, and $\sin \theta = t/ds$.

It is important to realise that fault movement is difficult to measure in field because it is impossible to trace precise points along or across the discontinuity surface. A precise displacement can be seen only in an aerial photograph or on a satellite imagery.

2.4.2 Movement along Faults

(a) **Rotational [Fig. 2.20 (c)]** : In the case of rotational movements, the straight lines on the opposite walls of the fault do not remain parallel to each other.

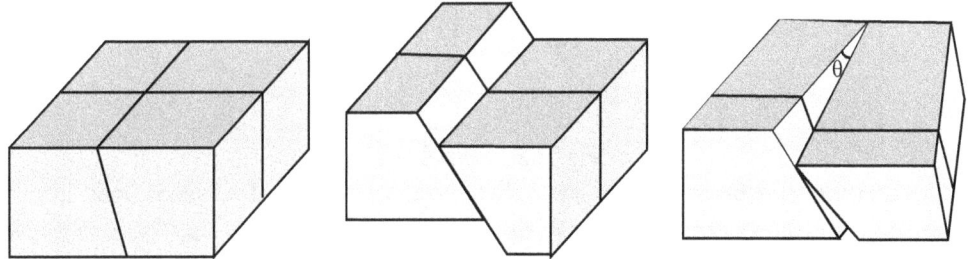

(a) Before faulting (b) Translational movement (c) Rotational movement

Fig. 2.20 : Movement along faults

(b) **Translational [Fig. 2.20 (b)]** : Translational movements are those in which all straight lines on the opposite sides of the fault remain parallel.

2.4.3 Classification of Faults

Faults can also be classified geometrically, i.e. simply by describing the fault, and genetically, i.e. by considering the orientation of major stresses.

(A) Classification based on attitude of fault plane in relation to attitude of adjacent rocks :

Theme of this classification is the relation of strike and dip of fault with strike and dip of adjacent beds. Three types of faults are,

(a) Strike fault : (Fig. 2.21)

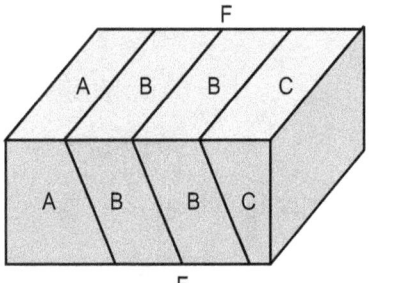 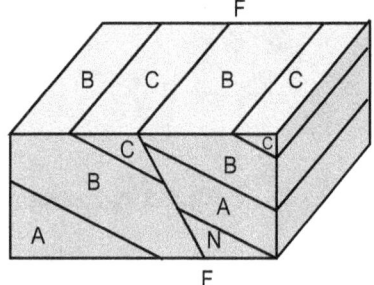

Fig. 2.21 : Strike fault

A strike fault is the one which strikes parallel to the strike of the adjacent beds. It is also called as *bedding fault*.

(b) Dip fault : (Fig. 2.22)

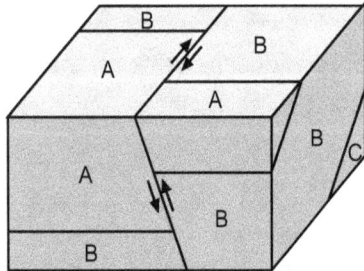 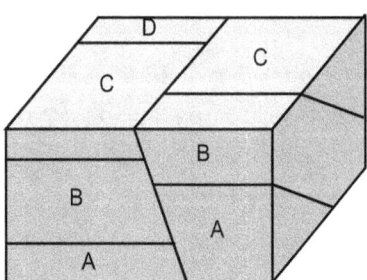

Fig. 2.22 : Dip fault

Strike of the fault plane remains parallel to the dip direction of adjacent beds. In other words, strike of fault is normal to strike of rock.

(c) Oblique fault : (Fig. 2.23)

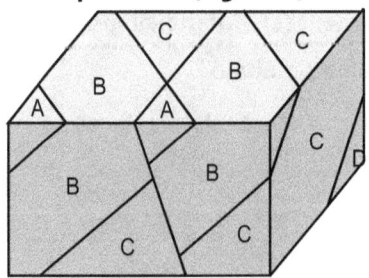 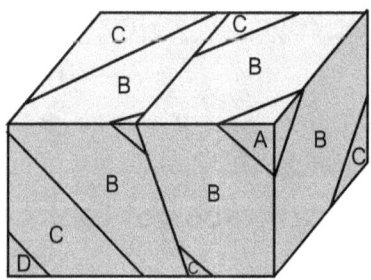

Fig. 2.23 : Oblique fault

In the case of oblique or diagonal fault, strata strikes oblique to fault.

(B) Genetic classification : The classification is based on the relative movement along the fault. Three major types are recognised :

(1) Normal or Gravity fault : When hanging wall moves down in relation to footwall, the fault is called Normal or Gravity fault [Fig. 2.24 (a)].

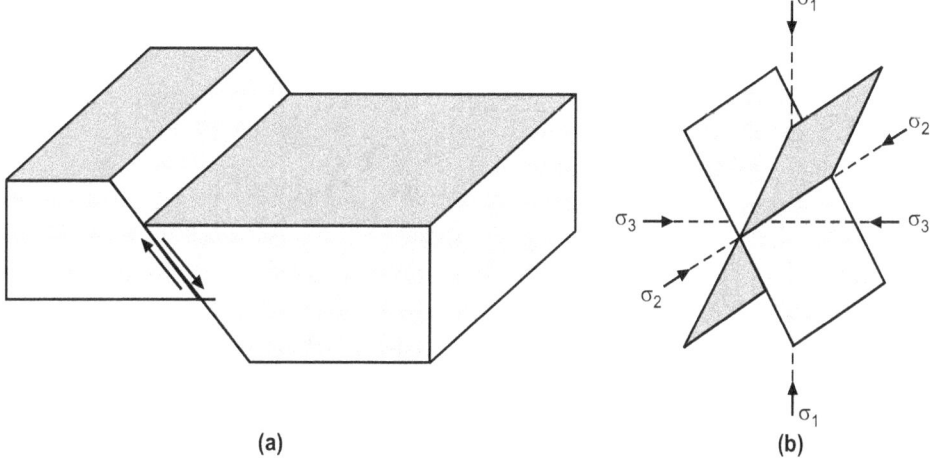

(a) (b)

Fig. 2.24 : Normal or Gravity fault

Here, the major compressional stress is vertical and corresponds to gravitational load. The fault generally dip more than 45° · σ_3 i.e., minimum compressional stress direction is horizontal. [Fig. 2.24 (b)]

(2) Thrust or Reverse fault :

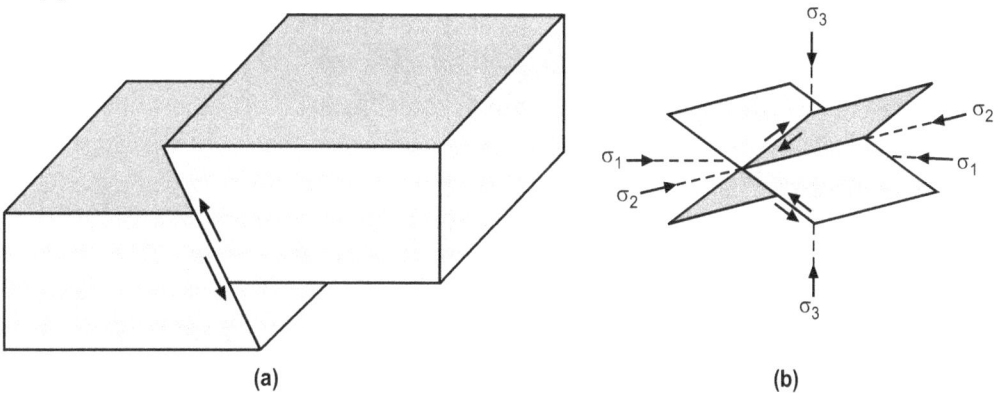

(a) (b)

Fig. 2.25 : Thrust or Reverse fault

When the hanging wall moves up in relation to footwall, the fault is known as thrust or reverse fault [Fig. 2.25(a)]. Here σ_1 is horizontal and σ_3 is vertical [Fig. 2.25 (b)]. The precise distinction between thrust and reverse fault is made on the basis of dip of the fault plane.

  (i) **Reverse fault :** Dip amount is more than 45°.
 (ii) **Thrust fault :** Dip amount is less than 45°.
(iii) **Overthrust fault :** Dip amount is less than 10°. The actual slip movement in this case is very large.

(3) Strike-slip fault : (Wrench fault) (tear fault)

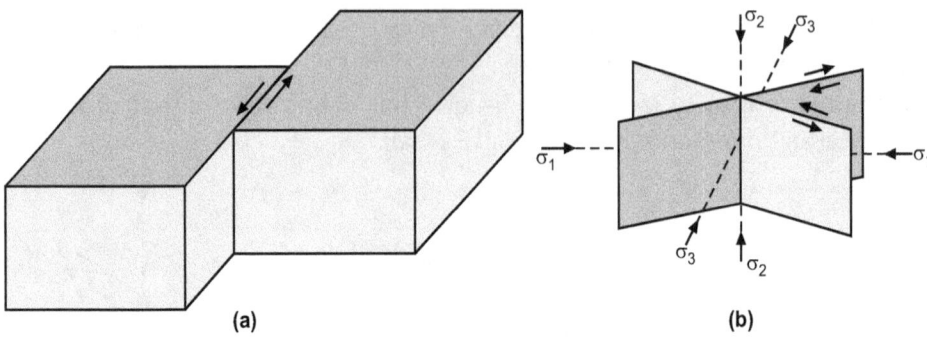

Fig. 2.26 : Strike fault developed in a stress field

Slip is along the strike of a fault plane [Fig. 2.26 (a)]. Dip-slip component is very small. Here, both σ_1 and σ_3 are horizontal and σ_2 i.e. intermediate stress is vertical. [Fig. 2.26 (b)]

(C) Other fault types :

(1) Horst and Graben : Graben (German Trench) is a depression which is formed due to two normal faults. Horst (upthrow) is a special type of fault, where the area is uplifted due to the presence of two thrust faults. [Fig. 2.27 (a)]

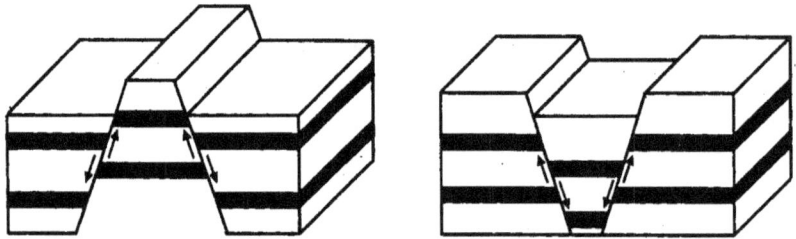

Fig. 2.27 (a) : Horst and Graben

(2) Step fault : When the area is bounded by many normal faults, so that movement is along one definite direction, the resultant structure gives a stair-like or step-like appearance, known as a *step fault*. [Fig. 2.27(b)].

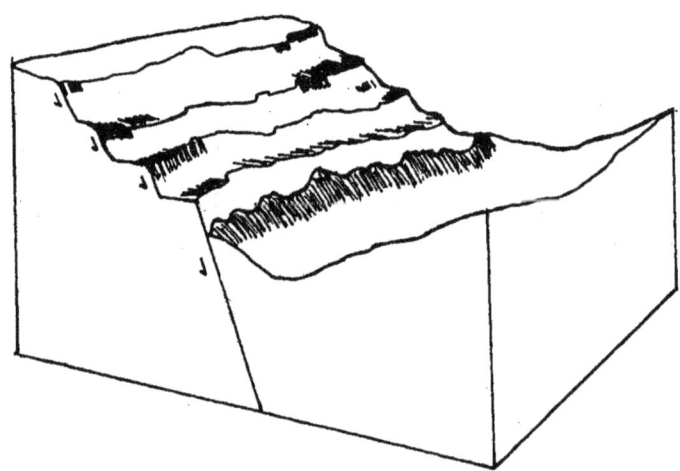

Fig. 2.27 (b) : Step fault

2.4.4 Field Recognition of Faults

Faults are easily recognised in the stratified rocks by actual displacement of strata, especially when the fault is normal or oblique to strike of bedding. But in the case of strike fault, such criteria is not valid. In such cases, faults may be recognised based on the following criterias :

(i) **Slickensides :** These are shining or striated surfaces caused by polishing action or due to friction of the opposite wall along the fault.

(ii) **Gouge, pulvarised rock :** It is similar to clay. This zone is generally softer than adjacent parts and gives rise to topographic depressions.

(iii) **Brecciated rock :** It is known as fault braccia where a zone of broken and crushed rock fragments mark the presence of the fault.

(iv) **Crushed rock :** Another evidence in favour of faulting is in the form of abnormal silicification in the strata.

In igneous rocks, faults may be identified by mineral growth or mineralisation, calcite, pegmatitic veins etc. without which recognition of fault is very difficult. In metamorphic rocks, fault delineation can be made by very careful observations. It may be in the form of repetition of strata or abrupt change in strike direction.

2.4.5 Seismic Faulting and Associated Features

Shearing may take place along fault planes, fault zones/shear zones by slow ductile processes, which do not give rise to seismic events. On the contrary, seismicity is associated with an abrupt sliding on a fault plane within a period of few seconds.

From the Fig. 2.28, it can be seen that seismic faulting can occur only at the depth more than 5 km; if fluid pressure (P) approaches that magnitude of total confining pressure (S_3).

i.e. $\lambda_e = P/S_3 = 1.0$

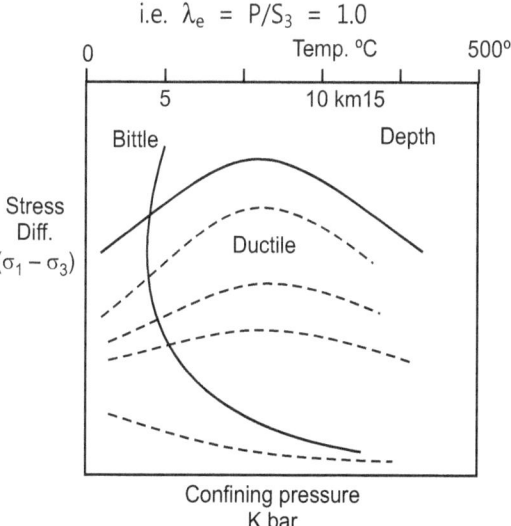

Fig. 2.28 : Seismic faulting

2.4.6 Active and Passive Faults

Faults capable of slippage during a short span of time, are recognised as active. These faults are episodic and the intervals of non-slippage range from a few years to hundreds or thousands of years.

To decide whether a fault is active, or not, it is necessary to check the historical evidence or history of past events. Often neo-tectonic movements may be observed along the fault. On the other hand, it is likely that a fault has remained undisturbed for thousands of years. In such cases, the fault may be labelled as passive or dead.

How to recognise active faults in the field ?

(1) Recent geologic deposits, unconsolidated alluvium, soil etc. are the useful sources for the recognition of recent crystal movements because they are widespread and young in geological sense. Thus, if a fault has displaced these recent deposits, clearly indicating a fact that the displacement is younger than the material. On the contrary, an inactive fault may be covered by deposits that are undisturbed. Thus, uninterrupted beds of alluvium may be considered as free from recent crystal movements.

(2) In many cases, topographic criteria may be used to ascertain whether the fault is active or dead. The most prominent feature is a fault scarp. This range from vertical cliffs to inconspicuous gentle slopes. As gentle slopes are rapidly obliterated, their presence may be a representation of recent faulting or of recurrent movement.

Straight stream channels or offset stream channels may be considered as another potential evidence.

2.4.7 Reactivation of Faults

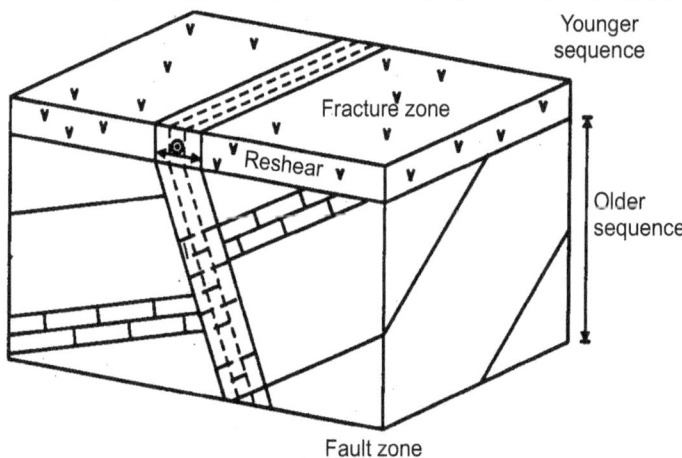

Fig. 2.29 : Reactivation of faults

Reactivation of faults is a common phenomenon, but very difficult to recognise. It is often observed that the prominent rupture zone is repeated in stratified rocks of different age. The rupture in different stratigraphic horizons may be represented by a fault, silica veins, a fracture zone, cataclasite, mylonite etc. Some splays of brittle fracture or a fracture zone may become reactivated due to recurrence of older fault zone (Fig. 2.29). The process of recurrence of a rupture zone in different stratigraphic horizons may be explained by considering Fig. 2.30.

From the Fig. 2.30, it is seen that initial failure occurs at the peak stress (S_p) which the rock can sustain, followed by a sharp decrease in the ability of the rock to sustain a differential stress.

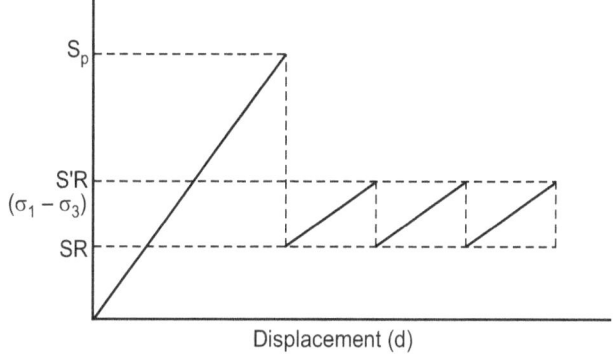

Fig. 2.30 : Recurrence of a fault

If $\sigma_3 = 0$ (rock mass is not subjected to a confining pressure), the differential stress which the failure plane is able to support is small.

If confining pressure exists (closed system, overburden), the rock mass is able to sustain a differential stress (SR, residual strength), the magnitude of which is explained by the frictional resistance to sliding on the fracture plane.

Subsequent displacements take place in a succession of shocks, in which the differential stress increases in S'R; here an increment of slip takes place and the differential stress again falls to SR.

The change in stress in the system brought about by reshear or reactivation causes seismic activity. Faults are initiated or ruptured only once and may reactivate many times. Hence, the factor of reshear drop associated with seismicity is crucial.

2.4.8 Effects of Faulting on Disrupted Beds

As mentioned earlier, presence of faults may be interpreted by studying various structures seen in the field (Section 2.4.3). In addition to those, an abrupt change in strike or dip, omission or repetition beds indicate that faulting has taken place. Similarly, vertical fault movements may produce a fault scarp; which is a steep slope joining the land on the upthrown and downthrown sides. Thus, the fault trace follows a course that is controlled by the attitude of fault and its topography.

Normal or reverse faulting of horizontal beds bring higher and lower layers against each other, the throw being equal to the change in the elevation of beds.

The effects of faulting on inclined beds are complicated and are influenced by the attitude of fault and the dip of beds.

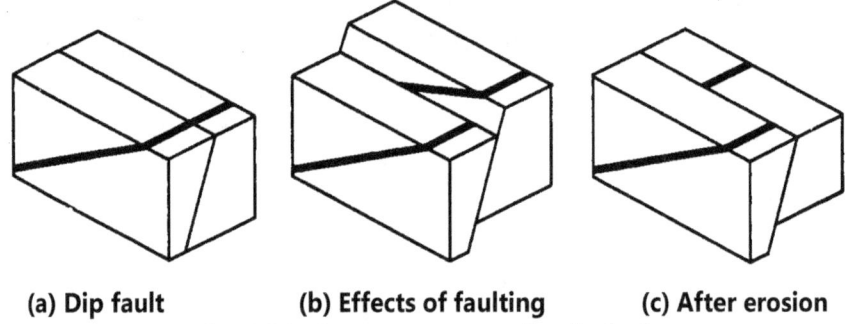

(a) Dip fault   (b) Effects of faulting   (c) After erosion

Fig. 2.31 : Outcrop pattern of a dip fault

A dip fault displaces the outcrop of inclined bed laterally and thus younger beds on the downthrown side are brought against older beds on the upthrown side (Fig. 2.31).

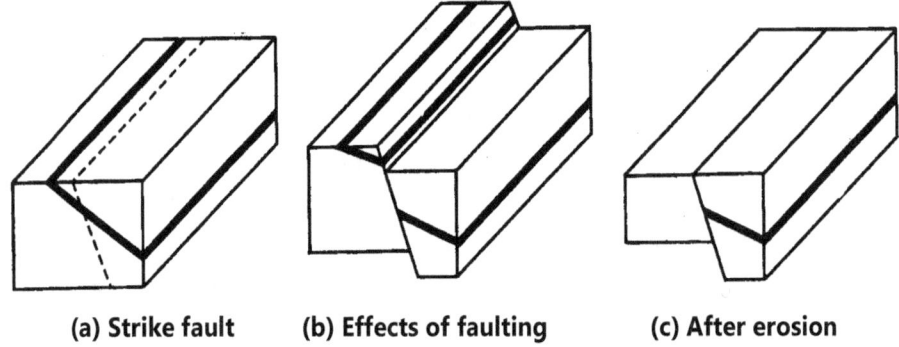

(a) Strike fault   (b) Effects of faulting   (c) After erosion

Fig. 2.32 : Outcrop pattern of a strike fault with dip-slip

A strike fault if steeper than dip of beds; affects the form of omission of beds (Fig. 2.32).

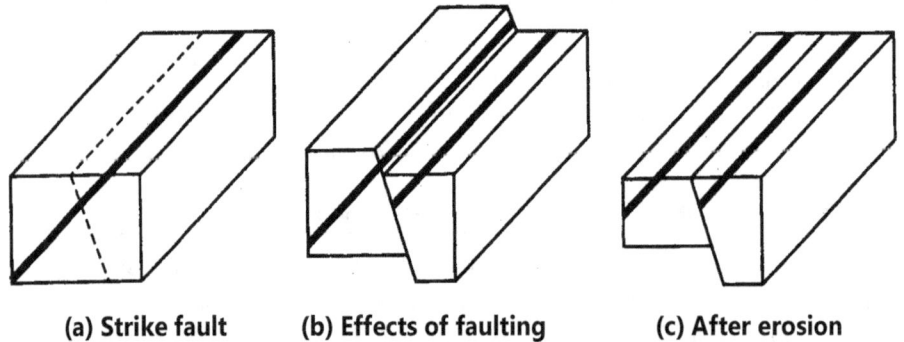

(a) Strike fault   (b) Effects of faulting   (c) After erosion

Fig. 2.33 : Outcrop pattern of a strike fault with dip in opposite direction

In case, the strike fault dips in opposite direction as compared to dip of beds, it is observed that beds are repeated (Fig. 2.33).

The effects of faults on folded strata are different.

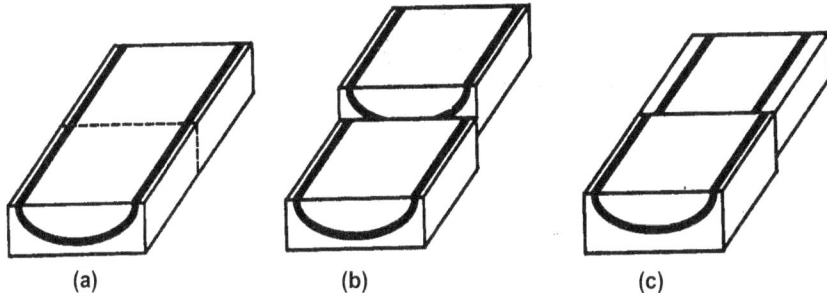

Fig. 2.34 : Outcrop pattern of a syncline

It would be evident from Fig. 2.34 that in the case of synclinal structure, the width of a syncline is increased on the downthrown side and the width of anticline is decreased accordingly.

2.5 JOINTS

Joints are the ruptures or discontinuities along which a negligible or no visible movement is observed. These may be formed due to tension or shear stresses acting on a rock mass. The cause of the stress may be in the form of contraction, compression, unusual uplift, subsidence, earthquakes or other earth movements. Joint may also be defined as *'a break of geological origin in the continuity of a body of rock along which there is no visible movement'*. Joint occurs at the outcrop scale in all rocks and thus constitutes the most abundant structural element in the crust of the earth. A group of parallel joints is called a set and joint sets intersect in the form of a joint system. Joints can either be open filled or healed.

A study of joints is very important from engineering point of view. Close spaced joints are found to be dangerous in tunnelling. In quarry operation, the ease of dressing and block operation is largely influenced by joints. A well-drilled in massive rocks is less productive than the well-drilled in jointed rocks.

Attitude of joints is measured by its strike and dip similar to the bedding plane. The strike is the direction of horizontal line on the surface of the joint and dip is the inclination of the joint plane. Joints may be classified genetically or geometrically. Geometric classification is purely descriptive and does not indicate the origin of the joints.

2.5.1 Geometric Classification

Joints are classified on the basis of the attitude of bedding plane (Fig. 2.35).

Strike joints are those that strike essentially parallel to the bedding plane. The inclination of strike joint may differ from the dip of a bedding plane. Bedding joints are parallel to the strictly bedding plane.

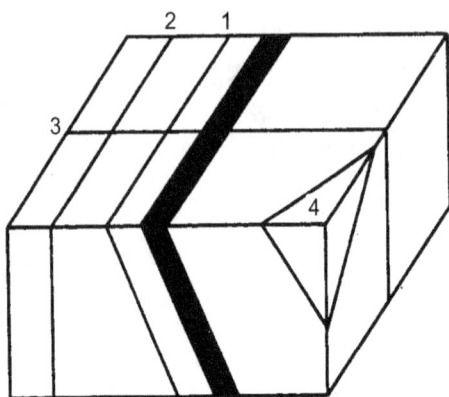

Fig. 2.35 : Geometrical classification of joints

Dip joints are those that strike normal to strike of the bedding plane. In other words, dip joints are parallel to the dip direction of the bedding plane.

Oblique or diagonal joints are neither parallel to the strike of bed, nor in the dip direction of bed. Thus, these joints strike oblique to rock strata.

2.5.2 Genetic Classification

In this classification, origin of the joints is discussed. The reasons for the development of joints are as follows : (a) unloading process, (b) cooling of magnetic material, (c) gravitational forces, (d) tectonic forces.

(a) Unloaded joints (also called as sheeting or topographic joints) : Joints may be formed due to released stored stresses consequent on deep burial. The weight of great thickness of overburden exert a tremendous pressure on deeply buried rocks. In other words, the underlying rocks are constantly under lithostatic pressure caused by the overburden. However, once the overburden is removed, pressure exerted on deeper rocks reduces appreciably. As a result the concealed rock gets expanded vertically in the form of tension joints which are developed parallel to ground surface. Thus, the joints are known as *topographic joints*; and are commonly seen in massive rocks.

The sheet or topographic joints are usually close spaced. It is seen that perpendicular distance between two successive joints is few centimetres and these are traceable for a distance of few metres (persistence). Thus, these joints may act as inflow zones or passage ways for ground water movement.

(b) Cooling joints : Another common mode of formation of joint is the contraction observed in a cooling igneous body. Basically, these, joints are tension cracks formed due to shrinkage of rock. The best example of this is, columnar jointing in basaltic rocks. During the process of cooling, the tensional forces acting towards a number of centres are set in layers.

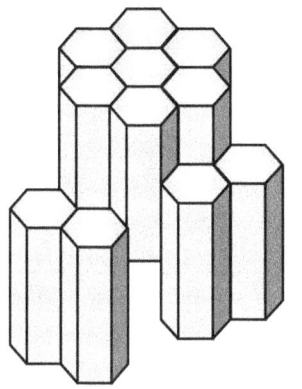
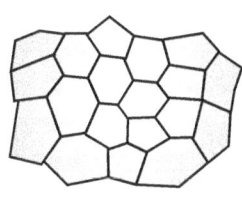

Fig. 2.36

These forces tend to open a series of joints which ideally assume a hexagonal pattern and as cooling proceeds towards central zone of mass, the joint develop in depth [Fig. 2.36 (a)].

In other words, during the process of cooling, a uniform tensional stress may be formed in the plane parallel to the contracts giving rise to hexagonal cracks [Fig. 2.36 (a) and (b)].

(c) **Tectonic joints :** Many a times, joints are syngenetic to folding or major faults and thus owe their origin to the same compressive forces which produce the folds faults.

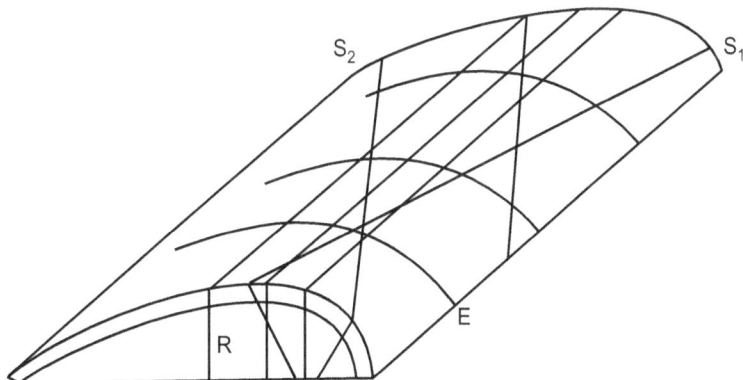

Fig. 2.37 : Diagram illustrating development of Release (R), Extension (E), and Shear (S_1 and S_2) joints along the crest of an anticline

Extension joints are always perpendicular to fold axes and are commonly developed in the direction of maximum compressional stress (Fig. 2.37).

Joints parallel to the axial plane of the folds are known as **longitudinal joints**. These may be tension fracture or release joint similar to those formed in the direction of maximum strain (Fig. 2.37).

Cross joints are always oblique to fold axis. In some cases, the two cross joints forming the conjugate sets intersect in the direction of intermediate stress. These joints are known as **shear joints** (Fig. 2.37).

(d) Superfacial movements : In many cases, joints are formed due to superfacial movements e.g. glaciers, crevasses etc.

2.5.3 Discontinuities

The majority of the rock masses exposed on the surface and at shallow depth behave like discontinuities and the discontinuities largely control the mechanical behaviour. It is therefore essential that both the structure of the rock mass and nature of its discontinuities are carefully described in addition to lithological description of the rock type.

The term 'discontinuity' covers large number of planar surfaces (Table 2.1) that vary in dimensions from small fissures to large faults.

Table 2.1 : Mechanical classification of discontinuities

Characteristic	Faults	Shear joints	Tension joints	Bedding planes	Dykes and sills	Igneous
1. Occurrence	Generally unique	Sets	Sets	Sets	Generally unique	Unique
2. Continuity	High	Medium	Low	High	High	High
3. Length	Extremely long	Long to short	Medium to short	Very long	Very long to extremely long	Very long
4. Condition	Tight, smooth to polished surfaces	Tight, smooth to polished surfaces	–	Tight smooth to rough surfaces	Often gradational tight	Open
5. Infilling	Cataclastic material	Gouge	-	-	Igneous rocks	-
6. Movement	Slickensides	Slickensides	–	Slickenside	Slickensides	–
7. Fracture angle	Varies, Depending upon nature of fault	–	–	–	–	–
8. Friction angle	–	Peak 30°- 50° Residual 20°- 40°	Peak 40°- 50° Residual 30°- 45°			
9. Other	–	–	–	May be horizontal, inclined or vertical and folded	Often fractured	Sometimes faulted

In general, a discontinuity represents a plane of weakness within a rock mass, across which the material is structurally discontinuous. Each discontinuity survey depends on clarity and quality of data. Rock masses and discontinuities can be described by outcrop description, drill core and drill hole description and aerial photos-satellite imageries.

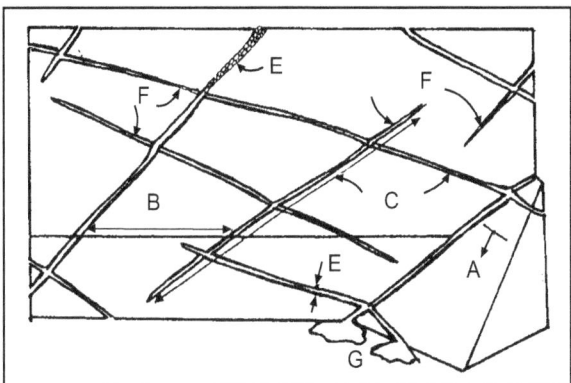

Fig. 2.38 : Measurement of discontinuity characteristics
A : Discontinuity, B : Spacing, C : Persistence, D : Block size, E : Aperture, filling,
F : Roughness, G : Seepage.

Commonly the following ten parameters are accurately measured to quantify discontinuities and rock masses.

(a) Orientation :

The orientation of a discontinuity in space is described by its strike direction, and amount and direction of dip. The measurements are important for several reasons. For example, failure by sliding is most likely to occur along planes dipping towards a slope rather than away from it. It is desirable to measure a sufficient number of orientations to mark prominent joint sets in the area (number, n = 150 to 200).

Measurements may be carried out by scan line method or random method. In the scan line method, first a traverse or scan line is drawn on the outcrop fate, aerial photograph or even on oriented field photograph. It is advisable in case of field photographs to take overlapping photos considering the important aspect of dip of beds and orientation of every discontinuity is measured (Fig. 2.38). Though the method is time consuming, discontinuities that are repetitive along one or two directions and continuous may be easily quantified. To get better results, three to four traverses are taken at different directions in the same sampling station.

In Random method, measurements are carried out on many discontinuities irrespective of their size and continuity. Though large number of readings are taken, but as measurements are made randomly, plots prepared from this may give biased idea about attitude of prominent discontinuity.

Data collected may be presented by rose diagram, histogram and projection methods.

Rose diagrams : In this graphical method, strike orientations are presented on a simplified compass rose from 0 – 360° with radial lines at 5 – 10° interval. Rose diagrams offer a good method of recording data when combined with the relevant map. As it involves no representation of dip angle, the range of dip may be shown outside the circumference (Fig. 2.39).

Results obtained from rosette diagrams are more informative if length of discontinuities is plotted alongwith orientation [Fig. 2.39 (b)].

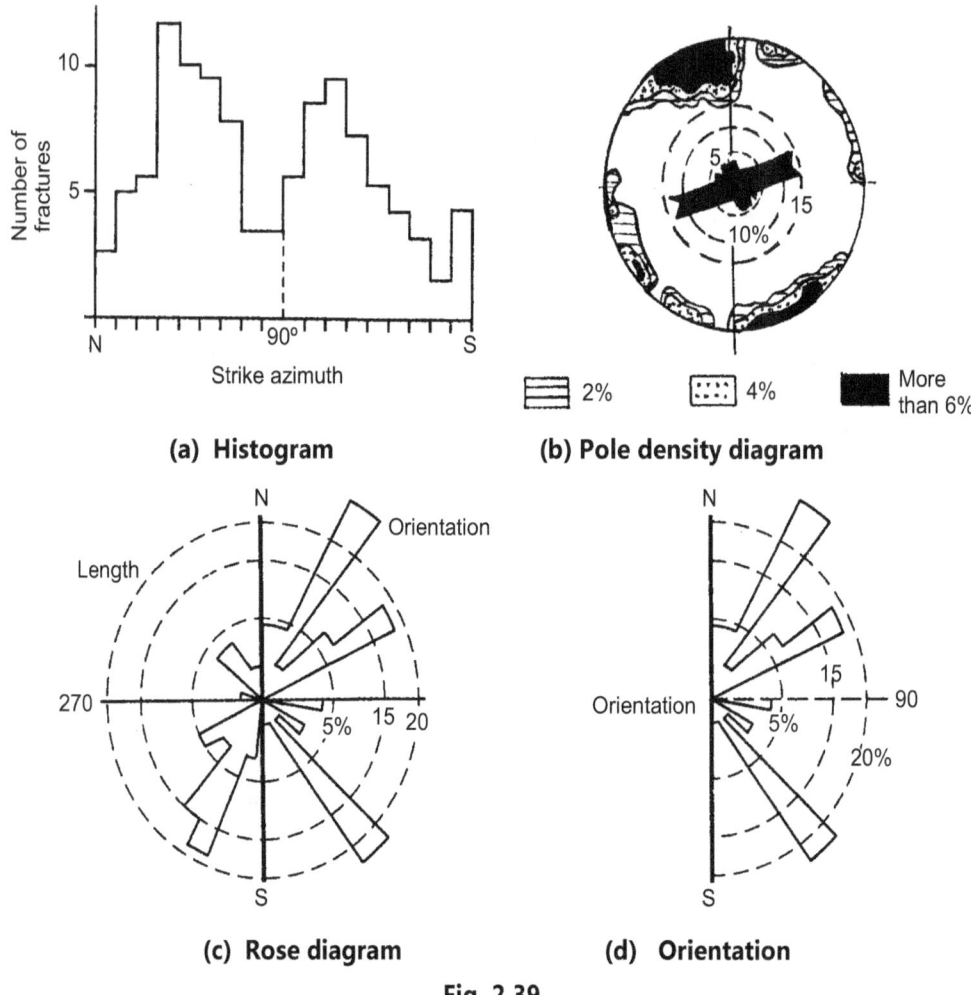

Fig. 2.39

A *Histogram* is similar to a rose diagram but it is plotted on a square grid instead of a circular grid. In this strike, orientations are plotted on x-axis and frequencies on y-axis [Fig. 2.39 (c)]. The method helps in recording minor changes in orientations without exaggeration than the rosette diagrams.

Projection method [Fig. 2.39 (d)] is useful in differentiating low and steep dipping discontinuities. The diagram is simply a contoured diagram in which contour value increases towards centre. The central value of highest concentration of poles can be taken as representing the mean orientation of given set of discontinuities.

(b) Spacing :

Spacing is the perpendicular distance between adjacent discontinuities that largely control size of individual blocks (Fig. 2.40).

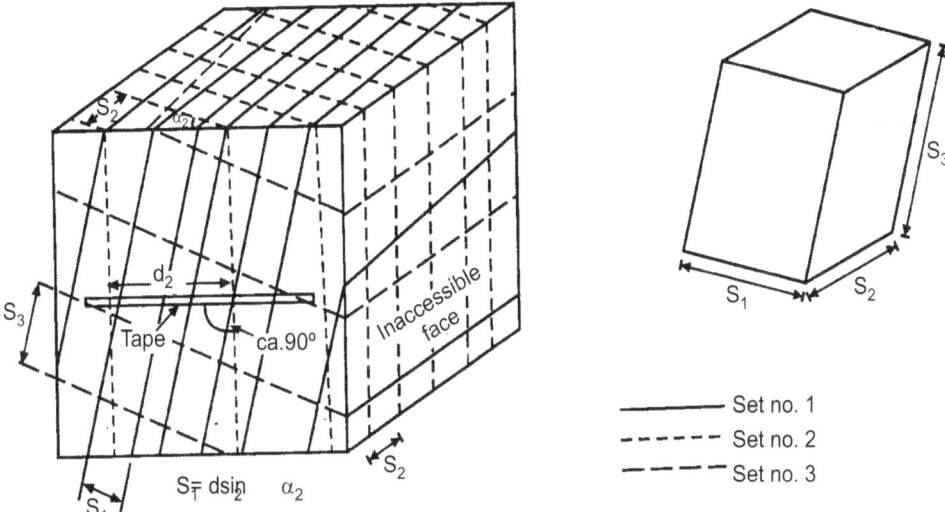

Fig. 2.40 : Measurement of joint spacing from observation of a rock exposure

The spacing of individual discontinuities and associated sets has a strong influence on the seepage characteristics and permeability. Several closely spaced sets tend to create conditions of low mass cohesion, whereas widely spaced discontinuities yield interlocking conditions.

Spacing is measured by using scan line / traverse method (Fig. 2.40). In this, distance (d) is measured between adjacent discontinuities and the spacing is calculated from the equation

$$s = d \cdot \sin \theta$$

where, s = spacing

d = modal distance measured

θ = angle between the scan line and the observed discontinuity, if any.

The distributions may be presented as histograms, one for each set. The spacing is described by the following terms.

Table 2.2 : Terminology for spacing

Description	Spacing
Extremely close spacing	< 2 cm
Very close spacing	2 – 6 cm
Close spacing	6 – 20 cm
Moderate spacing	20 – 60 cm
Wide spacing	60 – 200 cm
Very wide spacing	200 – 600 cm
Extremely wide spacing	> 600 cm

(c) Persistence :

Persistence is *the trace length of a discontinuity observed in an exposure or aerial photograph*. Though this is a very difficult parameter to quantify, it is one of the most important rock mass parameter in rock slopes, dam foundations and tunneling particularly those discontinuities that are unfavourably oriented. In rare instances, rock outcrops are small compared to the length of persistent discontinuities and the real persistence may only be guessed. The modal trace lengths measured for each set may be described by the following terms (Table 2.3)

Table 2.3 : Assessment for persistence

Description	Trace length
Very low persistence	< 1 m
Low persistence	1 – 3 m
Medium persistence	3 – 10 m
High persistence	10 – 20 m
Very high persistence	> 20 m

Another important factor in the measurement of persistence of a discontinuity is to trace the kind of termination which could be beyond the exposure (x_1), within the exposure (x_2) or against other discontinuity (x_3). This helps in deciding systematic and non-systematic discontinuities.

Termination index for a domain may be calculated as follows :

$$T_r = \frac{\Sigma x \cdot 100}{2n} \%$$

where,
T_r = Termination index
Σx = ($x_1 + x_2 + x_3$)
n = Number of discontinuities observed

(d) Roughness :

The roughness of discontinuity walls can be characterised by 'waviness' and 'unevenness'. Waviness refers to large scale undulations which cause dilation during shear displacement, while unevenness is small scale roughness that tends to be damaged during shear displacement. Often surface roughness alters dip of the bed locally. It can be measured in the field by linear profile method.

In this method, initially accessible discontinuities which are potential sites of shear failure, are selected. Measurements on attitude of discontinuities and places of dip alterations along planar surfaces are recorded accurately. Generally, two measurements are to be carried out; d_1 : tangential distance along actual dip of the discontinuity, and d_2 : perpendicular distance from the assumed straight edge to the surface of a discontinuity. Repeat the procedure at many places along the discontinuity surface. The recorded data are to be plotted to the same scale and same inclination to decide the surface roughness. The prepared profile may then be compared with the photograph of the relevant surface.

The description of roughness should be based on small scale (cm) and intermediate scale (m). Generally, three categories are recognised at intermediate scale which are further divided into terms used as small scale.

1. Stepped   :   Rough, smooth, slickensided
2. Undulating :   Rough, smooth, slickensided
3. Planar   :   Rough, smooth, slickensided

The main purpose in describing roughness of the walls of discontinuities is to allow estimation of shear strength.

Barton (1976) proposed the following empirical expression to derive the shear strength (τ) along joint surfaces.

$$\tau = \sigma_n \tan [JRC \log_{10} (JCS/\sigma_n) + \phi_b]$$

where,
σ_n = Effective normal stress
JRC = Joint roughness coefficient
JCS = Joint wall compressive strength
ϕ_b = Basic friction angle.

Barton (1976) recognised values of JRC range from 0 to 20 from the smoothest to roughest surface (Fig. 2.41).

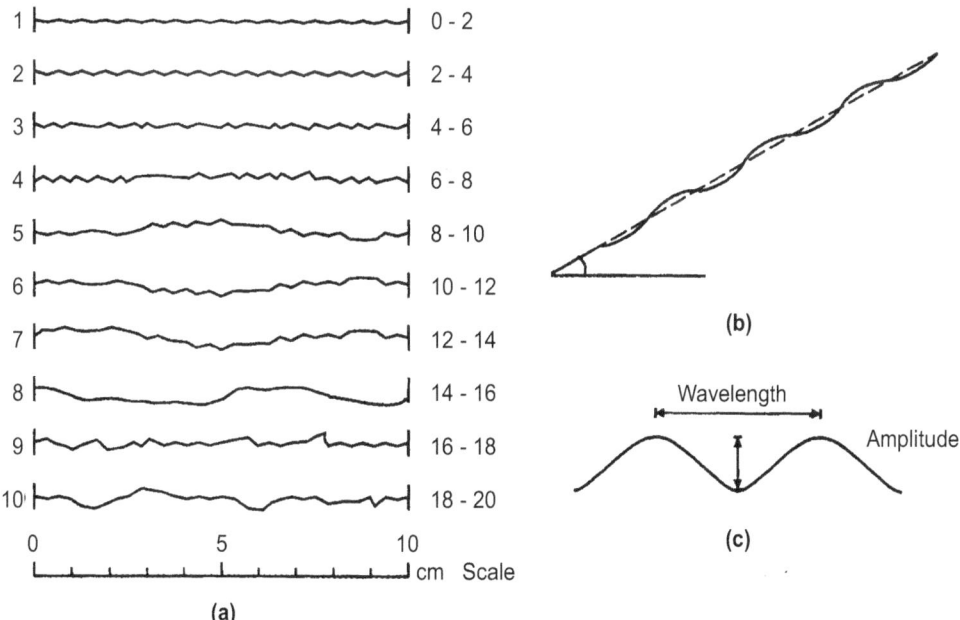

Fig. 2.41 : Measurement of surface roughness (a) Surface waviness due to presence of irregular discontinuity. This results in alteration of dip angle locally (b) Measurement of surface roughness (c) Typical roughness profiles for a range of joint roughness coefficients

The JCS is equal to the unconfined compressive strength of the unweathered rock. This may be reduced to 75% when the walls of the joints are weathered.

(e) Wall strength :

Rock masses are frequently weathered and altered by hydrothermal process. Physical weathering results in opening of discontinuities, the creation of new planar surfaces and also widening of the discontinuities. Chemical weathering is intense near the walls of discontinuities which results into appreciable reduction in the wall strength. It results in discolouration of the rock and leads to alteration of silicate minerals to clay minerals. Thus, initially the grade of weathering of the rockmass as a whole should be described (Table 2.4) followed by the description of the rock material consisting walls of individual discontinuities (Fig. 2.42, Table 2.4).

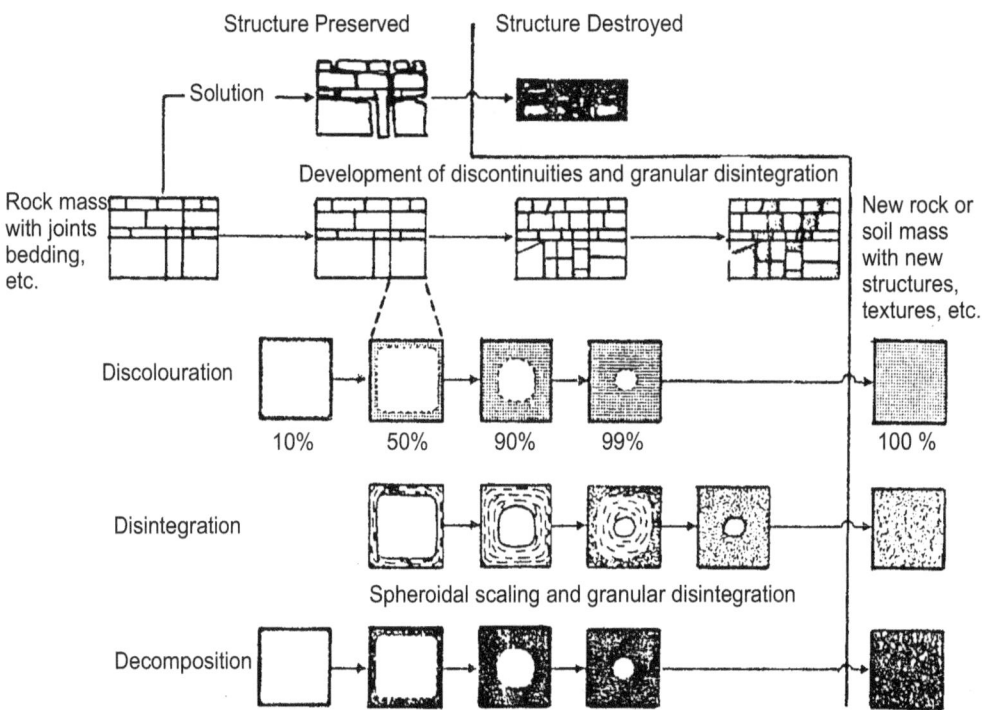

Fig. 2.42 : Idealized diagram of the stages of weathering of a rock mass

Table 2.4 : Weathering grade of rock forming walls of discontinuities

Term	Description
Fresh	No visible sign of weathering
Discoloured	The colour of the fresh rock is altered.
Decomposed	The rock is altered partially to soil in which original fabric is preserved.
Disintegrated	The rock is friable but mineralogical changes are few. Rock is partially altered to soil.

A more detailed account of the walls of discontinuities may be available if manual index tests (recommended by ISRM, 1978) are performed on material representative of the walls (Table 2.5). It is possible to ascertain presence of critical discontinuities on the basis of kind of material available for tests.

Table 2.5 : Grade of weathering based on manual index tests (ISRM, 1978)

Grade and Description	Field identification [R : rock, S : cohesive soil]
R_0 – extremely weak rock.	Easily scratchable by fingernail
R_1 – very weak rock.	Can be peeled by a pocket knife or crumbles under blow of a geological hammer.
R_2 – weak rock.	Can be removed by a pocket knife with difficulty. Shallow impact marks develop under firm blow of geological hammer.
R_3 – medium strong rock	Can not be scrapped with a pocket knife, specimen may be fractured with single blow of geological hammer.
R_4 – strong rock	Specimen requires more than one blow of geological hammer to fracture it.
R_5 – very strong rock	Specimen requires many blows of geological hammer to fracture it.
R_6 – extremely strong rock	Specimen can only be chipped with geological hammer.
S_1 – very soft clay	Easily penetrated several inches by fingers.
S_2 – soft clay	Easily penetrated several inches by thumb.
S_3 – firm clay	Can be penetrated several inches by thumb with moderate efforts.
S_4 – stiff clay	Easily scratchable by thumb but penetrated only with great effort.
S_5 – very stiff clay	Easily indented by thumbnail.
S_6 – hard clay	Indented with some difficulty by thumbnail.

(f) Aperture :

Aperture is the perpendicular distance separating the adjacent rock walls of an open discontinuity in which the intervening space is filled by air or water. In the field, aperture is difficult to measure as the separations seen in the field are inherently disturbed due to blasting or surface weathering. Aperture may be described by following terms (Table 2.6).

Table 2.6 : Description of Aperture

Aperture	Description	
< 0.1 mm	Very tight	'Open'
0.1 to 0.25 mm	Tight	features
0.25 to 0.50 mm	Partially open	
0.5 to 2.5 mm	Open	'Gapped'
2.5 to 10 mm	Moderately open	features
> 10 mm	Wide	
1 to 10 cm	Very wide	'Open'
10 to 100 cm	Extremely wide	features
> 1 m	Cavernous	

(g) Filling :

Filling is the term for material occupying the adjacent rock walls of discontinuities. The perpendicular distance between adjacent rock walls is called 'width' of a filled discontinuity. The filling material may be calcite, quartz, clay, silt and fault gouge. As a result, filled discontinuities exhibit large variation in their behaviour particularly in their shear strength, permeability and deformability.

Following are the observations to be carried out on the filling material :

- Mineralogy of filling material
- Particle size
- Width
- Surface roughness
- Water content and permeability
- Filling strength
- Degree of weathering
- Swelling potential
- Effect of shear displacement, if any.

A continuous unfill will have an important role in the behaviour of rockmass, whereas an unfill discontinuity may provide little support. The mineral composition of finer material should be checked particularly if active or swelling clay minerals are suspected. Presence of water in filled material may significantly alter shear strength of the planar surfaces.

The width of filled material and surface roughness may also influence the shear strength along the discontinuity. In case of very narrow width of material, the peak strength of discontinuity will be influenced by the shear strength of the rock and surface waviness. On the other hand, 'wide' width of the filled material will control the frictional properties of a discontinuity.

In case of complex filled discontinuities, it is essential to make accurate field sketches of the wall rock (Fig. 2.43).

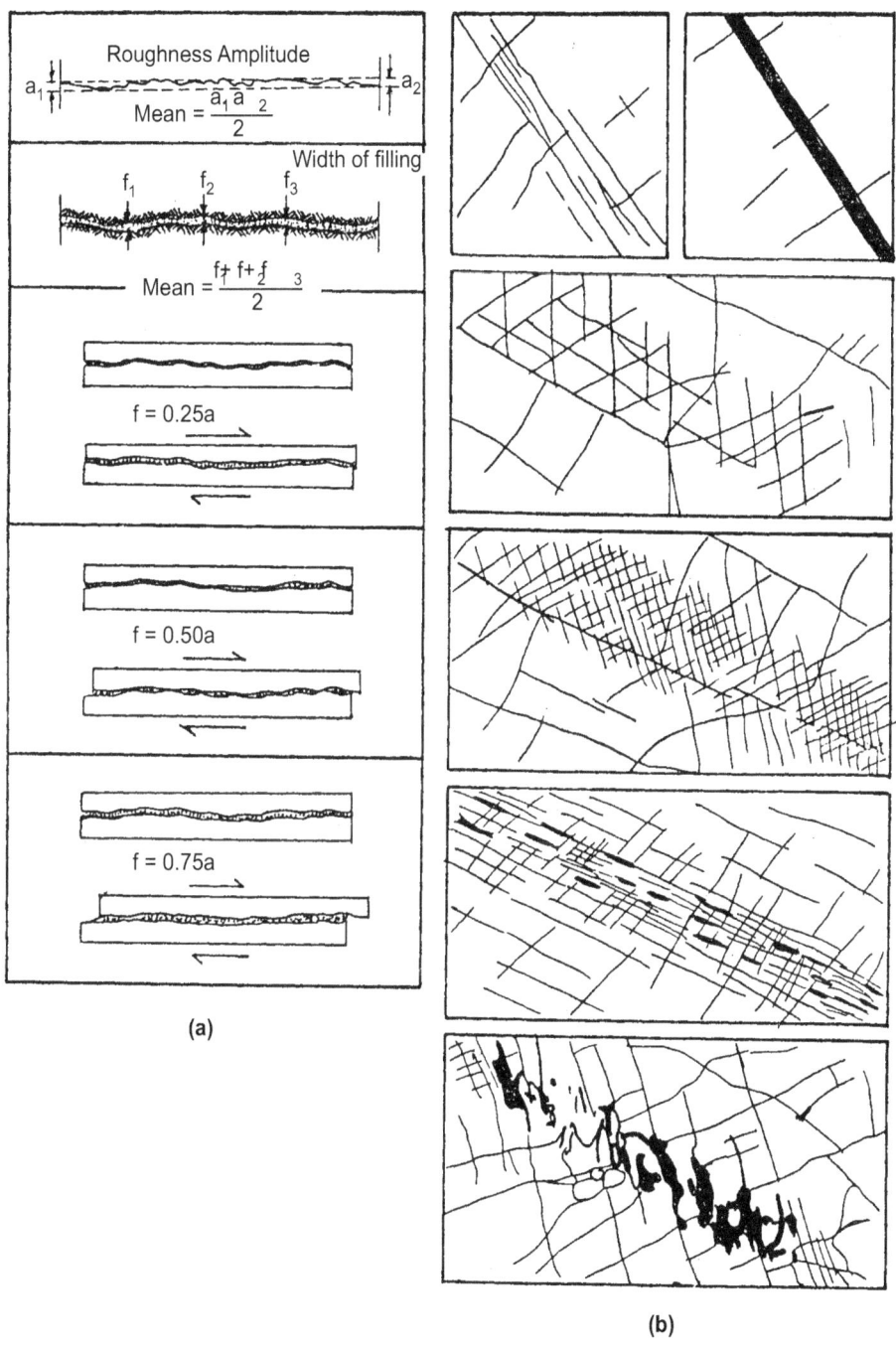

Fig. 2.43 : Field examples of filled discontinuities
(a) In the case of simple filled discontinuities, the amplitude of the wall roughness and the thickness of the filling can help to indicate the amount of shear displacement required for rock contact (stiffening) to occur. (Zero volume change assumed during shear) (b) Examples of field sketches of complex filled discontinuities

Hydrothermal alteration of gouge material may sometimes complicate the mineralogical identification as these products are not associated with the petrography of the crushed rock.

(h) Hydrogeology :

Description of local hydrogeological condition with detailed account on rainfall, surface run-off, seepage from individual discontinuities, groundwater movement, aquifers, aquicludes, dykes and inflow zones is of prime importance in discussing the stability of many man-made structures.

The hydrogeological investigations are to be carried out using toposheets, aerial photographs and seasonal field visits. General procedure on this is given in Unit 5 (b).

Seepage from individual open and filled discontinuities can be described by following terms.

Table 2.7 : Assessment of seepage from open and filled discontinuities

Seepage rating	Discontinuities	
	Open	**Filled**
I	The discontinuity is very tight and dry.	The filling material is over-consolidated and dry.
II	The discontinuity is dry with no trace of water flow.	The filling material is moist, but no free water is present.
III	The discontinuity is dry, but evidence of inflow seen.	The filling material is wet, occasional drops of water.
IV	The discontinuity is damp, but no free water is present.	The filling material shows signs of continuous flow of water.
V	The discontinuity shows seepage, occasional drops of water, but no free flow of water.	The filling material is washed out locally, considerable water flow along outwash channels.
VI	The discontinuity shows a continuous flow of water.	The filling material is washed out completely, very high water pressure is experienced.

(i) Number of sets :

The mechanical behaviour and appearance of rock mass is affected by the number of sets of discontinuities that intersect one another. It is particularly an important parameter in rock slope stability and tunnelling. In this, systematic joints should be separated out from non-systematic joints. Data in the form of orientation, spacing alongwith number of sets in a domain is useful in engineering classification of rock mass.

(j) Block size :

Block size is decided by spacing, number of sets and persistence. The number of sets and orientation determine the shape of the resulting blocks. Rock quarring and blasting efficiency are likely to be a function of block size.

Block size can be described by block size index (Bi) which is a representation of average dimension of typical rock blocks. The fractured rock mass can be idealised either as a collection of prismatic blocks, plates or bars (Fig. 2.44) according to the ratio of their relative distances. Commonly the block number increases with the increase of discontinuities within the volume of the rock mass.

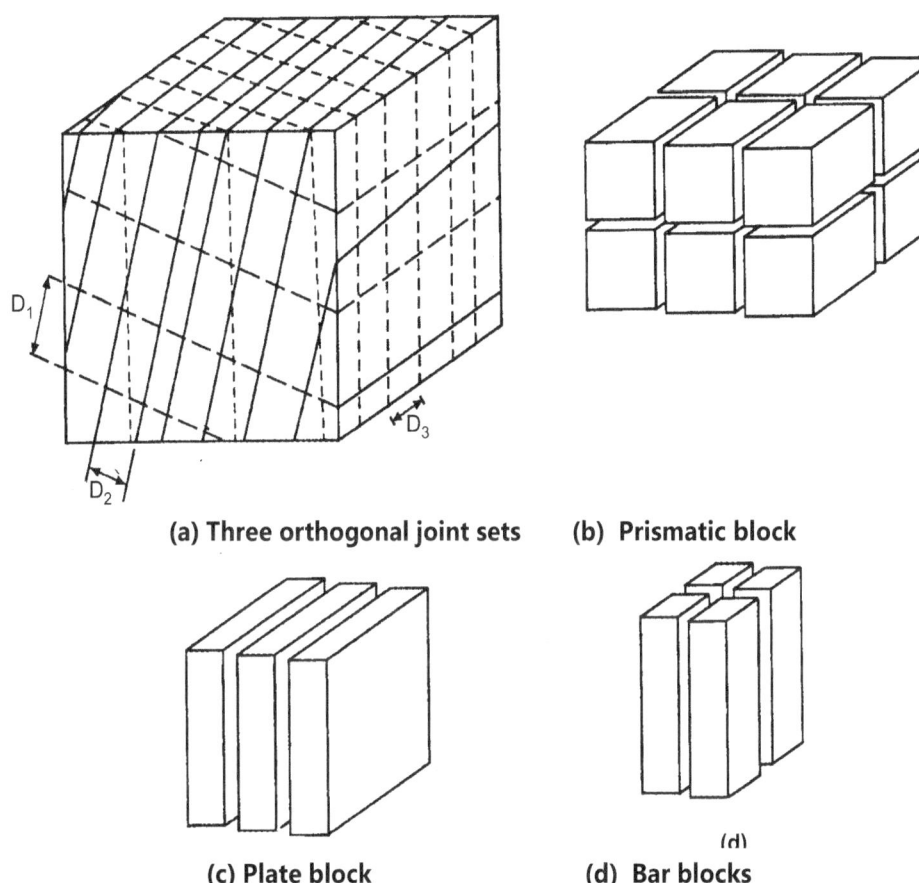

(a) Three orthogonal joint sets (b) Prismatic block

(c) Plate block (d) Bar blocks

Fig. 2.44 : Block size

To find out volumetric joint count (J_c), it is necessary to measure the sum of the number of joints per metre for each joint set present, which gives an impression of each block size (Table 2.8).

Table 2.8 : Description of block size

Description	J_c (Joints/m^3)
Very large blocks	< 1.0
Large blocks	1 – 3
Medium sized blocks	3 – 10
Small blocks	10 – 30
Very small blocks	> 30

2.6 UNCONFORMITY

An unconformity is a surface of erosion or non-deposition, usually the former, that separates younger strata from older strata. The development of an unconformity involves several stages. The first stage is deposition of older rocks followed by uplift and sub-aerial erosion, and on these eroded edges, younger rocks get deposited (Fig. 2.45). An unconformity indicates the influence of three important factors.

(1) **Time :** An unconformity develops during a period of time in which no sediments were deposited. It indicates unrecorded time.

(2) **Deposition :** Any break in deposition, small or large in extent, is an indication of unconformity.

(3) **Structures :** Structurally, unconformity is considered as a planar structure separating older rocks from younger rocks.

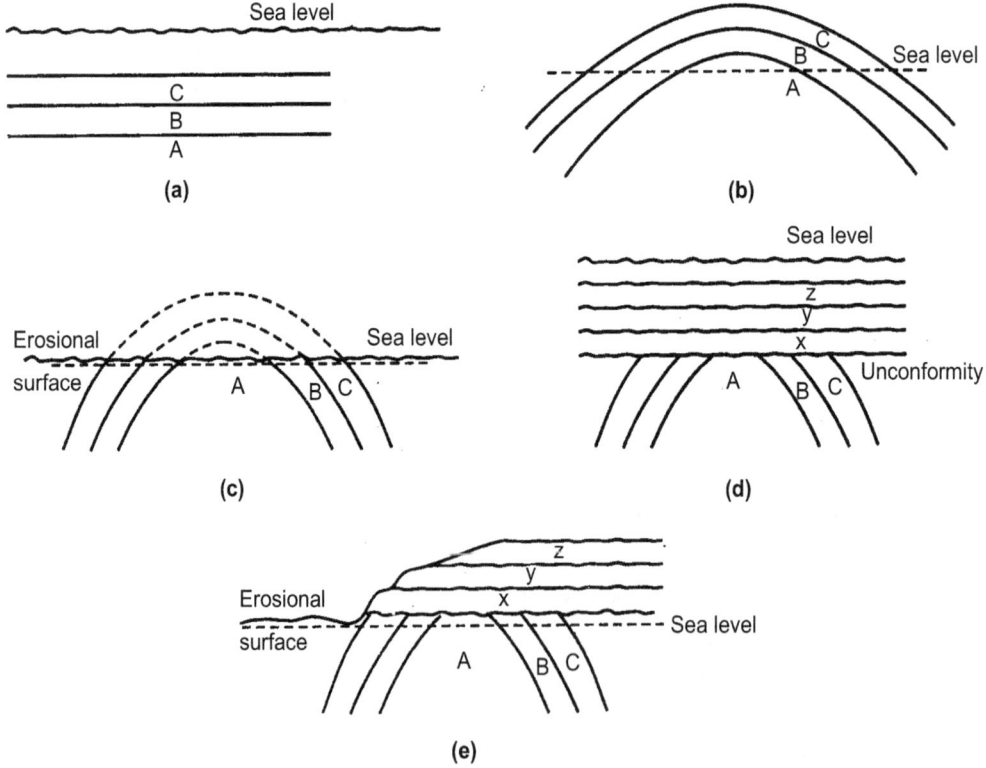

Fig. 2.45 : Development of an unconformity

Thus, the surface of an unconformity is commonly parallel to the surface of younger rocks or makes an angle with the upper strata. Four types of unconformities may be recognised.

(a) **Angular unconformity (Fig. 2.46)** : The older rocks dip at a different angle to the younger rocks. Also includes the case where unfolded, younger strata rests on the older folded strata.

(b) **Parallel unconformity (Fig. 2.46)** : The beds on opposite side of unconformity are parallel. It is also called disconformity in which the geologic time involved is large.

(c) **Local unconformity** : It is a minor type of unconformity representing a small time, period of non-deposition in geologic history. It is also called as non-depositional unconformity.

(d) **Non-conformity (Fig. 2.46)** : In this, sediments are deposited on top of igneous rocks or metamorphosed rock which are exposed on the surface by weathering and erosion. It is also called as Heterolithic unconformity.

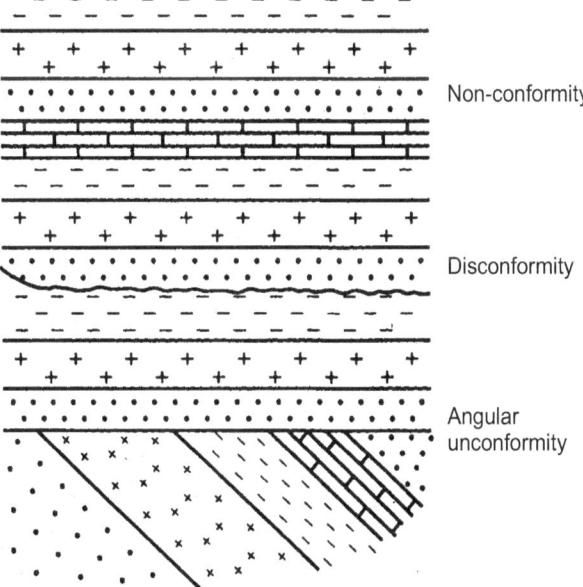

Fig. 2.46 : Type of unconformities

Overlap : This term is used when progressively younger members of upper series deposit on the older series [Fig 2.47 (a)].

Overstep : This is reverse of overlap i.e. lower beds of the upper series extend further than the younger ones [Fig. 2.47 (b)].

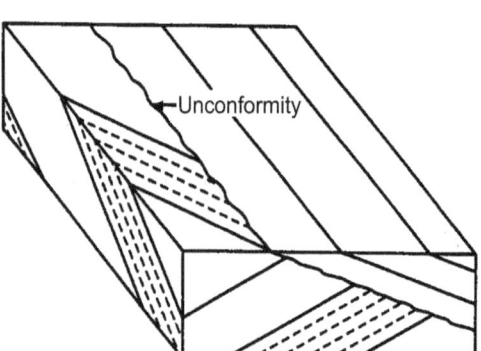 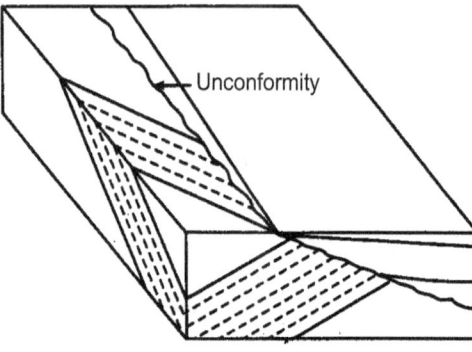

(a) Unconformity with overlap   (b) Unconformity with overstep
Fig. 2.47

2.6.1 Recognition of Unconformity

An unconformity may be identified by a careful observation in a single outcrop. The outcrop may be due to artificial opening or quarrying operation or it may be a natural exposure. The angular unconformity can readily be recognised in a vertical section due to angular relationship of two series. If the identification is not possible in a single outcrop, the study of aerial photo can provide a useful tool in the recognition.

A sharp contrast in the degree of induration indicates the unconformity.

A significant change in the degree of folding and also intensity is further suggestive. If rocks with a distinct difference in the grade of metamorphism is recorded in the same area, an unconformable relation of intensely metamorphic rocks with mild metamorphosed rocks may be visualised. Further, if the order strata consists of plutonic rocks, which is separated by upper sedimentary or metamorphic rock, is directly suggestive of presence of an unconformity, and in some cases, the most important criteria is recognition of fossil record. A significant change in the fossil record may predict an hiatus in the otherwise homogeneous formation.

2.7 FOLIATION AND LINEATION

The structures developed in the rocks at a deeper structural level of orogenic belts are different from those found at shallow structural level in the earth's crust. The variation is possibly due to increased temperature and great lithostatic pressure at the deeper level. Structure characteristics of these factors are in the form of intricate folding and sets of new planar surfaces (cleavage, schistosity etc.).

2.7.1 Foliation

A foliation is a set of new planar surfaces produced in a rock as a result of intense deformation. It include variety of structures such as slaty cleavage, schistosity, gneissose banding and close spaced fractures. Most of these structures are discussed in the appropriate section (schistosity - Metamorphic rocks).

Some other types of foliations are as follows :

(a) **Fracture cleavage :** A fracture cleavage consists of parallel close spaced fractures. It is characteristic of low temperature conditions under brittle deformation regime and is peculiar of sandstone or limestone etc.

(b) **Crenulation cleavage :** These are small scale folds shown by very thin layers or laminations within a rock. The structure is commonly associated with later structures, which possess a strong cleavage or schistosity as a result of earlier deformation.

2.7.2 Lineation

Lineation includes a set of linear structures produced in a rock as a result of deformation. Common examples of lineation are elongated pebbles in a deformed conglomerate, slickenside striations, crenulation fold axes, mineral rods etc.

PART (B)

2.8 PLATE TECTONICS

Careful measurements made in mines and drill holes round the world indicate that the rate of temperature increase with depth varies from 15° to 75°C/km, averaging about 30°C/km. The increase in temperature with depth is called *geothermal gradient*. Heat is produced in the interior due to presence of many chemical elements which are naturally radioactive e.g. uranium, thorium and potassium which undergo transformation to lead, lead and argon respectively. During the transformation, a tiny amount of heat is generated. Thus, radioactivity is a constant source of energy available in the interior.

The generated heat moves through conduction (the process by which heat can move through solid body without deforming the body) and convection (the process by which hot, less dense materials rise upward and are replaced by cold, downward and sideways flowing materials). The Earth's internal convection currents shape the surface of the Earth. The most important effect of convection currents inside the Earth is Plate-tectonics, the slow lateral movement of the Earth's outermost shell. It is the lateral movements that splits and moves continents, triggers, earthquakes, causes volcanoes and builts mountains (Fig. 2.48). The term 'plate' is used because the lithosphere moves as a number of separate plate like pieces. The plate range in width from several hundred to several thousand kilometres (Fig. 2.48). A total of six large plates and numerous smaller plates are recognised, all moving at a rate ranging from 1 to 12 cm/year. The plate may be completely continental (e.g. Eurasia plate) or oceanic (e.g. Pacific), or it may be partly continental and oceanic (e.g. Indian plate).

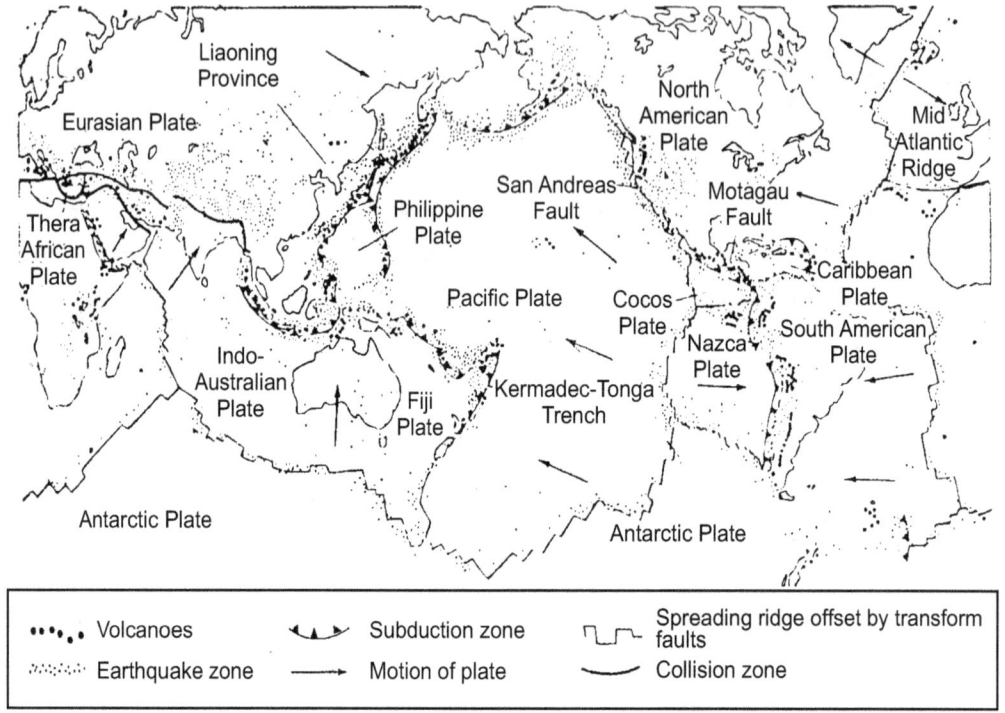

Fig. 2.48 : World map showing the relation between the major tectonic plates and recent earthquakes and volcanoes. Earthquake epicentres are denoted by small dots and volcanoes by large dots.

Plates move over the face of the Earth, each describing a circular path round its pole of rotation. In doing so, they move away from one adjacent plate, towards another and between a further pair. The relationships result in three types of plate boundary (Fig. 2.49, 24.50 and 2.51).

2.8.1 Divergent Plate Boundaries

It is also known as spreading centre. In this, two plates move apart and thus a fissure develops, allowing hot molten material to rise on the surface from deep interior or mantle (Fig. 2.49). This type of boundary is also known as pull-apart, constructive or divergent plate margins. For example, mid-oceanic ridges.

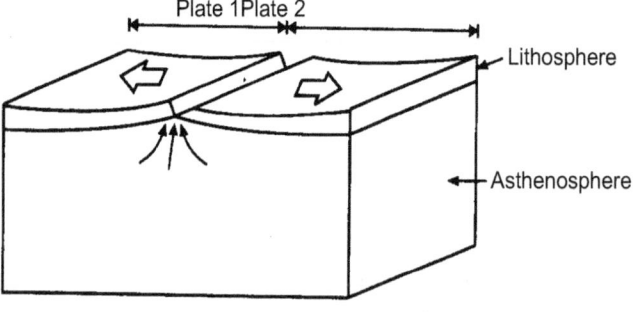

Fig. 2.49 : Divergent plate boundaries

These form the longest continuous mountain system on the earth. Their length is 64000 kilometres, width is 400 to 4800 km and elevation upto 3000 metres from their base. Two parts of this system are known to the mid-atlantic ridge and the east pacific rise. Presence of mid oceanic ridge can be best exemplified by the island, iceland.

2.8.2 Convergent Plate Boundaries

It is also known as closing centre. Here two plates move towards each other. As a result, the denser plate either sinks below the lighter plate, recognised as subduction zone (for example trenches) [Fig. 2.50 (a)] or the two plates must colloide so as to form a collision zone (for example, Himalayas) [Fig. 2.50 (b)]. The plate boundaries are also called as destructive or convergent margins. It is interesting to note that major destructive earthquakes are located along these margins.

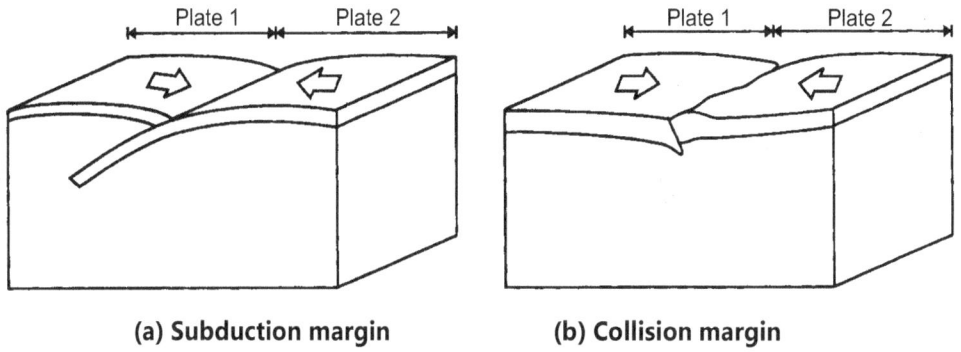

(a) Subduction margin   (b) Collision margin

Fig. 2.50 : Convergent plate boundaries

2.8.3 Transform Faults

These are regional fractures or shears in the lithosphere (Fig. 2.51) where two plates slide past each other, for example, San Andreas Fault.

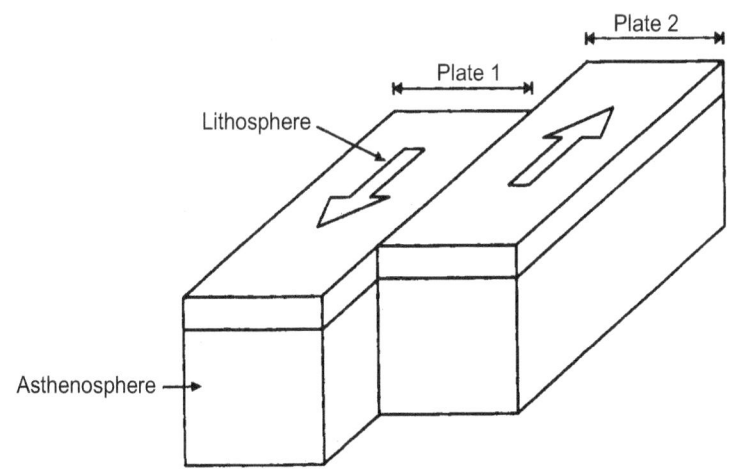

Fig. 2.51 : Transform fault system

The new plate material or rocks originated at divergent plate margins then moves away from the constructive margins. As a result, continuously new crust is developed along these margins. The newly formed crust moves towards destructive margin, undergoes the process of subduction and returns to the mantle. The lighter or continental plates remain on top and are carried as a superficial traveller. However, on the other hand, the denser or oceanic crust is uniformly formed and destroyed. Thus, it is significant that the oldest continental rocks are 3800 million years old while the oceanic crust is younger than 200 million years.

2.9 MODE OF OCCURRENCE

Igneous rocks occur either as intrusive (below the surface) or as extrusive (surface) rocks. The primary shapes and relationships of bodies of these two are fundamentally different.

(a) The Extrusive Rocks : The extrusive group of rocks include all the material errupted on the surface of the earth, which cools quickly to form extensive sheets. The flows rest on older rocks and may be covered by younger flows or sediments.

The extrusive rocks commonly follow the surface topography and exhibit a horizontal or subhorizontal disposition, provided they do not undergo the orogenic movements.

Some products of volcanic erruptions do not emerge quitely, but are blown out of the volcano, as showers of solid fragments broken from earlier lavas or from the walls of the volcano. The errupted material falls back on the earth's surface to form pyroclastic rocks.

(b) The Intrusive Rocks : The intrusive rocks appear to have been emplaced into openings of various kinds below the earth's surface and have crystallized under different physico-chemical conditions. These rocks must be younger than the country rock which they intrude. The form and extent of these rock bodies show a considerable variation. They are described as concordant if the contacts of the intrusive body are more or less parallel to the bedding of the intruded rock (Fig. 2.52) and discordant if the intrusive body cuts across the older beds (Fig. 2.52).

(1) Discordant Intrusions : The discordant intrusions may show varieties of forms, some of them are as follows :

(a) Dykes : A dyke (wall or stone) is a thin tabular body which commonly exhibits cross-cutting relationship with the country rock (Fig. 2.52). It occurs in the form of a parallel wall like masses of near vertical attitude. Dykes can be traceable for a distance of several kilometres, with the width upto few metres only.

Dykes occur along the discontinuities. In case, the dyke is softer or weaker than the country rock, it erodes easily giving rise to negative topographic relief. On the other hand, if the dyke is strong, higher resistance to weathering may be visualised and thus a positive topographic relief in the form of a mound may be observed. Such dykes may act as a natural band or dam.

Ring dykes are co-axial, conical sheets of uneven thickness, dipping away from a common centre and having arcuate outcrops.

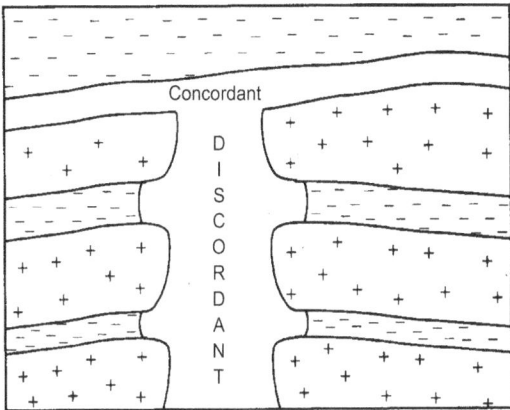

Fig. 2.52 : Igneous intrusions

(b) Batholith : Batholiths are great igneous intrusions of great dimension and commonly of granitic composition. It literally means 'deep-rock' and possesses the following characteristics :

(1) The intrusion cover a large area, probably more than 100 km².
(2) Broaden downward.
(3) Floor may be recorded at a depth of several kilometres.
(4) The walls are parallel to the strike of the country rock.

e.g. Mount Abu, Singhbhum Granite, Clospet Granite.

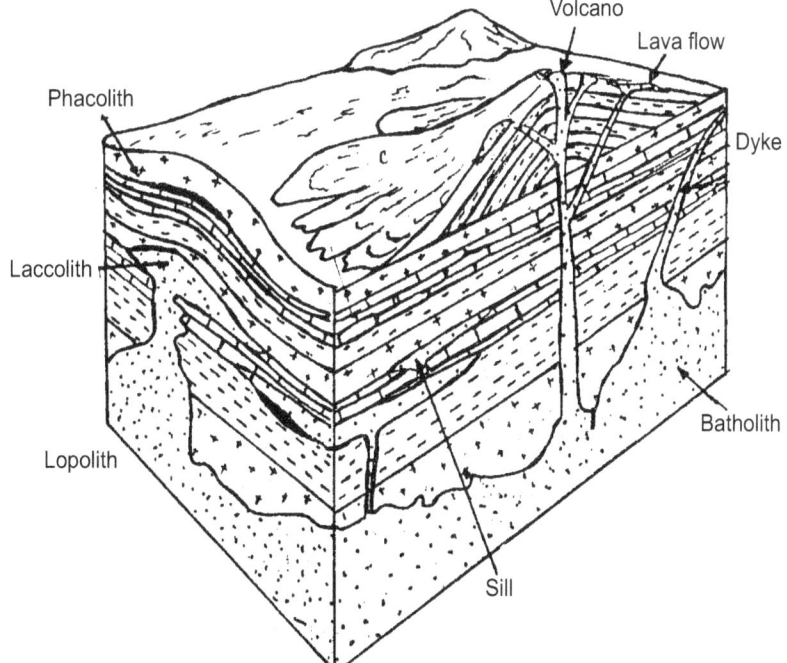

Fig. 2.53 : Diagrammatic representation of mode of occurrence of igneous rocks

(2) Concordant Intrusions :

(a) Sill : Sills are tabular bodies that are parallel to the bedding of the country rock (Fig. 2.52). It may range in size from tiny mass smaller than an inch to hundreds of metres in thickness. Most of the extensive sills are of dolerite and other basic igneous rocks.

Sills may be often confused with lava flows. The following table gives the points of distinction between a sill and lava flows :

Table 2.9

Sill	Lava Flow (after Johnson, 1976)
1. Upper surface is finely crystalline or glassy.	1. Upper surface is scoriaceous, the vesicles are often filled with secondary minerals.
2. Both upper and lower surface show chilling effects.	2. Chilling effects an indecisive evidence.
3. Baking effects may be seen on both upper and lower contacts with the country rock.	3. Baking is partial and seen only on the lower surface.
4. No cavities.	4. Amygdules are seen on upper surface and pipe amygdules on lower surface.
5. Small bifurcating veins may be seen.	5. Veins are absent.

(b) Laccolith : A laccolith has a flat base and a domed top. The dome like structure raises the overlying sediments so that they dip away from the centre of the intrusion. They are occasionally circular or elliptical in ground plan. Such intrusions are also called as forceful intrusions (Fig. 2.53).

(c) Lopolith : A lopolith is a saucer-shaped body of basic rocks in a structural basin. The sediments, into which the body is intruded, dip towards the centre of intrusion. A lopolith is characterised by thicker portion at the centre and thinner towards the margin. The peculiar shape of the intrusion develops due to collapse of country rock and subsequent rising of the injected magma through the collapsing layers (Fig. 2.53).

(d) Phacoliths : The phacoliths are confined to the crests of anticlines or to the troughs of syncline. These are commonly associated with plunging folds and thus in plan also they are cresent shaped (Fig. 2.53).

PART (C) : GROUNDWATER

INTRODUCTION

Groundwater is subsurface water that fills voids in soils and permeable geological formations. It is an important source particularly in arid regions. Groundwater is uniquely suited as drinking water; in general, it is widely distributed, inexpensive, easily available and usually requires little pre-treatment.

Groundwater in engineering geology is important because of the effects, its presence can have on the stability and durability of major engineering works.

Groundwater does not exists in isolation, but is an internal link in the hydrological cycle.

2.20 TYPES OF SUBSURFACE WATER

Groundwater supplied by rain or snow or by infiltration from rivers and lakes is described as magmatic water. Water entrapped in the pores of sedimentary rock at the time when the rock was deposited, is distinguished as connate water. In this also included is water entrapped in the cavities of extrusive igneous rocks at the time when the magma was ejected on the surface. It may be derived either from ocean water or from land water, while water entrapped into interstices of rocks and that remained with the rocks since, their burial is described as fossil water. It is believed that part of the stream and hot mineral laden water liberated during igneous activity arises from great depth and reaches the surface. Such a kind of 'virgin' water is known as **juvenile water**.

2.11 SURFACE RUN-OFF AND INFILTRATION

Water falling on the surface of the earth, flow through channels, known as run-off. It includes both water flowing on the surface and also below the surface.

Surface run-off is controlled by climatic and physiographic factors. The climatic factors include type of precipitation, rain intensity, duration, distribution and direction of rainfall etc. while the topographic factors include type of soil, area, shape, slope and orientation of basin, drainage network and use etc.

Infiltration : The rate of infiltration is controlled primarily by soil heterogeneities including structure of soil material, moisture content, compaction of soil, structural non-uniformity, vegetation cover and more importantly by the structure and composition of subsurface layers.

2.12 VERTICAL DISTRIBUTION OF GROUNDWATER

The vertical distribution of groundwater is controlled by the type of rock, geological structure, porosity of the rock and nature of soil material. Based on availability of dry pores and amount of water available, two major zones are recognized, zone of aeration or vadoze zone and zone of saturation or phreatic zone (Fig. 2.54).

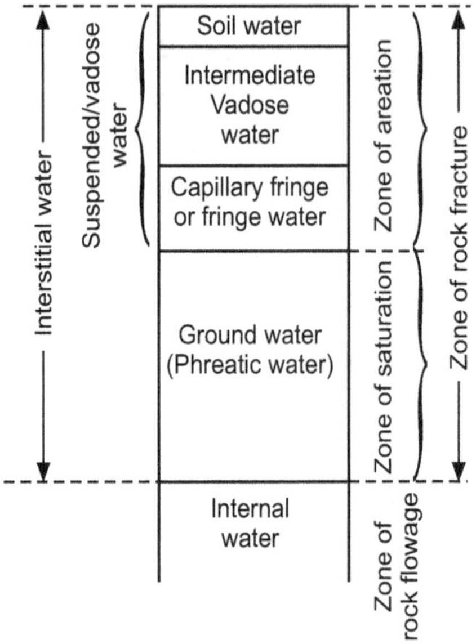

Fig. 2.54 : Vertical distribution of groundwater

Zone of Aeration : In this zone pores or voids are dry or partially filled, thus, known as zone of aeration; which is further divided into three gradational zones (Fig. 2.54). Soil water defines a near surface zone where wide fluctuations in water content due to evaporation, minor precipitation through rainfall, and the discharge and intake of water through the physiological functioning of water take place. In this zone, suspended water flows downwards through unsaturated pore spaces under the influence of gravity to the water table. Above water table occurs capillary fringe conditions where due to surface tension or capillary pressure water movement is rapid. Here reactions with rock forming minerals take place and oxidising conditions usually prevail.

Zone of Saturation : The uppermost level of water table or phreatic surface seen in a borehole or a dugwell is demarked as the zone of saturation. In this, pores or voids are saturated with water. It is also called as a *phreatic zone*.

The vertical extent of groundwater varies with the type of rock, its geological structure and its mass porosity.

2.13 MOVEMENT OF GROUNDWATER

Groundwater is an integral part of the hydrological cycle (Fig. 2.55). Water evaporated mainly from the ocean and falling on the land as rain, seeps into the ground and entres the aquifer. Some of the slowly moving groundwater reaches streams and contributes to the fluvial water they carry to the ocean, where the cycle begins again.

Most of the groundwater upto a few hundred metres of the surface is dynamic. However, as compared to the velocities of fluvial water which is measurable in metres to kilometres per hour, groundwater velocity that may be expressed in centimetres per day, is very slow. Furthermore, the movement is largely controlled by geometry of rocks.

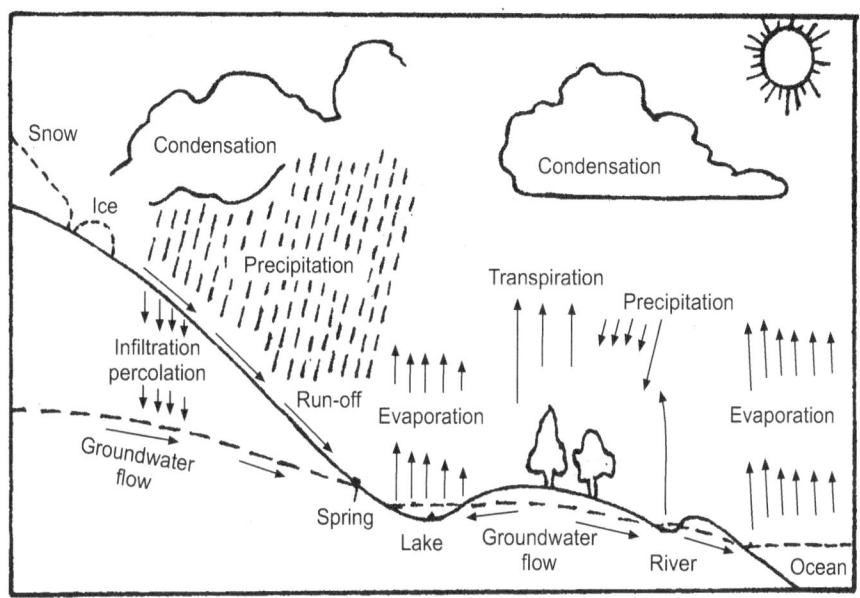

Fig. 2.55 : The hydrological cycle

2.13.1 Porosity and Permeability

The open spaces, voids or interstices in earth materials are important from the view point that they store and transmit groundwater. The size, shape, type and arrangement of the pore spaces are the chief factors in controlling storage capacity and transmissivity of the earth materials. Two types of rock interstices are recognised :

(a) Intergranular pores characteristics of clastic sedimentary rocks, volcanics rocks and both consolidated and unconsolidated materials [Fig. 2.56 (a)]. Origin of this type is attributed to the origin of rocks, also known as primary porosity.

(a) Primary sand and gravel   (b) Secondary permeable sedimentary rock   (c) Fractured rock

Fig. 2.56 : Types of porosity

(b) Intragranular pores resulting from joints and other secondary opening [Fig. 2.56 (b)], also known as secondary porosity, which is divided into two categories :

(1) Crystalline igneous and metamorphic rocks, indurated clastic rocks etc. that store and transmit water in joints and interconnected fractures [Fig. 2.56 (c)].

(2) Jointed and bedded rocks that are subject to chemical weathering and as a result solutional channels develop partially along the fractures and bedding planes. [Fig. 2.56 (b)].

Permeability is the quantity of water flowing per unit time through a unit cross-section under a unit hydraulic gradient.

In other words, it is a measure of how easily a solid allows fluids to pass through it. Commonly, a rock with low porosity is likely to have low permeability. However, a high porosity does not indicate proportionally high permeability. It can be said that size of pore spaces and the molecular attraction of rock surfaces play an important role in deciding permeability. Molecular attraction is a force that exists between a solid surface and a film of water.

(A) Movement of groundwater is different in the zone of aeration and in the zone of saturation. Permeability of soil is less compared to that of the regolith or weathered rock due to higher proportion of clay fractions. As clay retains part of the moving water and the remaining water seeps downward upto the water table under the influence of gravity.

In saturated zone, the movement of groundwater, known as percolation, is similar to the flow of water when a saturated sponge is squeezed gently. Here, the movement of water is controlled by the structure, size and shape of bedrock. Commonly water table follows the topographical gradients (Fig. 2.57).

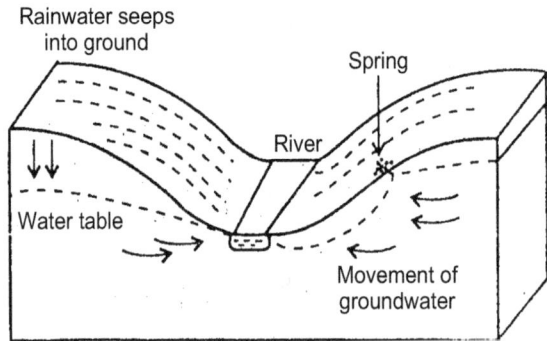

Fig. 2.57 : Movement of water in a uniformly permeable rock

In other words, water percolates from areas where water table is high towards the area of low relief shown by surface streams or lakes.

(B) Recharge and discharge are two very important components of groundwater. Recharge or replenishment occurs when rainwater enters the ground in favourable areas where precipitation seeps downward beneath the surface and reaches the zone of saturation. These areas are known as *recharge areas* (Fig. 2.58). On the other hand, *discharge* *areas* are those areas where dynamic subsurface water is discharged to streams, or lakes or swamps.

Recharge area covers larger surface area as compared to discharge area.

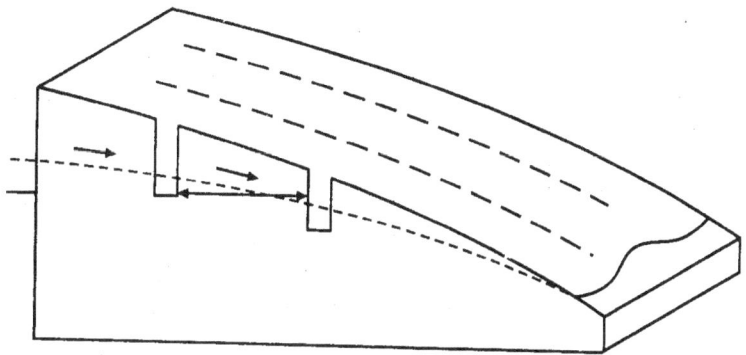

Fig. 2.58 : Hydraulic gradient

(C) Experimental studies have indicated that steeper the ground slope, faster is the movement of water. The hydraulic gradient or the slope of water can be determined by measuring the difference in the elevation of two points (h_1 and h) on the water table and dividing this by horizontal distance (d) between the points. In other words, the velocity of groundwater (V) is proportional to hydraulic gradient.

i.e. $$V \propto \frac{h_1 - h_2}{d} \qquad \ldots (2.1)$$

However, velocity of groundwater is also controlled by permeability of the rock or sediment through which water flows. By considering this, Henri Darcy, a French engineer, expressed an equation in which the permeability with the acceleration due to gravity and viscosity of water is expressed as a coefficient of permeability (k).

i.e. $$V = \frac{k(h_1 - h_2)}{d} \qquad \ldots (2.2)$$

It is seen that discharge (Q) in stream is a function of both stream velocity (V) and cross-section area (A). However, in case of groundwater, the cross sectional area is defined by an interconnected system of pores and not by an open channel. Thus, the equation,

$$Q = AV$$

may be rewritten by using (2.2)

$$Q = \frac{Ak(h_1 - h_2)}{d} \qquad \ldots (2.3)$$

The above equation is known as Darcy's Law. In this equation we consider A i.e. cross-sectional area as constant, by measuring discharge (Q), and hydraulic gradient ($h_1 - h_2/d$), it is possible to calculate the third parameter, i.e. k.

The above concept is difficult to apply to naturally occurring earth materials because permeability is the most variable of the materials properties measured in geological engineering.

2.14 NATURAL DISCHARGE OF GROUNDWATER

Natural discharge of groundwater takes place where the ground surface intersects the water table. It is called seepage if the flow from hydrologic unit is spread diffusely over marshy ground and the discharge is called a spring if it is concentrated as a channel through fissure or through a favourable geologic unit. Occurrence of springs may be recognized in a number of geologic conditions, some of them are illustrated in Fig. 2.59.

A valley spring [Fig. 2.59 (a)] occurs where the water table intersects the valley floor, that shows the presence of pervious rock.

A contact spring [Fig. 2.59 (b)] occurs at the boundary of two beds. Here, the underlying rock is impervious and the overlying rock is pervious. In Deccan trap Basalts, contact springs are commonly developed along the contact of compact and amygdaloidal basalt. In this, the amygdaloidal basalt acts as an impermeable blanket below the compact basalt. These springs are also called as stratum springs.

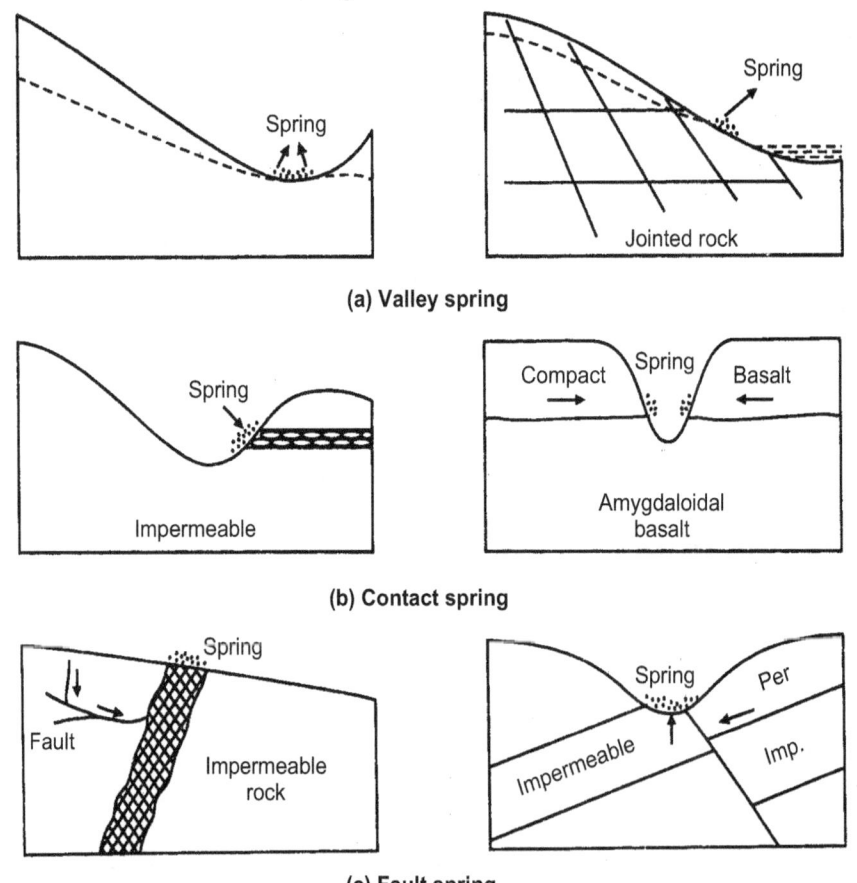

Fig. 2.59 : Natural discharge of groundwater

If an impermeable dyke is observed in a permeable rock, one may find presence of a contact springs at the intrusive contact.

Fault spring [Fig. 2.59 (c)] occurs when permeable rocks are juxtaposed against impermeable rocks.

It can be said that a vertical or a horizontal change in permeability is a common factor that contributes localisation of spring.

2.15 AQUIFERS

An aquifer is a body of highly permeable rock lying in the zone of saturation. Equivalent terms for an aquifer are reservoir rock and water bearing formation.

Based on geologic conditions, the aquifers are classified into two major categories, viz. Unconfined aquifers and confined aquifers.

(1) Unconfined aquifer : An aquifer having an upper surface coinciding with the water table and is in direct contact with atmosphere is called an unconfined aquifer. A special category of unconfined aquifer is called perched water body (Fig. 2.60), which can be formed due to the presence of an impermeable layer of rock or sediment in the zone of aeration below a permeable layer so that the impermeable layer holds the water.

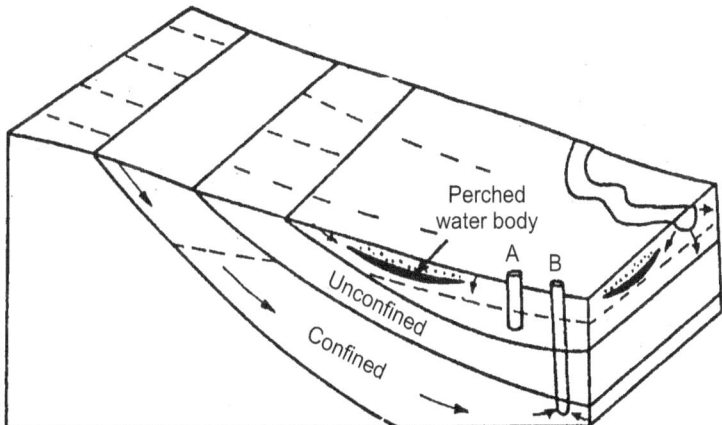

Fig. 2.60 : Aquifer system; note that well A pumps water from unconfined aquifer, while well B pumps water from concerned aquifer. Also note occurrence of punched water body at higher elevation due to presence of impermeable layer (dark layer)

(2) Confined aquifer : An aquifer that is bounded by aquicludes/impermeable layers called a confined aquifer (Fig. 2.60). In this, the aquifer is constantly under great hydrostatic pressure. If a well is drilled to tap the aquifer, the difference in pressure causes the water to rise to well. The water can rise the same elevation as the water table, in recharge area and if the elevation of water is lower as compared to recharge area, the water flows out of well without pumping. Such an aquifer is called **artesian aquifer** and the well is called **artesian well**.

Artesian conditions develop in various geologic conditions (Fig. 6.35). However, ideal artesian condition exists when the permeable layer is sandwiched in two upper and lower impermeable layers (Fig. 2.60).

2.16 WELLS

A well may either be a large diameter dug well or bore well that supplies water if it intersects the water table.

When water is pumped out of well the rate of withdraw initially exceeds the rate of recharge of groundwater. As a result, a conical depression in the water table surrounding the wells may be observed known as cone of depression. If the rate of pumping balances the rate of inflow or recharge, the hydraulic gradient stabilizes.

2.17 EXPLORATION FOR GROUNDWATER

Exploration programme starts as a basic geological exercise of mapping surface exposures, faults, discontinuities, intrusions etc. together with extrapolations from visible evidence. The programme is an integrated approach to groundwater prospecting. The techniques are used to –

(a) locate groundwater potential areas,

(b) get an idea about aquifer characteristics and

(c) understand the chemical quality of water.

Following are the techniques widely used for groundwater prospecting.

(1) Geomorphology : Geomorphological methods are based on the utilization of geologic data that may be supplemented by geological field reconnaissance i.e. the method to obtain information by visual observation and other detecting methods. The study of toposheets is also useful in this investigation which gives information about the kind of landforms seen in the area; some of these landforms may be potential areas of groundwater.

(2) Photogeology : Air photo interpretation is based on the fact that the occurrence of groundwater is closely related to the topographical and geological features such as, moisture, zones, fracture zone, weak dyke, ox-bow lakes, drainage patterns, vegetation etc. These are the direct indicators of subsurface conditions. Along with aerial photographs, infrared photographs and imageries are used for groundwater investigation. Infrared photography and thermal imagery can detect very slight temperature variations. Because groundwater is cooler than surface water, it is possible to identify it by such techniques.

(3) Geobotonical studies : Proper identification of flora showing close affinity towards groundwater often helps in locating the shallow conditions. Careful investigations carried out on plants have indicated the presence of three major types of flora :

(a) **Phreatophytes :** Plants growing on the water from the zone of saturation e.g. Ficus Globerata (Umber), Eugenia a Jambolana (Jambhul).

(b) **Xerophytes :** Plants growing on the water from the zone of aeration or vadose water zone;

(c) **Halophytes :** Salt resistant plants.

Though this technique is less time consuming and economic, it is of a limited use, unless views in conjection with information obtained by other methods are used.

(4) Hydrogeological surveys : These include :

(a) **Complete well inventory :** Complete well inventory is carried out by collecting detailed information about the altitude of wells, depth of water table, temperature, collection of Lithologs of existing wells, inflow zones etc.

Careful observations on topography, elevation of wells and depth of water table are indicative of movement of groundwater. Information on geological contacts, quantitative estimation of discontinuities may provide clues on inflow zones or recharge areas of groundwater. Accurate interpretation of lithologs may indicate water bearing characteristics of different horizons.

(b) **Pumping test :** Pumping tests are carried out to obtain information about the performance of wells (specific capacity) and three dimensional parameters of aquifers such as storativity and transmissivity. Storativity deals with storage capacity of an aquifer and transmissivity is the capacity of an aquifer to transmit the water.

The principle of pumping is simple. Water is pumped out from a well for a specific time and at a definite rate. The effect of pumping on the water level is measured in the pumped well and in the observation well in the vicinity. After pumping is stopped, rise of water level in the pumped well and in the observation well is measured. This gives an idea about specific capacity of the well and storativity and transmissivity of an aquifer.

Confined aquifers are more amenable to pump or recharge testing than unconfined aquifers. Confined flow to wells is described by a simpler set of boundary conditions. In general, water is released from storage throughout the entire thickness of confined aquifer. Flow lines towards full penetrating wells are parallel to the confining bed. In unconfined aquifers, the mobility of upper boundary is difficult to explain because the flow of wells is likely to contain vertical flow components and pore spaces do not drain instantaneously as heads are lower.

In general, spatial and temporal variations of aquifer properties, errors in measurement and heterogeneity of boundary conditions all contribute to uncertainty in pumping test results. However, careful and repetitive tests do produce estimates of hydraulic properties useful for engineering applications.

It must be remembered that in rocks, with porosity and permeability developed by weathering, jointing or karstification, pumping tests produce change in hydrogeologic characteristics in local domains. In case of non-systematic jointing, fracturing, the symmetry of the cone of depression may be distorted due to variations in aperture of joints from virtually infinite hydraulic conductivity in one direction to absence of permeability in other direction. As a result, this may be a constraint in the interpretation of pumping data.

(5) Geophysical investigations : Geophysical methods include magnetic, gravimetric, seismic and electrical resistivity methods. Magnetic and gravimetric methods are not useful in groundwater prospecting, as neither magnetic anomalies in the earth's magnetic field nor specific gravity on the earth's surface is related to the occurrence of groundwater. However, it may be used for obtaining indirect information on aquifer boundaries and also for mapping complex bedrock topography.

The electrical resistivity is the most important method for hydrogeological studies. The resistivity of rocks depend primarily on composition, structure, water content and chemical content of groundwater. The method is used specifically for investigating groundwater conditions at shallow to moderate depths, and thus is well suited to the study of lithology, the location of aquifers and investigation of rocks below the aquifer [refer section 4.6]. To achieve greater success, the electrical resistivity method requires two favourable geological conditions. First, the various geological formations should possess contrasting resistivity characteristics and secondly, heterogeneity should be less. The method is useful in the case of multi-layered sequence also. However, all geophysical field work necessarily requires an investigator to possess good knowledge about the geology of the region.

(6) Tracer techniques : A tracer is a certain substance added to a material in a chemical, biological or physical system to mark that material for study, to observe its progress through the system or to determine its final distribution. For any hydrological system to be evaluated, the choice of tracer depends on the accuracy involved, the need for in-situ detection, the resources available, consideration of safety and health and also on their behaviour in the terrestrial environment to be studied. The performance of a tracer is influenced by its absorption phenomena, chemical instability, temperature of water and degradation.

Water may be hard or soft depending on the proportion of calcium and magnesium bicarbonates dissolved in it. Noxious elements from rocks, if flows through, also get dissolved in the water making it unsuitable for consumption.

The travel distance of a tracer may vary from few metres to several kilometres. The tracers used are chemical tracers, fluorescent dyes, radio isotopes, nuclear tracers etc. Commonly, the isotopes are useful for determining areas and conditions of recharge and the sources of dissolved constituents. Nuclear tracers are useful in measuring various hydrological properties which govern the movement of groundwater.

2.18 WATER QUALITY AND GROUNDWATER POLLUTION

(1) All groundwater contains both anions and cations in solution. Analysis of many wells and springs show that the compounds dissolved in groundwater are mainly chlorides, sulphates, and biocarbonates of calcium, magnesium, sodium, iron and potassium (See Table 2.10). The nature and concentration of these compounds are influenced largely by the geology of the intake areas and also on the composition of the aquifer.

Table 2.10 : Drinking water action levels

Characteristic	Action level	
Arsenic	0.05	mg/l
Cadmium	0.005	"
Chromium	0.05	"
Cyanide	0.1	"
Fluoride	1.5	"
Lead 0.05	1.5	"
Mercury	0.001	"
Nickel	0.1	"
Nitrate and Nitrite nitrogen	1.0	"
Nitrate nitrogen	1.0	"
Selenium	0.01	"
Chloride	250	"
Sulphate	400	"
Hardness as $CaCO_3$	500	"
Total dissolved solids	1000	"
Aluminium	0.2	"
Copper	1.0	"
Iron	0.3	"
Magnanese	0.1	"
Sodium	200	"
Zinc	5.0	"
Chlorophenols	0.1	µg/l
DDT	200	"
Heptachlor	30	"
Lindane	3.0	"
Monochlorobenzene	3.0	"
1, 4-dichlorobenzene	100	"
2, 4 – D 0.1	Bq/l	
Gross alpha activity	0.1	Bq/l
Colour	15	TCU
Turbidity	5	NTU
Taste	not objectionable to 90% of consumers	
pH	6.5 to 8.5	

Water may be hard or soft, depending on the proportion of calcium and magnesium bicarbonates dissolved in it. Noxious elements from rocks, if flows through, also get dissolved in the water making it unsuitable for consumption.

(2) Groundwater is polluted due to the following major sources :
- (a) Seewage disposal including septic tanks;
- (b) Domestic waste disposal sites;
- (c) Agricultural waste disposal;
- (d) Organic wastes: oil, solvents, pesticides;
- (e) Sea water incursion;
- (f) Hazardous waste;
- (g) Inorganic fertilizers;
- (h) Fish farming;
- (i) Mining activities etc.

In general, it can be said that these sources of pollution cause a substantial damage to the overall quality of groundwater. These are listed in Table 2.11.

Table 2.11 : Induced effects on ground water quality and quantity

Causes These change composition of Water, directly or indirectly	Consequences	Effects Q_1 : Qualitative Q_2 : Quantitative
(a) Construction		
(1) Sealing of surface excavation	Reduction of intilitration and recharge.	Q_1
	Lowering of groundwater level.	Q_1
(2) Building on flood plain	Increase in run-off.	Q_1
(b) Waste water disposal		
(1) Introduction of waste water seepage	Introduction of pollutants.	Q_2
(2) Introduction of waste hea	Change in water temperature.	Q_2
(c) Agriculture		
(1) Irrigation, drainage,	Alteration of estimated run-off, Increase in seepage.	Q_1
(2) River regulation	Rapid water removal.	Q_1
(3) Fertilizers, slurry disposal, use of insecticides, storage of potential water pollutants.	Introduction of pesticides, insecticides, hercicides and inorganic ions like $\overline{Cl}$, $\overline{NO_3}$.	Q_2

(d) Production of raw material		
(1) Mismanagement of water rsources.	Lowering of groundwater table.	Q_1
(2) Changes in flow direction of groundwater.		
(3) Decrease or removal of protective cover.	Increased access by pollutants to groundwater.	Q_2
(e) Supply of drinking and domestic water		
(1) Excessive demands	Lowering of water table.	
	Upward trend of deepseated salty groundwater (coastal areas).	Q_1 Q_2
(f) Transport		
(1) Interruption or damming of groundwater flow by underground construction (e.g. metro)	Rise in run-off.	Q_1
(2) Salting of roads, road cleaning	Introduction of salt, petrol etc.	Q_2
(3) Sealing of surface.	Reduction of infiltration.	Q_1
(g) Others		
(1) Piping dam construction.	Total prevention of hydraulic connection of groundwater with surface water.	Q_1
(2) Siting of fishponds in region with wells.	Introduction of nutrients interruption of ecosystem	Q_2
(3) Leaking disposal sites	Infiltration of polluted water into ground and surface water.	Q_2

2.19 GEOLOGICAL WORK OF GROUNDWATER

In the regions underlain by highly permeable rocks, groundwater through chemical weathering develops characteristics.

(1) Solution : As soon as rainwater infiltrates the ground, it initiates the process of weathering. An important part of chemical weathering involves dissolution of minerals and rocks to form solution. For example, limestones.

The carbonate groups of minerals are readily dissolved by carbonic acid. As a result, groundwater becomes charged with calcium cations and bicarbonate anions (see, section 2.1). It can be said that the dissolution rate can exceed the average erosional reduction of the surface by mass-wasting, sheet erosion and streams.

(2) Chemical cementation and replacement : The conversion of sediment into sedimentary rocks is primarily a function of groundwater. Substances dissolved in water are precipitated as cement in pore spaces. This acts like a binding agent and thus transform the loose sediments into a cohesive rock.

Replacement is a process by which fluid dissolves matter already present and at the same time deposits from solution an equal volume of different substances. Replacement takes place approximately on a volume for volume basis. For example, petrified wood. The new material commonly preserves minute textures of replaced material.

(3) Caves and caverns : Caves are seen in many sizes and shapes. A very large system of interconnected cave chambers is called a **cavern**. For example, the Carlsbad caverns in SE New Mexico include one chamber 1200 metre long, 190 metre wide and 100 metre high.

Formation of a cave is purely a chemical process involving dissolution of carbonate rock by circulating groundwater. The sequential growth in a cave system may be as follows :

(a) Initial dissolution along discontinuity network by percolating water.

(b) Enlargement of a cave along the most favourable route of water.

(c) Deposition of carbonate material on the cave walls while a stream occupies the cave floor.

(d) Continued deposition of the carbonate on the walls and floor of the cave after the stream has stopped flowing.

The rate of development of a cave is controlled by the rate of dissolution, composition of circulating groundwater and discontinuity network.

The caves may often show presence of stalactites, stalagmites and columns. These are deposited by successive drops of water. As each drop forms on the roof of a cave, it loses a certain amount of carbon di-oxide gas and precipitates a particle of calcium carbonate.

Caves are generally formed in the upper zone of saturation. Thus, with decrease in water level these shift into the zone of aeration. Dissolution could then give rise to deposition.

Sinkholes are large dissolution cavities open to sky. They may be formed due to roof collapse catastrophically and may be located at the intersection of joints.

(4) In arid regions, large quantities of calcium carbonate formed by decomposition of country rock (for example, basalt) which are then transported in solution and get deposited in the form of nodules, concretions etc. known as Kankar.

2.20 GROUNDWATER MANAGEMENT

From the human point of view, groundwater is a vital resource particularly in arid regions and on islands where it may be the only fresh water available. Groundwater is greatly suitable for drinking purpose. In general, it is widely distributed, easily available, inexpensive and requires very little treatment. This resource is prone to pollution and over exploitation. The extraction of excessive quantities of groundwater can result in drying up of wells, land subsidence, salt water invasion and inevitably the loss of the resources (Fig. 2.61).

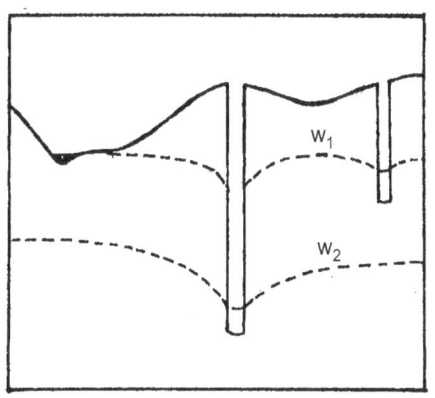
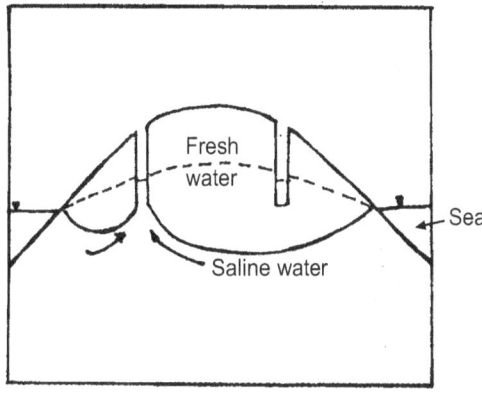

(a) Lowering of water table from w_1 to w_2 (b) Sea water intrusion

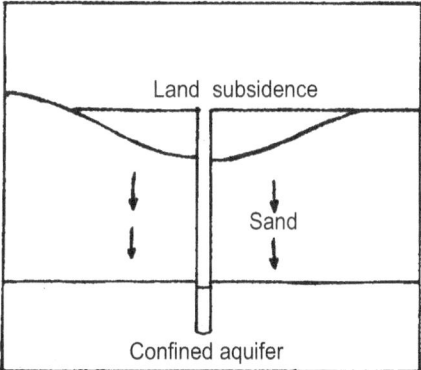

(c) Land subsidence due to compaction

Fig. 2.61 : Some of the effects of over-exploitation

A full assessment of water resources is a necessary prerequisite for effective groundwater protection. For the proper groundwater utilization, protection and conservation, the following base-line information is required: location, water quality and potential yield of major aquifers, existing and potential sources of pollution, aquifer's natural degree of protection and the location and extraction rates of wells.

However, the building up of a data base on the subsurface environment is a slow, time consuming, continuing and often complicated process. In the areas, where little information is available, remote sensing and/or geophysical methods are useful for developing preliminary geological database, depth of groundwater, water quality and existing land use. Direct subsurface measurements require the creation of network of observation wells.

Once the initial database is generated, systematic subsurface monitoring is essential to keep record of long term trends. It includes the periodic measurement of groundwater levels and water quality in a network of wells at key locations. Furthermore, records of the rate of exploitation of groundwater must be maintained. Commonly, the rate of removal should be less than the rate of recharge structure. It can serve as a medium for the dispersal of pollutants from the source.

2.21 ARTIFICIAL RECHARGE OF GROUNDWATER

Groundwater recharge or replanishment depends on several variables including rainfall, rate of infiltration, topographic variations, rate of evapotranspiration etc. It is estimated that out of total rainfall, about 91 per cent is carried along the slopes as surface run-off, while the remaining 9% only infiltrates down as groundwater recharge. However, this estimation varies from place to place. Furthermore, it is observed that the rate of exploitation of groundwater exceeds the rate of recharge of groundwater. Hence, in order to increase groundwater reserves, the basic requirement is to increase the rate of infiltration and decrease annual surface run-off. Following methods are used to increase groundwater recharge :

(1) Surface methods : (a) Percolation tanks and (b) Contour bunding.

(2) Sub-surface methods : (a) Subsurface dams and (b) Injection method.

2.21.1 Surface Methods

In this method, surface flowing water is diverted to groundwater. Two different techniques are used in this method :

(a) Percolation tank : The technique of constructing percolation tanks on permeable rocks is effectively used in Maharashtra. These are small bunds or dams constructed across the small streams at or near foothills of high grounds. However, utility of percolation tanks depend on their proper location and other factors like amount of rainfall, temperature fluctuations, rate of evaporation etc. of the place.

In this, the upstream side is permeable or porous. Similarly, downstream side has permeable rocks. In other words, it is necessary to determine hydrological parameters of exposed rocks. Furthermore, the catchment area should be sufficiently high and the rate of evaporation must be less. The most favourable site is a confluence of two streams.

Success of a percolation tank is decided by quantitative analysis of wells located along downstream direction. The analysis is to be carried before and after monsoon. Similarly, effectiveness of a percolation tank is studied by the analysis of crops in the command area.

(b) Contour bunding : Groundwater recharge is a function of many factors in which slope of basin is the most crucial one. In the case of steep slopes, surface run-off is rapid and vice-versa. Thus, if along steep slopes trenches like burrows are constructed, then the velocity of running water is likely to be appreciably reduced. As a result, water gets accumulated in the trenches (Fig. 2.62) which contributes to groundwater, through the process of infiltration, rate of which is decided by the bedrock.

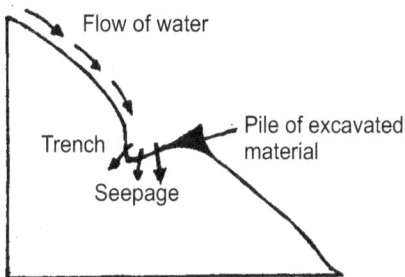

Fig. 2.62 : Recharge of groundwater through contour bunding method

After heavy rainfall, trenches are filled with water and it spills over. Thus, more trenches are generally constructed along the slope on downstream direction.

2.21.2 Subsurface Methods

(a) Subsurface Dams : In Maharashtra, subsurface dams are constructed in river beds which produced appreciable rise in groundwater level. In this, the applicable concept is fairly simple. It is seen that, the subsurface movement of water is controlled by topography and geology. Groundwater generally follows topography. Thus, subsurface run-off can be explained by Darcy's law. By constructing subsurface dams, movement of groundwater is controlled and as a result, rise in water level is observed.

As mentioned earlier, subsurface dams are constructed in river beds. Commonly, a pit is excavated across the river bed. Length of the pit is decided by the width of river channel and depth is decided by the depth at which groundwater is encountered. The excavated trench is then filled with material of low permeability, for example; clayey soil/concrete, and the upper surface is again filled by excavated material. In this, the artificial impermeable dyke acts as a barrier which converts the dynamic water into static water.

(b) Injection Method : In this method, water is forced or pumped inside the aquifer. The injection is controlled by four factors :

(1) aquifer characteristics : strorativity, transmissivity

(2) supply of recharge well

(3) presence of water organisms

(4) physical and chemical similarity of water.

However, this method is difficult to apply in the case of confined aquifers.

2.22 HUMAN IMPACT ON GROUNDWATER

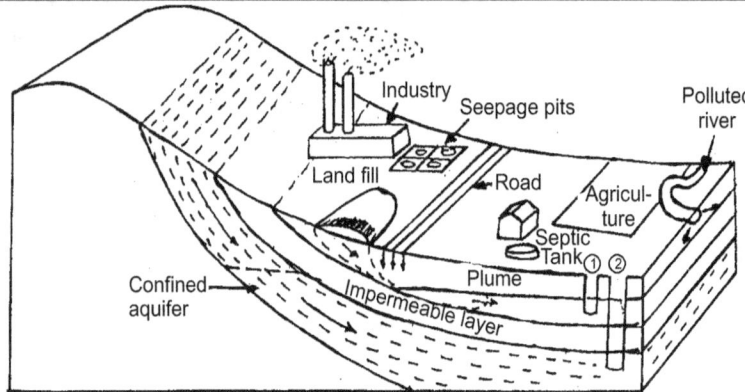

Fig. 2.63 : Human impact on groundwater; with the increase in industrial sector, urbanization, agriculture etc. large amount of contaminants often form an underground plume Well 1 is greatly polluted, however Well 2 receives clear water as it originates from a deeper confined aquifer whose recharge area is undeveloped

A very broad extent of human influence on groundwater has been recognized (Fig. 2.63). In this section only four major influences are discussed.

(1) Urbanization : Urbanization perhaps exercises the most drastic and rapid impact on the groundwater. The effects of urbanization are due to modifications caused in the natural drainage network with a denser, more efficient and permanent network and the covering of the large areas of the catchment with impermeable surfaces.

Urbanization tends to reduce groundwater levels because rainfall is quickly removed from the basin. Similarly, water quality changes in and downstream of urban and industrial areas, this may be due to the discharge of polluted waste water or washing of pollutants from the catchment areas.

(2) River impoundment : Small scale reservoir development has a locally significant impact on hydrological parameters; however, the effects of large scale structures on major rivers are more alarming (See Fig. 2.63).

(3) Deforestation : The removal of forests is responsible for increase in the surface run-off (upto 17 per cents, a case study from Finland) because evapotranspiration is higher in these areas. Flood magnitudes tends to increase, once the forest cover is reduced and reduce losses often means the ground water table rise.

The removal of trees changes surface and groundwater quality by modifying microchmates; changing patterns of atmospheric deposition of chemicals, providing a large supply of decaying vegetation and raising soil moisture content.

(4) Agricultural activity : Recent experiences shows that over exploitation of groundwater used for agriculture has reduced groundwater reserves. Similarly, increasing usage of synthetic fertilizers is responsible for changing the quality of water. Although, these non-point sources cause degradation of surface and groundwater quality over large areas, point sources such as septic tanks, cattle pens, manure piles etc. can cause short term seasonal effects.

2.23 GROUNDWATER AND ENGINEERING

Groundwater is important in three major operations (1) it may pose a problem to construction, (2) it may acts as an erosional agent, and (3) it may be critical to the functioning of a structure.

(1) Construction : Construction may be very difficult or even impossible at times due to excessive water present. This may be seen even in case of smaller construction projects. Similarly, the influence of subsurface water on soil may be equally troublesome.

(2) Erosional agent : Subsurface water is influencial in two major operations (a) destabilization of soil particles and (b) landslide, seepage pressure etc.

The latter process may be visualised in the adjoining areas of reservoirs due to increased pore pressure. The surface of the impounded water alters the level of water table in the adjacent slopes. These slopes experience a higher degree of saturation than under normal conditions. Thus, the slopes become unstable because of increased pore water pressure.

(3) Affecting the functioning of a structure : Subsurface water can be a critical factor that influences the functioning of a structure. It can serve as a medium for the disposal of pollutatnts from the source.

EXERCISE

1. How are rocks faulted ? Describe with a neat Fig., various parts and types of faults.
2. How are rocks folded ? Give various parts of a fold. Describe how a fold passes into a fault ?
3. Write notes on : (i) Fold morphology, (ii) Distinction between a fault and a joint, (iii) Reverse and normal faults, (iv) Horst and Graben, (v) Seismic faulting, (vi) Effects of faulting on disrupted beds, (vii) Tectonic joints, (viii) Columnar joints, (ix) Sheet joints, (x) Types of unconfirmity, (xi) Unconfirmity with overlap.
4. Explain the different features resulted due to action of compressional type of tectonic forces.
5. Write short note on angular unconformity and non-conformity.
6. Describe various types of unconformities with neat sketches.
7. How rocks are folded ? Describe various parts and different types of folds with neat sketches.

8. Explain 'SILL' and 'PHACCOCITH' as igneous intrusions.

9. How rocks are faulted ? Describe various types and parts of a fault.

10. What different features are developed due to tensional type of tectonic forces ? Explain with suitable examples and diagrams.

11. Describe any two modes of formation of igneous rocks.

12. Orogenic and epierogenic processes.

13. Write Notes on : (i) Depth zones of groundwater, (ii) Recharge and discharge of groundwater, (iii) Spring, (iv) Aquifers, (v) Exploration for ground water, (vi) Ground water and pollution, (vii) Geological work of ground water, (viii) Artificial recharge of groundwater, (ix) Groundwater and engineering, (x) Artesian condition, (xi) Pervious and impervious rocks.

Unit 3

GEOMORPHOLOGY, HISTORICAL GEOLOGY AND BUILDING STONES

PART (A) : GEOMORPHOLOGY

INTRODUCTION

Geomorphology is the science of expression of the Earth. The systematic description and analysis of landscapes and the processes that change them is essential in many fields besides engineering. Discussion on the origin of land is a common ground for diversified scientific disciplines including geology, hydrology, pedology, ecology and agriculture. Landforms may be formed due to constructional or destructional processes; and they undergo slow, continuous changes in response to internal and external processes of the Earth. Thus, the study is generally aimed to explain the past, the present and to predict the future, and also to have some understanding of the nature and rate of change. The analysis of such relationships provide valuable information useful to the society as several induced environmental hazards arise due to poor understanding of natural processes. Geomorphologists and engineers attempt several strategies to overcome these problems. It is a well known fact that major cities in India are situated on broad mature valleys developed by major river systems. Similarly large population of the world lives close to the coast. Minor changes in the system in such areas often lead to disasters. These changes may be natural or induced. Most important amongst these is urbanisation in the low lying areas of river valleys and rise in sea level, may be local or eustastic. Applied geomorphology is an essential element in their prediction and managerial perception and in planning how best to minimise their consequences.

Intensity of geomorphic expressions varies from one region to another influenced by climate, vegetation, composition and structure of rocks, elevation and also tectonic stresses.

3.1 WEATHERING

Rocks and minerals exposed to conditions at the earth's surface are broken down by the process known as *weathering*. In other words, weathering is the breaking down and alteration of material near the earth's surface to products that are more in equilibrium in modified physicochemical conditions. Weathering is physical/mechanical i.e., disintegration of rock without or partial chemical alteration; chemical (decomposition), which involves irreversible chemical changes; and biological weathering, affected by growth or movement of plants and animals. Although the processes involved may be distinct, these often act together and takes place in situ.

Weathering modifies the surface of attacked rock and results in a trend towards more stable minerals and rocks. As new minerals are continuously being formed with considerably changed properties, the new rocks also show a substantial change from its parent nature.

The rate and intensity of weathering depends on several factors of which important are climate, rock composition and structure, topography and also time. Thus, the effects of weathering vary according to the local conditions.

3.1.1 Mechanical or Physical Weathering

Physical weathering is the breaking down of material by mechanical methods brought about by a variety of causes. In this, failure occurs when stresses, between and within grains, set up by weathering agencies, exceed the strength of rock causing a rupture or a series of fissures. Different modes of mechanical break down are as follows :

(1) Sheeting, spalling and unloading : Sheeting is the division of rock into sheets by joint like cracks that are parallel to the ground surface. The process is commonly seen in massive granites and sandstones.

Sheeting is related to pressure relief phenomenon. Rock masses that are deeply buried or subjected to tectonic stresses, acquire a significant amount of 'locked in' strain energy. Some of this strain is released when lithostatic pressure or over burden is reduced. As a result of this, cracks parallel to ground surface, are formed. The discontinuities developed are also called as *topographic joints*.

In some cases, as in tunnels or caves, cracks produce spalls with platy rock fragments. These are tension cracks formed parallel to the unloaded surface.

(2) Frost weathering : In cold climatic terrains, where temperature falls below 0°C, water freezes to ice which leads to form crystals promoting volume changes. Experimental studies have shown that water expands by **9 per cent** on freezing at 0°C and exerts a maximum pressure of **2000 km/cm^2 at – 22°C**. The exerted pressure is far greater than the compressive strength of rock. This process is called as frost weathering (Fig. 3.1).

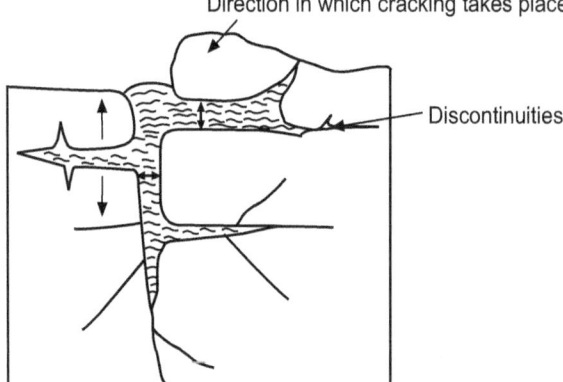

Fig. 3.1 : Frost weathering in a closed system, when water freezes, ice occupies more volume than water. This internal forces are created (arrow) which causes further cracking of rock

(3) Salt weathering : The growth of salt crystals from solution through the process of evaporation may produce disruption effects like frost weathering. The process takes place in soil or in porous rocks.

Weathering by salt crystals involves three groups of processes : (i) thermal expansion of salt crystals, (ii) hydration of salts and (iii) growth of salt crystals.

The growth of gypsum ($CaSO_4 \cdot 2H_2O$) is troublesome in industrial areas. In these areas, the air is polluted by sulfurous smoke from fossil fuel which, if reacted with rainwater becomes a dilute sulphuric acid that corrodes limestone and marble buildings. The product is gypsum which crystallizes in cracks, dislodges thin pieces of rock and accelerates chemical reaction. Salt weathering may take place during summer.

(4) Insulation weathering : The process is characteristic of arid condition where temperature fluctuations cause expansion or shrinkage of rocks. A rise in temperature during day time causes the rock to expand. A fall in temperature during night time results in shrinkage. Due to cyclic variations in temperature and as rock is a poor conductor of heat, a thermal gradient is set up between the surface and inside of a rock. Rocks are made up of different minerals which have variable rates of expansion and contraction. Darker minerals absorb heat faster than lighter minerals. Thus, due to uneven expansion and contraction, internal stresses are created within a rock that may lead to the formation of tiny cracks and eventually to granular disintegration.

(5) Cavitation : Cavitation is restricted to states such as base of high waterfalls. It occurs when water has a very high velocity. This consists of formation of air bubbles in turbulent water when the local pressure becomes less than the vapour pressure. The collapse of air bubbles produces shock waves like a hammer blow on a very small area, which help to weaken and disintegrate the attacked rock.

(6) Abrasion : The weathering away of rocks may simply be possible by mechanical abrasion. This may be because of friction or due to impact or by sliding of rocks against one another. Abrasion is the most active process of weathering in glaciated terrains, in wind transport and in river erosion.

3.1.2 Chemical Weathering

It includes a range of chemical reactions which alter the composition of rock materials, the volume of the rock and the strength and the coherence of the rock. Chemical weathering is either concentrated at the rock surface or along discontinuities. [Fig. 3.2 (a) and (b)]. Many features that are characteristics of physical weathering may also result from chemical weathering (granular and block disintegration). These two processes of weathering often operate in conjunction. Another distinctive feature of chemical weathering is its ability to penetrate more deeply into the rock than physical weathering which is essentially near surface or surface phenomenon.

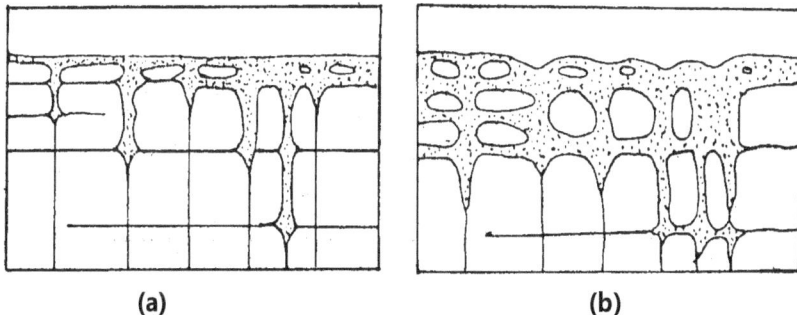

(a)   (b)

Fig. 3.2 : Breakdown of country rock along the discontinuities

(1) Solution : In the presence of water, many solids break up into individual molecules and distribute themselves in suspension between the molecules of the water. Solution is the first stage of reaction of chemical weathering. Commonly salts of Na (Sodium) and K (Potassium) are very soluble. Gypsym is less soluble and carbonate is still lesser. Solution may lead to precipitation that can lead to volume change and enhance physical weathering. Sulphurous and sulphuric acid in industrial atmosphere can give rise to an artificial weathering and production of soluble salts (see section 3.1).

The common reaction is between limestone and water which gives a solution of calcium bi-carbonate.

$$CaCO_3 + CO_2 + H_2O = 2CaHCO_3$$

Limestone   Calcium bi-carbonate

The intensity of weathering can also be determined by the analysis of run-off water in rivers or streams. They commonly have carbonates, and in warmer areas silica is also present indicating variable rate of solubility in different climatic conditions.

The fundamental reactions are as given in Table 3.1.

Table 3.1 : Common chemical weathering reactions

(1) Solution : Dissolution of carbonate minerals by carbonic acid

$$CaCO_3 + H_2CO_3 \longrightarrow Ca^{2+} + 2(HCO_3)^{1-}$$

Calcite carbonic acid   Bicarbonate ions

(2) Oxidation : Iron oxide changes to goethite

$$4FeO + 2H_2O + O_2 \longrightarrow 4FeO \cdot OH$$

Iron oxide   Geothite

(3) Carbonation : Production of carbonic acid by solution of carbon dioxide.

$$H_2O + CO_2 \longrightarrow H_2CO_3 \longrightarrow H^{1+} + HCO_3^{1-}$$

Carbonic acid   Bicarbonate ions

(4) Hydration : Dehydration of geothite to form haematite

$$2FeO \cdot O_3 \longrightarrow Fe_2O_3 + H_2O$$

Geothite   Haematite

(5) Hydrolysis : Potash feldspar is converted to kaoline.

$$4KAl\ Si_3O_8 + 4H^{1+} + 2H_2O \longrightarrow 4K^{1+} + Al_4\ Si_4\ Si_4\ O_{10}\ (OH)_8 + 8Sib_2$$

Potassium feldspar   Kaoline

(2) Carbonation : Carbonation is the process whereby the carbonic acid (H_2CO_3), a common constituent of ground water, attacks rocks and causes a chemical reaction (Table 3.1).Carbonation is often an initial step in certain types of weathering e.g. in the breakdown of feldspar.

(3) Hydration : Hydration is the addition of water to a mineral. For example, Iron oxides may absorb water and modify themselves into iron hydroxides or hydrated iron oxides. It is an important process in the formation of clay minerals. Being an integral part of exothermal reaction, it usually causes a considerable increase in the volume. Hydration normally takes place simultaneously with oxidation or carbonation.

(4) Oxidation – Reduction : Iron bearing minerals contain iron in the ferrous state e.g. pyrite (FeS_2), siderite ($FeCO_3$). On contact with water that has oxygen in solution, the ferrous iron oxidises to the ferric state and forms insoluble hydroxides or ferric oxides. Only oxygen free, chemically reducing alkaline water permits iron to remain in more soluble ferrous state. When aerated water reacts with iron bearing minerals, the reaction becomes more complex. In this process, new compounds are formed, some of which are almost insoluble.

Weathering by oxidation takes place with water as an intermediater. Unprotected iron surface stay clean and bright in dry air. But iron rusts or oxidises quickly in moist arid conditions. Rain water and circulating ground water always contain enough dissolved oxygen to oxidize metalic iron and to change the ferrous iron in mineral compounds to the more oxidized ferric state. Thus, the original mineral structure is destroyed. The oxidation-reduction reactions of water with compounds of aluminium, magnesium, manganese etc. are similar to the reaction of water with iron oxides.

(5) Hydrolysis : In hydrolysis, both the minerals and water molecules decomposes and react to form new compounds in an aqueous solution. It is the most important chemical weathering reaction of silicate minerals (Table 3.1).

The most common weathering reaction of hydrolysis is of feldspar, which is as follows :

$$2KAlSi_3O_8 + 2H_2CO_3 + 9H_2O \longrightarrow Al_2Si_2O_5(OH)_4 + 4H_4SiO_4 + 2K^+ + 2HCl_3^-$$

Orthoclase Carbonic acid　　　　　　　Kaolinite　　Silicic acid in solution

The plagioclase feldspar undergo decomposition more easily than orthoclase in carbonated water. In this, the end products are clay mineral, silica in solution and bi-carbonates of K, Na or Ca in solution.

Another important chemical reaction is the base exchange capacity. It involves mutual cations such as Ca^{++}, Mg^{++}, Na^+ or K^+ between an aqueous solution rich in one cation and a mineral rich in another. The rate of exchange depends on the chemical activity, abundance of cations, acidity, temperature etc.

3.1.3 Biotic Weathering

The process of weathering is influenced by plants, animals and bacterial actions. It is a combination of physical and chemical weathering.

In the simplest case, breaking of particles may be due to the pressure exerted by growing roots, along the planes of discontinuities.

The decomposition of plant materials, particularly in humid conditions, often forms humic acids which break down to rock minerals by the process known as **chelation**. The process increases the solubility of iron compounds which may be absorbed by growing plants. Weathering by humic acids is an important process in the formation of deep weathering in the tropical conditions.

3.1.4 Weathering of Rock Forming Minerals

Weathering of rock forming minerals depend on many factors including chemical composition, structure, crystal size, shape, crystal perfection etc. It is convenient to classify these minerals according to their ability to resist chemical weathering. Quartz is considered to be the most stable or resistant mineral. The susceptible unstable minerals include olivine, pyroxene and plagioclase feldspar. In general, the minerals which are more stable are light coloured and the minerals prone to weathering are dark coloured. The major alteration products are as follows :

Table 3.2 : Weathering of common rock forming minerals

Parent mineral	Process product	Weathering	Disposition
(1) Quartz			
	No chemical weathering	Sand grains	Sand stone
(2) Potash Feldspar			
$KAlSi_3O_8$			Some is transpoted to ocean, some is used by plant life and some is taken by certain clays.
K	$+CO_2$ (Carbonation)	K_2CO_3	
Al, Si, O	$+ H_2O$ (Hydration)	Clay $(Al_2Si_2O_5(OH)_4)$	Shale
		Soluble and Colloidal silica	Chert (Chalcedony)
SiO_2			
(3) Plagioclase Feldspar			
Ca	$+ CO_2$	$CaCO_3$ (Calcite)	Limestone
Na	$+ CO_2$	Na_2CO_3	Dissolves in ocean
Al, Si, O and SiO_2	as above		
(4) Mica	Same as potassium feldspar		

(5) Ferromagnesium Minerals

Depending on composition; weathering products are same as potassium feldspar.

Fe	+ O (oxidation)	Haematite Fe_2O_3 Limonite (FeO (OH))	Iron ore
	+ O + CO_2 (Oxidation and hydration)		
Mg	+ CO_2	$MgCO_3$	Some replaces calcium in limestone to form dolomite and some goes into certain clay minerals.

3.1.5 Structure, Climate and Rock Weathering

The susceptibility of rocks to weathering depends on their physical properties controlled largely by mineral composition, texture and deformation structure and also largely on the climatic condition. Details of rock properties that control degree of weathering are given in Table 3.3.

Table 3.3 : Resistance to weathering related to rock properties

Rock Properties	Physical weathering		Chemical weathering	
	Resistant	Non-resistant	Resistant	Non-resistant
1. Mineral composition	High feldspar, Ca Plagioclase, low quartz, $CaCO_3$ and homogeneous composition	High quartz content, Na Plagioclase, heterogeneous composition	Uniform mineral composition, high silica, low biotite, high orthoclase, low metal ion content	Mixed /variable mineral composition, high $CaCO_3$ content, low quartz, high Ca plagioclase high olivine.
2. Texture	Uniform texture crystalline, clastics, gneisses	Coarse grained, variable textural features, schistose.	Uniform texture, crystalline, clastics, gneiss.	Porphyritic, schistose
3. Porosity	Low porosity, free draining, low internal surface area	High porosity, poorly draining, high internal surface area.	large pore size, low permeability, low internal surface area.	Small pore size, high permeability, high internal surface area.
4. Bulk properties	Low absorption, Fresh hard rock	High absorption, Partially weathered rock	Low absorption, high compressive and tensile strength, fresh hard rock.	High absorption and partially weathered.

... Contd.

5. Structure	Non-foliated, clastics, thick bedded.	Foliated, fractured, soluble, thin bedded.	Strongly cemented, dense grain packing, massive, siliceous cement.	Calcareous cement, poorly cemented, thin bedded, fractured soluble.
6. Examples	Plutonic rocks, quartzite, sandstone, gneiss, limestone	Poorly cemented sandstone, basalt, limestone marble, schists	Crystalline rocks, plutonic igneous, quartzite, gneissses	Calcareous rocks, volcanic, claystones, slates, marbles, schists, cherts.

Rocks generally exhibit differential rate of weathering. Some rocks are massive, some have strong structural features that control mechanical disintegration and chemical decomposition. Their permeability varies from place to place in the same rock and in different rocks. Fractures break rocks and create surface of zero cohesion.

Mineral and chemical composition also controls weathering. For example, different textural types of identical granite have varying resistance to weathering and erosion. Table 3.3 clearly depicts the same. In addition to factors mentioned above, several other properties are known to affect the weathering characteristics and durability of rock. The properties like coefficients of volume expansion, thermal conductivity, diffusivity and tensile strength are very important in determining the resistance of rocks. As a result it is observed that each rock types has a distinctive weathering pattern. Limestones are smooth, grey and deeply pitted by solution. Shales spilt and crumble. The weathering appearance of rock is so useful that it is included among the diagnostic criteria for defining stratigraphic units which are the basic units of geologic mapping.

Climate Influence on Rock Weathering :

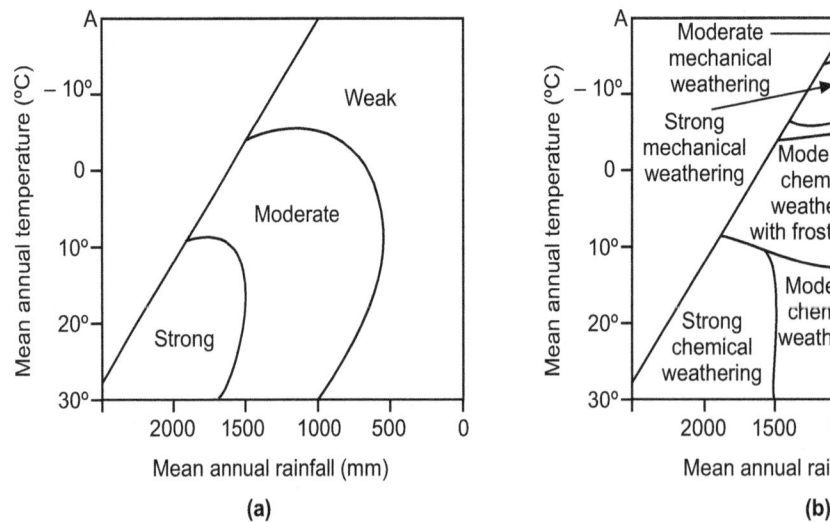

Fig. 3.3 : Climate and weathering (a) Regions of chemical weathering, (b) General classification of weathering regions

It is commonly observed that climate has great influence on the behaviour of rock. Granite may be a resistant rock in arid climate, but in humid tropical climate porphyritic granite in particular is least resistant. There exists a definite relationship between climate and weathering pattern of rocks (Fig. 3.3).

In the tropics, hydrolysis and residual clay mineral formation reach to depths of 100 m or more.

The great depth of weathering is due to temperature and abundant precipitation. Though both types of weathering occur simultaneously, chemical weathering is more pronounced. It is so intense that clay minerals are desilicified. A typical reaction of kaolinite in a great excess of water is –

$$Al_2Si_2O_3(OH)_4 + 5H_2O \longrightarrow 2Al(OH)_3 + 2H_4SiO_4$$

Kaolinite   water   Gibbsite   Silicic
                      (mineral   acid in
                      of bauxite) solution

The actual form of silica is not certain. Some are in amorphous or colloidal form and may reprecipitate at the water table in seasonally dry tropical regions to form chalcedony or opal. Gibbsite, the aluminium hydroxide residual, recrystallizes slowly as insoluble hydrated alumina.

i.e. $$2Al(OH)_3 \longrightarrow Al_2O_3 \cdot 3H_2O$$

Gibbsite is the major mineral in the heterogeneous earthy material of hydrated aluminium oxide, called **bauxite**. Tropical weathering of poor quality iron, aluminosilicates produce a layer of earthy or nodular bauxite.

The chief climatic controls are related to water and temperature. Water involves the total amount of precipitation, intensity of rain, proportion of precipitation that forms run off and precipitation-evaporation ratio. Temperature involves mean temperature, temperature range and fluctuations about freezing points. The other important factors which changes appreciably from place to place are cloud cover, relative humidity, drying winds and climatic changability. However, the relationship between climate and weathering is often very difficult to determine because all over the globe climatic changes are interpreted in the past from those prevailing at present.

Weathering of plutonic rocks : Plutonic rocks are usually strong and durable for any engineering purpose when they are fresh. But decomposition of these rocks to considerable depth from accumulated weathering over geologic time is a common experience. Granitic rocks usually weathers to a mixture of clayey regolith; and igneous rocks may produce extremely compressible clay soil. Most important reaction in plutonic igneous rocks is weathering of feldspar and mica.

$$4KAlSi_3O_8 + 2H_2CO_3 + 2H_2O \longrightarrow Al_4(OH)_8 Si_4O_{10} + 2K_2CO_3 + 8SiO_2$$

Orthoclase   Kaolinite

Orthoclase feldspar is converted to kaolinite clay, silica and soluble potassium carbonate. The later two will be carried in solution to be deposited nearby fractures in a rock or transported into a stream and carried into the ocean. If improper drainage is available, the potassium may be retained in the clay mineral to form illite or fine mica, called *sericite*.

$$CaAl_2Si_2O_8 \cdot 2NaAlSi_3O_8 + 2H_2O + 4H_2CO \rightarrow Al_4(OH)_8 Si_4O_{10} + Ca(HCO_3)_2 + 2NaHCO_3 + 4SiO_2$$
$$\text{Plagioclase} \qquad \text{Kaolinite}$$

Plagioclase feldspar has end members called albite and anorthite. This mixture is found in many acid igneous rocks. The calcium plagioclase weathers more rapidly than sodium plagioclase. It is generally broken down to kaolinite clay, and soluble bicarbonates of sodium and calcium.

$$4KMg_2Fe(OH)_2 AlSi_3O_{10} + 2H_2CO_3 + O_2 \longrightarrow$$
$$\text{Biotite}$$

$$Al_4(OH)_8 Si_4O_{10} + 2Fe_2O_3 \cdot H_2O + 4KHCO_3 + 8Mg(HCO_3)_2 + 8SiO_2 + 8H_2O$$
$$\text{Kaolinite} \qquad \text{Limonite}$$

Weathering of biotite mica yields kaolinite and limonite, soluble silica and soluble bicarbonates of potassium and magnesium. If weathering takes place in impermeable horizons, the Mg, Fe or both may be retained by the clay minerals to produce montmorillonite instead of kaolinite. It may be said that an early sign of weathering in granitic rocks is brown decolouration of biotite, resulting from formation of limonite around its margins.

Quartz and muscovite mica are resistant to weathering and are generally retained in the residual soil.

Minerals in basic and ultrabasic rocks are more easily attacked in weathering. As they are richer in Fe and Mg minerals, they tend to produce montmorillonite clays. In these rocks, decaying is possible even upto deeper levels.

3.1.6 Weathering Profiles and Weathering Grades

The important features of weathering profiles are seen in a quarry face, a cliff face or may be in a well section. One of such features is the junction between weathered rock and fresh parent rock. Another feature may be seen in the form of gradation from soil to unweathered parent rock.

The weathering profile may be formed by mechanical or chemical weathering. It appreciably varies from place to place because of variations in the controlling factors including rock type and structure, topography, climate etc.

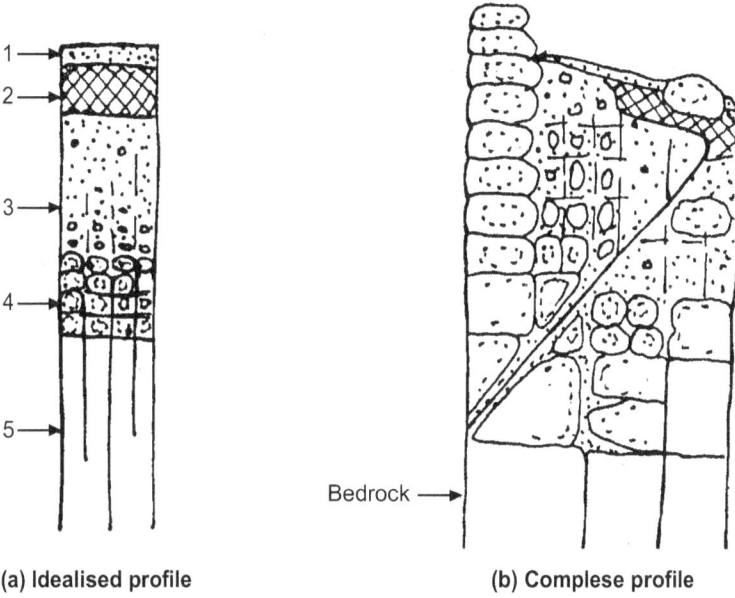

(a) Idealised profile (b) Complese profile

Fig. 3.4 : Generalised weathering profile

The generalised sequence commonly observed in the profile is as follows. (also see Fig. 3.4)

(1) Soil horizon.

(2) Intensely weathered zone or structureless regolith. The complete weathered material, saprolite is called regolith.

(3) Saprolite – In-situ weathered rock is called saprolite retaining rock structure.

(4) Moderately weathered zone, presence of higher proportion of country rock.

(5) Fresh parent rock or unweathered rock.

It must be remembered that this sequence may not be observed under all climatic conditions. Often a sharp change from weathered material and fresh rock may be observed.

(a) Igneous and metamorphic rocks : The weathering profile seen on metamorphic rocks is complicated as compared to that on igneous rocks. This is possibly due to their uneven distribution or differing lithology. Hard resistant rocks (quartzite or gneiss) are often interbedded with weaker rocks like phyllite or schist. The resistant layers form ridges or hills. While weaker horizons produce valleys. On the other hand, in granites, weathering profiles are simple because the joint networks are comparatively simple. The profile on basalt is similar to that on intrusive rocks. The higher proportion of ferromagnesium minerals in basalt results in soils rich in iron and clay minerals.

(b) Sedimentary rocks : The sedimentary rocks commonly show variations in composition in profile as well as laterally. Thus, the profiles seen on sedimentary rocks are extremely variable both vertically and laterally. The depth of weathering may be high. In karstitic terrain, deep solution cavities filled with soft clay, are of a common occurrence; and thus have an appreciable control on slope stability. These pockets develop along joints, faults and bedding planes.

Weathering profiles on mudrocks are extremely variable. Fissures are invariably important structures at all stages in the weathering of mudstones/shales. The weathered zone is usually thin with low strength and low permeability at the surface overlying a join and fissured rock of higher permeability. The transition from soil to rock is gradual.

(c) Classification of the grade of weathering : As a rock weathers, its porosity increases significantly. Its capacity to transmit fluid also increases and with this in a decreases the resistance of rock in a span of time. Based on field observations carried out on rocks at in-situ in different weathering profiles indicate six fold classification for weathered rocks (Table 3.4).

The following classification is simple to use in the field. In general, a detailed account of from top soil to fresh unaltered rock when seen in profile is given very accurately. Often accuracy is to the precision if thin sections of different horizons are prepared and observed carefully under microscope.

Table 3.4 : Engineering grade classification of weathered rocks

Grade	Degree of decomposition	Field recognition		Engineering behaviour of rocks
		Soft rocks (Soil)	Hard rocks (Rocks)	
VI	Soil	The original soil is altered completely to new product.	The rock is discoloured and completely altered to a soil in which original fabric of the rock is completely destroyed. Also associated with volume change.	Bad foundation material, erodes easily.
V	Completely weathered	The soil is discoloured and altered with no trace of original fabric.	The rock is discoloured and altered to a soil, but has partially preserved the original fabric.	Unsuitable for foundation of concrete dams or large structures. During construction, careful monitoring is required.

... *Contd.*

IV	Highly weathered	The soil is altered to a great extent with occasional relicts of original rock.	The rock is discoloured, discontinuities may be air filled and have discoloured surfaces. The original fabric of the rock near discontinuites is altered.	Similarly to grade V. Erratic presence of boulders makes it unreliable/ unsuitable for large structures.
III	Moderately weathered	The soil is composed of large discoloured lithorelicts of original rock separated by altered material.	The rock is discoloured, greater surface area covered by original fabric. Discontinuties may be open and discolouration along them may not be as intense as in grade IV.	Suitable for small structures, but behaviour structural features particularly in large openings need to be monitored.
II	Slightly weathered	The material is composed of angular blocks of fresh soil which is slightly discoloured. Some altered material starting to penetrate inwards from discontinuities separating blocks.	The rock is slightly discoloured adjacent to discontinuities. The discoloured rock may be slightly weaker than fresh rock.	May be suitable for large structures. Suitability depends on discontinuties : their attitude, spacing, block size, aperature, surface waviness etc.
I	Fresh rock	The parent material is unaltered and homogeneous throughout the exposure.	The parent rock shows no discolouration and homogeneous throughout the exposure.	Similar to grade II.

3.1.7 Weathering and the Evolution of Landforms

Varieties of land expressions are developed in response to different weathering processes controlled by climate, structure and rock properties. Following are the evolutionary processes in the formation of landforms.

1. Constant volume weathering
2. Weathering with expansion
3. Differential weathering
4. Fragmented rocks and residual deposits
5. Limestone and solutional landforms
6. Slopes

1. Constant volume weathering : Constant volume weathering takes place at depth below the earth's surface. In many areas of deep weathering it is observed that many original features are preserved as 'ghost' structures in the weathered material. For example, presence of quartz veins, original banding etc.

2. Weathering with expansion : Massive rocks like granite, sandstones and basic igneous rocks tend to produce slabs of rock, several tens of metre in thickness. Landforms produced due to unloading are called as *exfoliation*.

The dominant feature of unloading is the production of large and thick curved slabs of rocks and exposure of domal shaped rock beneath. The detached individual slabs are few metres in thickness and partings between the slabs is parallel to the ground surface, called topographic joints.

Exfoliation describes several processes and several landforms that have in common the possession of more or less concentric shells of rock over an inner core. Exfoliation may be divided into the following divisions.

Spheroidal weathering : Spheroidal weathering is a process accelerated due to combined action of physical and chemical weathering. It is seen in the form of fresh road cuts where rounded boulders of even dimensions are developed in rows running in several directions. The pattern results from intersecting joint sets (generally three sets) that control the slow movement of water through the rock (Fig. 3.5).

It is seen from Fig. 3.5 that the effectiveness of chemical weathering increases as surface area exposed to weathering increases. The increase in surface area is due to subdivision of larger blocks into smaller blocks controlled by attitude of joints and spacing. Increase in surface area increases the secondary porosity and in turn permeability of the rock. Solutions moving along joints separating nearly cubic blocks of rock attack corners, edges and sides. Corners become rounded and eventually the blocks are reduced to spheres. Once a spherical form is achieved, the energy of attacks becomes uniformly distributed over the whole surface so that no further change in form occurs.

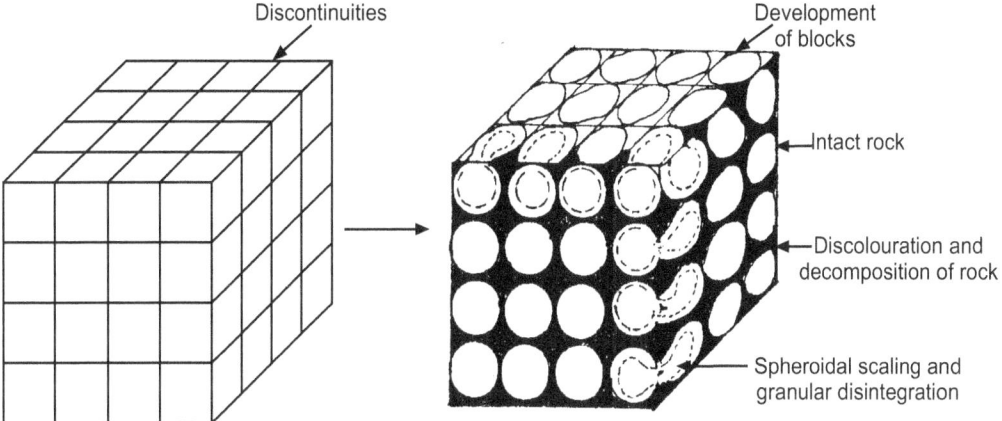

Fig. 3.5 : Spheroidal weathering

Spheroidal weathering is very often seen in Deccan Trap Basalts.

Flaking : Flaking is also called as spalling, scaling and onion skin weathering. It is caused by fine growth of salt crystals, chemical decay of minerals and periodic temperature changes.

The growth of salt crystals in layers or pockets below the surface of porous rocks can give rise to flaking. The flakes are found to be backed by a layer of salt upto 2 mm thick. Flaking by hydration also produce uniform thickness slabs.

Individual blocks that weather by flaking becomes rounded because the process attacks corners and edges more than the faces.

Some soils give rise to a hummocky surface, the mounds and depressions making various patterns of different sizes. The mounds are often circular about one metre across and separated by flat depressions about two metres across. The surface of mounds is calcareous and has a low density. However the soil in the depression is non-calcareous and similar to soil formed in the lower profile. Thus, the mound owe its origin to calcareous subsoil. This is possibly related to swelling characteristics of certain minerals. It is seen that when the soil dries and cracks and pieces of top soil fall down the cracks. When the soil becomes wet it swells possibly due to presence of montmorillonite mineral. If dried the soil shranks, extent sideways pressure which is relieved by movement upwards. The cracks or lines produced by upward pressure is later filled up by the carbonate solutions.

3. Differential weathering : Differential weathering results due to structural or lithological differences in rock. It occurs on all scales.

Often many kinds of hollows produced by weathering occur on horizontal, sloping or vertical surfaces. They are called as **weathering pits**. They may be developed due to flaking, granular disintegration or even due to alterations.

Cavernous weathering, meaning window, occurs on steep slope. They generally extend upwards and backwards into the rock, but do not grow downward. They may be formed due to flaking or granular disintegration.

When the weathering rock has a pattern of joints filled by iron material which may be more resistant than the host rock and thus stand out on a weathered surface as a boxwork or honeycomb. In such cases the enrichment in the iron of the boxwork may be at the expanse of the rock which loses cement and crumbles more easily and thus the different hardness is due to part of the weathering process.

Many weathering pits are surrounded by a raised rim that stands above the surrounding rock surfaces. They are formed in varieties of rocks and also in different climatic conditions. On a larger scale, differential weathering can give rise to mushroom rocks, and pedestal stones. Similarly differential weathering and erosion on dykes of igneous rock can give rise to depressions (trenches) or walls (natural dams) depending on whether the dyke is softer or harder than the surrounding rock (Fig. 3.6).

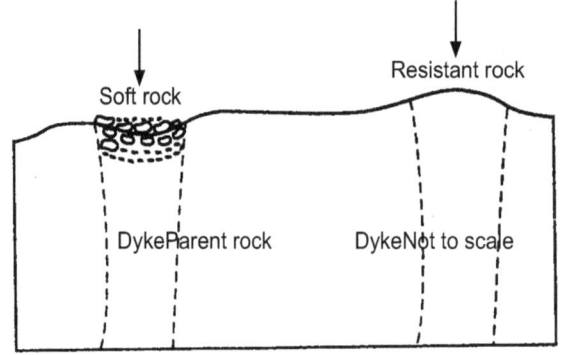

Fig. 3.6

Weathering can carve individual boulders into a wide variety of shapes. The most important being formation of tors of granites (Fig. 3.7).

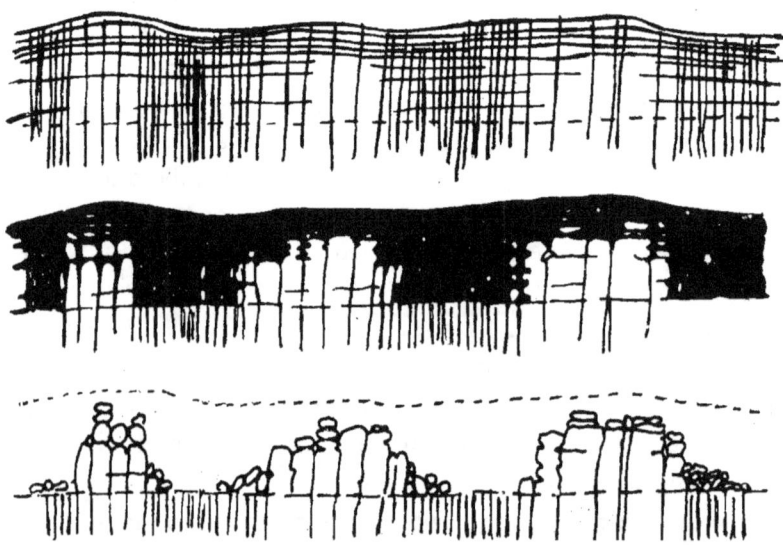

Fig. 3.7 : Evolution of a group of tors, note that spacing of discontinuities (joints) is important in deciding size of individual tor

Tors are small hills or heaps of boulders, usually upto 20 metres in elevation, rising abruptly from the surrounding low lying areas. It is observed that during the course of erosion, the basal surface of weathering may be exhumed and the corestones left behind as soft material of the regolith is washed away. This stripping gives rise to kind of differential weathering probably formed due to sub-aerial weathering to produce tors of uneven dimensions (Fig. 3.7). Development of tors is also controlled by joint orientation and spacing. Once exposed, tors decompose very slowly, while the underlying jointed rock is brought within the vadose zone of intense weathering and thus decays rapidly.

In many areas, large plains may be formed by alternate deep weathering and stripping, called **etch plains**. The etched plains may undergo several cycles of weathering followed by stripping. Many irregularities in the depth of etching could give rise to tors.

4. **Fragmented rocks and residual deposits :** The particles and deposits of particles produced by weathering are often features of landforms. For example : loess deposits, talus and scree deposits.

Talus is the waste produced by the action of running water which undergoes deposition on the steep slopes or at the foot of a cliff. Scree are the debris derived by frost action. The surface of scree slopes is at the angle of repose for the fragments that make up the scree, the larger the fragments the steeper the slope. They often occur in more or less continuous sheets along valley slopes in the form of cones or fans. Scree and talus surfaces are often mobile and there is no soil formation by vegetation while weathering continues unabated.

Typical residual deposits are also discussed in sedimentary rocks.

5. **Solutional landforms :** Solution gives rise to small and large landforms particularly in limestone areas, called as Karst topography. Solution tends to make original planar surface irregular by producing pits. When limestone dissolves very irregularly, boxwork may be produced by differential weathering at the surface or in caves. When a stream flows over limestone particularly in active areas asymmetrical scallops may be produced. (5 to 50 cm in length, aligned in the direction of water flow and concave with steepest side upstream). In areas where water is stagnant, symmetrical scallops are created.

Caverns are irregular hollows formed by solution. Another characteristic of limestone country is development of sink holes (small caves).

Commonly the limestone is not equally soluble in all directions possibly due to changes in lithology.

The most glaring morphological feature in limestone is development of caves. Most caves have a marked horizontal development indicating that their position follows the water table in limestone country. In plan, many caves have a distinct joint controlled pattern.

Caves are either excavated in vadose zone or phreatic zone above water table. Those excavated in vadose zone have plans approximately like normal river systems with regular down hill gradient and their passages are marked by meanders, asymmetrical scallops and a general lack of phreatic feature. On the other hand, caves formed in phreatic zone may be distinguished by lack of regular gradients, boxworks, blind passages and asymmetrical scallops. In rare instances, caves in vadose zone are recognised with the help of bridges of insoluble rock like chert.

Solution pipes are depressions which are circular in cross section with vertical wall and when excavated they closely resemble man made wells. They generally appear to be formed at joint intersections.

Limestone landforms are controlled by lithology and climate. Most of them are seen in hard limestones of low porosity but with very developed joints.

6. Slopes : Landscapes are very largely made up of hillslopes, form of which depends on combined action of weathering, erosion and mass movements. Here only the aspects related to weathering are discussed and other aspects are dealt in appropriate sections.

Four basic elements of slope are recognised (Fig. 3.8) : The waxing slope, the free face, the debris slope and the pediment slope.

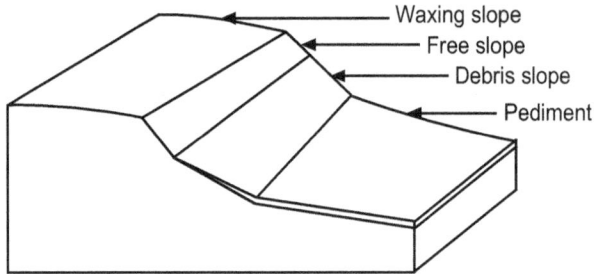

Fig. 3.8 : Elements of a fully developed hill slopes

The waxing slope (Fig. 3.8) is the convex crest of a scarp formed possibly due to creep; and is constantly under modification.

The free face (Fig. 3.8) is the outcrop of barren rock exposed below the waxing slope. It is the most active element in backwearing of the slope as a whole. Weathering is rapid and it discourages accumulation of debris.

The debris slope (Fig. 3.8) is covered with detritrus derived from free face. On this kind of slope there is usually a reduction in particle size with distance downslope.

The pediment is the basal slope element made up of hard or soft rock of uneven weathering index.

3.2 FLUVIAL PROCESSES

Fluvial geomorphology is very important in major civil engineering operations. The most fundamental landforms seen on the earth's surface are developed by fluvial action, though other processes also substantially contribute to their modification and development. An understanding of applied fluvial geomorphology, including quantitative study of sediment load, is essential where a dam is to be constructed across a river valley as a part of hydroelectric and irrigation projects. The study is useful in calculating the life of a reservoir. In rare cases, the river may flood, overflow their banks and an abnormal sediment load may be deposited over their flood plains. Here, an understanding of artificial channelisation may be beneficial which helps to reduce the problem by speeding up the escape of the flood water. The required information is derived from quantitative estimations of discharge variations in rivers, the nature and amount of sediment load etc.

The capacity of a river to carry sediment load and to erode its channels, laterally as well as vertically, is evaluated by the amount of energy it possesses.

A river has a potential energy controlled by the amount of water present (volume) and the head of the water (vertical distance above sea level). The kinetic energy (an energy of movement) generated by the river is evaluated by the flow of water and its velocity i.e. discharge. Thus, an increase in the discharge of water and its velocity leads to an increase in river energy. Rivers may show substantial spatial as well as temporal variations.

3.2.1 Fluvial Classification System

Rivers normally flowing into channels cut either into bedrock or in alluvial (recent) sediments. Rivers in bedrock tend to follow a stable course while those in alluvium have a strong tendency to change their position and behaviour. Failure to understand the natural behaviour of alluvial river systems can lead to damaging effects particularly if artificial changes are introduced in the system.

Bedrock channels are likely to be much more irregular than alluvial channels.

Whether in alluvium or bedrock, the **thalweg**, or line connecting points of maximum water depth in a general downstream direction along the channel is seldom straight.

In humid regions, rivers are called **effluent** as they receive water also from groundwater. Rivers in arid regions generally lose water to ground in addition to losing it by evaporation and they often dry up completely without reaching the sea. They are called **influent** streams.

The shape of river and channel segment is used to describe different terms. Some segments are straight in plan view. Sinuous channels develop in bedrock and alluvium either by rounding the corners of zigzag channels or alternately eroding and depositing sediment as pools and riffles along former straight reaches. The sinuous channels are called meanders. Rivers that carry large amount of coarse sediment construct midstream bars at frequent intervals and divide into numerous intersecting and shifting channels, called as braided or anastomosing.

3.2.2 Fluvial Erosion

Erosion by a river or a stream is the process of continuous removal of weathered material from in-situ.

The most common process of stream erosion is mechanical abrasion or corrosion. The rate of corrosion depends on the volume of water, the gradient, hardness and softness of bedrock. The coarse disintegrated particles of hard rock are rolled and dragged along the channel floor, slowly removing away exposed rock outcrops.

Pot holes are often created in the beds of the fast flowing rivers due to strong eddy motions by swirling action of pebbles. The sheer hydraulic power exerted by rapid river flow, referred as pot-hole drilling may also be responsible for shattering of bedrock in the channel. The process becomes easier if joints and bedding planes are widened by localised corrosion or chemical attack.

Erosion by a river or a stream is influential in three interactions; viz vertical downcutting, lateral erosion and headward erosion.

(1) Vertical downcutting : Vertical downcutting is peculiar of the fast flowing rivers that transport a large bed load. The bed load is used to abrade and pot hole the channel floor, which leads to the formation of deep narrow gorges.

However, river water cannot continue to flow when there is no slope and there is also a limit below which a river cannot excavate its own bed. Thus, no further conversion of potential energy to river work is possible. The ultimate base level is the sea level into which the rivers must flow. But for smaller streams, temporary base levels are created by lower limiting planar surfaces produced by lakes, resistant rock masses etc.

(2) Lateral erosion : Once the temporary base level is attained, the kinetic energy of the river is used for lateral excavation causing bank erosion. However, the role played by weathering and slope transport in the process of valley widening is substantial. As a result of these interactions meanders or sinusoidal bents are developed.

(3) Headward erosion : Headward erosion is prominent where river profile (for details, see section 3.2.4) is steep. It is associated with waterfalls where an alternate sequence of hard and soft rock is observed. Thus, on steepend valley sections, the rapidly flowing water increases the rate of erosion with the result that steepened section migrates upstream.

In the case of waterfalls, erosion is concentrated at the base of the fall and may involve sudden burst of trapped air bubbles. This process is known as cavitation. This leads to retreating of the fall and periodic collapse of hard rocks so that in course of time, the fall may be abandoned.

3.2.3 Fluvial Transport

The theoretical maximum load that a stream can transport is labelled as its capacity; while, competence is the measure of a river's ability to transport a maximum grain size of disintegrated particles. It depends on the factors like velocity, the shape and size of particles, temperature of water etc.

The weathered material (disintegrated and decomposed) is transported in three forms :

 (a) **Bed load :** Bed load is often a permanent load situated in the river channel. It includes the gravel and large size fragments, transported close to the channel floor by rolling or sliding.

(b) **Suspension load :** Clay, silt and sand particles transported during moderate/high flow, are called as suspension load.

(c) **Solution load :** The decomposed material available in solution or colloidal mixtures is called dissolved or solution bed.

3.2.4 Fluvial Gradation

The concept of stream gradation is controlled and influenced by many factors including discharge, sediment load, base level, channel width, depth, bed roughness etc. The fluvial system is said to be graded if the stream channel system adjusts its gradient and attains an average steady state of operation for a measurable period. The system is then said to have achieved an equilibrium state of operation. The equilibrium may be achieved in a process of a gradational steps (Fig. 3.9). Thus, the concept of a river in graded system may be visualised by first imagining an ungraded river that flows over a tectonic landscape, newly raised from the other normal land or from the floor of the sea (Fig 3.9 (a)). Rainfall varies over the landscape, water flows down-slope along easy water carrying paths. Drainage networks are eroded and valleys are broadened by mass wasting on slopes along the deeper channels (Fig. 3.9 (b)).

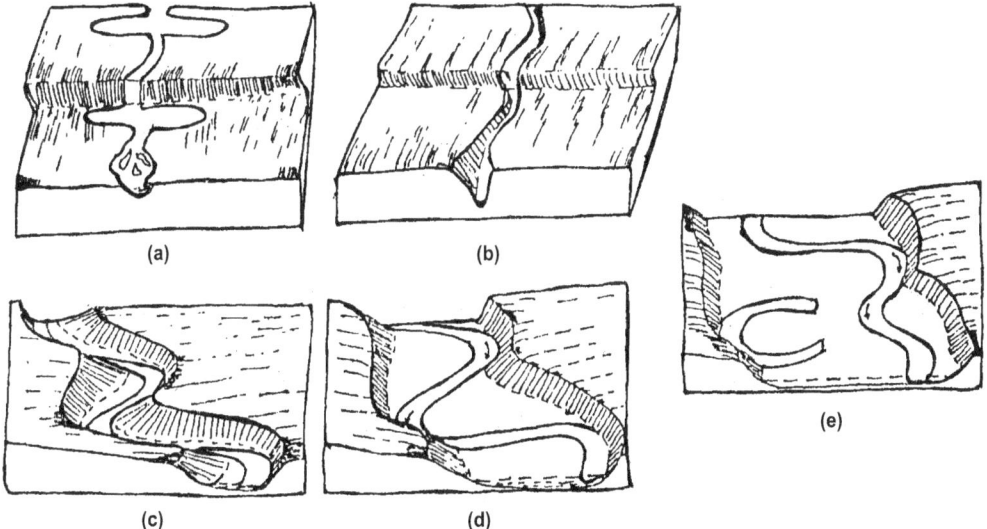

Fig. 3.9 : (a) Initial stage, stream is flowing on a pre-existing topography.

(b) Youthful stage, vertical downcutting

(c) Maturity stage, meandering channel, lateral cutting

(d) Widening of channel, flood-plain development

(e) Old stage, near peneplain, ox-bow lakes

In this way, the initial channel originates and begins its travel towards the sea. The gradation processes may be marked in the smoothness of river profile (stages 1 to 6, Fig. 3.10) Irregularities in profile are related to the presence of lakes, rapids, falls or beds of hard rock which provide temporary base levels so that profile flattens off on approaching these features, and then steepens again below them. Here, the velocity of a river or a stream rapidly increases and thus abrasion of bedrock becomes intense. As a result, falls are cut back and the rapids are trenched, while the lakes are filled by sediments. As a continuous process, the lakes disappear and falls are transformed into rapids while the rapids are reduced to a gradient of minimum irregularities, (stage 2, Fig. 3.10). Simultaneously, tributaries are also being introduced into the land mass, excavating the drainage area and converting the original landscape into a fluvial land form system.

In the initial stages, the stream's energy is utilized in excavating the floor (downcutting) so that very little or no debris accumulates in the channel. However, continuous excavation contributes to an increasing supply of rock debris to the channels. Thus, there comes a stage when the supply of bed exactly matches the stream's capacity for transport. This stage is called the graded condition (stage 3, Fig. 3.10).

After attaining this stage, the stream continues to excavate on the outsides of the bank (lateral erosion) and the first indication of having attained a graded condition may be visualised in the development of a flood plain valley [(Fig. 3.9 (c)]. On the outer side of a bend, the channel shifts laterally into a curve of a large diameter and erodes the outer bank. On the inside of the bend, the alluvium accumulates in the form of point bar deposits [(Fig. 3.9 (d)]. As a continuous process, the flood-plain valley is widened and meanders or sinusoidal bends are developed [Fig. 3.9 (d)]; occasionally they produce cut-offs, leaving crescentic mort or ox-bow lakes [(Fig. 3.9 (e)]. Because of flood plain development, the deeper valley gradually disappears and forms an open valley with soil covered slopes.

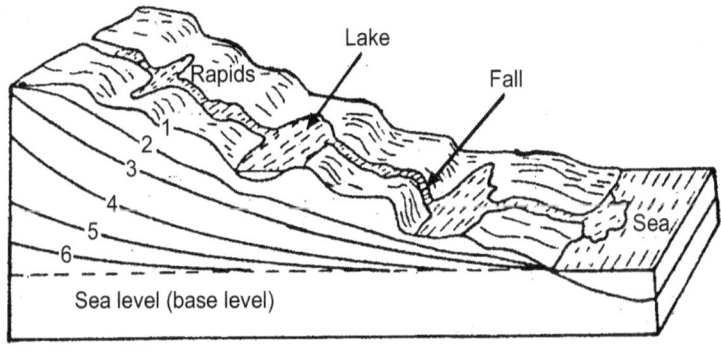

Fig. 3.10 : Evolution of a stream

The profile, if plotted, of such a stream, is referred as a graded profile (stage 4, Fig. 3.10). However, the profile may not be very smooth, if considered the effects of major tributaries which cause abrupt increases in the discharge and load from point to point along the main stream. Thus, at each confluence point, the profile of a graded stream is segmented. Irregularities of profile may often be due to a distinct change in bedrock from place to place, for example, a sandstone shale sequence. Theoretically, the goal of the erosion process is to reduce land mass to penultimate base level. After a time span of millions of years, the land surface is reduced to an undulating surface of minimum elevation known as **peneplain** (stage 6, Fig. 3.10).

Thus, the history of the fluvial system from the initial period to peneplain surface, is considered, in three stages.

The youth stage of a river system is characterised by steep gradients giving rise to gorges or narrow, steep sided valleys [(Fig. 3.9 (a) and Fig. 3.11] water falls and rapids are common and the river profiles are not in equilibrium. The rapidly flowing streams consume their energy in the process of excavation and thus there is no flood-plain.

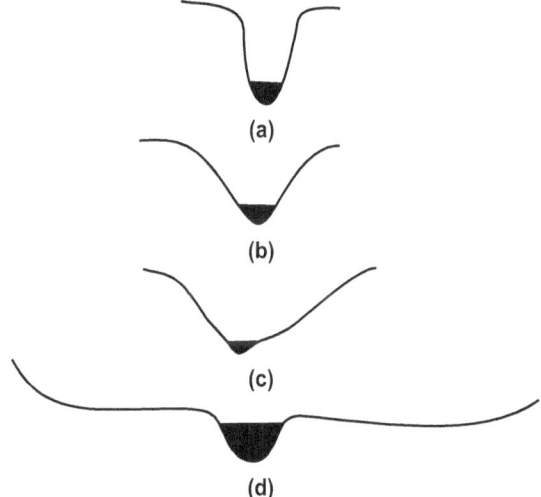

Fig. 3.11 : Stage of valley erosion,
(a) Extreme youth : Vertical downcutting characterised by canyons, rapids, waterfalls and seldom lakes.
(b) Youth : Characterised by V shaped valleys, falls, rapids and also lakes.
(c) Maturity : Lateral cutting, valley flood is broader than the river channel.
(d) Old : Development of a flood plain valley is very broad with gentle slopes.

In the maturity stage, the gradient is moderate and the valley is deeper and wider. The stream is in equilibrium and said to possess a flood-plain along with meandering curves [Fig. 3.9 (d) and Fig. 3.11].

In the old stage, the gradient is still lowered; the valley is widened and lateral cutting by the migrating meander belt becomes the main erosional process. A broad flood plain, characterised by large meanders, braided or anastomosing stream, is formed (Fig. 3.9 (a) and Fig. 3.10). Irregularities are minimum and thus the condition of base levelling or peneplanation is almost achieved.

3.2.5 Fluvial Morphology

Every river is seen as a three dimensional body. In order to understand the concept of river evolution it is necessary to explain the elements of channel geometry i.e. plan view, cross section and longitudinal profiles; and to understand their mutual dependence. They are also part of an 'interconnected system' which is further controlled by the external factors (natural base factors, tectonics, lithology, climate), discharge and sediment load.

(a) Plan view : Three channel patterns are recognised : straight, meandering and braided. (Fig. 3.12).

In nature, geometrically straight channels are rare. Channels are thus called straight if they exhibit a very small river evolution over a certain distance. Two main factors govern the straight nature of a channel : a steep gradient and a narrow course caused by geological and morphological influences. Elongation due to steep gradients is typical in geologically young mountain ranges and tectonically active regions. In small scale maps minor morphological features are suppressed to an extent that the whole river gives the impression of a straight course.

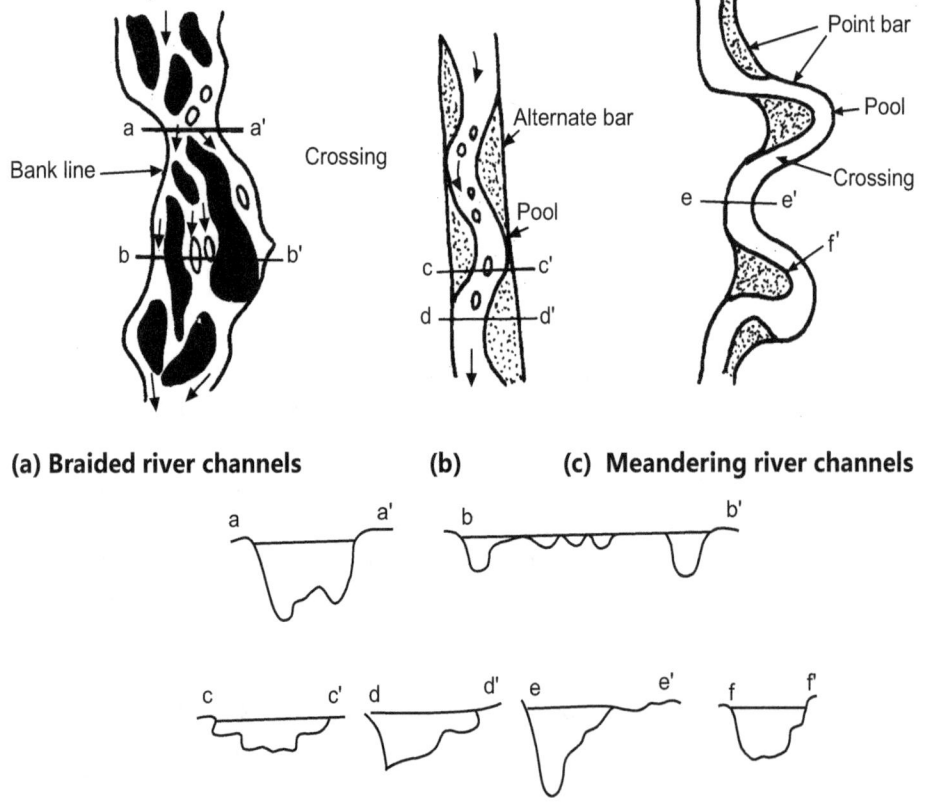

Fig. 3.12 : River channel patterns

Meandering river channels : Sinuous river channels are usually referred as meanders. More precisely a meandering stream is the one whose channel alignment consists essentially of pronounced bends with deep pools in the outer side and shallow crossing in the short, straight reach connecting the bends (Fig. 3.12 (c)). The thalweg flows from a pool through a crossing to the next pool, forming the sinuous curve of a single meander loop. As is seen in Fig. 3.12 (c), the pool tend to be triangular in section with point bars located on the inside of the bend. In the crossings, the channel is more rectangular with greater width and shallower depth. At low flows the local slope is steeper and velocities are greater in the crossing than in the pool. At low stages the thalweg is located very close to the outside of the bend. At higher stages the thalweg tends to straighten. It moves away from the outside of the bend and encroaches on the point bar partially. With increase in time meanders widen their loop at various rates and move downstream. The latter process is described as migration. The phenomena of widening and migration can be developed separately but usually they are interlinked. Migration to a large extent, is controlled by erosional resistance of the bedrock.

When the meander loops approach each other due to their lateral erosion, a cut-off is established at the contacts that leads to the establishment of ox-bow lakes (Fig. 3.13).

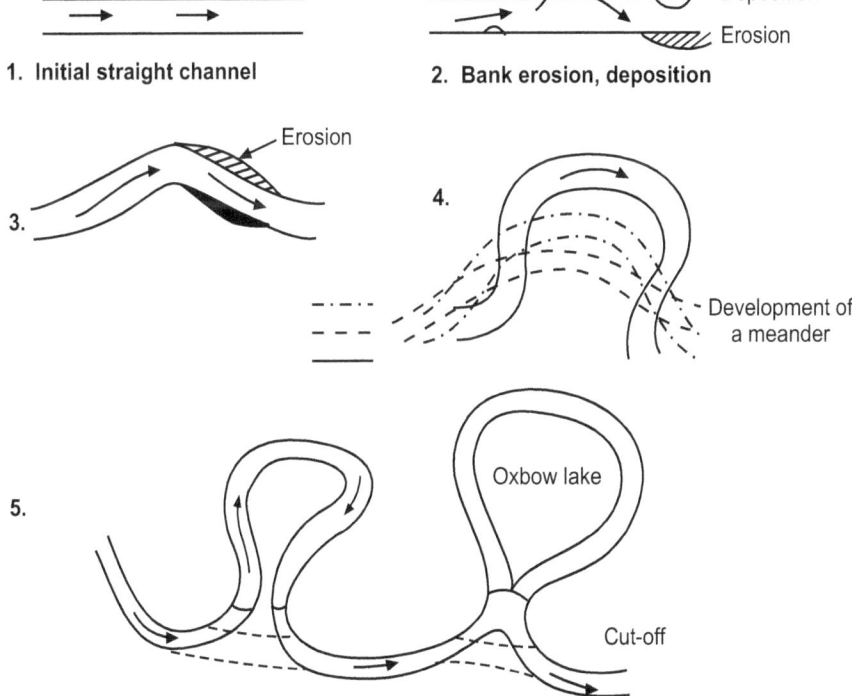

Fig. 3.13 : Development of ox-bow lake

Each cut-off shortens the course and thus leads to an increase of the gradient in the area which proportionally increases the energy potential of the river and accelerates the widening of the loops. (Fig. 3.13)

Meandering pattern is very common in alluvial streams (Fig. 3.14).

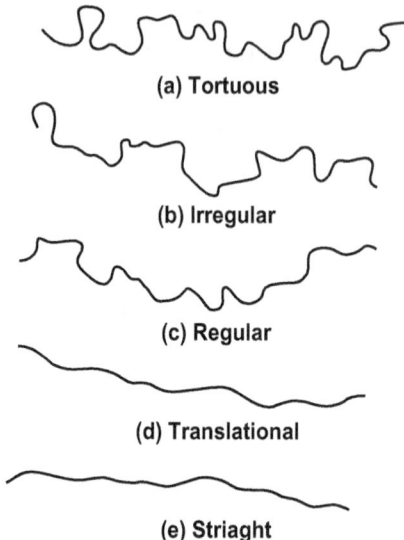

Fig. 3.14 : Rivers in alluvium, classification based on their geometry

In tortuous meandering channels, bends are deformed and smoothness which is typical of meander bends is absent [Fig. 3.14 (a)]. Irregular meanders consist of a pattern of low amplitude and wavelength [Fig. 3.14 (b)] superimposed on a larger pattern. It is suggested that smaller meanders may be related to the periods of low perennial flow, while the larger owe their origin to the mean annual flood. The regular pattern [Fig. 3.14 (c)] shows regular waveform in plan. The transitional pattern is characterised by very flat curves [Fig. 3.14 (d)] and the straight pattern has minor bends without any irregularity [Fig. 3.14 (e)].

Braided river channels are commonly encountered in areas with strong bedload transport. The river is split in numerous diverging channels which reunite again and change their appearance with every major flood [Fig. 3.12 (a)]. While one channel is being filled up, the water scours a new path until the next flood leads to its starvation and widens another. The two primary factors that may be responsible for the braided condition are overloading and steep slopes. Disturbances of a braided reach can be caused by variation in one of these basic parameters. If changes in the supply of bedload are reduced for any reason, braided river quickly lose their characteristic features. Degradation starts to prevail and the network of braided sections is replaced by a stretched channel that cuts itself into the bottom and causes the former channel to fall dry.

(b) Longitudinal sections : The longitudinal profile of a river is one of the most important morphological element, to mark the earth's surface. Their development controls the morphological character of a landscape. The longitudinal profile represents its gradient of the bottom at each point as a reaction to tectonic, lithological and climatic factors. The gradient in the upper reaches is steep, it decreases gradually downstream and is very low at the base for the erosion or at sea level. Thus, every longitudinal profile is divided into upper, middle and lower reaches (Fig. 3.15).

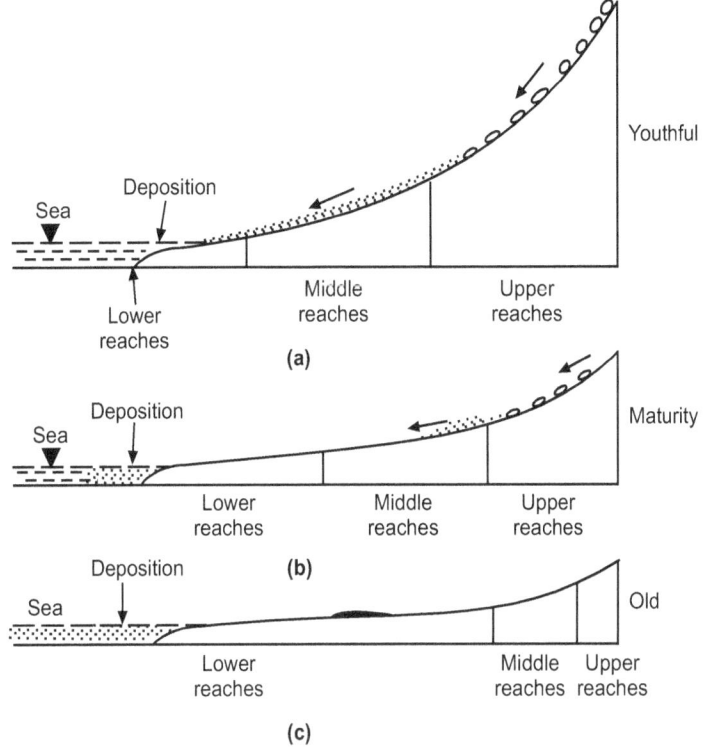

Fig. 3.15 : Stages of denudation

Erosion is predominant in upper reaches, transportation in the middle and accumulation in the lower reaches. It is seen from the Fig. 3.15 that slope and distance of longitudinal profile varies consistantly with stages of denudation. This roughly corresponds with the youthful, maturity and old stage of a river system (Fig. 3.9 and 3.10). In case of a river in youthful stage where erosion is predominant, its slope is steep and distance of upper reaches is much more than that of middle and lower reaches. [Fig. 3.15 (a)]. In the maturity stage, slope is gentle and distance of middle and lower reaches is more than upper reaches [Fig. 3.15(b)]. In the old stage elevation difference between source and month is not significantly large. Lower reaches cover about 80% of the profile compared to middle and upper reaches [Fig. 3.15 (c)].

(c) **Cross-sectional view :** Cross-section on rivers is a direct expression of the controlling forces of erosion and transportation. In every phase of development, a river will show the appropriate cross-sections (Fig. 3.11). Direct or close relationship to the river is developed only for the gorge, the canyon or the V shaped valley. Lateral erosion gradually becoming predominant. This gives rise to valley widening (Fig. 3.11).

In a gorge or V shaped valley of narrow width, the river occupies the entire width of the valley, the bed is rocky and covered by large boulders. While U shaped broad valley indicates that the river has developed its flood plain and except during the flood-time, the river occupies deepest portion of the valley. A characteristic of many low land river is development of levees (Fig. 3.17).

3.2.6 Fluvial Deposition

Deposition of sediment takes place when the velocity of a stream is abruptly reduced because of sharp change in gradient. It occurs where a river flowing smoothly along a steep mountain slope reaches the ground of minimum undulations or plains. Such deposition results in the development of semi-permanent landforms.

The fluvial landforms are developed by fluvial processes of overland flow and channel flow. Thus, rock fragments that are removed from country rock are transported by running water and deposited at favourable sites to form entirely different sets of landforms. A deposition at landform once formed, may be eroded with the result that a new generation of erosional landforms are developed, which we may observe in the present environment.

(a) Alluvium : Alluvium is unconsolidated or semi-consolidated sediment of comparatively recent geologic age that was deposited by flowing water. It covers the bedrock floors of river valleys. Alluvial gravel rarely forms ridges; for example, Tapti Alluvium.

Alluvium deposits may be 'Active Alluvium' and 'Redict Alluvium'. An active alluvium is that sediment now capable of being transported by the stream that flows on it and the depth of which is defined by the flood scour depth of the modern channel. The deeper and coarser alluvium that is not being excavated by the modern streams, is known as 'Relict Alluvium'.

(b) Flood-plain deposits : Sedimentation in flood-plain valleys is explained by lateral migration of channels across the flood plain and by over bank deposition during flood times. Each process gives rise to a distinct suite of deposits and related landforms [Fig. 3.16 and 3.17]. These are summarised in Table 3.5.

Table 3.5 : Flood-plain deposits

Site of Deposition	Characteristics	Name
(1) Channel	(a) Consists largely of bed load and similar sediment forming bars.	Transitory channels.
	(b) Immobile larger particles that are armouring the channel bed. They may be moved only at very high discharge.	Lag deposit
	(c) Accumulations filling aboundoned channels. Particles may be fine or organic.	Channel fills
(2) Channel	Points and alternating bars that have been presented as a result of channel shifting.	Lateral accretion deposits.

... Contd.

(3) Over bank	(a) Fine grained sediments deposited from over bank flood water; including levee and bank swamp deposits.	Vertical accretion deposits.
	(b) Bedload material spread on to flood plains when levees are breached by flood waters.	Splays
(4) Valley margin	(a) Bedload with coarsest material at the fan apex; may have lenses of mudflow deposits.	Fan deposits.
	(b) Deposits derived from slope wash and soil creep, at the base of hill.	Colluvium
	(c) Landslide, rockfall debris at the base of hill, often interbedded with colluvium.	Mass movement deposits.

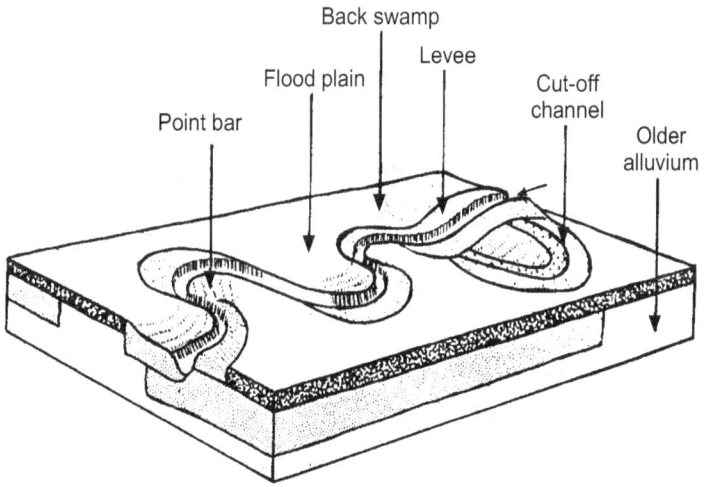

Fig. 3.16 : Flood plain deposits developed by meandering stream

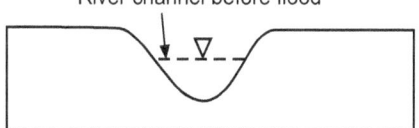

(a) River channel before flood

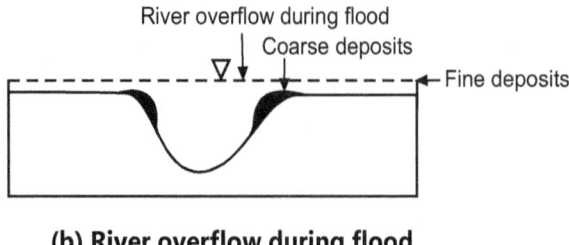

(b) River overflow during flood

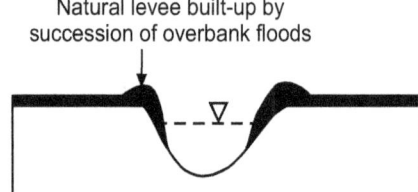

(c) Natural level built up by succession of overbank floods

Fig. 3.17 : Development of natural levees

Flood-plains are built in two fundamental ways by lateral accretion and vertical accretion. Point bars (Fig. 3.16) are the most important deposits of lateral accretion. As a meandering channel migrates across the flood-plain cut bank on the convex side is eroded (Fig. 3.13 and 3.16). The derived load is carried a short distance downstream and deposited as a submerged bar, usually on the same side of the stream due to collapse of the convex side. This gives rise to point bars, a sub-dued relief of low ridges and intervening swales that contain record of many cycles of meandering channel migration. It is seen that deposition at point bars is controlled to a large extent by velocity of water and grain size of particles. The crest of point bars is usually close to the level of the flood-plain. The rate of migration of a meandering channel is a function of erodibility of a river.

As a continuous process of migration, a meandering channel becomes increasingly sinuous untill it is cut-off either at the neck or in between two point bars (Fig. 3.16) to produce ox-bow lake or mort lake. It is a temporary feature which eventually fills with organic matter and sediment deposited from overbank flows (Fig. 3.13).

Large rivers with gentle gradients and an essentially suspended load typically have meandering channels on broad flood plains. When the river is in flood, the velocity in the overbank water may be very low and flood water may spill over slowly towards valley margins. Under these conditions, flood plain deposition is largely by vertical accretion. The abrupt loss of velocity at the edge of flooded channel cause coarser deposition on the natural levees (Fig. 3.17) which grade laterally into backswamp deposits. The levees usually show an asymmetrical section with relatively steep banks against the river [Fig. 3.17 (c)]. When levees extend well above flood-plains they may be breached during floods, called as a **crevasse** and delta like deposit formed on the flood plain, known as *crevasse splay*.

(c) Alluvial fans : The deposits are largely composed of well developed rounded quartz with silts and clays. Flood plain valleys develop due to lateral migration and vertical accretion.

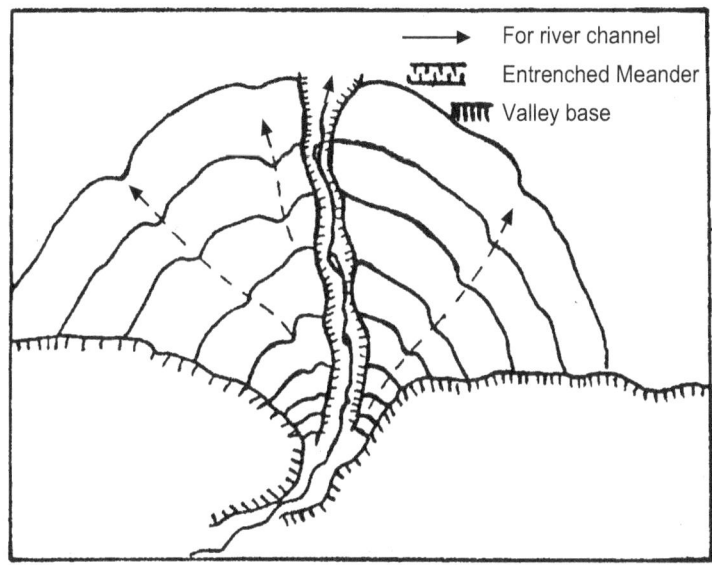

Fig. 3.18 : Geometry of an alluvial fan

Lateral migration occurs with both braided and meandering channels. Braided rivers normally change course when overbank flow spread on the flood plain as a result a new channel system is formed; while abondoned system becomes fossilised and may be filled with fine material and organic matter. Such channel changes tend to be catastrophic. Meandering channels migrate as the outer bank is eroded by undercutting and collapse, and on the inner side of a channel point bar deposition occurs in the form of a cross stratified deposit. The crests of point bars are usually close to the level of the flood-plain.

The rate of migration of meandering channel is a function of erodibility of a river; e.g. the rate of lateral migration of Kosi river is 760 metres/year over several centuries; while in case of Brahmaputra it is 900 metres/year.

An alluvial fan is commonly formed where a high flowing stream experiences sudden loss of velocity at the break of slope between very steep valley wall and the flood-plain. A cone-shaped mass of coarse alluvium with an apex at the point where the stream leaves the mountain slope, gradually accumulates (Fig. 3.18). Their surface morphology is characterised by radiating, branching distributary channels most often braided than meandering. Fans are aggradational. One radial channel may carry most of the discharge until its gradient becomes oversteep by deposition, and the stream may abruptly shift to a low gradient radius. As a continuous process, a uniform conical form is developed because of homogeneous development along all radii. Alluvial fans are characteristic of glacial or arid intermontane regions.

(d) Deltas : Deposition in a flood-plain of a river is often temporary and as an end-process most of the sediment load is carried into the sea or to a lake. Here, the velocity of the running water is checked and a major part of the load is deposited in a triangle-shaped area with apex pointing upstream. The part of the delta which stands above water level is actually a continuation of a flood-plain and is built outward into the sea by successive accumulation of load. Not all deltas have the same shape. The shape is influenced by river discharge and load, grain size, flood frequency and intensity, climate, salinity, temperature etc.

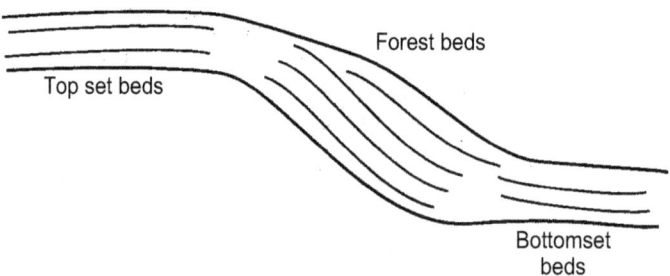

Fig. 3.19 : Delta profile

The cross-section of a simple delta shows three basic depositional features: bottom set beds, foreset beds and topset beds (Fig. 3.19). The foreset beds are made up of the coarser material and each bed is inclined. The bottomset beds are accumulated beyond the foreset beds and consist of thin, horizontal to sub-horizontal lamellae of fine grained sediments while the top set beds, consist of the coarse material of horizontal disposition.

(e) Fluvial terraces : Most flood-plains have a low relief surface like a succession of steps rising up the valley sides. The surface of each terrace demarcates, the position of the flood-plain at an earlier stage in the history of a river valley (Fig. 3.20).

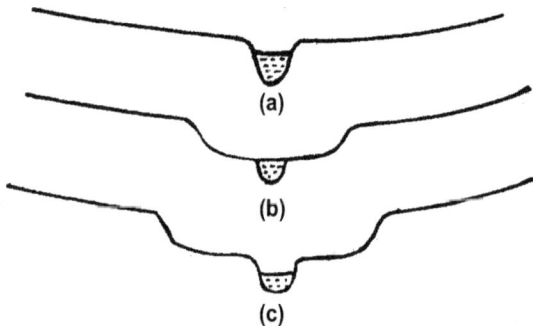

(a) An uplift caused the river to downcut forming a V-shaped valley,
(b) Further erosion widens the valley and old terrace is seen on both sides, and
(c) A new uplift caused further downcutting.
Fig. 3.20 : Fluvial terrace

Alluvial or fluvial terraces may represent aggradation alternating with downcutting and as a result of continuous erosion, the terraces themselves are relics of earlier flood-plain. Thus, the higher terraces are older and are formed when the river had flowed at its highest level. It is important to note that fluvial terraces are cut, not built, by rivers.

The studied fluvial terraces, their longitudinal profile may converge or diverge downstream. Convergence indicates possible rejuvenation because of tectonic uplift. Divergence indicates a progressive lowering of base level more rapidly than the average erosion rate.

Generally, the alluvial (fluvial) terraces are fertile agricultural land which may easily be used for urban growth.

3.2.7 Erosional Landforms

During the process of erosion, the river may give rise to a number of landforms developed under variable conditions. Origin of these landforms is influenced by many factors including composition and structure of rocks, pre-existing morphology, climate, eroding agent etc. Major landforms are as below :

(a) Waterfalls : Waterfall and rapids are amongst the most important fluvial landforms and are potential sites for hydroelectric power generation. A waterfall is a site where water falls vertically; a cataract is a step like succession of waterfalls; while rapids are short steep slopes in the long profile of a stream. These normally occur due to three reasons :

(1) Those resulting from differential erosion of rocks with varying resistance. (Fig. 3.21)

(2) Those which results from deposition in a stream channel (Fig. 3.21).

(3) Those caused by vertical slips in the longitudinal profile (Fig. 3.21).

Horizontal or moderately dipping sequence may contain a resistant layer; such as sandstone, dyke. The resistant rock then forms a cap rock while weaker underlying beds are rapidly eroded (Fig. 3.21 (a)].

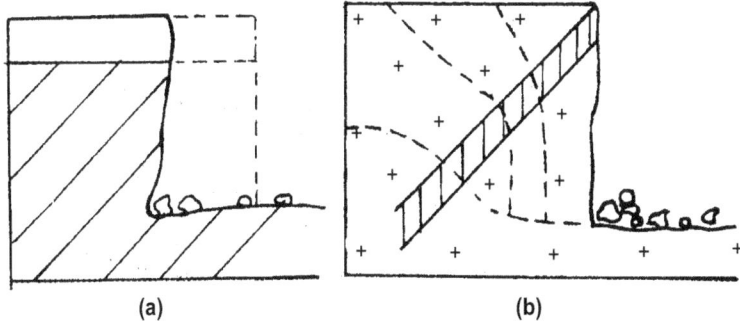

(a)   (b)

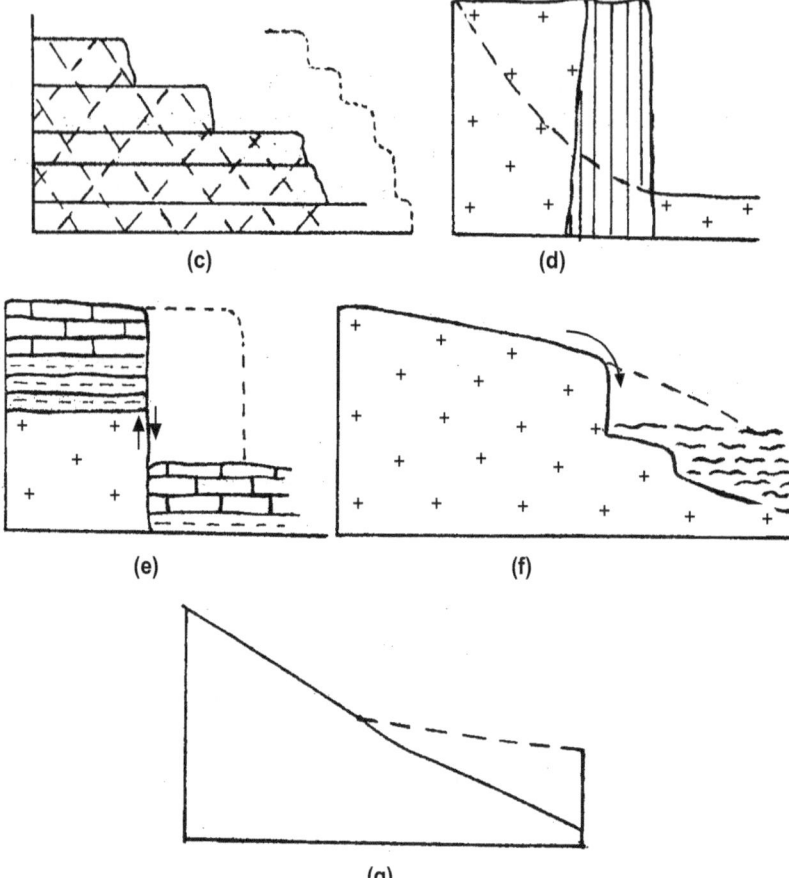

Fig. 3.21 : Causes and controls on the location of waterfalls. Successive positions of waterfalls are indicated by numerals. Note the plunge pools and the tendency to undercut the cap rock in the uppermost diagrams

Step falls develop in rocks with a more uniform erodibility where undercutting occurs along individual bedding planes [Fig. 3.21(b) and (c)]. Single falls also occur where vertical beds juxtapose rocks of varying resistance e.g. dyke [Fig. 3.21 (d)]. Falls are also observed in an area of tectonic uplift [Fig. 3.21(g)], faulting [Fig. 3.21(e)], steep coast [Fig. 3.21(f)].

Rates of waterfall recession are very variable. Retreat is frequently along lines of weakness (faults, joints). In sedimentary rocks, the dip may also control the lifespan of a waterfall, as falls in beds dipping upstream will be gradually reduced in height while horizontal or downstream dipping beds will maintain the falls. It can be said that elimination of waterfall is aided by high velocity, erosive capacity, cavitation and undercutting of cap rock.

(b) Structure controlled landforms : The typical structure controlled landforms shown in Fig. 3.22 are best seen in sedimentary rocks terrains.

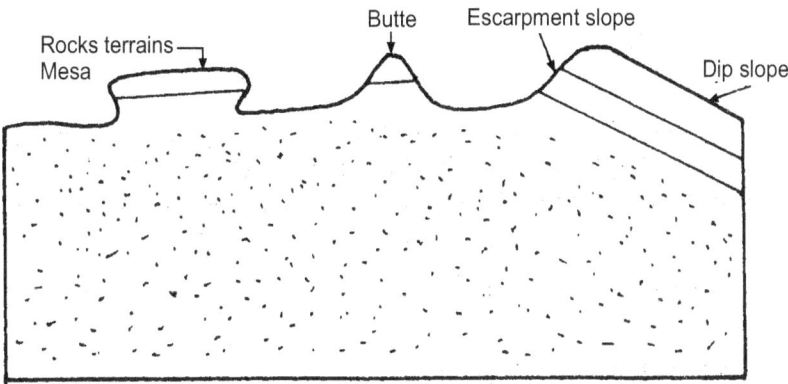

Fig. 3.22 : Structure controlled landforms

If an alternate sequence of tilted hard and soft rock is observed, in such a case after erosion, the outcropping edge of a resistant rock will form an escarpment, while the dip slope is parallel to stratification [Fig. 3.20]. In case, the hard resistant rock is horizontal and caps a broad flat topped table land, it is known as **Mesa**. However, if the diameter of cap rock is lesser than the elevation of a hill above the adjoining areas, the hill is known as **Butte** [Fig. 3.22].

A cuesta is an asymmetrical hill with a gentle dip slope and a steep escarpment slope, while a hogback is an symmetrical hill with the amount of dip slope comparable with the amount of escarpment slope (Fig. 3.22). In case of flat irons, the dip slope is steeper than the escarpment slopes.

Generally, the escarpment streams are steep and short with high gradient. On the other hand, the dip slope streams are gentle and long with low gradient. As a part of continuous process, a stream flowing along the low elevation between an escarpment slope and dip slope, will migrate along down dip direction. Similarly, weathered material may easily be transferred along steeper escarpment slope than along gentler dip slope. Thus, the entire ridge and valley system migrate in downward as well as lateral direction. *The process is known as homoclinal shifting* [Fig. 3.22].

(c) River capture :

Stream capture or piracy is associated with growth of main river and subsequent streams. It is a very common phenomenon controlled by variable geological factors, more likely in areas of weakened and rapidly erodable rock. Fig. 3.23, suggests how this process could occur. Diagnostic features of river capture include,

(a) The sharp change of river course at the site of the diversion; known as the elbow of the capture.

(b) The presence of a col marking the course of the diverted stream prior to the capture, known as the wind gap.

(c) The misfit geometry of the beheaded stream, which is normally abnormal for the valley it occupies.

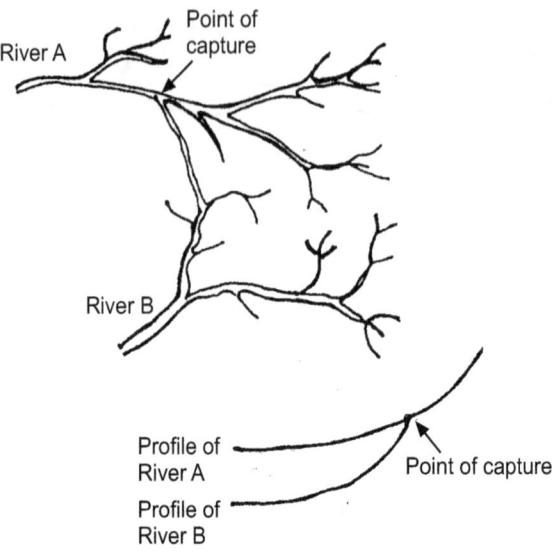

Fig. 3.23

The effects of a capture on the hydraulic geometry of the capturing stream and the beheaded stream can be typical. It is observed that the capturing stream has a relatively steep longitudinal profile in a low order tributary stream at the capture, whereas the beheaded stream has a gentle low profile.

3.2.8 Rejuvenation

A graded stream exhibits a major change in the activity when crust of the earth is subjected to orogenic movements and is uplifted as compared to surrounding areas. Following the uplifting, the river undergoes the process of vertical downcutting in an attempt to re-establish equilibrium grade at a lower level. The process is known as rejuvenation or reactivation. Thus, the features similar to youthful stage of a river may be formed in the graded stream. Therefore, it is also called as **rebirth of a river**.

In case rejuvenation occurs in a peneplain area, a steep sided **narrow gorge** on either side of which lies the former flood-plain is developed above the present channel depth. The flat surface characteristic of flood-plain is known as **rock terrace**.

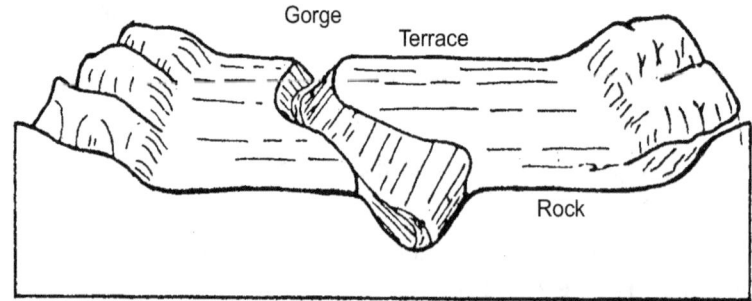

Fig. 3.24 : Incised or Entrenched Meander, a feature indicative of river rejuvenation

Similarly, where the graded stream had developed meanders on a broad flood plain, the process of uplift responsible for rejuvenation causes the meanders to begin active erosion again and excavate its own flood-plain to form entrenched meanders or incised meanders (Fig. 3.24).

Another possible indication of rejuvenation is presence of waterfall/rapid.

3.2.9 Drainage Basins and Patterns

A drainage basin is a limited clearly defined area developed by major river and its tributaries. The divides marking the boundaries between the drainage basins are usually the dominant morphological features e.g. any major mountain range. The water can run off to two sides at uneven velocities controlled by local gradients. In addition, there are also local divides found between various tributaries to the principal river right upto the smallest creeks. Thus, on satellite imageries or on small scale topo sheet a river system gives rise to a tree like branched system; growth of which is controlled by several factors including physical properties of rock, structure and climate. Based on the geometry of tree like branched system on local or regional scale several drainage patterns are recognised (Fig. 3.25). Some of them are summarised in Table 3.6.

Dendritic type is the most frequently developed pattern belongs to the river systems essentially controlled by the bedrock (Fig. 3.25). The main river corresponds to the trunk of a tree, the tributaries of various orders to its branches and twigs. This pattern is called dendritic pattern. In this, the tributaries join the subsequent streams at highly diverse angles.

Table 3.6 : Significance of basic drainage patterns

Drainage Pattern	Significance
1. Dendritic	Horizontal, uniformly resistant bedrock; surface run-off is much more and permeability of rock is less.
2. Trellis	Dipping or folded sedimentary rocks, areas of parallel fractures. Type pattern is recognised in areas where small tributaries are essentially of the same size on opposite sides of long parallel major stream.
3. Rectangular	Joints and / or faults at right angles.
4. Radial and annular patterns	Structural domes and basins; anticlines and synclines.

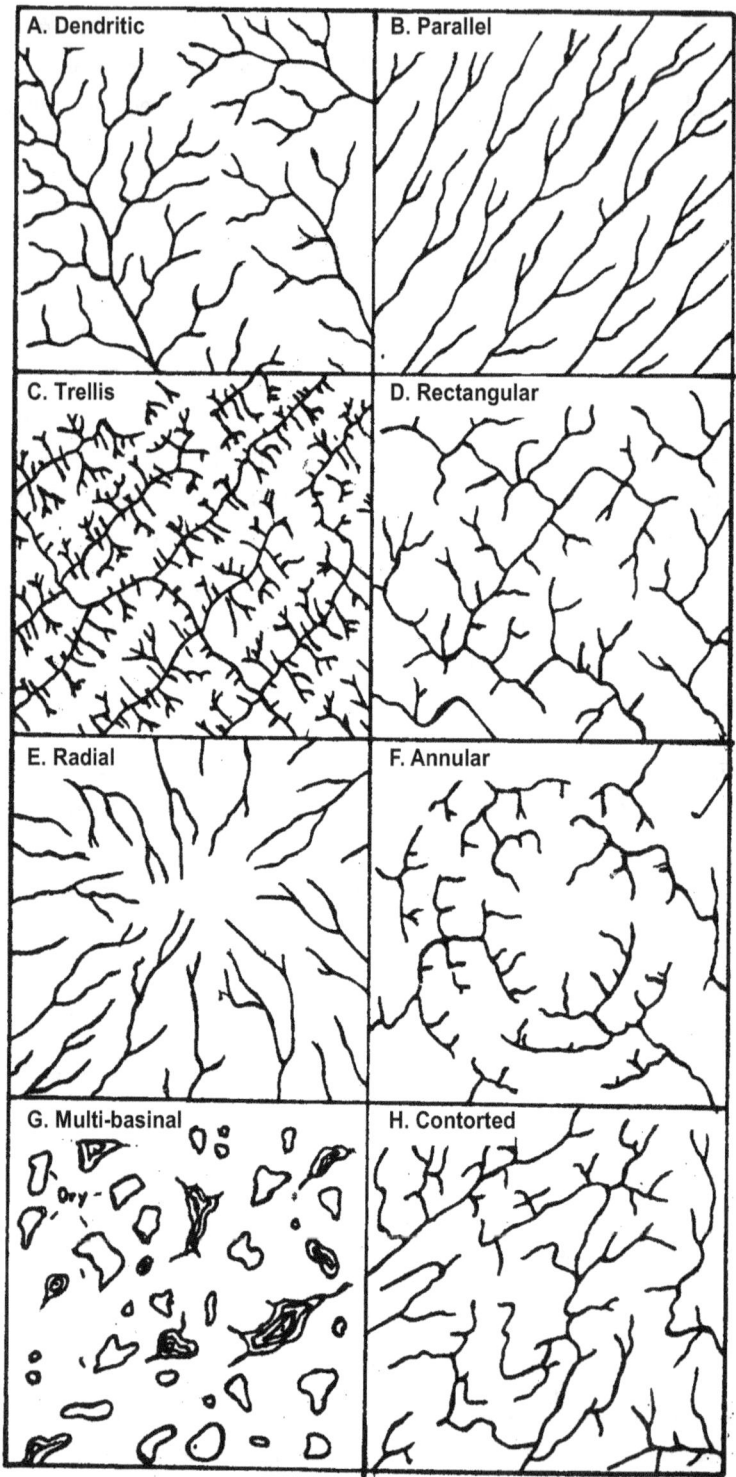

Fig. 3.25 : Basic drainage patterns

Trellis or angular pattern is governed by the succession of escarpments and intervening valleys parallel to the bedding resulting from the differences in weathering and erodibility of these alternations of lithology. The pattern is also developed in areas where horizontal homogeneous massive rocks are cut by parallel fracture zones and intersecting major fault. As a result, the main river follows the easily eroded major fault while the tributaries are controlled by the fracture zones (Fig. 3.25 B, C and D).

Radial and Annular patterns are found in areas of domes, basins, volcanoes, and granite domes (Fig. 3.25 E and F). In the areas of ascent, erosion selectively carves out the harder rocks. Over the rock sequences dipping away from the center a circular topography is developed with concentric valleys and ridges. The consequent streams here flow away radially over the bedding surfaces. They end in the larger subsequent streams which follow the circular strike of the ring structures until they reach a cross cutting gorge through which they flow out and away from ring structures (Fig. 3.25 E and F).

Drainage pattern of the radial or similar types can also be found around plunging axes of anticlines and synclines.

Rivers of high plateaus and Table lands :

These streams may be considered as a special type of mountain rivers. In this system, the river either adjust themselves to the topography and to the geological structures or they form the topography in accordance with the sequence exposed. Following types are recognised (Fig. 3.24).

- **Consequent** streams following the natural slope of the land surface.
- **Subsequent** streams flowing into the consequent streams from the sides at right angles to dip and parallel to strike.
- **Resequent** streams as tributaries to the subsequent streams more or less parallel to the main consequent stream.
- **Obsequent** streams flowing against the dip of the beds.
- **Insequent** streams which show no clearcut relation to the dip of the beds.

All these types are schematically shown in Fig. 3.26.

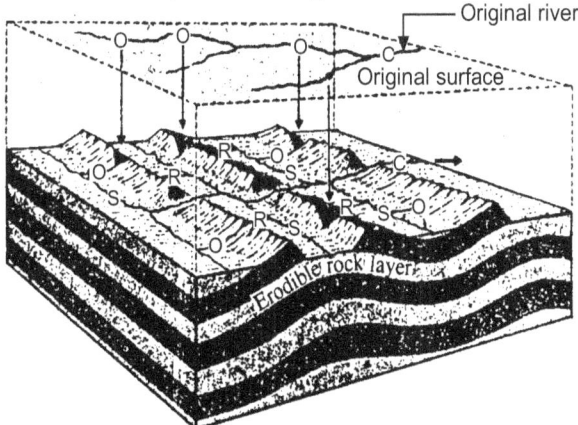

Fig. 3.26 : Development of consequent valley system over an initial landscape. With later erosion subsequent streams become prominent. C — consequent, S — subsequent, R — Resequent and O — Obsequent rivers and valleys

3.2.10 Geological Hazards of Running Water

A typical river valley consists of a channel, a flat area (flood plain) and sloping valley sides. Most of the time, the flow is restricted to the channel, but in case of high flow when the channel cannot carry the water, it spreads towards the margin of valley causing flood. This is the normal expected behaviour of a river. People who live or build structures on flood plains must expect these floods. In other words, the main effect of urbanization is to increase run-off, which, in turn, causes increased erosion followed by deposition of eroded material in downstream areas. The resulting flooding, erosion and deposition may also occur in urbanised area. In a given drainage basin, a rainfall will cause an increase in the inflow of the main stream. The length of the time lag and the amount of increase in the flow will depend upon the amount and intensity of the rainfall as well as on the characteristics of the river. Fig. 3.27 shows an example. Urbanization of a drainage basin will increase both the peak run-off and the total run-off because man made structures reduce the infiltration.

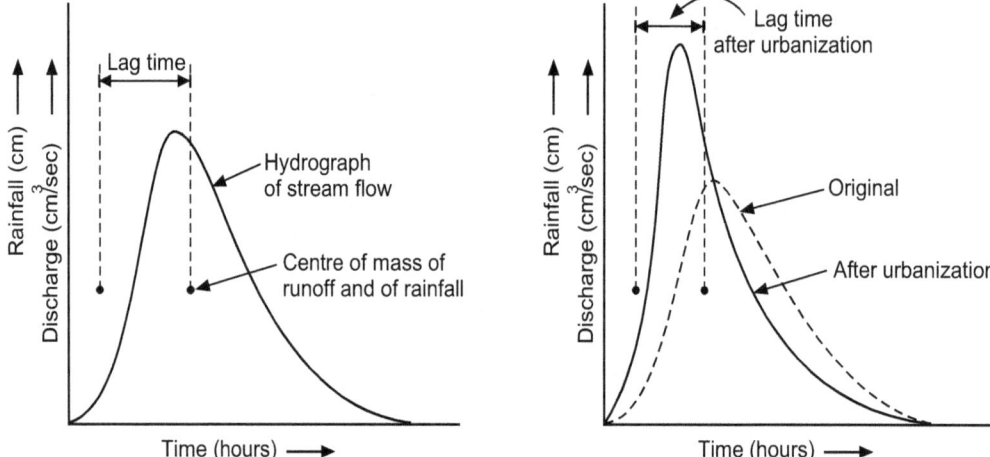

Fig. 3.27 : The effect of urbanization of stream flow.
After urbanization, the peak flow is higher and occurs sooner

The increase in discharge causes increased erosion. The initial effect is a deepening of the channel and removal of accumulated sediment load leading to increase the river capacity so that it can carry more water without flooding. As the main stream deepens, the tributaries also deepens because of lowering of their base level. Gullies may appear at many places in the drainage basin.

The increased run-off means less infiltration and proportionally lesser recharge of groundwater supply.

A dam causes changes in a stream. Dams have finite lives because of sedimentation in the reservoirs. This upstream deposition causes problems especially for farmers whose agriculture ditches are silted up. On the other hand erosion occurs on downstream side. As a result, stream deepens its channels. The tributaries also deepen proportional to the main stream.

The increased erosion caused either by urbanization or dams may make the water muddy. The maximum amount of erosion occurs during the construction phase of urbanization when the natural slope of ground is altered.

3.3 COASTAL PROCESSES

The coastlines of the world (more than 4,40,000 km in length) represent one of the most dynamic of natural environments and one of the most important contexts in which human activity and geomorphological processes interact. These coasts may be the sites of erosion or deposition. Erosional coastlines typically have cliff lines which may be preserved, occasionally, in the geological record as unconformity surfaces. Wave cut platforms of bedrock eroded sub-horizontally at beach level occur along many erosional coastlines. Constructional coastlines have a higher preservation potential if the area is a region of subsidence. They may be sites of accumulation of clastic sediments, carbonate deposits or evaporites.

3.3.1 Morphological Features of Coastlines

The shoreline fluctuates rapidly from time to time influenced by waves and tides.

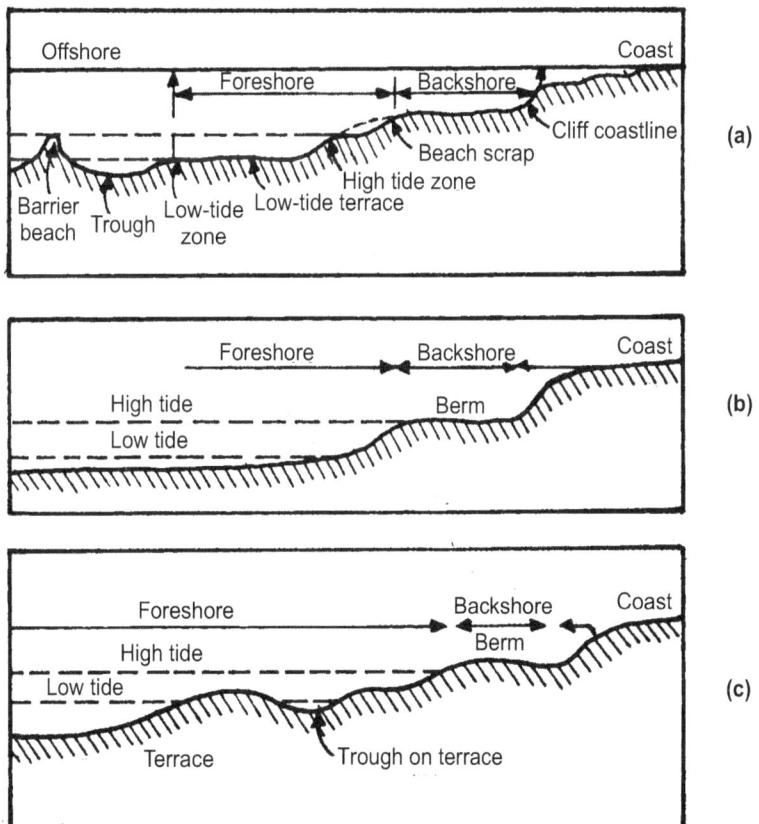

Fig. 3.28 : Shore zone morphology (a) section illustrating terminology used to describe beach slopes and associated features, (b) section through a beach with a backshore, (c) section through a beach having a terrace exposed at low tide

The shore zone is the zone affected by wave action. It is conveniently divided into : (a) the offshore, the shallow bottom seaward of the breaking waves, (b) the nearshore, between low tide level and the breaker zone, (c) the foreshore, which extends from low tide level to the limit of high tide, storm wave effects, and (d) the backshore from the limit of frequent storm waves landwards to the base of a cliff, dune or vegetated beach ride. The shorezone is represented in Fig. 3.28. Coastal environment may be divided into **the beach zone, the perched zones on steep slopes above the sea, esturies and deltas.**

The beach zone or shore is the area of loose sediments extending from low water level to maximum water level reached by tide water or swash. The upper limit is marked by dunes or by permanent vegetation. The loose sediments consist essentially of sand. Beaches at the lower edges of sea cliffs and include large rock fragments eroded from the cliffs and worn smooth by wave attack. Beaches that consist entirely of pebbles or cobbles are known as **shingle beaches**, other shores may consist of mud and rapidly convert to marshes.

A cliffed shore zone includes both land and sea areas. These may be active or inactive/passive. Active or live cliffs are those where marine erosion is active and the cliff surface is vertical or very steep [Fig. 3.29 (a)]. In many cases, wave action is restricted, (sheltered bays) because of the presence of a large cliff foot. Cliffs are reduced in angle over geologic time so that they are no more subjected to erosion, are known as inactive or dead cliffs [Fig. 3.29 (b)].

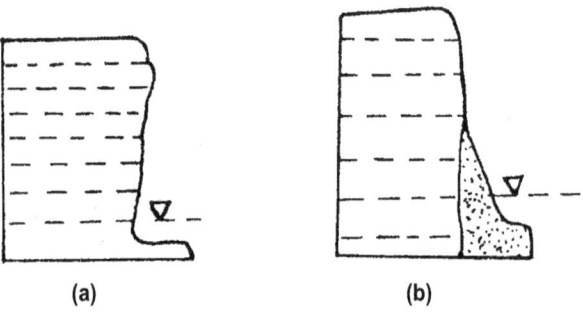

Fig. 3.29 : The cliff faces

The cliff profiles are strongly influenced by geological structures including angle and direction of rock dip, discontinuities and composition of a rock.

In case of horizontal beds, cliffs are vertical [Fig. 3.30 (a)]. Often the rocks dip gently towards sea and joints are vertical or normal to the bedding plane [Fig. 3.30 (b)]. In this, joints are widened because of weathering and the cliff may be seen partially overhanging. Thus, columnar masses are removed to give large boundary accumulations at the cliff base.

Where beds are sloping towards sea (20° or more) and joints are parallel to bedding plane, the cliff profile is represented by smooth rock slabs [Fig 3.30 (c)], width of which is decided by the spacing between joints.

Where the beds dip inland and traversed by irregular joints, there is a greater stability; as the rock mass remains in-situ even when loosened [Fig. 3.30 (d)]. The resultant cliff is very steep. On the other hand, where dip is steeper and joints developed are normal to the bedding planes, the joints can act as slip planes and the resultant cliff will be less steep [Fig. 3.30 (e)].

In general, it can be said that marine erosion is influential along lines of structural weakness, bedding planes etc. As a result, cliff faces are rather smooth in profile, otherwise the profile of a cliff is irregular.

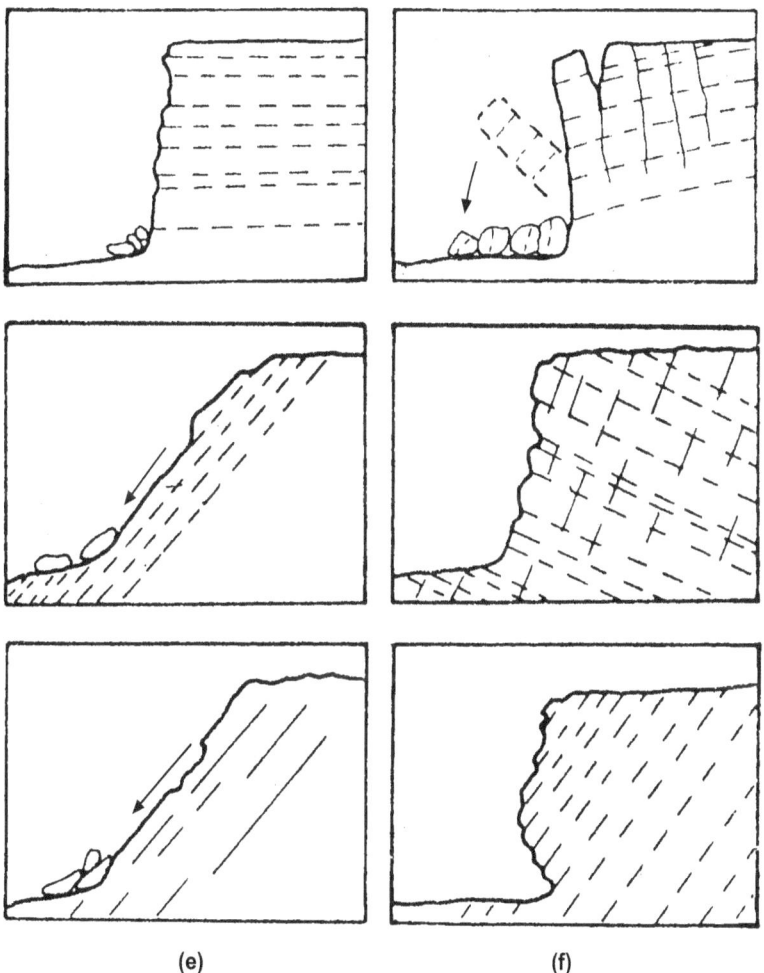

(e)   (f)

Fig. 3.30 : Influence of geological structure on the development of a cliff

On the other hand, the form of a constructional coastline is determined by the supply of sediment, the wave energy, the tidal energy and the climate. Sediment accumulation occurs where the waves break on a beach dune ridge and in backshore areas of the coastal plain.

Where wave energy is sufficiently strong, sand and gravel material may continuously be reworked on the foreshore. At the top of the beach, a ridge called as a berm marks the division between the backshore and foreshore (Fig. 3.28).

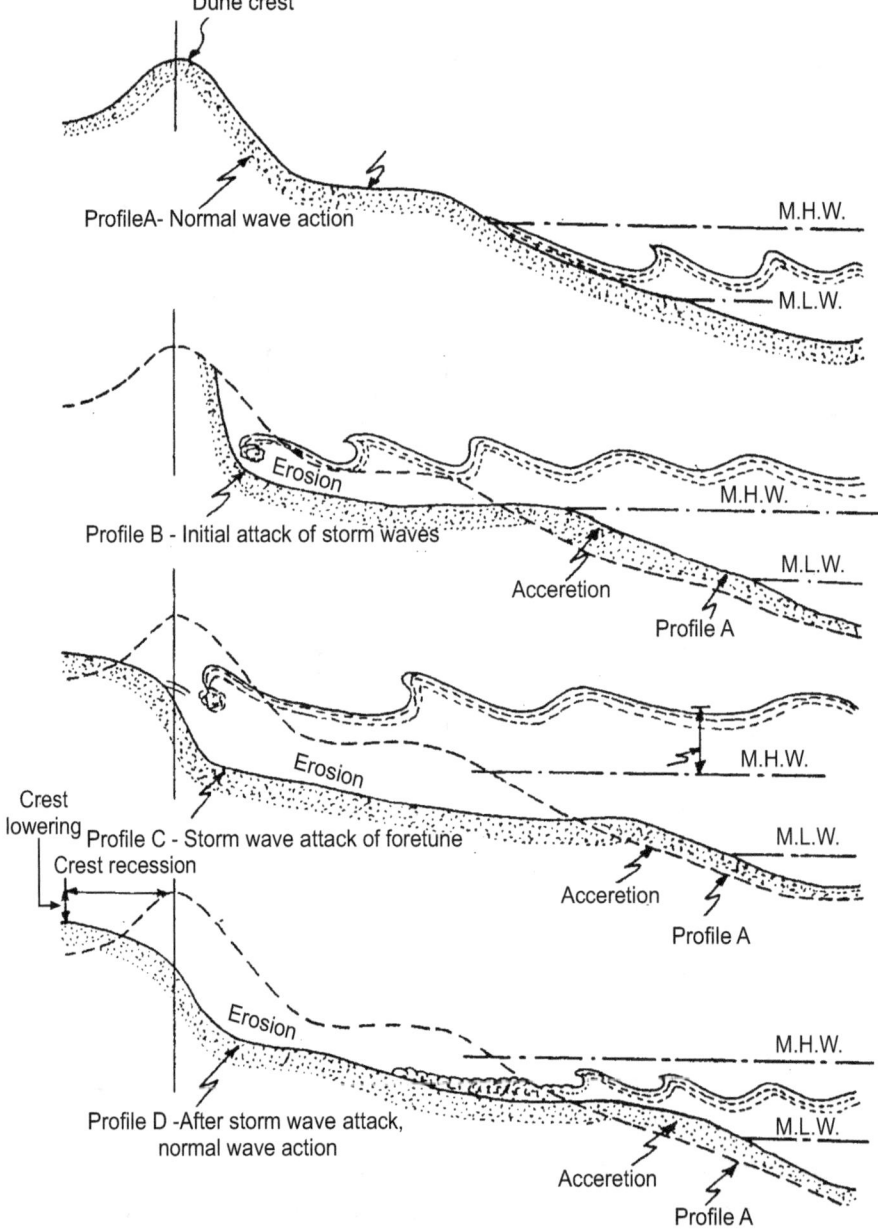

**Fig. 3.31 : Profiles of a beach showing low storm waves erode a shoreline.
M. H. W. = Mean High Water; M.L.W. = Mean Low Water.
(From U.S. Army coastal Engineering Research Center, 1984)**

Water only washes over the top of the berm under storm surge condition. Sediment carried by the waves over the berm crest is deposited on the landward side forming layers which dip gently landward. Sand washed up the beach and the backshore area is further subject to reworking by wind action. Onshore winds may remove sand from the top of the beach and redeposit it as **aeolien dunes** (Fig. 3.31).

Lagoons are areas of quiet condition and low energy sedimentation. They are permanent bodies of water with limited access to the open ocean (Fig. 3.32).

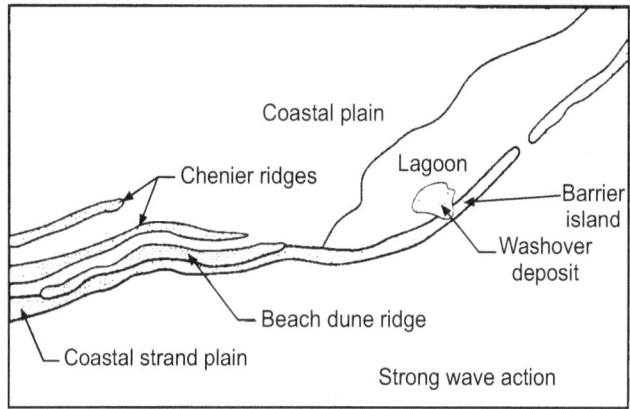

Fig. 3.32 : Morphological features of a wave dominated coastline

Coastal plains are low-lying areas adjacent to seas (Fig. 3.32). They are part of coastal environment and often influenced by the adjacent oceanic action when storm surges result in excessive flooding by sea water.

A barrier island is a beach detached from the main coast to form a ridge of sediment parallel to the coast. Long linear barrier islands form easily along coast with a low tidal range and high wave energy (Fig. 3.32).

Behind some beaches a series of ridges are often seen parallel to the coastlines (Fig. 3.32), called **chennier ridges**. They are relicts of former beaches which have been left inland as the shoreline prograded. They are composed of sandy or shelly debris and are separated by areas of finer grained sediments which forms a marshy land.

Perched zones are the parts of the coastal zone above base level; and at the crest or close to the edge of the scarp or on the scarp itself. Coastal zone may often exhibit the presence of a succession of terraces separated by cliff representing old sea cliffs. Base of each cliff marks a former sea face.

An estuary is that portion of the lower course of a river system that experiences tides. Estuaries with their associated marshes are drowned valleys. Marsh grasses spread rapidly over the soft muds of estuaries and coastal flats. In tropical areas, mangroves are developed in place of marsh grass.

Deltaic environment differ from estuaries in many ways. The details of delta are given in sub-section 3.2.6 and hence not discussed here.

3.3.2 Shore Processes

The sea effects change through storm waves, surge waves and certain currents with minor factors are the standing waves and coastal winds.

Waves :

There are two main types of waves : waves of oscillation and waves of translation. The waves of oscillation are found outside the breaker zone. The water particles follow a more or less circular orbit with no or little change in position. Waves of translation have only a crest without a complimentary trough. The wave particles are displaced forward without a compensating backward motion. Objects are directly moved ahead.

The orbit of wave of oscillation becomes smaller with depth. On approaching the shore, the orbital energy is restricted to a smaller depth of water, resulting in increased orbital velocity and amplitude of waves. Waves generally break when the depth of water below the trough is a little greater than half the height of the wave.

Short steep waves generated by storms near the coast tend to destruct a beach down by removing material from just the still water level and carrying it into deeper water. Long low waves tend to rebuild beaches by bringing material in from shallower water and depositing it just above the still water level.

On an irregular coast, headlands are subjected to more concentrated wave attack than intervening embankment due to wave refraction. Waves slow down as they enter shallow water. The remainder of the wave, running more freely on either side, thus envelopes the headland. As the wave breaks, first at headland and progressing around the sides, the wave energy is concentrated inward on the headland. Erosion is more rapid at the headlands. Along many rocks cliffed coasts, selective wave attack at the base of a cliff may excavate caves. Enlargement of a cave may so thin the roof that it collapses.

Currents and Drifts :

Littoral or longshore currents :

Longshore currents and to a lesser extent, tidal currents have direct effect on coasts. Littoral currents are caused by obliquely approaching waves which may transport enormous quantities of sediment along the shore. The littoral transport takes place on the beach zone, in the surf zone and in a zone beyond the breakers down to depth of 30 m.

Beach drift is the movement of sediment along the beach. When an obliquely approaching wave breaks, the surf is thrust obliquely towards the shore and the swash rushes obliquely up the beach. The swash returns as backwash under the influence of gravity. Longshore drift also occurs in the surf zone where sediment and material placed in suspension by the breaking waves are moved laterally parallel to coast.

Tidal currents : The tides caused by the gravitational attraction of the moon are regular and predictable at any area. The range of tide varies from place to place. The range is greatest when the sun, moon and earth are in line with the moon either between the sun and the earth (no moon) or on the far side of the earth from the sun (full moon). Tides are also influenced by lattitude, distribution and configuration of the continents and weather.

3.3.3 Shoreline Changes

Shoreline changes may be slow or fast, erosional or depositional and may be associated with rise and fall of sea level. They may be monitored using topographic maps, bathy metric charts, aerial photographs and satellite imageries.

The most important change is seen in the form of fluctuations in sea water level. It may be local or worldwide. The most recent fluctuations are related to waxing and waning of the great ice sheets during pleistocene times. It is estimated that during times of maximum glaciation there may be lowering of sea level as much as 130 m than now. Similarly, during interglacial stages, sea level may rise by 60 – 90 m than now. Alongwith sea level fluctuations, tectonic forces are also responsible in elevating some coastal areas and depressing others. Thus, it is quite likely that some coastal areas may be subjected to flooding and others to deposition.

Problems associated with coastal erosion and sediment transfer are often associated with coastal flooding. There may be extensive damage in terms of settlements, human lives and damage to properties.

When sea level rises substantially, one obvious result is development of estuaries. Additionally, the submergence of areas of complex relief gives rise to many islands. On the other hand, raised beaches are formed due to falling sea levels. They generally take the form of raised wavecut platforms or raised beach platforms of variable width and backed by a degraded cliff, on which beach deposits and the raised beach proper are preserved. The latter is identifiable by the presence of typically rounded beach cobbles and pebbles, beach sands and marine shells. In addition to raised beach platform, the modern wavecut platforms may be eroded across at two to three levels indicating proportional changes in sea level.

3.3.4 Preventive Measures

The emplacement of engineered structures in the shoreline zone is one of the strategies that may be adopted in any coastal management schemes. The protection schemes can be placed in three major categories : (a) those that inhibit direct wave attack which include seawalls, bulkheads, reventments and breakwaters, (b) those designed to inhibit the transport of sand by currents which include jettis built at bays and inlet and groins, and (c) those that change the beach zone topography such as sand dunes and artificial beach nourishment.

Seawalls, Reventments and Bulkheads :

These structures are built parallel to shores, separating the land from wave action. Their purpose is to absorb wave energy and to prevent direct attack on man-made structures. They may consist of concrete, riprap, steel and timber.

Breakwater : Breakwaters are structures that protect a harbour portion of the shoreline. They impose artificial condition on approaching waves, i.e. there is refraction and diffraction of the waves which absorb and dampen wave energy. However, beaches downdrift from the structure may be excessively eroded by the sand – starved currents.

3.4 GLACIAL PROCESSES

The importance of ice in erosion, transport and deposition is visualised by the present day extent of ice sheets and ice caps which cover an area of about 15 million km² of the earth's surface. Three major types are recognised; extensive ice caps or ice sheets, valley glaciers and mountain glaciers. In addition to the areas covered by ice, there are extensive land surfaces (North America, Siberia etc.) which experience a very cold climate with severe winter freezing and a comparatively warm summer. Thus, the accumulated snow is removed by melting each year. Such land is characterised by periglacial environment which covers an area of 20 per cent of the earth's land surface.

3.4.1 Profile of a Glacial Valley

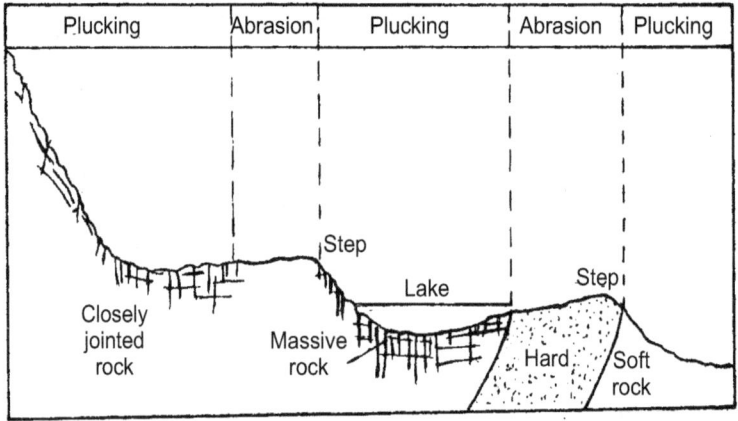

Fig. 3.33 : Typical long profile of a glacial valley

(a) Glacial valleys are commonly U-shaped with broad valley floors (valley troughs) bounded on both sides by gently sloping valleys. Glaciers and ice sheets are believed to erode mainly by two processes, that is, abrasion and plucking.

Abrasion is the *process of scratching and polishing of the rock surfaces*. It is effective when basal sliding is prominent (Fig. 3.33). The particles used in abrasion are subject to a considerable wear and are finally reduced to sand and silt that can be easily washed out along with the finer particles by basal melt water streams which gives to the stream their milky appearance. Thus, the landforms resulting from abrasion are striated, polished or scratched.

Plucking is the *process of excavation or detachment from bed rock or large fragments upto a metre or more in diameter*. It is an effective process where the rock is jointed or the rock is weakened by some other process. As a result, irregular rock-faces with the appearance of having been quarried are developed on the down slope valleys (Fig. 3.33).

Jettis and Groynes : Jettis are built at inlets to protect navigation channels whereas groynes are often built beyond the breaker zone. They are like dams, permeable or impermeable, high or low, long or short.

However, both structures prevent longshore material from entering the channel. As a result sand is generally deposited on the updrift side.

(b) The unsorted disintegrated fragments are transported by the glaciers on the ice surface (supraglacial), within the ice (englacial) and at the base of glacier (sub-glacial) (Fig. 3.34).

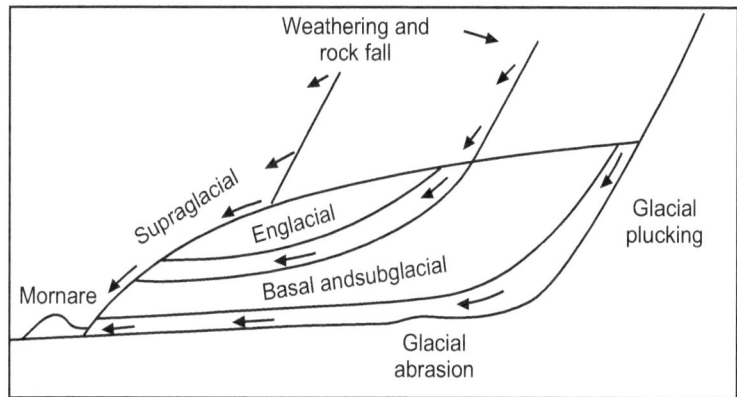

Fig. 3.34 : Transportation characteristic of glaciers

From the (Fig. 3.34), it is seen that sub-glacial material is derived from plucking and abrasion. As a result, the transported debris become fine grained. The supraglacial material can fall directly on to the glacial margins.

(c) The sediment load is transported and deposited by melt water. Supraglacial material tends to be concentrated along the margins, known as *lateral moraine* or may be along the central line of the glacial as *medial moraine*. These two grow into ice ridges upto 30 metres above the glacial surface. Sediment can also be deposited at the base of the glacier, while the englacial material melts out at the glacial surface near the snout, thus forming one metre thin layer of ablation moraine. These two gives rise to ill-sorted till deposits or tillites.

(d) The cross-sections of large glacial valleys often show the presence of a valley in valley with the peculiar shaped trough entrenched into a more open lower valley. This may perhaps be preglacial river valley. Due to overdeepening of the main valley, tributary valleys are formed, occupied by smaller and temporary glaciers. These valleys are known as **hanging valleys**. The almost vertical trough is succeeded down valley by horizontal to sub-horizontal benches or rock basins bounded on sides by solid massive rocks (rock steps). The features are well-illustrated in Fig. 3.34. Such profiles are formed due to the process of overdeepening so that basins or depressions coincide with exposures of weak jointed rocks. While the hard massive rocks that are abraded on the up glacier slope and are plucked on the down glacier slope (Fig. 3.34). These mounds are known as **roches moutonnes**.

Glacial cirques are long depressions, bounded by steep head and side walls. When seen in plan, they are arcuate in shape. The most important features of a cirque are : smooth abraded floor, plucked walls, small lakes formed due to melt water and typical uneven rock walls which are smoothened on inner side and plucked on other side.

3.4.2 Glacial Deposits

Two kinds of glacial deposits are recognised, namely, till or unstratified drift and stratified drift. Commonly one type grades into the other. Till is deposited directly by ice, whilst stratified drift or tillite is deposited by melt water issuing from the ice.

Deposits of till consist of a variable proportion of unsorted rock debris ranging from fine rock flour to boulders. Angular sharp fragments are of common occurrence. The compactness of a till varies according to the degree of consolidation, amount of cementation and size of grains.

A moraine is an accumulation of drift deposited directly from a glacier which gives rise to till. There are different types of moraine deposited by valley glaciers. Lateral moraine is a collective rock debri which a glacier wears from its valley sides and which is supplimented by material that falls from the valley slopes above the ice.

A medial moraine develops from the merger of two lateral moraines. Terminal moraine is a material which is deposited at the snout of a glacier when the rate of wastage is balanced by the rate of outward flow of ice. Terminal moraine are usually discontinuous with smooth curved outline. Ground moraine is formed when basal ice becomes overloaded with rock debris and is forced to deposit some of it. As a result, ground moraine is distributed irregularly.

Stratified deposits of drift are often subdivided into two sub-categories namely, those develop in contact with ice and those accumulate beyond the limit of ice, forming in streams, lakes and even in seas. Locally, the sediment possess a wide range of grain size, shape and sorting. They often exhibit sharp changes in their physical properties.

The tills and stratified deposits of drift give rise to number of landforms.

Kames are mounds of stratified drift which originate as a fan built against the snout of a glacier where a tunnel in the ice, along which meltwater travels, emerges.

Eskers are long, narrow, sinous, ridge like masses of stratified drift which are unrelated to surface topography. They represent sediments deposited by stream which are flown within channels in a glacier. They are composed of sands and gravels. Eskers may be exposed for a length of few tens of kilometres with a width upto 200 m.

3.4.3 Glacial Hazards

Glacial hazards are grouped into two broad catagories : avalanche, and glacial outbursts and flooding. The time involved in the different types of glacial hazard varies significantly (Table 3.7)

(a) Avalanches : The rapid movement of detached masses of ice and snow under the influence of gravity is a very serious hazard in mountain areas. There may be a clearcut distinction between ice, snow and slush avalanches.

Ice avalanches which usually occur at a glacier snout, arise from the instability of ice on a steep slope in which ice separates by detachment and sliding. It may be caused due to crevasse formation and occurrence of an earthquake.

Table 3.7 : Types of glacial hazard

Time	Hazard	Description
Minutes	Avalanche	Slide or fall of large mass of ice, snow and/or bedrock
Hours	Glacial outburst	Catastrophic discharge of water under pressure from a glacier.
Days to week	Flood	Areal coverage mostly by water.
Minutes to years	Glacial surge	Rapid increase in rate of glacial flow.
Years to Decades	Glacial fluctuations	Variation in ice front due to climate changes.

Snow avalanches occur when the weight of a snow mass exceeds the frictional resistance of the surface on which it lies. They are originated due to several factors including metorological condition, snow structure and mechanics, structural weakness in snow masses melting and overriding. Geomorphologically, the important terrain conditions are slope inclination, length, orientation and roughness.

Slush avalanche is a water saturated form of rapid mass snow movement. It is generally associated with weak cohesionless coarse grained snowpacks. The process do not require steep slopes in the beginning and it develops in drainage channels, depressions and open fields.

Avalanche location may be predicted from historical evidence relating to previous avalanche combined with topographic data. As a result, it is possible to produce hazard maps of avalanche prone areas.

Glacier floods result from the sudden release of water impounded in, on, under or adjacent to a glacier. Water pressure may build up within a glacier to an extent where it exceeds the strength of ice with the result that the ice is ruptured. This leads to development of internal drainage channel. Progressive enlargement of internal drainage channels also leads to an increase in discharge. Eventually, water which is dammed by ice may cause the ice to become detached from the rockmass where it rests. The ice is then buoyed up, allowing the water to drain from the ice-dammed lake. Discharge of several thousand cubic metres per second may occur from such lakes. Generally, these outbursts occur during summer season. The resulting flood often carry huge quantities of debris.

Glacial fluctuations are encountered in response to climatic changes. The advance of a glacier into a valley can lead to the river which occupies the valley being dammed with land being inundated as a lake forms. This may lead to a disaster of the ice dams.

3.5 EOLIAN PROCESSES AND LANDFORMS

Wind is a comparatively minor agent of erosion essentially due to low density of air as compared to that of rock and water. Rock fragments are 2000 times heavier than the air. Thus, the moving air exerts a very low pressure which may be responsible for the transportation of very fine particles.

Eolian processes are most common in arid regions where lack of vegetation makes erosion, transportation and deposition very easy. The eolian processes are also prominent in the humid tropical zones, precisely the coastal parts.

(a) Wind erosion occurs either by deflation, the process of removing loose sand and dust or by abrasion. It produces small characteristic landforms.

When an alternate sequence of hard and soft sedimentary rocks is subjected to wind erosion, the underlying weak rock is excavated forming tabular masses of hard rock upto 30 metres in height. The resultant feature is known as **Zeugen** [Fig. 3.35 (a)]. Another form is **yardang**, an elongated ridge formed parallel to wind direction. Yardangs show basal undercutting at their upward wind ends [Fig. 3.35 (b)].

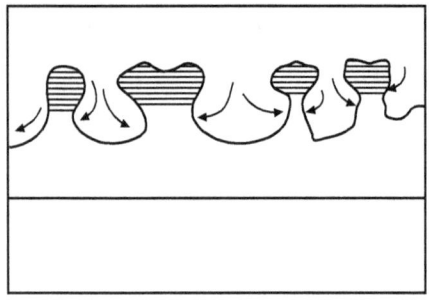
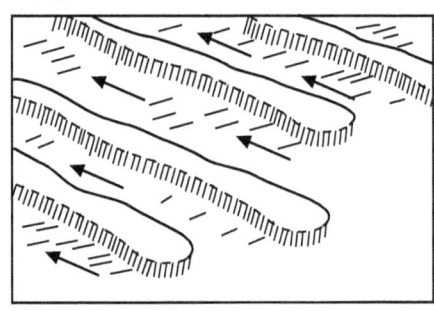

(a) Zeugen　　　　　　　　　　(b) Yardangs

Fig. 3.35 : Typical features of wind erosion

An important feature resulting from wind erosion is deflection hollow. This attains a depth of 130 metres below sea level and is considered as a regional feature to have involved the removal of 3000 cubic kilometres of rock. These are formed along structurally weak zones and with the presence of moisture along them may lead to localised chemical weathering. As process continues, the basin floor becomes wet and marshy.

(b) The arid regions show a large accumulation of wind blown sand, thus forming sand dunes of various scales and forms. The dunes may cover an area of a few hundred square kilometres, known as **whale backs**. These are best developed in Sahara. Smaller dunes are commonly of two types, the **transverse crescentic (barchan) and the longitudinal (seif)**.

Barchans are formed prominently due to unidirectional wind [Fig. 3.26 (a)]. These are characterised by gentle wind ward slope of 10 to 15 degrees and comparatively steeper leeward slope of 25 to 30 degrees.

Once the structure of a dune is formed, the fresh sand is then transported up the gentle wind ward slope, over the dune crest and on to the steep lee slope of the dune. Thus, the dune migrates down wind direction [Fig. 3.36 (a)]. The rate of migration is slowest at the centre and more rapid at its extremities. Thus, horns are formed.

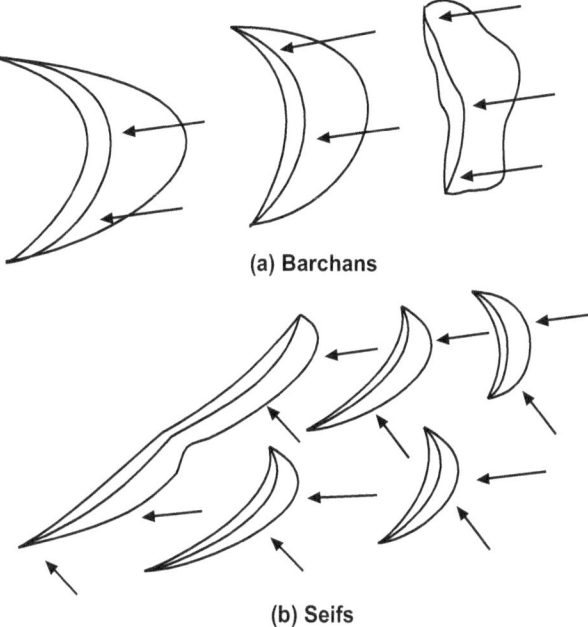

Fig. 3.36 : Types of dune

The longitudinal dunes are known as seif which are developed parallel to the wind direction. They are asymmetrical in profile. The seif may be formed because of combined action of main wind and cross-wind [Fig. 3.36 (b)] over two adjacent barchan dunes.

(c) **Loess :** Loess is usually fine grained unstratified soft yellowish or brownish colour material. It varies in mineral composition from one location to another, but commonly it is made up of quartz, other silicate minerals and calcite. The wind blown deposits are mostly observed in North China, Europe and North America. In these areas, the loess plains have developed rich black soils suited to cultivation of grains.

From the grain size analysis, it is evident that 5 to 10 per cent of the particles fall into coarse clay grade and about the same proportion may be very fine sand and the average grain size fall in the range of 0.005 to 0.006 mm, equivalent to silt size particles. The deposits are formed due to combined effect of deflection and saltation.

Though loess deposit is stable in natural state, but when reworked or exposed in artificial cut, it looses its original cohesion and undergoes rapid erosion.

Loess has seldom shown stratification, if present, is believed to be developed in water. The unstratified loess form vertical cliff walls eventhough the material is soft enough to cut with a knife.

3.6 LAKES

Lakes form when there is supply of water to a topographic low on the land surface. They are very sensitive to climatic changes. Lakes have a huge variety of different characteristics. They may be very large or very small, deep or shallow, natural or man made. Freshwater or saline, perennial or seasonal. They vary in size from small cut off channel or ox-bow lake to as large as inland sea. For example, Caspian Sea in Central Asia with a total area of 3,71,800 km^2 and Lake superior, North America with an area of 83000 km^2.

Large lakes often exhibit characteristics very similar to those of seas or oceans. Wind blowing over large lakes can generate waves of sufficient size to result in erosion process similar to those at the sea coast. Another similarity between lakes and seas is the creation of deltas where rivers flow into them and lakes even have a type of tidal movement known as **seiche**.

Lakes may be formed through several processes. A significant number of lakes are formed as a result of crustal or tectonic movement, volcanic activity or as a result of changes in relative sea level. Tectonic activity involves subsidence or downfaulting of a block of a land e.g. Lake Victoria in East Africa and Lake Baykal in Central Asia (1949 m deep)

Craters are frequently created by volcanic eruptions and under suitable circumstances, these hollows may be filled with water after volcanic activity is ceased e.g. crater lake in ovegon with a diameter of 9 km. In rare instances, a lava flow or accumulation of other volcanic material may block a valley to form a lake.

A second group of processes responsible for lake formation involves erosion of various kinds. Moving bodies of ice are probably the most important of these erosion agents. They form deep rounded hollows known as circques of corries that have a rock in deepened basins scoured out by glaciers. They are called ribboned lake. In lowland areas, glacial topography often produce landforms that favour formation of temporary lakes.

Another type of erosion that produces lakes is solution particularly in karst topography where rock material is dissolved in acidic water. The process may give rise to steep sided hollows known as swallow holes upto 30 m deep which can fill up with water if they either lie below the water table or become clogged with inwashed clay.

Deflation, the erosive action of wind in desert regions, can also produce hollows of substantial size. If the hollows are eroded down to a level below that of water table, they become shallow swamps or saline lakes.

There are rare examples of lakes that have developed in the impact craters of large meteorites. Lonar lake in Buldhana district, and Ashanti crater in Ghana are best examples in support of this.

A third group of processes which form lakes involves various types of deposition. Glacial deposits are often laid down in irregular sheets, in which the numerous hollows may fill up with water. Kettle lakes are lakes formed in hollows produced by the melting of blocks of ice.

River deposits also form lakes. Common examples' occur where ox-bow lakes form due to meander cut-off; and the building of natural levees on both sides of river channels which prevent flood waters flowing back into the river channel creating flood plain lakes. In coastal areas, this action produces delta lagoons though these are partly sealed by marine deposits.

Lacustrine Deposits :

Deposition in lakes is controlled by depth and chemistry of water, and sediment supply. The shallow lake margins are generally sites of the coarsest sediment deposition (Fig. 3.37).

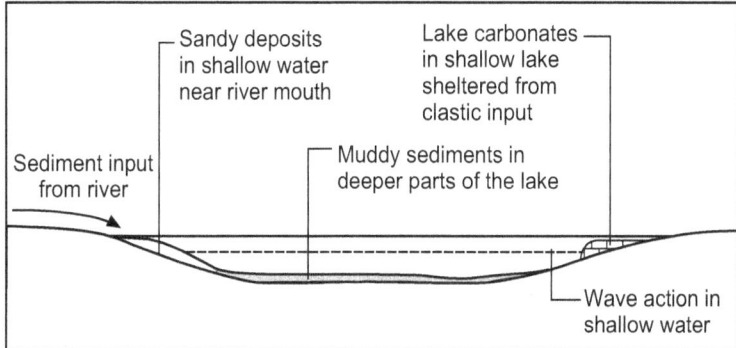

(a) Sedimentation in lacustrine condition

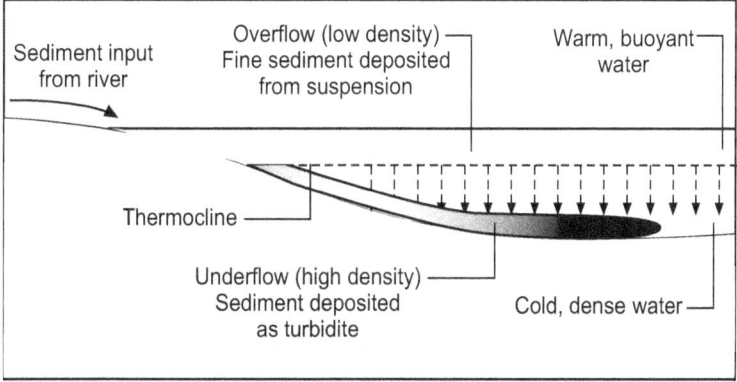

(b) Distribution of sediments in lakes related to lake stratification

Fig. 3.37 : Depositional pattern in lakes

Where a sediment laden river enters a lake, a delta forms as coarse material is deposited at the river mouth. Away from the river mouth, the lake shore deposit depends on the strength of winds generating waves and currents in the lake basin. Strong wind driven currents can redistribute sandy material around the edges of lake (Fig. 3.37). On the other hand, weak wind driven currents lake deposits tend to be fine grained. At the centre of lake, sedimentation takes place due to density variation and sediment dispersal. Generally, muddy sediments undergo deposition in deeper parts of the lake. Often inorganic precipitation of lime mud results from evaporation, temperature variations and chemistry of water.

Eliminations of Lakes :

Lakes are always temporary features. They may disappear after earth tremors (temporarily), lowering of water table, sedimentation and also due to tectonic forces.

Climatic changes may produce changes in lake level. For example, ice dammed lakes may disappear if the water is able to escape under the ice or if ice melts.

One interesting aspect of lakes that have been filled by sediment and vegetation, is that they provide important information regarding the geomorphological, vegetational and climatic history of the surrounding areas. In Deccan Trap Country, at many places muddy sediments of lacustrine origin are faithfully preserved.

PART (B) : HISTORICAL GEOLOGY

Historical geology, the history of the earth, is the most important goal of geology. The planet earth has a great history, traceable from its birth, about 4500 million years ago, to the recent alluvium. The history may be explained on the basis of countless volcanic eruptions, formation of thick piles of sedimentary sequences, complex deformations and associated metamorphism, abundance of fossils etc. The history may be determined with the help of conventional methods.

It is commonly based on the following four factors :

(1) Relative and absolute age of rocks exposed in different areas;
(2) Orogenic and epionogenic movements;
(3) Paleogeography i.e. the distribution of land and sea in geological past; and
(4) Synthesis of all.

Age of rocks may be decided by studying fossils (relative age) or by radioactive dating (absolute). The mutual relation and succession of various rocks, their ages and relation with rocks of different area deals with stratigraphy (Fig. 3.38).

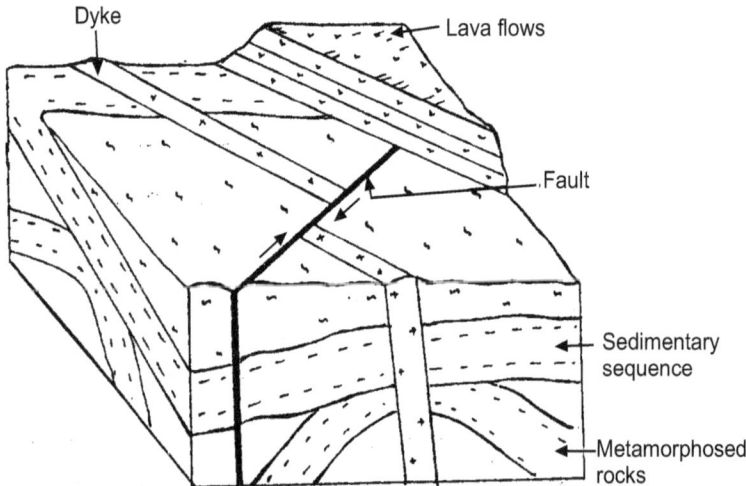

Fig. 3.38 : Schematic representation of how relative ages of rocks and geological events may be determined from geometrical relationship and contact of some rocks

Stratigraphy is the study of stratified rocks and their properties. However, stratification is not only restricted to sedimentary rocks, but is also seen in igneous rock, particularly in volcanic rocks and seldom in plutonic rocks. With all these bedded rocks, one may set up age relations between beds. Thus, stratigraphy involves studying and describing sedimentary sequences, and on the basis of this, interpreting the geological history represented. In order to reconstruct an environment of deposition or to develop the stratigraphy on a regional scale, it is necessary to correlate sedimentary formations from different area of investigation. The requisite information falls into the following three main groups :

(1) Rock composition and structures resulting from sedimentological processes;
(2) Fossil content; and
(3) Presence of radioactive elements.

The passage of time since the formation of the Earth is divided into geochronological units. These are divisions of time which may be measured in years or referred to by name. Geologic time is normally expressed in millions of years or thousands of year before present. The abbreviations used for dates are 'Ma' for millions of years before present and 'Ka' for thousands of years before present. A hierarchical set of terms for the geological time units has been established.

Eons : These are the longest periods of time, with the history of the earth now commonly divided into three eons : the Archaeozoic Eon up to 2.5 Ga (thousands of millions of year before present, called gigayears), the Proterozoic Eon from 2.5 Ga upto 570 Ma and the Phanerozoic Eon upto the present.

Eras : There are three divisions of the Phanerozoic : the Paleozoic Era upto 248 Ma, the Mesozoic Era from 248 Ma until 65 Ma and the Cenozoic Era up to the present.

Periods : The basic unit of geological time is the period and this is the most commonly used division while reffering to Earth history. The mesozoic era, for example, is divided into three periods : the Triassic period, the Jurassic period and the Cretaceous period. The tertiary was formerly considered to be an Era and the sub-divisions (paleocene through the pliocene) were considered to be periods. It is now common to consider the Cenozoic Era to be made up of two periods : The Tertiary (divided into sub-periods, the Paleogene and the Neogene) and the Quaternary period.

Epochs : These are the major divisions of periods. For example, the Paleogene sub-period is divided into the Paleocene Epoch, the Eoceue Epoch and the Oligocene Epoch. Similarly, the Neogene sub-period is divided into the Miocene Epoch and the Pliocene Epoch.

Stratigraphic Units :

Stratigraphic classification promotes understandings of the geometry and sequence of rock bodies. The development of stratigraphy requires formulation of law of superposition, cross cutting relations, isotopic dating, fossil assemblages and unconformities to explain sequential arrangements among rock bodies. Sufficient care is required in defining the boundaries of a unit so as to distinguish one material body from those adjoining it. Thus, units showing differing characteristics do not coincide with other units and therefore, distinctive terms are needed to identify different stratigraphic units.

Four principal categories of units have been used widely in traditional stratigraphic works, namely, lithostratigraphic, biostratigraphic, chronostratigraphic and geochronologic.

- A lithostratigraphic unit is a body of strata which is distinguished and defined by its lithological characteristics and its stratigraphic position relative to other bodies of rock.
- A biostratigraphic unit is a body of rock which is defined and characteristed by its fossil content. The fossil content is used to place the rock in an ordered succession relative to other rocks which contain fossils of older or younger age.
- A chronostratigraphic unit is a body of rock established to serve as a material reference to all rocks formed during same span of time.
- A geochronologic unit is a division of time distinguished on the basis of rock record preserved in a chronostratigraphic unit. For example, carboniferous period. This is a rather conceptual unit.

3.7 PRINCIPLES OF STRATIGRAPHY

The stratigraphic principles are based on three fundamental concepts viz., (a) Uniformitarinism, (b) Order of superposition, and (c) Fossil assemblages.

3.7.1 Uniformitarinism

The concept of uniformitarinism is based on the simple theory of evolution of earth. In the simplest form by observing the present day environmental characteristics, it is possible to interpret the ancient environmental conditions. In other words, the theory can be explained by one sentence i.e. "present is the key to the geological past".

3.7.2 Order of Superposition

This concept, postulated by Steno in 1669, can be easily applied to determine the relative ages of various layers of sedimentary and other associated rocks. In simple terms, this can be explained as in the case of horizontally disposed sedimentary sequence. The rocks at the bottom are definitely older than the rocks at the top elevation. If, for example, we consider one cycle of deposition, the lamillae, deposited during initial stages would be older than the lamillae deposited during late stage. If the strata is structurally deformed, then intensely deformed sequence is older than the moderately deformed sequence or, the top and bottom of the strata can be determined by the primary sedimentary structures like graded bedding, ripple marks, current bedding etc.

3.7.3 Fossil Assemblages

An individual sequence not only explain distinct petrological characters but also exhibits a fossil assemblage which is typical and distinctly different from underlying and overlying sequences. During the evolution of the earth's system, certain fossils attained similar characteristics and with progressive evolution, the form of the organisms became more complicated. Though some species are long-lived and have a great range in time, there are certain others which have a very short time range and each of these (for example, graptolites and ammonoids) are highly valuable indicators of a particular time in geologic past.

However, fossil assemblage of similar age is controlled by environment of deposition and sedimentation process. The conditions which control deposition or sedimentations are depth of water, chemical composition, settling velocity of water etc.

By considering in details, all principles of stratigraphy, the entire geological succession may be evaluated which is represented graphically in vertical columns with the older rocks written at bottom followed upward by comparatively younger strata, and finally on the top the youngest rock is to be written.

3.7.4 Absolute Ages of Rocks

The most reliable method of determining the absolute age of rock is based on the concept of decay of radioactive elements. The radioactive element commonly undergo the process of decay giving rise to their stable daughter elements. Thus, for each element, a certain half-life period is defined, which is the time taken for the decay of half the parent element. The study is carried out on various minerals having radioactive elements. It is confirmed that as soon as the minerals are formed, the radioactive elements begin to decay. At any time, after the crystallization of minerals, the quantity of parent elements and daughter elements can be determined in the laboratory by using sophisticated equipments. Since the half-life period of radioactive element is known, the time taken for the creation of decay element can be easily calculated. The time corresponds to crystallization or formation of mineral and hence the age of rock can be elucidated. Half-life period of certain radioactive elements to their daughter element is given in table 3.8.

Table 3.8

Parent Element	Daughter Element	Half-life Period
U^{238}	$Pb^{206} - 8He^4$	4.468×10^9 years
U^{235}	$Pb^{207} - 7He^4$	0.704×10^9 years
Th^{232}	$Pb^{208} - 6He^4$	14.01×10^9 years
Rb^{87}	Sr^{87}	50×10^9 years
K^{40}	$Ar^{40} - Ca^{40}$	11.9×10^9 years
C^{14}	N^{14}	5570 years

3.8 GEOLOGICAL TIME SCALE

Geological history of the earth's surface is represented by many cycles of depositions, volcanic eruptions, erosion and also by tectonic movements. Age of the earth is believed to be 4500 million years and the oldest rocks exposed on the surface have an age of 3800 million years (approximately). The history also suggests an evolutionary pattern of organisms from primitive simple form to complicated forms. Thus, for convenience, a standard geologic scale is prepared essentially on the basis of evolution of organisms. It is quite interesting to note that organisms are seldom preserved in rocks older than 570 million years (m.y.). Thus, on the basis of life that existed on the surface of the earth, all the rock successions are grouped into two major, broader divisions such as Azoic (devoid of life) and Phanerozoic (life with hard parts preserved). The boundary between these two is marked at 570 m.y. Azoic is further divided into : (a) Archaean (Age upto 2500 m.y.) and (b) Proterozoic (2500-570 m.y.). Although Proterozoic rocks show remains of some organisms, no hard part organisms are preserved.

The Phanerozoic are further classified into three major eras made up of smaller periods based on the basis on the presence of fossil assemblages. The three major eras are : Paleozoic (Palen-early, zoic-life), Mesozoic (Meso-middle) and Cenozoic (Ceno-new). These eras consist of ten periods. The tabular geologic time is given in Table 3.9.

Table 3.9 : The geological time scale (From Harland et. al. 1989)

EON	Era	Period		Epoch	Age (ma)
P H A N E R O Z O I C	Cenozoic	Quaternary		Holocene	0.01
				Pleistocene	1.65
		Tertiary	Neogene	Pliocene	5.3
				Miocene	24
			Palaeogene	Oligocene	36
				Eocene	57
				Palaeocene	65
	Mesozoic	Cretaceous			144
		Jurassic			208
		Triassic			245
	Palaeozoic	Permian			280
		Carboniferous			360
		Devonian			408
		Silurian			435
		Ordovician			505
		Cambrian			570
EON					
Proterozoic					2500
Archaean					

Names of the most of the periods are derived from their type areas from where the rock were first described. The name 'Cambrian' is derived from the area 'cambria' of Welsh Province of Great Britan; 'Devonian' from Deveshine of Great Britain, 'Permian' from the same name Province in U.S.S.R., 'Jurassic' from the Jura mountains, Switzerland. The names of Carboniferous and Cretaceous are derived from typical rock names in the type areas. Carboniferous deals with coal and Cretaceous with chalk (Limestone). The names Ordovician and "Silurian" are derived from the old tribes (Srdovic and Silurs) living in Great Britain. Tertiary and Quarternary represent the stages of organic evolution. Details of each period are given in Table 3.10.

Table 3.10 : Brief history of the earth

Period	History
Quaternary	This, the latest geological period, continues upto and including the present day. It is characterised by four major ice ages alternate with warmer intervals. Mammals increased and adapted and man evolved to dominate the earth.
Tertiary	The opening of Cenozoic (recent life) era witnessed an explosive growth of mammals. Flowering plants increased rapidly and as the climates later cooled, grasslands appeared. The period also witnessed extensive volcanic activity.
Cretaceous	Dinosaurs remained dominant until they and many large reptiles becomes extinct at the end of this period. First true birds and mammals fluorished. The period also witnessed widening of the Atlantic Ocean; and thus separation of Africa from Southern America initiated.
Jurassic	On land the Dinosaurs fluorished, and the air was first conquered by flying reptiles and later by primitive birds. The period also shown traces of some flowering plants. Considerable volcanic activity was associated with the opening of the Atlantic Ocean.
Triassic	The Mesozoic era witnessed breaking and separation of different continents. On land, conifers became the dominant plants. This was a period of great diversity among the reptiles and the first dinosaurs and giant marine reptiles occurred. Small primitive mammals also evolved.
Permian	Desert conditions prevailed over the continents. The reptiles spread widely and the modern insect evolved. Several marine organism became extinct. But on land, conifers developed.
Carboniferous	Mountain building, folding and erosion continued. Richly forested swamps and deltas in North America and Europe were submerged and formed large coal deposits. Extensive glaciation spread over the southern hemisphere. Insects fluorished. First reptile appeared.

... Contd.

Devonian	A period of extensive evolution. Land was covered by early seed plants. Fish grew in variety and size and the first amphibians developed. Mountain building movement reached a peak as evident from many fold belts.
Silurian	The first appearance of jawless fish, and first vertebrates (animals with backbone). The late Silurian period evidenced the growth of the first land plants. This was a period of extensive carbonate sedimentation in shallow seas. Important changes in sea levels produced unconformities and attendant changes in fossil fauna.
Ordovician	The period was characterised by mild climate and seas still covered most of the areas. There was extensive sedimentation and important mountain building processes. Reef building algae were common and corals, sponges and molluscs abundant.
Cambrian	The transition is well documented as evident from the sudden appearance of abundant fossils. This marks the beginning of the Palaeozoic (ancient life) era. In the early widespread shallow seas, early marine life developed, Trilobites were abundant.
Proterozoic	Proterozoic mark the wide spread sedimentation, recognized in Peninsular India as Purana sedimentary sequence. Stromatolites were abundant. Traces of life are generally rare.
Archaeans	The greatest part of geological time is represented by the Archaeans and the Proterozoics. The crust, land masses and sea formed and great volcanic activity occurred. Archaean rocks form shield areas of all the continents. Life is rarely preserved.

3.9 GEOLOGY OF INDIA

On the basis of physiographic expression, India is divided into three distinct parts viz., (a) Peninsular India, lying on the south of Indogangetic plains and consisting of very old and stable part of the earth's crust in geologic history, (b) Extra-peninsula : consisting of Himalayan ranges which is the youngest mountain range in geologic past, and (c) Indo-Gangetic plains consisting of alluvial plains between Peninsular and Extra-Peninsular regions. These three parts show a great deal of variation both in geology and physiography.

Peninsular region exhibits mountains of circumdenudation i.e. relict mountains. The country is comparatively flat with low gradients and has matured valleys. The Extra-peninsula is the region of fold mountain chains. Its rivers exhibit presence of deep and steep-sided gorges and are in youthful stage. The Indo-Gangetic plain has recent alluvium sediments deposited by the Himalayan rivers.

In this chapter, a brief outline of geological characteristics of peninsular India is only discussed. The geological details of extra-peninsular region are out of scope of the present work.

3.9.1 Peninsular India

The rocks of peninsular India show great variations in age, traceable from the Archaeans to recent Alluvium deposited by many streams. The geography of the region is extremely variable and comprises of a complex association of plateau mountains with widely distributed drainage, peneplained ancient folded mountains, elongate graben like valleys and recent coastal plains. Thus, the peninsular India has a great geological history. The important groups of rocks in the peninsular India are given in Table 3.11.

Table 3.11

Standard scale	Major geologic events in Peninsular India
Recent	Alluvium
Quaternary	Laterite and Bauxite
Cretaceous to Eocene	Deccan Trap Basalts exposed in parts of Maharashtra, Gujarat, Madhya Pradesh, Karnataka, Andhra Pradesh etc.
Carboniferous to Jurassic	Gondwana sedimentary sequence exposed in parts of Bihar, Bengal, Maharashtra, Orissa etc
Proterozoic	Purana sedimentary sequences – Cuddapah : Andhra Pradesh – Vuidhyan : Madhya Pradesh, Utter Pradesh etc. – Kaladgi : Karnataka, Maharashtra – Delhi : Metamorphosed sequence : Rajasthan – Metamorphosed rocks in Maharashtra – Eastern Ghat metamorphosed rocks along east coast of India – Singhbhum Iron-Ore Group, Bihar and Orissa
Archaeans	– Volcani sedimentary of Karnataka, Andhra Pradesh, Maharashtra, Goa etc. (Dharwars) – Granulities of South India.

(a) Archaean Rocks :
  (1) Volcani - Sedimentary sequence classified as Dharwars exposed mainly in parts of southern India.
  (2) Metamorphosed rocks exposed in parts of Maharashtra, Madhya Pradesh etc.
  (3) Singhbhum - Iron Ore group of rocks exposed in Bihar and Orissa.

(b) Proterozoic Sedimentaries :
  (1) Aravali metasediments exposed in parts of Rajasthan, Gujarat, Utter Pradesh etc.
  (2) Purana sedimentaries including Cuddapah Group (Andhra Pradesh), Vindhyans (Madhya Pradesh) and other sedimentary basins of small areal extents.
  (3) Eastern Ghat Group of rocks exposed along east coast India.

(c) Mesozoic sediments :

Gondwana Group exposed in parts of Maharashtra, Madhya Pradesh, Orissa, Uttar Pradesh, Bihar, West Bengal etc.

(d) Cretaceous - Tertiary :

Deccan Trap Volcanics exposed in parts of Maharashtra, Gujarat, Karnataka, Madhya Pradesh etc.

(e) Quaternary : Laterite and Bauxites.

These rocks show dominance of four structural – geomorphological trends, as NNW – SSE trending Western Ghats, NE – SW trending Eastern Ghats, E – W Satpuras and NE – SW trending Aravali ranges.

Archaean Geology :

(1) **Dharwar Super group :** The Dharwar Belt of South India is made up of two principal components : An assemblage of metamorphic rocks called as Dharwar Group and a variety of granites and gneisses. The Dharwar Group rocks are typically exposed in parts of Karnataka, Konkan, Goa etc. with its type section and at around Dharwar, North Karnataka. The rocks include slates, phyllites, banded iron quartzite, chlorite schist, hornblende schist, amphibolites, crystalline limestones etc. They have a regional strike of NNW-SSE with fluctuations from N – S to NW – SE. These rocks are intensely deformed by more than three orogenic phases.

The gneisses and granites, called as Peninsular Gneisses, are older than Dharwars (3000 m.y.). These are exposed in vast areas covering mostly the South India Craton.

Dharwarian rocks have some of the most important economic mineral deposits, such as copper (Chitaldurg district), gold (Kolar and Hatti), manganese (Goa, Hospet), iron ore (Goa, Hospet, Hasan) etc.

Building stones : The gneisses, granites, quartzites and crystalline limestone are excellent building stones. They are most durable and resistant stones. Most of the temples in Karnataka and especially ruins of Hampi are constructed out of granites and gneisses. Furthermore, some feldsparthic gneisses and granites have given rise to good kaoline which is very useful for many construction purposes.

The other important deposits are Asbestos, Magnesite, Mica etc.

(2) **Singhbhum belt :** The rocks exposed in parts of Bihar and Orissa include some of the oldest rocks and very large economic deposits. The region is a major shear zone and thus rocks are intensely deformed. The older metamorphics (3200 m.y.) consists of pelites, hornblende schists, gneisses etc. The Iron-Ore Group (2700 m.y.) is younger than the Older Metamorphic Group which includes a folded sequence of shales, sandstones, banded quartzites, basic etc. intruded by granite gneisses, dolerites and granites. The area recognises many economic deposits like copper (associated with uranium), iron-ore (one of the largest deposits) etc. The mica deposits of Bihar is one of the largest in India.

Building stones : The banded gneisses and granites of Bihar and Orissa have provided excellent materials for temples, forts, places etc. The most important localities are Ranchi, Hazaribagh, Gaya of Bihar and Sambhalpur district of Orissa.

(3) Aravali – Delhi belt : The Aravali – Delhi belt extends from Gujarat through Rajasthan to Delhi for a distance of 800 km. The sequence shows a great variation in metamorphism and composition traceable from argillaceous rocks (partially metamorphosed) to phyllites to high grade schists. The dolomitic limestone of Zawar area is reputed for lead – zinc deposits. The rocks have a regional strike of NE – SW with steep dips. The area recognizes regional folds often disturbed by smaller dislocations. Aravali succession is intruded by granite and ultrabasics. The granite phase is recorded in the form of Mount Abu Granite (Erinpura Granite).

Building stones : The crystalline limestones and marbles of Rajasthan have been extensively used as building and ornamental stones. The Makrana marble is used in the Taj Mahal of Agra, Dilwara Temple, Mount Abu, Victoria Memorial; Kolkatta, etc. The usual Makrana marble is white with cloudy streaks and grey patches. The Motipura marble, Baroda is a green serpentine marble with rose and pink bands. It is extensively used in Gujarat. Other important locations are Mewar, Raialo (Jaipur), Alwar (Sachcharoidal marble), Umrar (Bundi) etc. Many a times, the flagstone of Jaipur used as paving stone, while slate quarried from Ajmer are used for roofing and paving purposes.

The most important economic deposit is of mica. It is mined at Jaipur, Bhilwara, Ajmer etc. The mica is generally colourless, but light green and ruby coloured varities are also common.

(4) Sausar and Sakoli : The Nagpur, Bhandara, Durg and Chindwara districts in Central India expose another important suite of Precambrian rocks. Sausar and Sakoli are two different chronologic sequences in which sausars are represented by gneisses, marbles, quartzites, gondites, quartz schists and amphibolites. The rocks are intensely deformed giving rise to a regional overturned isoclinal fold and recumbant of schists, quartzites, states and phyllites. The rocks are folded and show a high degree of metamorphism. Regional strike for these rocks is approximately E-W.

The area recognises very important economic deposits of manganese found in a rock known as Gondite. Sometimes, the manganese horizons attain a thickness of 6 m or more of sold manganese ore (Lihangi, Mansar). The Balaghat – Nagpur region contains the richest ore and maximum reserves in India.

Building stones : The most important construction material is available in the form of gneisses and granites and are quarried from Balaghat, Bhandara and Chindwara. The multicoloured marbles from Jabalpur, Narasingpur, Chindwara and Nagpur are used for architectural purposes.

Proterozoic Sedimentary Sequences :

The proterozoic sedimentary rocks known as 'Puranas' (older) were deposited on the eroded irregular edges of Archaean basements. A large pronounced unconformity known as Great Eparchean unconformity separates the Proterozoic and Archaean successions. The Puranas are exposed in parts of Karnataka, Andhra Pradesh, Tamil Nadu, where two important sequences are the 'Cuddapahs' and the 'Vindhyans'.

(a) The Cuddapahs : The rocks of the Cuddapah Group are exposed in a large cresent shaped basin with its type section exposed around Cuddapah, Andhra Pradesh. Geographically, the region, about 300 km, along its length and 140 km across, is characterised by a few north-south parallel ridges. The sequence comprises over 6000 m thick succession mostly of quartzites, shales, and varieties of limestones. The rocks in the basins are undisturbed in the western part but show intense folding and as increasing metamorphism towards eastern margin. These are introduced by sills of dolerite and basalts.

On the basis of the presence of local inconformities, the Cuddapahs are divided into four groups, namely Krishna, Nallamalai, Chiyar and Papagharis which are further classified on the basis of cycle of deposition.

The Cuddapah supergroup recognises an important deposits of Barytes which produces an average of 15,000 tonnes of Baryes per year. The area also recognises smaller but good quality deposit of asbestos which is exposed at Pulivendla, Cuddapah district.

Building stones : The quartzites of Pulivendla and Nagari are used as building stones. The rock is well-bedded and yields rectangular blocks and slabs. The Cuddapah shales have yielded good quality refractory clay. Another important rock is dolomitic limestones, which is quarried from Cuddapah. It is very good flooring material and is widely used as paving stones, fence stone, step and table tops.

(b) The Vindhyans : The Vindhyans derives its name from the great Vindhya mountains, a prominent plateau like range of sandstone to the north of Narmada Valley. The basinal rocks cover an extensive area of 1,00,000 sq.km in Central India and further north, extending from Delhi and Gwalior. The sequence consists of a cyclic deposition of sandstones, shales and limestones which is divided into two broad classes, upper and lower, essentially on the basis of the degree of deformation. The lower Vindhyans are deformed and metamorphosed. In Rajasthan, the Vindhyans are affected by the main boundary fault which has a throw of 1500 m and which brings the Vindhyans in contact with highly folded Aravalis. This fault can be traced for a distance of 1500 km.

The most important economic deposits confined to the Vindhyan supergroup are of Diamonds (Location Panna).

Building stones : Some of the limestones of lower Vindhyans quarried from Sabalgarh are used for interior decoration due to a peculiar spherulitic structure, the concentric shells of which show various colours. The limestones of Guintur district are excellent building and ornamental stones e.g. Buddhist sculptures, Amaravati. However, these limestones are the most important raw material for the lime and cement industry.

The Vindhyan sandstones, because of their regular bedding, uniform grain size, attractive colour, high durability and easy workability, are extensively used as building stones. The stones have cream-light, grey and red colours and often show creamy impurities, or spots, e.g. Buddhist stupas of Sanchi, Sarnath etc. The stones used in Fatehpur Sikri, new administrative building of New Delhi etc. were quarried in many areas in Bharatpur, Jaipur, Bicaner, Mirzapur etc.

Some of the Vindhyan friable sandstone yield very good sand for the manufacture of glass.

(c) Eastern ghat : The Eastern Ghat rocks are exposed along the east coast of India from Orissa to Tamil Nadu with a very prominent NE – SW regional strike for over 1200 km. The low lying hills are made up of gneisses, Charnockites and Khondatites. The rocks show very high degree of metamorphism.

Charnockites are hyperstone (pyroxene) bearing granite exposed in parts of Tamil Nadu. They are commonly known as Nilgiri Gneiss and Mountain Gneiss as they formed the higher peaks of south India. Khondatite is a typical schistose rock named after the Khondes tribe of Visakhapattanam (Andhra Pradesh) and is made up of quartz, feldspar and granite. It is exposed in parts of Andhra Pradesh, Orissa, Bihar and Tamil Nadu. Khondatites are often associated with manganese rich gneisses which have workable deposits of manganese ore.

Building stones : The charnockites are considered as most durable and strongest stones in the world, and thus have been used in harbour construction in Mumbai and Chennai. Most of the temples of Tamil Nadu are constructed of charnockites. The Khondatites are not highly durable as they weather to a sandy rock and produce red and brown streaks in ground mass. But still, they have extensively used on building and temple construction e.g. Puri and Konark temples. Similarly, the talc and chlorite schist are suitable for carving doorwoods, windows etc. For example, Sun God in Konark temple.

(d) Other sedimentary sequences : The other smaller sedimentary basins-are Kaladgi (exposed in Belgaum and Bijapur district, north Karnataka, and parts of Sindhudurg, Ratnagiri and Kolhapur districts of Maharashtra), Bhima (Gulbarga and Bijapur districts, north Karnataka), Pakhal (Godavari valley, Andhra Pradesh) etc.

The Bhimal limestone is a major raw material in cement manufacture. It is quarried at Shahabad, Wadi, Gulbarga district etc. Similarly, at places like the Kaladgi limestones are used for cement industry (Bagalkot, Lokapur, Kaladgi etc.). The most common building stone in these areas is sandstones/quartzites. e.g. Golgumbaj, Bijapur. In Sindhudurg district, the friable Kaladgi sandstones are used as silica sand and glass sand in the foundry and the manufacture of glass respectively.

The Gondwana group : The 'Gondwana' sequence represents 6000 to 7000 metre thick succession of fluviatile and lacustrine deposits with glacial deposits at its base. The deposition of this involved a large cycle of continental sedimentation which was started in Permian period and closed in cretaceous period indicating a span of 180 Ma. During this time, there existed a single continent 'Gondwara land' which included India, Africa, South America, Australia and Antarctica. The term 'Gondwana' was introduced by Medlicott in 1872 after the tribe name 'Gonds habitant' in Madhya Pradesh. These rocks exposed in peninsular India are confined to three river valley grabens, the Narmada-son, Damodar, the Mahanadi and the Godavari.

Beginning of the Gondwana sedimentation is marked by glacial deposits, Tillites, which are exposed at Talchir (Orissa) and also in Godavari Valley, indicative of glacial condition prevailed during Carboniferous times. With the change in climatic conditions and retreat of glaciers, the area was filled in by swamps rich in vegetative matter the condition favourable for deposition of coal bearing horizons. After the deposition of coal bearing strata, the area again evidenced change in environmental conditions evidenced due to deposition of ironstone shale, iron carbonates (reducing conditions), variegated clay and ferrugenous sandstones (oxidising conditions) in different terrains. This is followed by deposition of coal bearing strata (Raniganj basin, Damodar valley), which yielded the superior quantity coalseams. The Triassic Godwana consists of repetitive cyclic deposition of arkosic sandstones and shales while the younger Gondwana are made up of varieties of sandstones deposited in fluvial environment. Therefore, it can be said that the Gondwana sedimentation received a great change in environmental conditions throughout the deposition which is also reflected in the variation of plant fossils preserved in these rocks.

The most important economic deposits in Gondwana is of coal. Most of the workable coal seams are in the Damodar valley. The recent estimation of reserves of coal in Gondwana are approximately 1,45,000 million tonnes. The Gondwana is useful for refractory purposes, making bricks, pottery, china-ware etc.

Building stones : The Barakar, Raniganj, Kamthi and Panchmarhi sandstones are used as building material. It is fine grained and suitable for carving, e.g. temples of Puri, Bhuvaneshwar and Konark.

3.10 DECCAN TRAP BASALT

Towards the close of Cretaceous, a large part of peninsular India was affected by fissure type of volcanic erruptions that formed several hundred metres thick horizontal to sub-horizontal piles of lava flows. This great volcanic material covers an area of 5,00,000 square kilometres in parts of Maharashtra, Madhya Pradesh, Gujarat, Karnataka and Andhra Pradesh and is known as 'Deccan Traps'. The term 'Trap' is used to describe the typical step-like topography created by the flat topped weathered basalts. These are also known as Plateau Basalt. It can be said that this was the largest geological activity evidenced in peninsular India with notable exception of the metamorphics and the granites of the Archaeans.

Deccan Trap Basalts, often seen exposed along with volcanic Breccia, ash and volcanic tuffs, suggest central type of explosive action of same intensity. Similarly, volcanic vents are found at a number of widely separated localities. However, the erruption of the main mass of lava was of a passive type i.e. fissure type erruption.

3.10.1 Horizontality of the Lava Flows

The most important aspect of the Deccan Trap Basalts is their remarkable horizontal disposition which is uniformly seen throughout their wide areas, with a notable exception of flows neighbouring Mumbai. In this area, the Basalt attains a dip from 5° to 50° (approximately).

3.10.2 Thickness

The Deccan Trap Basalts attain their maximum thickness near the Mumbai coast where they are estimated to be 2500 metres approximately. Their thickness decreases further north as well as south.

The individual flows vary in thickness from a few centimetres to about 120 metres. It is observed that an individual flow shows a typical tabular geometry as seen from its greater persistent with their thickness. Individual flows may be traceable for a distance of about 10 kilometres or more. This is best possibly seen on the vertical faces of the Sahyadri scarps.

3.10.3 Petrology

From pure geological point of view, the Deccan Traps, possess uniform composition. However, due to differential cooling, these exhibit heterogeneity in field characteristics and as a result show a great variation in their engineering properties.

Major mineral constituents of the basalts are augite and labradorite (calcium – plagioclase). Its average density is 3.9. The basalts are generally dark grey to brownish in colour.

Other varieties of rocks associated with the basalts are Syenites and Diorite (near Jawhar, Thane district), Gabbro and other alkali rocks near Murud.

3.10.4 Petrography

As mentioned earlier, basalts are composed of augite and labradorite. It commonly shows ophitic to subophitic texture. The rocks often show phenocrysts of feldspar embedded in fine grained ground mass or interstitial glass matter. The glass is often liable to alteration into chloropbaeite. Olivine is often present as a major mineral constituent.

Among the most important secondary minerals due to hydrothermal activity during cooling of the lava, that are found in cavities, are the zeolite, stillite, apophylite, heulandite, calcite, crystalline quartz, rock crystal and other varieties of silica like chacedony, agate, jaspar etc.

3.10.5 Types of Basalt

Basalts are the products of differential cooling of hot lava material. Hence, eventhough their mineral constituents are identical, these show great variation in texture and structure due to change in cooling rate. Below are some of the common varieties :

(1) Vesicular basalt : Basalts often show a typical porous appearance, also known as scoriaceous basalt. The pores are ellipsoidal or spheroidal in shape; and commonly their diameter is small (not more than few centimetres). Pores are isolated or poorly inter-connected. The rock is free from joints. It is considered as an aquicluide.

(2) Amygdaloidal basalt : Commonly the vesicles are filled with secondary minerals like zeolites, quartz, calcite or other silica minerals. The dark coloured mesocratic rock thus exhibits the presence of light coloured cavity filling minerals and the structure is known as **amygdaloidal**. Thus, the rock is called amygdaloidal basalt. It is also known as zeolitic basalt. The cavities are often pipe shaped or tabular which are formed by rising gas bubbles. These rocks are known as pipe amygdaloidal basalts and are restricted at the bottom of many flows.

(3) Compact basalt : This is a typical aphinitic basalt and may easily be recognised in the field by its characteristic jointing pattern. Flows of compact basalts are vesicular or amygdaloidal at their bottom or top.

(4) Porphyritic basalt : Often laths of plagioclase are enclosed in glassy ground mass. Their size varies from 1 cm to 10 centimetres. The typical basalt is known as porphyritic basalt.

(5) Basalt glass : Basaltic rock is seldom pitch black in colour; and under microscope it exhibits the presence of palagonite or chlorphaeite. The rock has a typical holohyaline texture. It is also known as Tachylytic Basalt. On exposure, it alters to red bole or red bed.

(6) Volcanic breccia : Volcanic breccia is made of pyroclastic fragments embedded in basaltic matrix. The fragments are commonly basaltic in composition and their borders are often altered or zeolitized. Under the microscope, matrix is typical glassy. These are the products of central type of erruption and are always isolated in distribution. The flows are irregular or gently dipping.

3.10.6 Field Characters of Basalts

As mentioned earlier, Deccan Trap Basalts occur as a thin tabular horizontal to sub-horizontal flows. An individual flow contact may be marked by using certain criterias like distribution of vesicles, grain size, jointing etc. In general, it can be said that the compact basalts occur as thick extensive flows while amygaloidal basalts occur as thin, irregular flows. Their irregularity in space is often, possibly, due to pre-trappean topography.

In the amygdaloidal flows, the top is usually vesicular, middle is appreciably compact and the bottom showing cylindrical pipes filled with secondary minerals. Vesicular and non-vesicular flows may alternate with each other.

(1) Jointing : The joints observed in the Deccan Trap Basalts are divided into three catagories :

(a) Fractures : These are tectonic in origin and believed to be regional in scale. Fractures can easily be recognised from normal joints on the basis of their persistence. Commonly, a fracture is seen to cut various flows of basalt without any displacement. The basalts across the fractures are undisturbed but are partially altered or decomposed. Due to which, apparent movement in basalt flows is observed. These are vertical or sub-vertical in nature and approximately N – S or NNW – SSE in orientation.

Due to differential resistance of basaltic flows and vertical to sub-vertical fracture, beautiful topographic features like Mesa, Buttle are observed in the Sahyadri ranges.

Aperture between walls of a fracture commonly varies from a few millimetres to 25 to 30 centimetres. These fractures are seldom tight. In general, depth of fractures is partially responsible in deciding of weathering.

(b) Cooling joints : Cooling joints are seen most commonly in the form of columnar joints in compact basalts. It is interesting to note that amygdaloidal basalt seldom contains joints and are massive. In plan view, columnar joints are hexagonal and horizontal distance between similar parallel walls varies from few centimetres to metres. Similarly, as the name suggests, the ratio of horizontal to vertical distance in the structure is normally more than 1 : 10. The presence of columnar joints produce beautiful topographic features; but from engineering point of view, these are very dangerous and unstable.

(c) Topographic or sheet joints : Sheet joints are formed due to removal of overburden or release of pressure. Generally, sheet joints are seen in massive rocks. Amygdaloidal basalts being free from discontinuities show the presence of these joints.

Sheet joints are the product of weathering and develop parallel or sub-parallel to ground slope. Normally, they are close spaced and the vertical distance between two successive cracks is in centimetres. Persistance of sheet joints is controlled by degree and intensity of weathering. Normally, sheet joints are traceable for a distance of few metres.

(2) Weathering : In general, it is observed that compact basalt shows presence of three sets of joints, two vertical / sub-vertical and one horizontal. As a result of this, the basalt flows are disintegrated into rectangular blocks and thus giving a characteristic blocky appearance to flow. This type of weathering, typical of compact basalt flows, is known as **spheroidal weathering**. As mentioned earlier, the degree, intensity and depth of weathering often influenced by persistence and penetration of fractures.

The Deccan Trap Basalts give rise to either a deep brown or red lateritic soil or black cotton soil. The black cotton soil, also called as regolith, is rich in humus and other nutrients like lime, magnesium and iron are present. It has a peculiar property of swelling and when dry, it develops fissures or cracks.

Another product of weathering is a hard, impermeable, brick coloured rock 'laterite'. It has a vermicular/pisolitic structure and with higher proportion of aluminium oxides, bauxites are formed.

3.10.7 Dykes

Dykes are abundant in the trappean country, but they are restricted to specific areas like north Maharashtra, western Maharashtra and Saurashtra. These are typical hypabyssal intrusions and are doleritic in composition.

In Gujarat, dykes show a distinct orientation in the direction ENE-WSW, while in western Maharashtra, the dyke system has a general N-S trend with minor deviations towards NW-SE.

Thickness of dykes considerably vary from few metres to 60 metres approximately and these can be traceable over a length of 30 to 40 kilometres.

The dykes exhibit two types of topographic expressions :

(1) Dykes are softer than country rock and show topographic lows. Commonly, these dykes possess three sets of joints : two vertical and one horizontal and the intrusive mass is broken into rectangular block. Such dykes allow easy movement of water.

(2) Dykes, harder than country rock, stand out as low mounds and act as a barrier or natural dam. Thus, they prevent flow of water and are believed to be impervious.

3.10.8 Inter-Trappean Beds

Between two lava flows, sedimentary beds of lacustrine origin are seldom seen. For example, upperhatti, north Karnataka. These beds are fossiliferous and are important in explaining the history of the periods of quiet large intervals between two successive erruptions. The beds are known as Inter-Trappean Beds. Usually, they are 1 to 3 metres in thickness and are traceable for a distance of 5 to 7 kilometres.

A very good exposure of Inter-Trappean beds is seen in Chhindwara district, Madhya Pradesh. Here beautiful silicified leaves, flowers, fruits, seeds etc. are preserved in abundance.

During the period of eruptive quiescene of lava, there came into existence some rivers and lakes and seldom there was modification in drainage pattern. The fluviatile and lacustrine deposits formed in them are intercalated with the lava flow. Thus, they are trapped between two successive fissure erruptions.

3.10.9 Age of Deccan Traps

As mentioned earlier, the Trap country is formed due to numerous fissure erruptions which involved a span of a few million of years. Thus, there is a vivid controversy about the exact age of the Deccan Trap Basalts. The fresh water or lacustrine fossils occurring in the Inter-Trappean Beds indicate the age of deposition close to the Cretaceous-Tertiary Boundary. Recent studies have suggested that major bulk of the Deccan Trap was formed at or around 65 m.y. ago.

3.10.10 Economics

Being hard, dense and durable, Deccan Traps are used as building stones and as road metal. As road metal, they are tough, wear-resisting and have good binding properties. They are also used as aggregate in cement concrete.

The cavity minerals observed in Deccan Trap Basalts are used as semi-precious stone. These include quartz, amethyst, agate and chalcedony etc.

The traps are often capped by Laterites and Bauxites. Bauxite frined from Kolhapur and Ratnagiri district is used as a chief-source for alumina. Laterite forms a good building stone.

PART (C) : BUILDING STONES

Engineering structures are constructed either on soil or on rock. But a distinct difference is noted in the behaviour of rock and soil. Rock is an aggregate of minerals and is interlocked or cemented to be a coherent material while soil is either form in-situ or transported and deposited elsewhere. As a result, rocks are better suited as than soils for building materials and for other purposes.

Many minerals and rocks are useful for the purpose of building stones, road metals, paving stones and dimension stones. These stones are commonly hard, compact and resistant to all sorts of weathering and erosion, and most important point is these should be locally available in sufficient quantity.

The group of minerals and rocks used in engineering industries are as follows : Building, paving crused and dimension stones, cements,

Sand and Gravel,

Carbonates, including limestones, Dolomites,

Asphalts and Bitumites,

Clay minerals.

3.11 STONES REQUIRED FOR BUILDING ROOFING

The important properties for the commercial utilization of rocks of various types are their durability, hardness, toughness, strength and ease of processing and quarrying.

The costly stones are cut, polished and sold in the market as 'Dimension Stones'. When the material is broken into even and small pieces, it is known as crushed stone. Building stones are generally dimension stones. Very few rock materials satisfy the requirements of dimension stone due to easy workability, exploitation and quarrying.

3.12 PHYSICAL PROPERTIES OF ROCKS

As mentioned earlier, most important physical properties of rocks essential for being considered as a suitable material for engineering purposes are durability, hardness, toughness, porosity and strength. These properties are dependent on the mode of occurrence, type and condition of rocks, groundwater condition, and when subjected to mechanical pressure on abrasion or impact.

3.12.1 Durability

Durability is the capacity of rock materials to withstand variable natural and induced forces for a measurable length of times comparable to the life of the structure. In this, the important factors that influence durability are climatic conditions, composition and structure of rocks. The building or dimension stones are subjected to alternate dry and wet climatic conditions.

Igneous rocks are the products of crystallization and are liable to decomposition or alteration, for example, spheroidal weathering. Similarly, in granites decomposition of feldspar to clay is a common phenomenon. Olivine bearing rocks are known for their alteration to serpentine and also to clays. As a result, durability of these stones decreases owing to instability of different minerals.

The clastic sedimentary rocks, especially sandstones due to their mineral composition are relatively durable rocks. Marble is a durable rock compared to limestones owing to its mosaic or interlocking granulose texture.

On theoretical grounds, quartz, amphiboles, feldspar are stable minerals and thus granites, syenites, diorites, gneissose rocks are more durable stones.

3.12.2 Toughness

Toughness is the resistance of rockmass to impact. The property is largely influenced by texture of rocks and on the individual tenacity of minerals. Thus, an interlocking, granular texture is capable of producing good building stone; sandstones are not tough, because the grains are not only rounded but seldom uncemented. Clacite, being soluble and easily workable, prevents marble from being tough.

3.12.3 Hardness

Hardness of rocks depends partially on hardness of individual mineral constituents and cohesion between particles. Granite consists of quartz, feldspar and accessories like mica and hornblende. Hardness of quartz is 7 and of feldspar it is 6. Further more, granite is a product of slow cooling. Thus, granite is usually harder than any other igneous rock. Sandstones without any cementing matrix are friable because of poor cohesion between individual particles. Pure marbles are relatively softer than dolomite marble because calcite is softer and soluble than dolomite.

3.12.4 Porosity and Permeability

Porosity and Permeability affects the coefficient of expansion and contraction of rock material.

Rocks with interlocked texture, like igneous rocks, marbles, quartzites and almost all the gneisses and schists, have virtually no porosity and are believed to be impervious. The sedimentary rocks like sandstones, shales and limestones contain a large percentage of porosity. Tiny pores in fine grained sandstones and shales allow surface water to get inside the pore and are said to be aquiclude.

Rocks often exhibit discontinuities of different kinds along which effects of weathering are pronounced. In such cases, permeability is greatly influenced by discontinuities.

3.12.5 Compressive Strength

The term strength refers to the ability of rockmass to withstand crushing when loaded. Commonly, three kinds of stresses are to be discussed in studying strength of rockmass; compressive stresses; which reduce volume of rockmass; tensile stresses which tend to produce cracks in rockmass and shear stresses which make the rockmass flow or slide past each other. Rocks in their natural conditions are seldom subject to torsion.

The compressive strength of rocks is influenced by their texture and mineral constituents. Igneous and metamorphic rocks with interlocking texture are stronger than schistose rocks, while in sedimentary rocks, the cement may have a substantial influence on the compressive strength. For example; sandstone, conglomerate. However, if cementing material is argillaceous (clay) or calcareous, the compressive strength is comparatively low. When cementing material is silica and mineral composition is due to quartz, approximately the highest compressive strength is obtained. Discontinuous rocks possess low compressive strength.

The compressive strength is also influenced by weak planes. Commonly normal to the direction of weak plane the highest compressive strength is obtained, while the strength is minimum along weak planes.

Saturation or moisture content is another factor that reduces compressive strength of rockmass. It is observed that the higher the porosity, higher the chances of saturation and inversely the lower will be the strength of rockmass when saturated.

Thus, based on unconfined compressive strength, the rocks may be divided into various classes. (Table 3.12)

Table 3.12 : Classification of building stones based on unconfined compressive strength

Strength classification	Rock types
Very weak	Weathered and ill sorted sedimentary rocks.
Weak	Weakly cemented sedimentary rocks, schists.
Medium	Competent sedimentary rocks, low density coarse igneous rocks.
Strong	Competent igneous rocks, some metamorphic rocks, and fine grained sandstones.
Very strong	Quartzite, dense, fine grained massive igneous rocks.

The above classification does not match with the conventional geologic classification.

3.12.6 Deformational Properties

Deformation of rock masses are more important in the discussion of stability of excavations than stress criteria. Testing of rock and rock masses indicates that failure strains are more consistent and therefore, more predictable than failure stresses. As a result, rock strain monitoring devices are used to overcome the uncertainty involved in predicting the stability of slopes and excavations. Such monitoring requires knowledge of the magnitude of strains and interpretation of stress from strain measurements requires a knowledge of Young's modulus and Poisson's ratio of the rock.

Young's modulus : Young's modulus is the ratio of normal stress to normal strain for a rock sample under given loading conditions; it is numerically equal to the slope of the stress strain curve. If the curve is liner the material is said to be linearly elastic.

Modulus of deformation : Modulus of deformation refers to deformation that is not perfectly elastic and implies inelastic deformation. This term would be appropriate for the stress-strain curve of a jointed rock mass. It is observed that the modulus of deformation for a rock mass can be much less than the Young's modulus of intact rock.

Poisson's ratio : Poisson's ratio is the ratio of the transverse normal strain to the longitudinal normal strain of an elastic body under a uniaxial load. The larger the Poisson's ratio of a rock, the larger is its lateral expansion. As in the case of Young's modulus, the experimental values of this ratio also depend on the character of the stress-strain diagram and sample conditions. Values available for Poisson's ratio fluctuates between 0.15 and 0.24 for granite, 0.16 and 0.23 for limestone, 0.08 and 0.20 schist, and 0.25 to 0.38 for marble.

Creep : The short term static rock behaviour does not characterize the ability of rock material to deform slowly with time or creep. The creep load rate under a specified load should be determined and compared to the life and purpose of the constriction creep occurs in most earth materials and on very gentle slopes.

3.12.7 Dynamic Rock Properties

If a rockmass is subjected to natural or induced vibrations, the transient dynamic stresses may exceed the existing static stresses by many orders of magnitudes.

A dynamic load is defined by the speed of its application. An explosion applied over a period of microseconds will create pressures for in excess of the static impressive strength of the rock. As rocks can resist a much greater magnitude of dynamic stress than static stress, failure predictions based on these are complex and must be applied with caution.

3.12.8 Index Properties

Index properties are used to classify rocks rapidly using many tests repetitions.

Point load strength index : The point load strength index is the ratio of the force required to fracture a core to the squared distance between the loaded points. The purpose of this test is to obtain a tentative strength of the material.

Slake durability : Slake durability is the resistance of a rock to accelerated wetting and drying. It is defined as *the percentage ratio of final to initial dry sample weights. Rocks with high clay content are susceptible to serious slaking.*

Swelling and shrinkage : Rocks with high clay content are commonly prone to swell or shrink owing to a change of water content. The heave produced by swelling of rocks causes widespread foundation problems. Wet clayey rocks can shrink on drying with equally disastrous results.

Rock Quality Designation (RQD) : The RQD (discussed in unit-4) is a modified core recovery percentage in which all the pieces of sound core over 10 cm in length are counted as recovery. Details are given in unit-4.

3.12.9 In-Situ Stresses

In-situ test are generally used to provide design data based on stress measurements. Gravitational stresses are those that arise from the force of gravity on a rock mass and at any point the vertical component is the product of density and depth. Tectonic stresses are stresses applied at the boundaries of rock masses and are generally thought to course earthquakes, mountain uplift and faulting. These stresses will be modified by topography and by variations in rock properties. *Residual stresses* are those that remain in the rock after it has been isolated from exterior loads.

3.13 INDIAN BUILDING STONES

The suitability of any building material is based along with other factors, on its availability in local environment. For example, in the parts of interior karnataka, most of the houses are constructed of laterite. The granites, granite gneisses, slates, crystalline limestone, marble, quartzite, charnoekite etc. are considered as very good building stones. Similarly, the banded gneissic rocks are extensively used for the construction of temples, palaces, bridges, hospitals etc.

Makrana marble quarried near Jodhpur, is considered as very important and elegant building stone. It is white in colour with cloudy streaks and grey partings. Makrana marble was used for the construction of most famous Taj Mahal and the most elegant Dilwara Temple, Mount Abu. Similar kind of marble known as Motipura Marble is being quarried in Gujrat. It is a serpentine marble, mottled with pink striations.

Limestones quarried in Madhya Pradesh contain sphourlitic structure in which semi-circular shells exhibit many colour shades. These are used for interior decorations. Similarly, sandstones are also used as decorative stones. These rocks are suitable for carving e.g. Buddhist sculptures, Badami carvings etc. The sandstones are excellent stones due to their homogeneity, regular bedded appearance; uniform grain size, high durability, easy workability and attractive colour. The most famous examples are Fatehpur Sikri, Rashtrapati Bhavan, Delhi secretariat etc.

The charnockites quarried in Tamil Nadu are considered as most durable stones because of their random grain growth, equigranular texture resistant mineral composition etc.

The Aravalli slate is another important roofing material. These are quarried near Ajmer. Another important occurrence of slate is reported near Cuddapah, Andhra Pradesh.

In Maharashtra, the Deccan Basalts are used extensively as building materials. The rocks are available in large masses and as they are mesocratic, they require no colour washing of the outer walls. Very often, basalts due to constant decomposition, alter to laterite. These are used as building stones; for example, Konkan area, Maharashtra.

3.14 CONCRETE AGGREGATES

3.14.1

Aggregates, in case of a material of construction, designates inert materials which when bound together into a conglomeratic mass by a matrix forms concrete, morter, plaster etc.

Precisely aggregates are not inert materials but are chemically and physically active and in many ways control the properties and behaviour of the mass into which they are incorporated.

Coarse aggregate used in concrete is crushed rock or natural rock fragments that are retained on a screen with 1/4 in holes. Fine aggregates are uniformly graded screening of crushed rock that passes through 1/4 in holes. The engineering properties of aggregate are controlled by their shape, size, surface texture and coating of the particles.

The shape of natural rock fragments largely depends on the presence and spacing of natural partings such as cleavage planes in minerals or discontinuity in rocks. If natural weak planes are absent or insignificant, the probability of breaking is equal in all directions and equidimensional products are produced. Mineral like quartz is devoid of weak planes and thus of quartz sand, both angular and rounded, are equidimensional. Feldspars have two cleavages and develop tabular particles when broken. Pronounced stratification, a characteristic of sedimentary rocks, also results in the production of planar or elongated pieces in the aggregates. Basalts tend to produce sharp angular particles. Flat or elongated aggregate particles tend to decrease the workability of concrete and thus more cement, water and crushed rock are required. Similarly sharp angular fragments make a harsh mix which increases the amount of cement required in concrete.

The surface of crushed material may show wide variation from very smooth, regular to striated, very uneven. The number of pores in an aggregate particle directly influences the bond between the material and cement. If pores are fine sized abundant, because of capillarity, these readily absorb water and tend to remain saturated after being enclosed by the cement mortar. Scarcity of pores contributes to the density of the rock, thus making it highly resistant to abrasion, a factor of significance particularly when the concrete is used for the construction of highway parements. The specific gravity of the rock material is important if the specifications require that the concrete have a certain minimum or maximum weight weak and absorptive aggregate usually possess a low specific gravity.

It is necessary that the constituent particles of a concrete mix resist both physical and chemical weathering. Highly porous aggregate deteriorates very easily. They produce weak bond in concrete or induce cracking, spalling or even blisters in the concrete. For example, micaceous minerals.

In many cases, particles in sedimentary deposits show coating of iron and clay minerals. It may be thin or thick, hard or soft and loosely or firmly bonded. Thin, soft and loosely bonded coating may be easily removed by screening and washing.

Following are the important properties of concrete aggregates.

Tenacity is the bond between the aggregate and concrete depends primarily on the structure of an aggregate particle and also on substances filling the pores of the particle. If the substances are soluble, they may be leached from the exposed concrete mass with a resulting decrease in concrete strength.

Volume changes in the concrete may be due to water sorption or high thermal expansivity of the aggregate. In the earlier case, presence of clay minerals (smectite and illites) as impurities in the concrete structure undergo volume change if allowed to absorb water. In the later case, with decreasing temperature tensile stresses may cause fracturing of the mortar or breakage of the bond.

3.14.2 Criteria for Cement-Aggregate Reaction

When concrete is setting and hardening, hydration of cement results in release of alkalies (oxides of sodium and potash). All silicate and silica minerals are attacked by these alkalies. Certain criterias are used to recognize the reactive minerals present in the aggregate.

Silica gels : The most important criteria for recognizing cement aggregate reaction in concrete, both in thin section and hard specimen is the presence of alkalic silica gels. These gels result from interactions between cement alkalies and susceptible rocks and minerals of the aggregate. They occupy pores voids in the cement paste, in cracks and layers upon external surfaces.

The gels in deteriorated concrete show large variation in physical properties controlled largely by water content and degree of carbonation. They are colourless, and transparent or white and porcelaneous. Often both types occur in the same deposit with the colourless type occuring as a shell surrounding the porcelaneous type. Rarely a gel body is homogeneous and made up of only one kind. The gels may be watery, viscous or even hard and brittle in nature.

The gels, chemically, composed mainly of silica and alkalies with minor amounts of CaO, Al_2O_3 and Fe_2O_3.

Reaction rims : The occurrence of alteration rims on aggregate grains of some specific rocks may be characteristic of cement aggregate reaction. They generally exhibit a greater transparency than the minor portion. They may result from combination of two processes, such as, removal of some of the rock constituent by dissolution and penetration of the alkalic silica gel into the interstices of the rock. This is particularly observed in volcanic rocks.

Reaction rims may weaken the peripheral zone of an aggregate particle. As a result, thin shell of rock substance may separate from the interior portion.

3.14.3 Criteria for General Deterioration

Micro fractures : The deteriorated concrete generally show fractures in larger frequency with greater persistance and width than observed in concrete of excellent quality. They may be air filled or filled by secondary deposits.

Calcium hydroxide : Hydration of portland cement produces calcium hydroxide which occurs in all concrete. It may be seen as tiny crystals throughout the cement paste, found as segregation of larger crystals, occupying fractures or voids of various shapes and commonly concentrated in openings adjacent to aggregate particles.

Calcium Carbonate : Carbonation is a common process particularly in fractured concrete which takes place due to penetration of water containing dissolved carbon in oxide. The crystals of calcium carbonate are tiny and may be seen in the form of bands bordering fractures.

Calcium sulphate : Gypsum ($CaSO_4 \cdot 2H_2O$) is formed in concrete as a result of severe attacks by sulphate solutions. It forms at the expanse of calcium compounds in the hydrated cement and may result in serious disintegration.

The above features may be developed during mixing and placing or from original properties of the cement and aggregate.

Presence of abundant irregular pores in concrete is attributed to excess water or lesser cement added to mixture. On the other hand, good quality cement may become porous and soft through leaching and decomposition of the cement.

3.14.4 Alkali-Aggregate Reactions

When water is added to portland cement in making portland concrete, highly alkaline environment is created which may react with the produce aggregate. This happens when a variety of siliceous minerals and rocks and certain dolomitic limestone are used as aggregates. Other factors in the discussion are the alkali type and content in the cement, amount of water available and grain size of particles.

The reaction produce cracking of the concrete due to expansion of the aggregate particles. In addition, the bond between the aggregate particle and the paste may be reduced by a silica gel reaction at the particle-past interface.

The various reactions are as follows :

(A) Alkali-silica reactions : In the alkali-silica reaction, aggregate expansion results from the formation of a silica gel that continues to increase in volume till in content to water. The rate of reaction is controlled by reactivity of the aggregate, proportion of reactive aggregate in the concrete, aggregate size, alkali content of the cement, temperature and availability of water. The reactive aggregates include chert, chalcedony opal, and crypto-crystalline quartz.

(B) Alkali-silicate reactions : The rocks like phyllite, greywacke and argillites are considered as expansive aggregate materials in the alkaline portland cement environment. Several common phyllosilicate minerals are talc, chlorite, kaolinite, serpentine and muscovite have been shown to swell in an aqueous alkaline environment.

(C) Alkali-carbonate reactions : The carbonate aggregates are not immune from alkali reaction problems. The process, called de-dolomitisation by which dolomite is converted to calcite and brucite in an alkaline environment often results in volume expansion.

$$CaMg(CO_3)_2 + 2MOH \rightarrow Mg(OH)_2 + CaCO_3 + M_2CO_3$$
Dolomite   Alkali   Brucite   Calcite   Carbonate

where M represents potassium, sodium of lithium.

The carbonate formed reacts with calcium hydroxide in the portland cement and water mix.

$$M_2CO_3 + Ca(OH)_2 \rightarrow 2MOH + CaCO_3$$

The reactions are controlled by several factors including approximately equal amounts of dolomite and calcite, finer size of calcite, alkaline nature of cement, and appreciable proportion of clay minerals (upto 20%).

The clay minerals help in generating swelling pressure in the mix. However in general, it may be argued that the limestones house often produced excellent record in portland cement.

PART (D) : GEOLOGICAL HAZARDS

3.15 GEOHAZARDS

A natural hazard is a potentially damaging event or the probability that such an event will occur within a given time period and area. **A natural disaster** occurs only if a natural hazard seriously disrupts the functioning of a community, causing widespread human, material or environmental losses that exceed the community's capability to cope without external relief (UNESCO 1993)

Our planet experiences numerous hazards throughout the year, including hundreds of floods, 10,000 earthquakes, landslides, avalanches, hundreds of volcanic eruptions, draughts, cyclones etc. It is calculated that over the last two decades, natural hazards have claimed about 3 million lives and made more than a billion people homeless (Table 3.13). Hence, our foremost task is to study these hazards and caution people about their occurrences and severity.

Table 3.13 : Estimated number of people affected by disasters, 1980 – 1990 ($\times 10^4$, excluding fatalities)

Disaster type	Africa	North & Latin America	Asia	Europe	Australia Pacific	Total
Droughts	1,34,618	30,297	7,87,237	–	71	9,52,233,
Floods	7,124	22,682	4,93,766	839	227	5,24,638
Windstorms	3,600	4,906	1,39,594	871	1415	1,50,336
Earthquakes	828	1,969	23,793	1808	12	28,410
Landslides	10	3,110	17	16	1	3154
Volcanoes	9	58	528	0	25	620
Wildfires	26	216	354	3	13	612
Tsunamis	–	–	1	–	–	1
Total	1,46,215	63,238	14,45,290	3,537	1,764	16,60,044

Two basic kinds of hazard exist : (i) produced by purely natural processes, and (ii) induced as a natural response to human activities. The nature of any hazard varies greatly. Based on their effects, three basic divisions are made :

Macro : effects are regional and severe.
Meso : effects are seen in district or city.
Micro : on the scale of an individual and his immediate environment (village or town).

The effects are influenced by length, mass and time. The details are given in Table 3.14.

Table 3.14

Scale	Dimension	Character of hazard
Micro	Length	Discontinuities, cleavage, compositional variations of rocks, i.e. local variations of small extent and continuity.
	Mass	Local problems caused by a few men.
	Time	Rates of change within the range of man's mobility.
Meso	Length	Volcanoes, deltas, major variation in rocks and stress in-situ, major structures i.e. variations which influence many peoples habit.
	Mass	Disturbance controlled by a communal effort.
	Time	Rates of change that approach the limits of man's mobility.
Macro	Length	Variations which affect complete regions.
	Mass	Disturbances beyond the control of man.
	Time	Rates of change which generally result in injury and death.

Man can live with problems on a micro scale. But the attempts for reduction in the intensity of geological hazards may well be tried. i.e. a macro problem may be reduced to a more acceptable meso scale and meso problems to a more manageable micro problems. Such a reduction is possible only if the cause and behaviour of these hazards are fully understood.

(A) Natural Geohazards : The natural geohazards arising from several natural processes is summarised in Table 3.15.

Table 3.15 : Dominantly Natural Geohazards and Problems

1.	Erosion	– Wind : Hurricanes, Cyclones and Dust storms
		– Rivers : Flash floods.
		– Unstable slopes : Snow avalanches, Mud and Debris flows, Rockfalls and Landslides.
		– Coastlines : Tsunamis and strom waves, shoreline erosion, excessive deposition.
		– Karstification and underground solution of bedrock.
		– Desertification.
2.	Problem Soils	– Expansive and compressible soil, Quick sand and Quick clay, Saline soil.
3.	Land subsidence due to crustal movements.	
4.	Sea-level changes	
5.	Earthquakes	
6.	Volcanism	

It must be remembered that every country is vulnerable to natural hazards.

(B) Human Induced Geohazards : Hazards may also occur in response to changes in the natural systems, for example, increase in severity of floods due to rapid urbanization. Some of these hazards are given in Table 3.16.

Table 3.16 : Dominantly Human-Induced Geohazards and Problems

1. Agriculture and forestry
   - Soil contamination
   - Salinization
   - Accelerated erosion and run-off
2. Mining
   - Land disturbance
   - Contamination of soil and water by mine drainage and tailing
   - Land subsidence, quarries and mine collapse
3. Oil and Gas Development
   - Spills and blow-outs
   - Groundwater contamination
   - Land subsidence.
4. Groundwater Development
   - Subsidence due to withdrawal
   - Aquifer draw-down
   - Salt water invasion and contamination
   - Water table rise
5. Waste Disposal
   - Radioactive waste
   - Hazardous chemicals
   - Sewage
   - Urban garbage
6. Impact of Construction and Development on Geological Environment and conditions
   - Rivers : Water removal for industrial, residential or irrigation purpose.
   - Dams and reservoirs : reservoir silting, decrease in river sediment load, erosion in downstream areas, chemical reactivity of groundwater with construction material, acid drainage from newly exposed bedrock and induced seismicity

(C) Before going into the details of individual events, let us consider definitions of different terms used.

(1) Natural Hazard (H) : The probability of occurrence of a potentially dangerous phenomenon in a specific time span and in a given area.

(2) Succeptibility / Vulnerability : Loss due to a natural hazard (V).

(3) Risk (R) : Expected loss due to the occurrence of natural hazard, $R = H \times V$.

(4) Intensity (E) : The population, properties etc. at risk in a given area.

(5) Total risk (R') : The expected number of lives lost, damage to property etc. due to an occurrence of a natural hazard. It is a product of Risk (R) and Intensity (E).

That is $R' = E \times R = E \times H \times V$

(D) Assessing the Risk : A risk assessment is an estimate of the likely losses from natural hazards in a community over time. Once the losses are known, a community can evaluate the benefits of various measures to reduce losses. The study is divided into different components.

Hazard Identification : In a hazard identification, a community recognises the specific physical phenomena or physical effects (e.g. ground shaking, flood water levels) to which it is exposed. Hazard zones can be mapped according to the frequency, location, intensity and probability of future hazardous events.

Preliminary hazard identifications can be carried out on the basis of existing geologic, geomorphic and soil maps, climate and hydrological data, topographic maps, historical records and published reports (Table 3.17). Hazard identification needs to be an ongoing process. New information about the frequency, probability and intensity of natural hazards is constantly produced and updated. In this, state of art technologies such as GIS should be used efficiently.

The following details are required for a Risk Assessment estimation :

- Locations of previous hazardous events.
- Severity of physical effects.
- Frequency or recurrence of events.
- Injuries and damage patterns.
- Location of populations and facilities (e.g. schools, factories, hospitals and dams) at risk.

Table 3.17 : Methods for identifying and avoiding hazard prone areas through geophysical and land use

Hazard	Specific action	Purpose of mitigation
(1) Earthquakes	(a) Regional investigation of the seismic or paleoseismic studies of the area; Geologic map of faults. (a) Local investigations of the active faults/fractures. (b) Study of aerial photographs, review of groundwater data.	Identification of area of high risk and reduce density of proposed structures.
(2) Expansive soils	(a) Determine swelling potential from different soil index properties; Plasticity index, Shrinkage limit, Liquid limit, Grain size, Colloid content. (b) Microzonation to establish swelling prone areas.	Identification of high risk area.
(3) Landslides	(a) Regional mapping and investigations; Topography, Geology, Precipitation. (b) Local investigations; soil borings, Geophysical surveys, in-situ tests. (c) Evaluate slide potential form; slope geometry, rock of soil strength, groundwater. (d) Microzonation to establish slide prone areas.	Identify potential slide area. Identify factors of safety.

Vulnerability Analysis : A vulnerability analysis considers the population, structures, engineering works and other facilities at risk in hazard prone areas. Much of the information on losses and the performance of structures is recorded during past disasters. The assessments must be undated periodically. The vulnerability changes continuously with population fluctuations and the construction of new houses, roads, industrial facilities and other infrastructure facilities. Satellite data in a computerised 'GIS' can be used to prepare and update these assessments.

Risk Evaluation : Hazard identification and vulnerability analysis, together, provide information on the risk a society faces over time. Thus, a systematic programme can be arranged on prevention, caution and emergency response measures.

3.16 EARTHQUAKE

An earthquake is an oscillatory movement produced due to release of strain energy below or within the crust of the earth's surface. It generates elastic vibrations or 'waves' which move out in all directions from the point of origin. Generally, the weak planes exposed on the earth surface and which are continuous to deep interior are the surface manifestations of an earthquake.

3.16.1 Focus and Epicentre

Before going into the details of earthquake mechanism, let us discuss two important terms (1) Focus, (2) Epicentre.

The point of origin of an earthquake is called as *focus* (Fig. 3.39). The point which is on the surface vertically above the focus is called *epicentre*. In other words, epicentre is the surface manifestation of the focus (Fig. 3.39). The intensity of the earthquake at epicentre is maximum and away from epicentre, the intensity is reduced. If the points of equal intensity are joined, a circular or elliptical line is formed called as isoseismal lines.

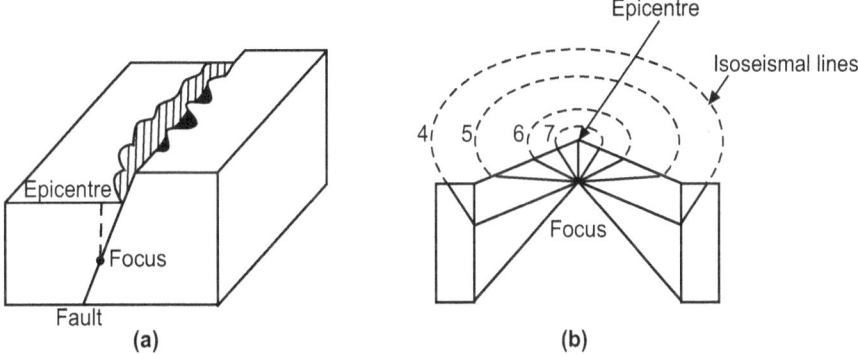

Fig. 3.39 : Focus, Epicentre and Isoseismal lines of an earthquake (a) Sketch of active fault scrap, (b) Intensity of earthquakes diminishes from epicentre. The lines of equal intensity are called isoseismal lines. The numerals shows that intensity decreases away from epicentre

3.17 TYPES OF EARTHQUAKES

Depending upon their causes, earthquakes are classified into three types :
(1) Tectonic Earthquakes (2) Non-tectonic Earthquakes (3) Induced Earthquakes.

(1) Tectonic Earthquakes : These are produced due to earth's movements along the fault plane. Earthquakes caused by volcanic eruptions are commonly feeble or of less intensity. Tectonic earthquakes are very severe and affects a large area. The tectonic earthquakes are further classified according to the focal depth (a) Shallow focus : Focal point is restricted to 0 – 60 km. Deep interior. (b) Intermediate : Focus is recorded in between 60 and 300 km. (c) Deep Earthquakes : Focus may reach upto a depth of 700 km.

(2) Non-tectonic Earthquakes : These occur due to various reasons such as volcanic eruptions, superficial movements like landslides or due to subsidence of ground below the surface etc.

(3) Induced Earthquakes : In certain cases due to disequilibrium in conditions at a place where tectonic stress already existed, earthquake may occur by movement along the fault plane. Earthquakes may also take place due to nuclear explosions. But more commonly, changes in conditions are due to the increase in fluid pore pressure through two ways. (1) artificial recharge by wells by injections of fluids. (2) construction of dams.

3.18 AREAS PRONE TO EARTHQUAKES

When the epicentres are plotted on world map it is distinct that the earthquakes are clustered around certain belts or regions. These are the regions of instability where adjustments are taking place. Two areas of seismic activity are most prominent such as, (a) the circumpacific belt which follows the West coast of North and South America, continued through the aleutan islands and south to Japan, East China, the East indies and New Zealand. (b) the mediterrinean himalayan belt which passes from Spain and Morocco through the Alpine Arc to the Balchans and Asia Minor, through Himalayan ranges to Burma and East Indies where it joins the first belt. It is suggested that about 80% of the recorded earthquakes occur in these two belts. (refer, unit - 1)

3.19 EFFECTS OF EARTHQUAKES

On average, about 200 large magnitude earthquakes occur in a decade – about 20 each year. As the world's population increases and areas previously almost uninhabited become increasingly settled, the possibility for earthquakes to cause damage increases. At the start of the century, less than one in three large earthquakes on the continent killed someone. The number has gradually increased throughout the century, roughly in line with the world's population, until in the 1990's, two earthquakes in every three now kill someone, as shown in the enclosed Fig. 3.40.

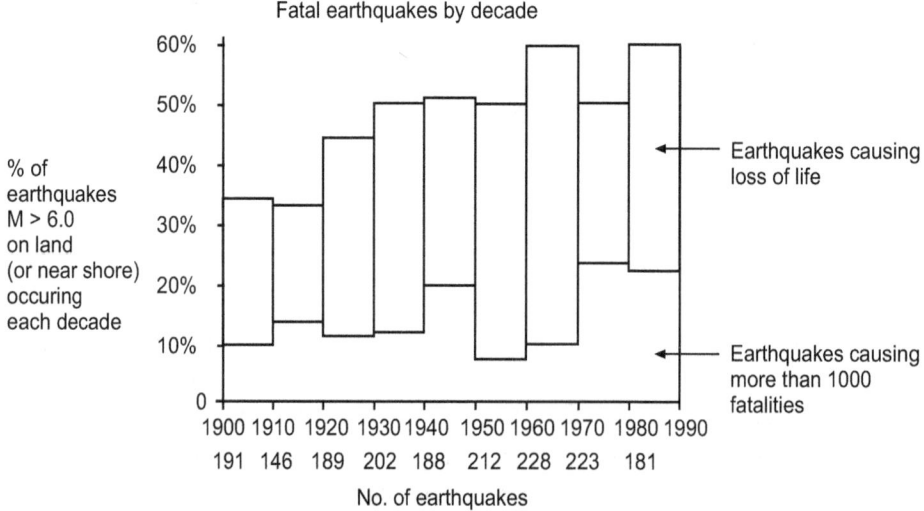

Fig. 3.40 : Earthquake problem in the 20th centaury

An earthquake is not only frightening but also destructive. The recent quake occurred in Killari destroyed the entire village and surroundings with thousands of people losing their lives. Most of the constructions, trees etc. were collapsed. Similar damaging effects were evidenced by the people of Utter Kashi in the year 1991.

The San Andreas fault which runs parallel to west of America is one of the major manifestations of earthquakes. The trace of this fault at the surface is distinctly seen on aerial photographs and satellite imageries, for hundreds of kilometre to the north and south of the San Francisco. In 1906, the area evidenced one of the most severe of earthquakes, when the opposite sides of the walls were moved by almost by 7 m. Surface streams were offset along the fault. Several buildings were collapsed. Bridges and other structures were erected at places. The area again evidenced another severe earthquake in 1971. The damaging effects were again very severe.

Indian subcontinent has witnessed 10 worst earthquakes in the 20th century with magnitude more than six (6). For example, in a short span of 50 years, four such earthquakes with magnitude more than 8 occurred (Assam earthquake, 1897 - 8.7, Kangra earthquake, 1905 - 8.6, Bihar earthquake, 1934 - 8.4, and Assam earthquake, 1950 - 8.7). These earthquakes are mentioned separately by Prof. C. F. Richter in his famous book "Engineering Seismology". A brief mention of these earthquakes is given below along with the kutch earthquake of 1819.

The **Kutch earthquake** of magnitude 8.3 took place on the west coast of India on June 16, 1819. The earthquake caused a fault scrap of 26 km long and about 3 m in height, called as **'Allah Bund'**. This was one of the earliest and largest earthquakes to have occurred in the aseismic areas of India.

The **Assam Earthquake** of June, 12, 1897 (M = 8.7) caused severe damage in an area of 500 km radius resulting into extensive liquefaction in the alluvial plains of Brahmaputra. It is noted that vertical displacement of 11-30 m were observed along 20 km N-S fault, thus producing a number of waterfalls and about 30 smaller lakes in the course of the river. The shaking in the meizoseismal area was so severe that it provided a model for specifying the modified Mercalli earthquake intensity of XII.

The Bihar earthquake of January 15, 1934 (M = 8.4) caused widespread damage in an area of 300 km radius (intensity X in 125 km long and 30 km wide area). The area evidenced extensive liquefaction, thus termed as 'slump belt' it was associated with fissuring liquefaction and formation of sand boils. One of the fissure was 4.5 m deep, 9 m wide and 270 m long.

The Assam earthquake of August 15, 1950 (M = 8.7) was one of worst earthquakes hit the Indians. In Arunachal Pradesh many incidences of landsliding took place. In the tiding valley, a 6.5 km × 0.5 km block slid down into the valley forming a new dam. Similarly a number of dams were formed which brought disastrous floods in Assam.

The 6.8 magnitude **Koyna Earthquake** of December 10, 1967 caused widespread damaged killing about 200 persons and injuring more than 1500 persons. It took place near to the 103 m concrete gravity dam at Koyna. Prior to this earthquake, the area used to be considered aseismic. This earthquake lead to the revision of Indian seismic zonation map where Koyna was brought in zone IV from zone I and Mumbai to zone III from zone I.

The **Uttarkashi Earthquake** of magnitude 6.6 shook the districts of Chamoli, Tehri and Uttarkashi on October, 20, 1991. The maximum earthquake intensity of IX on the modified mercalli scale was mapped to an area of about 20 km. Another earthquake of magnitude 6.8 rocked Chamoli district in the later part of 1998.

The most devastating earthquake on account of loss of human lives and damage to man made structures was recorded on September 30, 1993. The 6.4 magnitude earthquake is known as *Killari Earthquake*. The area was considered as aseismic and was placed in the zone I (lowest seismic zone) by the Indian code (IS : 1893 – 1984). Most of the damage was restricted in a relatively small area of 20 km (human lives more than 8000 were lost) as against the 500 km radius zone in one case of Assam earthquakes of 1897 and 1934.

The **Jabalpur Earthquake** of magnitude 6.0 is the first moderate earthquake to have occurred adjacent to a major Indian city in recent times.

Thus, it can be said that recurrence of seismicity is much higher in Himalaya area than in case of Indian peninsula.

Major earthquakes of the Twenteeth century are given in Table 3.18 along with the location, magnitude on Richter scale and the number of dead.

Table 3.18 : Major Earthquakes of the Twenteeth's century

Date	Location	Magnitude	Loss
19.4.1906	San Francisco	8.3	503
16.8.1906	Chili	8.6	20,000
28.12.1908	Italy	7.5	83,000
13.1.1915	Italy	7.5	29,980
16.12.1920	China	8.3	1,00,000
1.9.1923	Tokyo	8.6	1,00,000
22.5.1927	China	8.3	2,00,000
26.12.1932	China	7.6	70,000
2.3.1933	Japan	8.9	2,990
15.1.1934	India	8.4	10,700
31.5.1935	India	7.5	30,000
24.1.1939	Chili	8.3	28,000
26.12.1939	Turkey	7.9	30,000
21.12.1946	Japan	8.4	2,000
28.6.1948	Japan	7.3	5,131

... Contd.

5.8.1949	Eucador	6.8	6,000
15.8.1950	India	8.7	1,530
18.3.1953	Turkey	7.2	1,200
10.6.1956	Afganistan	7.7	2,000
2.7.1957	Iran	7.4	2,500
13.12.1957	Iran	7.1	2,000
19.2.1960	Morocco	5.8	12,000
21.5.1960	Chili	8.3	5,000
1.9.1962	Iran	7.1	12,230
26.7.1963	Yugoslavia	6.0	1,100
27.3.1964	Alaska	8.3	131
19.8.1966	Turkey	6.9	2,520
31.8.1968	Iran	7.4	12,000
28.3.1970	Turkey	7.4	1,086
31.5.1970	Peru	7.4	66,794
10.4.1972	Iran	6.9	5,057
13.12.1972	Nicaragna	6.2	5,000
28.12.1974	Pakistan	6.3	5,200
6.9.1975	Turkey	6.8	2,312
4.2.1976	Guatemala	7.5	22,778
6.5.1976	Italy	6.5	946
28.7.1976	China	7.8 – 8.2	2,42,000
17.8.1976	Phillippines	7.8	8,000
24.11.1976	Turkey	7.9	4,000
16.9.1978	Iran	7.7	2,50,000
23.11.1980	Italy	7.2	4,200
30.10.1983	Turkey	7.1	1,300
19.9.1985	Mexico	8.1	9,500
7.12.1988	Armenia	6.9	25,000
21.6.1990	Iran	7.7	40,000
16.9.1990	Phillipines	7.8	1,700
30.9.1993	India	6.4	10,000
16.1.1995	Japan	6.9	5,400

3.20 ELASTIC REBOUND THEORY

The theory postulates that when a force is applied to two adjacent fault blocks, friction is first sufficient to prevent movement parallel to the fault plane. As a result of continued forces, a zone on either side of the fault undergoes elastic deformation. When the continued forces reaches a magnitude that exceeds the frictional resistance of the fault surface, the elastically stored energy is suddenly released and the effects are recorded in the form of displacement along the fault plane (Fig. 3.41). Thus, it can be said that the earthquakes occur from a more or less continuous deformational process, the energy liberated being stored elastically in the rock instantaneously.

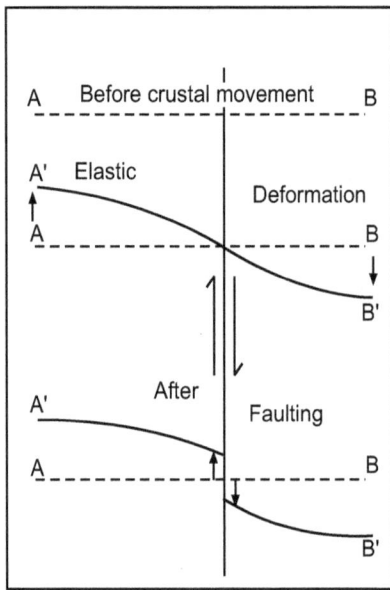

Fig. 3.41 : Diagram illustrating the concept of elastic rebound theory along a fault

The elastic rebound theory has many implications. The theory defines an absolute upper limit of elastic properties of the rock beyond which earthquake shocks may attain. It also indicate that an earthquake may be preceded by foreshocks and followed by after shocks.

3.21 EARTHQUAKE WAVES

The elastic vibrations are created when a fault slip takes place from the earthquake focus and travel in all directions. They are of three kinds. Primary wave, secondary wave and surface wave. Primary and secondary waves are also known as body waves.

(1) Primary or Compressional Waves : These are compressional or sound waves, consisting of longitudinal vibrations which give an oscillatory movement to the particles in the direction in which waves are propagated (p) (Fig. 3.42).

(2) Secondary Waves : These are shear waves which give transverse vibrations with an oscillatory movement at right angles to their path (s) (Fig. 3.42).

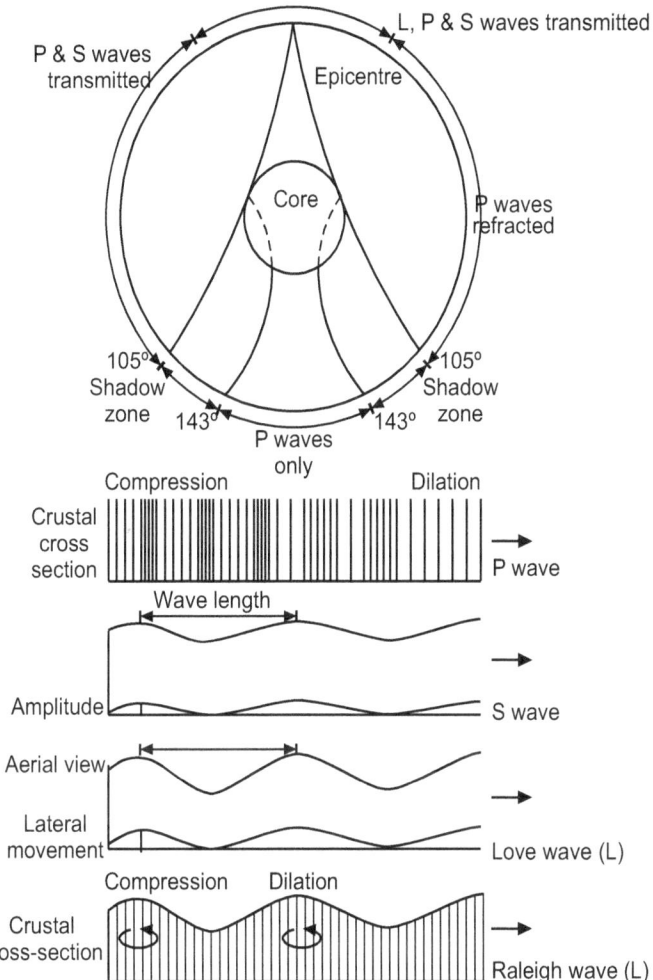

Fig. 3.42 : Propagation of earthquake waves

(3) Surface or Love Waves : These are shallow waves or waves of long period which travel around periphery of the earth (L). The influence of vibration causes horizontal as well as vertical movement (Fig. 3.42).

Velocity of these waves is largely influenced by three factors. (i) the Density - D, (ii) the bulk-modulus–K, i.e. the resistance to the change of volume without change of shape (iii) the rigidity – modulus, N, i.e. the resistance to change of shape without change of volume. It is suggested that for compressional wave, velocity is equal to $\frac{K + 4/3\,N}{D}$ and for shear waves velocity is N/D . Thus, it is seen that compressional waves travel faster than shear waves in the same medium. In fluid medium where rigidity is zero, there can be no shear waves and the velocity of compressional waves will be K/D. Therefore, from these statements, it can be said that P waves, the compressional waves, receive first on seismogram followed by shear or S wave and as L waves are surface waves these will be recorded last on the seismogram.

3.22 EARTHQUAKE INTENSITY AND MAGNITUDE

The severity of earthquake is evaluated by considering two factors,

(i) energy released during faulting, and

(ii) observed effects in the environment i.e. damage caused to human lives and property.

The energy released is measured on the basis of the amplitude of the largest wave recorded on the seismogram. The amplitude is measured in a linear (logarithmic) scale and the magnitude (M) is the logarithm of the amplitude.

The magnitude can be calculated by considering the largest amplitude of waves recorded on seismogram. When the largest amplitude of the body-wave pulse is used, the magnitude is called *body-wave magnitude* (M_b). When the largest amplitude of surface wave pulse is used, the magnitude is called surface wave magnitude (M_s). The relationship of these two is given by Howell (1973) as,

$$M_b = 2.5 + 0.63\ M_s$$

Magnitude is related to the amount of energy released by an earthquake. The empirical relation between two is postulated by many scientists, the one given by Bath (1966) is, $\log_{10} E = 12.24 + 1.44\ M$, where the energy is released in ergs. This scale is developed by Charlees F. Richter in 1935. The scale ranges upto 10 and energy released during any next number is 31.5 times greater than the previous number.

Table 3.19 : Richter scale

Richter Earthquake Magnitude	Approx. energy (equivalent of explosion of T.N.T.)
1.0	170 gm
2.0	6 gm
3.0	179 gm
4.0	5 tons
5.0	180 tons
6.0	5,687 tons
7.0	90,7000 tons
8.0	56,86,890 tons
9.0	18,04,93,000 tons

The other scale which is based on the destruction caused to human life and property, known as Mercallis. This is as follows :

Table 3.20 : Modified Mercallis scale

Intensity	Effects	Maximum acceleration of ground
I	Instrumental : Detected only by seismogram.	10
II	Feeble : noticed only by sensitive people.	25
III	Slight : Felt by people at rest especially on upper floors.	50
IV	Moderate : Felt by people while walking, sliding of loose boulders.	100
V	Rather strong : Felt generally, heavy furniture may move, most of those in sleep are awakened.	250
VI	Strong : Falling of loose objects, moderate to intense damage for ordinary structures.	500
VII	Very strong : Walls crack, plaster falls, moderate to intense damage for constructions.	1000
VIII	Destructive : Car drivers seriously disturbed, poorly constructed buildings damaged, chimney falls, changes in water wells.	2500
IX	Rumous : Some houses collapse where ground begins to crack; Underground pipes are broken.	5000
X	Disastrous : Landslides on steep slopes, ground cracks badly, railways bend, some wooden structures destroyed, water, splashed over banks.	7500
XI	Very Disastrous : Few buildings remain standing, bridges destroyed all services (rails, cables etc.) out of action, great landslides.	9800
XII	Catastrophic : Total destruction, objects thrown into air, ground rises and falls in waves.	

The relationship between Mercallis scale and Richter's scale is as follows :

Table 3.21 : Relation between Richter and Mercallis scale

Richter	Area evidenced (km²)	Distance	Mercallis	Ground acceleration
3.0 – 3.9	1,950	29 km	II – III	< 0.15
4.0 – 4.9	7,800	50 km	IV – V	0.15 – 0.04
5.0 – 5.9	39,000	110 km	VI – VII	0.06 – 0.15
6.0 – 6.9	1,30,000	200 km	VII – VIII	0.15 – 0.30
7.0 – 7.9	5,20,000	400 km	IX – X	0.50 – 0.60
8.0 – 8.9	20,80,000	720 km	XI – XII	> 0.60

3.23 LOCATING EPICENTRE AND FOCUS

When the time taken by the arrival of P and S waves in various seismological stations is plotted together against distance, they commonly fall on smooth curves.

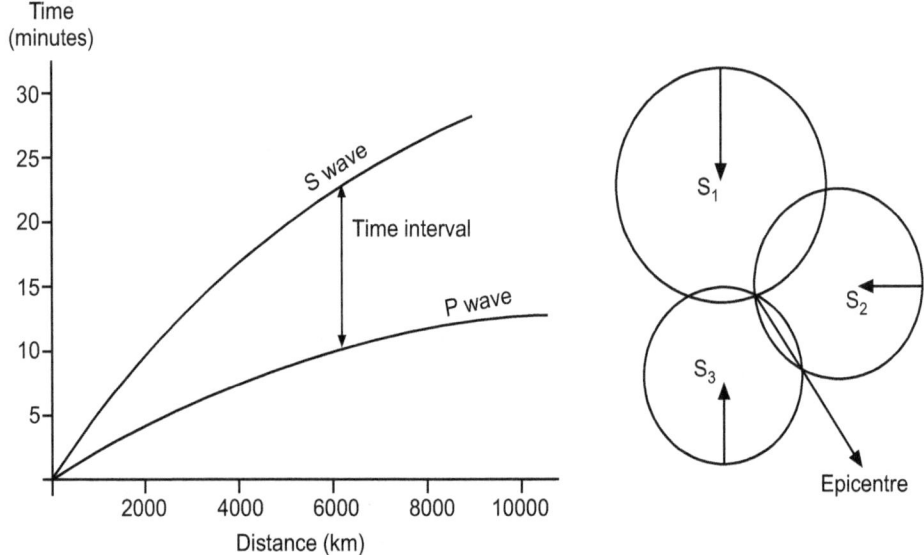

Fig. 3.43 : Locating epicentre

From the Fig. 3.43 it is seen that the time interval between arrival of P and S increases with an increase in the distance. Thus, when an earthquake is recorded at different stations, measurement of time interval between S and P waves gives an idea about the distance from the epicentre and station. A circle is drawn around each station with a radius corresponding to the respective distance of the epicentre.

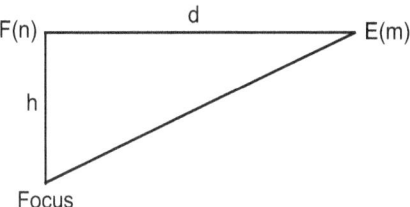

Fig. 3.44 : Locating focus

Intensity at E = m (known)
F = n (known)
Distance between E and F = d (known)

The focus point of an earthquake can be elucidated by considering the intensity at E i.e. epicentre, intensity at F, i.e. at a station and distance between these two i.e. d.

Thus, $\dfrac{n}{M} = \dfrac{h^2}{r^2} = (\sin \theta)^2$. The angle θ can be calculated.

Hence, $\tan \theta = \dfrac{h}{D}$

$H = D \cdot \tan \theta$

3.24 INTERNAL STRUCTURE OF THE EARTH

The study of many earthquakes indicated many significant records. It was found that P and S waves were not transmitted to stations situated at distances greater than 105 arc away from an epicentre (the distance is measured around the earth). But at 142 of arc from the epicentre, only P waves were recorded in the modified form and S waves were completely absent. Thus, the region between zone through which no P and S wave were transmitted, even though P waves were recorded. At 142 arc the velocity was reduced suggesting a change in the composition of material. The curve of P – S waves against depth in km indicated similar result. It was also seen that S waves were completely absent beneath a certain depth (Fig. 3.45). Thus, the material available at deep interior appeared to have no rigidity, as S waves did not transmit through fluid medium. Therefore, it is suggested that the earth's core is in liquid state which is surrounded by solid material, and the radius of the core is calculated as 3500 km. The boundary between the core and the overlying material is known as "Weichert Guttenberg discontinuity".

Density of the earth is 5.5. However, rocks exposed on and at shallow depth have an average density of 2.57 – 3.0 approx. The core thus must be heavy with a mean density to be about 12. The heaviest material on the surface is iron (density 7.8). Further, certain meteorites are made of nickel – iron alloys with an average density of 8.2. Thus, it is suggested that the core is composed of a mixture of nickel and iron in a fluid state under high temperature and pressure conditions. The velocity of P wave at a depth between 4900 – 5700 suggests a gradual increase which is further followed by steep increase in velocity. This favours the existence of transitional zone between outer core and inner core, which is known as "Lehman discontinuity". (Fig. 3.45)

Table 3.22 : Internal structure of the earth (a. Holmes, 1981)

Zones		Depth (and radius) in km	Velocity of P waves in km/sec	Density gm/cm^3	Pressure in 10^6 bars approximately in atmospheres
Crust	A	Sea level (6371)		2.7	
			—	2.8	—
				2.9	
Mohorovicic Discontinuity		33 (6338)			9000
			7.9 8.1	3.32	
		50 Low velocity	7.8		
		250 zone	8.1		
Upper	B				
Mantle		413 (5958)	8.97	3.64	1,40,000
	C	720 (Deepest earthquake)	10.87	4.29	2,70,000
		984 (5387)	11.42	4.64	3,82,000
Lower	D		13.64	5.66	
Mantle		2898 (3473) Oldham or Gutenberg Discontinuity			13,68,000
Outer Core	E		8.10	9.71	
		4703 (1667)		11.76	31,80,000
Transition	F		10.31		
		5154 (1216)		C. 14	C. 33,00,000
Inner Core			11.23		
	G	63 (centre)		C. 16	C. 36,00,000

From the Fig. 3.45 it is seen that the S waves are completely absent at a depth greater than 2900 km. Further, there is sudden fall in the velocity of P waves which marks the presence of Gutenberg discontinuity.

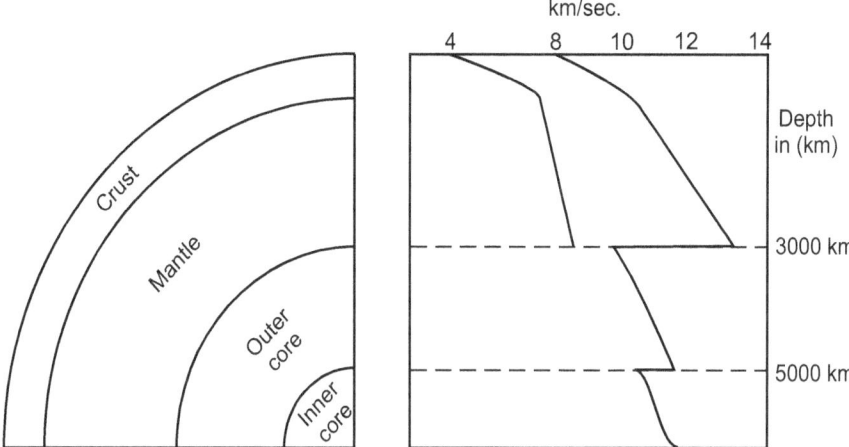

Fig. 3.45 : Schematic sketch showing delineation of internal structure of the earth based on velocities of P and S waves

At a depth of about 35 km, the change in the velocity of P and S waves is distinct. This is considered as a base of crust and beginning of mantle, which was first recognised by Mohorovicic in 1909, thus known as Mohorovicic discontinuity. When the velocities in the crust are compared with those calculated for rocks tested in the laboratory, it was found that the velocity recorded for superfacial and shallow depth material is similar to Granites and velocities recorded beneath this zone upto Mohorovicic discontinuity is similar to Basalt. Thus, the upper surface of the earth upto 15 – 20 km approximately consists of granite, called as SIAL indicating predominance of Silica and Aluminium. Whereas the lower portion is SIMA which is traced upto Mohorovicic discontinuity. This is indicative of dominance of Silica and Magnesium. The table given below summarizes the data of interior of earth. (Table 3.22)

3.25 EARTHQUAKE HAZARDS

Earthquakes produce many direct and indirect effects. Some of them are considered as secondary hazards e.g. landslides and tsunamis.

Fault displacement and ground shaking : Fault displacement, either rapid or gradual, may damage foundation of buildings on or near the fault area or may displace the land creating ridges and troughs.

Ground shaking causes more widespread damage particularly to the man made structures. The extent of damage is related to the size of the earthquake, shallow focus, capacity of rock or soil to absorb strain energy and the type of building being affected. After shocks may cause further damage. They may continue for a period of weeks or even a few months.

Ground failure : Seismic vibrations may cause settlement beneath buildings when soils consolidate or compact. Certain types of soils, such as quicksand or sandy soils, are more likely to fail during an earthquake.

Liquefaction is a type of ground failure which occurs when saturated soil losses its shear strength and becomes liquefied. Another type of ground failure that may result from earthquakes is **subsidence** or vertically downward earth movement caused by reduction in soil water pressure.

Landslides : Slope instability may cause landslides during an earthquake. Steepness of slope, weak soil and presence of water may increase instability of slopes. Liquefaction of soils on slopes may lead to disastrous slides.

Flooding : Tsunamis may be generated by marine earthquakes which may break over the coastlines with great destructive power. Other flooding may be caused by seiches or failures in dams and levees.

3.26 EARTHQUAKES PREDICTION

Table 3.23 : Recognition of active faults on descriptions of Historical, Geological and Seismological evidence

Evidence	Inactive	Potentially active	Active
Geological criteria	Geomorphic features typical of active fault are absent and geologic evidence indicate no recent movement along fault.	(1) Geomorphic features typical of active fault are eroded, subdued and inconsistent.	(1) The young deposits have been displaced or cut by faulting.
		(2) Fault may not be seen in younger alluvium, but may be found in older alluvium.	(2) Fresh geomorphic expressions are seen on fault face.
		(3) Water barrier may be found in older materials.	(3) Water barriers in younger sediments.
Historical criteria	No historic activity	No reliable record of event.	(1) Surface faulting and associated severe earthquakes.
			(2) Tectonic fault creep or geodetic indications of movement.
Seismological criteria	No activity	Alignment of some earthquake epicentres along fault trace but no reliable data.	Earthquake epicentres are aligned along individual fault with a high degree of confidence.

(a) Spatial Prediction : Almost all tectonic earthquakes occur along the active fault planes. The active faults are those along which movement has occurred in the recent geological past and future movement is expected. Thus, a key to identification of such faults is possible with the help of field mapping at sufficient scale showing known or inferred active faults. However, the geological indications favouring recent movement along the fault are rare. Fault showing displacement of stream, glacial moraine etc. can be considered as active (Table 3.23). The observations on San Andreas fault suggest important change in behaviour of rocks in different areas. Certain regions are seismically very active evidenced due to definite earth movements and other segments are passive. Such passive regions are most dangerous as the fault is locked and is storing energy. The accumulated strain would be released in the form of major earthquake if the stresses accumulated in the rocks exceed the strength of the rock. Thus, these seismic gaps are considered as potential for future great earthquakes.

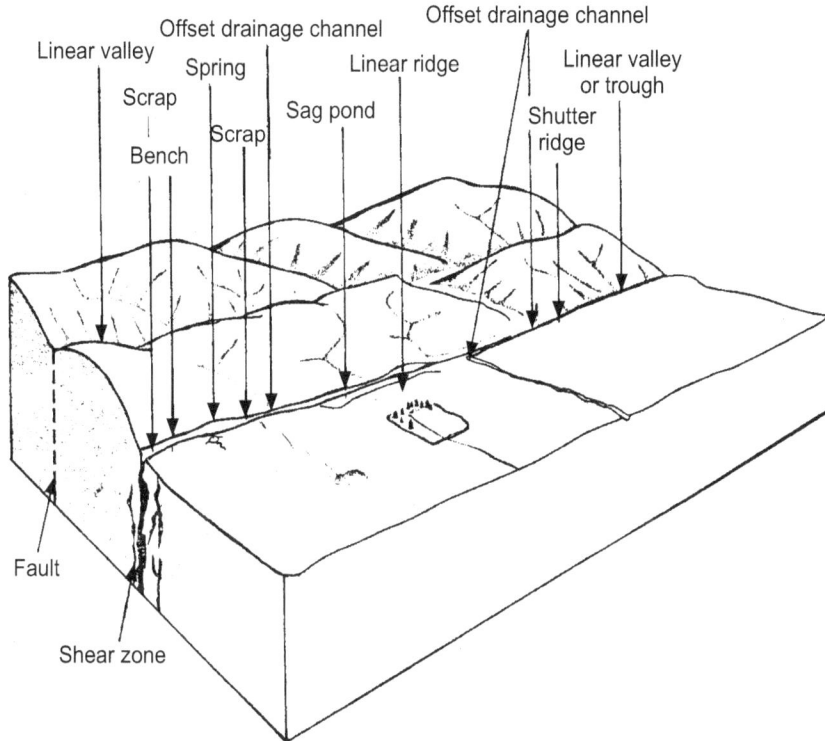

Fig. 3.46 : Common landforms along the active strike slip fault system

Neotectonics : The study of landforms affected by recent earth movements, neotectonics can often provide indirect indications of earthquake activities, particularly historic earthquakes. The science that deals with study of historical earthquake using morphotectonic signatures, is called **paleoseismology**. A possible relationship between morphotectonic features and earthquakes is faithfully shown in case of San Andreas fault and also in case of Alpine fault, New Zealand.

Drainage is one of the sensitive indicators of neotectonic events. Streams and rivers can either be displaced by such an event or have their gradients changed. In either case, response is very rapid. There now exists a long list of geomorphological indicators of earthquake (tectonic) activity (Table 3.23) some of which are also given in Fig. 3.46.

Often indications are given by river terraces (Fig. 3.41) and alluvial fans (Fig. 3.48) as morphological and sedimentological cleans to neotectonic activity which may be accompanied by earthquakes.

Table 3.24 : Geomorphological indicators of neotectonic activity

Direct :
Displacement of dated beaches.
Deformed shorelines.
Distortion of river terraces.
Deformation of alluvial fans.
Displacement of dated terraces.
Warping of plantation surfaces.
Fault scraps
Shutter ridges
Separation of river terraces.
Displacement of man-made structures.

Indirect Response :
Response of stream channels.
River capture.
Formation of lakes.

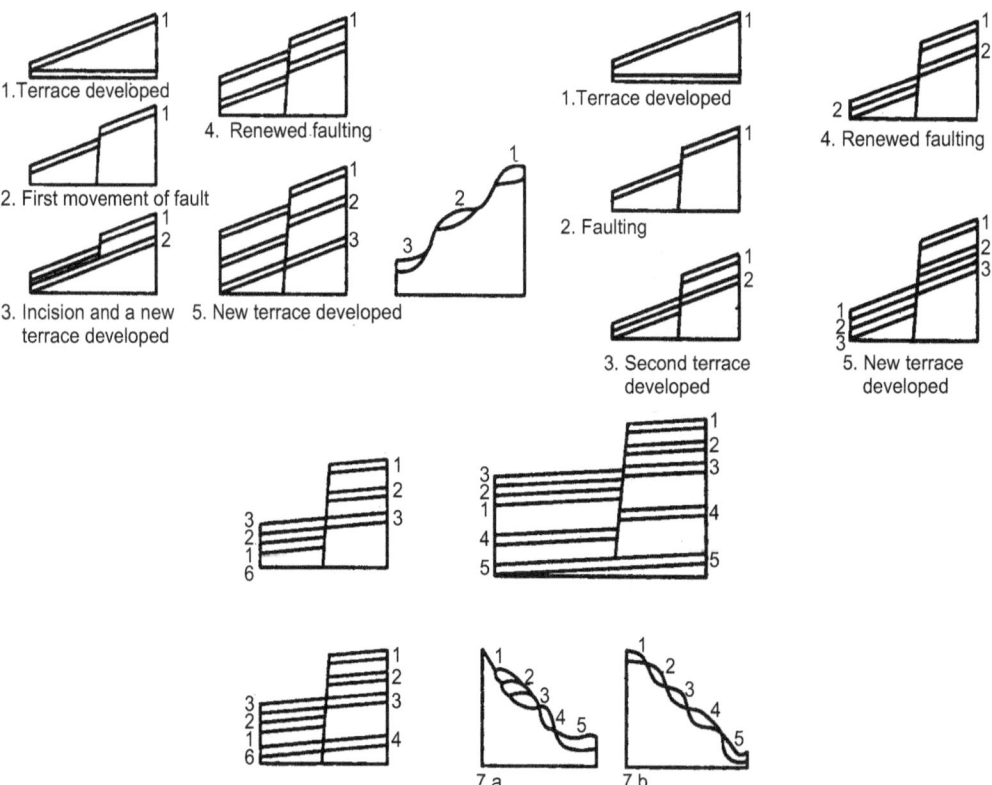

Fig. 3.47 : Effects of recent faulting on the river terraces

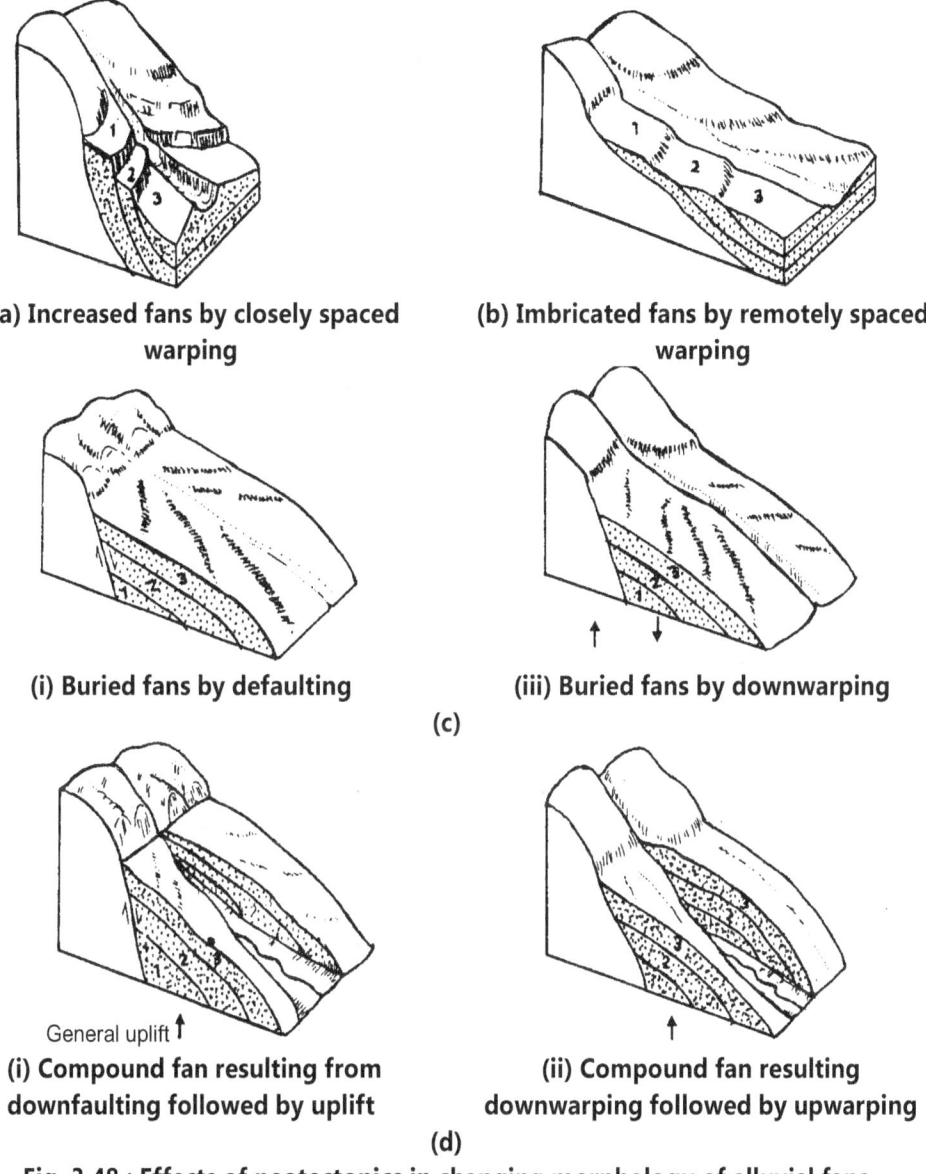

Fig. 3.48 : Effects of neotectonics in changing morphology of alluvial fans

The above mentioned indicators and by comparison with past earthquake events experienced in China, it has shown that earthquakes tend to occur in the following specific locations : at the ends of the faults, where faults make a sharp change in direction and at the intersection of active faults. Detailed geomorphological studies have indicated evidence of recent movement along faults in the form of behaved streams, deflected and offset streams, shutter ridges, pressure ridges, fault scarps and sag ponds (Fig. 3.48).

Liquefaction : The term liquefaction has been used in conjunction with a variety of phenomenon that involve soil deformation caused under undrained conditions. The generation of high pore water pressure under undrained condition is typical of liquefaction process. When cohesionless soil is saturated, rapid loading occurs under undrained conditions, so the tendency for densification causes excess pore water pressure to increase and effective stresses to decrease. Liquefaction phenomenon that result from this process can be divided into two major groups : Flow liquefaction and cyclic mobility.

Both flow liquefaction and cyclic mobility are very important. In the field, flow liquefaction occurs much less frequently than cyclic mobility, but its effects are usually more severe. Flow liquefaction produces flow-failures, which can occur when shear stress required for static equilibrium of a soil mass is greater than the shear strength of the soil in its liquefied state. The failures are characterised by the sudden nature of their origin, the rate at which they develop and the larger distance over which the liquefied materials often move.

Cyclic mobility is another phenomenon that can also produce large permanent deformation during earthquake shaking. It occurs when the static shear stress is less than the shear strength of the liquefied soil. The deformations produced by cyclic mobility are driven by both cyclic and static shear stresses. These deformations, termed as lateral spreading, can occur on very gently sloping ground or even on flat ground adjacent to water bodies.

Liquefaction susceptibility : Not all soils are susceptible to liquefaction. However, if the soil is susceptible, the matters of liquefaction initiation and its effects must be recognised. Four major criteria are used, namely, historical, geological, compositional and state criteria.

A great deal of information on liquefaction behaviour has come from post earthquake field investigations. It is observed that liquefaction often recurs at the same location when soil and groundwater conditions have remained unchanged. Thus, based on certain post depositional structures in soil, specific sites may be recognised.

Soil deposits that are susceptible to liquefaction are formed within a narrow range of geological environments. Generally, the geologic processes that sort soils into uniform grain-size distributions and deposit them in loose states produce soil deposit with high liquefaction susceptibility. Fluvial deposits, colluvium and wind worn deposits are likely to be susceptible to liquefaction than alluvial fan, alluvial plane, beach and lacustrine deposits. The older soil is often less prone to liquefaction than that of never deposits. i.e. Soils of Holocene age are more susceptible than soils of Pleistocene age, although susceptibility decreases with age within the Holocene.

Liquefaction occurs only in saturated soils. Thus, the depth of groundwater influences liquefaction susceptibility. Human made loose soil fills (loose compaction) are very likely to be susceptible to liquefaction.

Another important characteristic that influence liquefaction is compositional changes associated with large volume changes.

Liquefaction susceptibility also depends on the initial state of the soil (i.e. stress and density characteristics at the time of earthquake).

However, it may be remembered that although cyclic mobility is an earthquake related phenomenon, flow liquefaction can be initiated in a variety of other ways.

(b) Temporal Prediction : Upto certain extent, it is possible to predict the temporal occurrence of an earthquake. For example, the earthquake of the magnitude of 7.3 occurred in 1975 was successfully predicted by Chinese with the help of certain foreshocks that had began since 1971. They could not however predict the most severe earthquake of 1976; which destroyed the entire city of Tanghan. The observations made on certain regions suggested that before the occurrence of major earthquake, the area has evidenced numerous foreshocks or tremors. In addition, the following scientific methods are adopted for temporal earthquake prediction (Fig. 3.49).

(1) **Seismic wave velocity :** It is observed that the difference in arrival time between P and S waves decreases from normal.

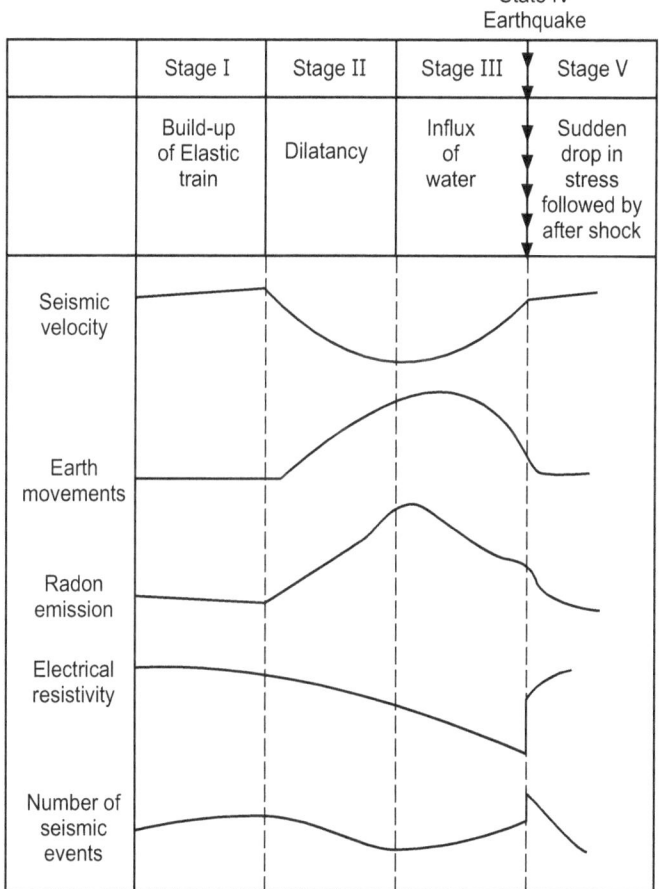

Fig. 3.49 : Temporal prediction of earthquakes

(2) **Radon gas :** Increase in radon concentration is observed prior to major earthquake. However, there is no adequate data to support this.

(3) **Groundwater levels :** Drop in ground water level in wells prior to major earthquake, as evidenced in Japan, China and California. It is suggested that prior to fault displacement, tiny cracks or fissures open up parallel to fault allowing water to move into the pore. This results in lowering of groundwater level in the area.

(4) Seismic activity : The abnormal seismic record in the area of 'locked segment" provide significant information.

(5) Crustal elevation changes : Uplifting or subsidence prior to earthquake e.g. San Andreas fault surveys carried out in the area north of Los Angeles (85,000 km^2) showed an uplift of 0.45 m between 1961 and 1977.

(6) Animals : Strange animal behaviour is observed prior to major earthquake.

Based on these methods Press (1975) postulated one model of 'Dilatency' which is a step further in the various process, which are used as precursors of earthquakes. (Fig. 3.49)

EXERCISE

1. Describe any two features resulting from river deposition.
2. Describe with neat sketches any one feature resulting from river erosion, river deposition and rejuvenation respectively.
3. Explain process of coastal erosion.
4. Explain factors controlling weathering.
5. Give an account of Deccan Trap Basalts with reference to varieities, distribution, structure and age.
6. Write Notes on : (i) Mineral wealth of Dharwars, (ii) Vindhyan building stones, (iii) Pre-Cambrian metamorphic rocks, (iv) Order of superposition, (v) Geological time scale.
7. Write a note on physiographic divisions of India.
8. Explain Field characters of Deccan Trap Basalt.
9. Write short note on : Youth stage of a river.
10. Write short note on : Climatic changes during Gondwana period.
11. Write note on Gondwana coal.
12. Describe two features developed due to river erosion.
13. Give comparative account of Peninsular and extra-peninsular division of India.
14. Give an account of Deccan Trap Basalt w.r.t. (i) Distribution, (ii) Varieties of Basalts.
15. Write note on : Eparchaean Interval.
16. Write a note on : Vindhyan Building stone.
17. Write a note on : Graded profile and base level of erosion.
18. Discuss the influence of mineral composition and texture on the suitability of a building stone.
19. Write notes on : (i) Dimension stones, (ii) Qualities of a good building stone, (iii) Engineering characteristics of building stones , (iv) Architectural appearance of building stones durability.
20. What are earthquakes ? How are they caused ? Explain seismic waves ?
21. Write notes on : (i) Tectonic earthquakes, (ii) Elastic rebound theory, (iii) Earthquake waves, (iv) Earthquake magnitude and intensity, (v) Internal structure of the earth, (vi) Earthquake, (vii) Recognition of active faults.

Unit 4

PRELIMINARY GEOLOGICAL STUDIES, REMOTE FUNCTION AND GEOPHYSICAL EXPLORATION

PART (A) : PRELIMINARY GEOLOGICAL EXPLORATIONS

INTRODUCTION

Geological investigations are necessary as they provide information regarding stability of an engineering structure which is to be constructed in the area of investigation. Site investigations are carried out by using basic knowledge of geology. This approach may be divided into a four-phase study.

Phase I : PRELIMINARY INVESTIGATION

A careful study of geology, geomorphology, history etc. is done with the help of available geologic maps and also by using conventional remote sensing techniques. This helps in identifying critical areas or routes in the area of investigations.

Phase II : FIELD INVESTIGATION

Intensive field work is done to check the geological map followed by collection, plotting and synthesis of structural and sedimentological data. Drilling bore-holes and test pits in critical areas, logging cores and examining pits: in-situ testing, taking oriented samples of laboratory analysis and testing. Evaluation of hydrogeological conditions.

Phase III : LABORATORY TESTING

Re-examination and testing of samples; comparison of results with the analysed structural data.

Phase IV : FIELD MEASUREMENT

Monitoring of critical areas to check the possible effects due to construction; for example: squeezing of rocks, heave etc.

In case of dam, tunnel construction, study of all phases is essential, while in the case of smaller structures like low rise housing development, first two phases are important.

In this chapter, each phase is discussed in brief but not by giving them separate status.

4.1 PRELIMINARY DESK STUDIES

Preliminary desk studies involve collection of documentary material relating to the history, topography, geology and hydrology of the area, in order to get an idea about ground condition and possible geotechnical problems and to allow the design of a site investigation programme. These three kinds of features can be graphically represented on maps and aerial photographs.

(a) Topographic Maps :

A topographic map is a representation of natural and man made features of an area by means of conventional signs upon a plane surface. A topographic map shows both horizontal distances between the features and their elevations above mean sea level. The configuration of land surface, called relief, can be represented on the map by means of contour lines. The map also shows drainage and culture by means of symbols.

Topographic maps are prepared on different scales (1 : 10,00,000, 1 : 2,50,000, 1 : 50,000 and 1 : 25,000). The most convenient scale available over recent years is 1 : 50,000. Though more detailed maps are available on 1 : 25,000 scale, however their coverage still is very limited. If the distances on the map are considerably decreased, it is said to be 'Low-scale' map (1 : 10,00,000 and 1 : 2,50,000). The opposite would be a 'Large-scale' map (1 : 50,000 and 1 : 25,000).

Elevation difference on the map is shown by contour lines. The contour interval is the vertical distance between the contours. Generally, the contour interval is 20 m in case of 1 : 50,000 and 1 : 25,000 maps, but in mountainous terrain, the interval is 40 metres. The shape of contours and value of contour lines are useful in interpreting geomorphic expression of an object (Hill, valley …).

Topography generally tends to reflect the structure and composition of the underlying rocks. The simplest case that may be illustrated is that of a region underlain by rocks of uniform resistance to erosion. If such a region is subjected to fluvial erosion, the drainage pattern will tend to develop dentritic drainage pattern. Thus, any homogeneous rock may give rise to dendritic drainage where surface run-off is more. For example, horizontally bedded sedimentary rocks and large bodies of igneous rocks.

A more general case may be illustrated by beds of alternating hard and soft rocks that have been thrown into large anticlines and synclines. This type of structure is characterised by a topography consisting of arcuate asymmetrical ridges (hogbacks). As the bedding planes of sedimentary rocks represent units of equal resistant to erosion, it is reasonable to argue that on inclined bedded layer an erosional surface will develop which approximately parallels the plane formed by intersection of dip and strike, called as **dip slope**. The side opposite to dip slope is not influenced by the bedding plants and is usually steeper than the dip slope. Thus, the dip is normally away from the direction towards which the steeper side of the escarpment faces.

Faults are usually difficult to interpret from topographic maps.

(b) Geological Maps :

A **geological map** is a two dimensional representation of the distribution and structure of rock in an area with as much detail as is commensurate with the scale on which the map is constructed. In practice, the smallest rock unit that can be lineated on the scale adopted is usually the formation. But as formation usually consist of more than one rock type, the average areal geology map does not as a rule exhibit the distribution of distinct rock types. Small scale maps are sufficient to establish the principal rock types in the area, the broader structural frames and the main outlines of the history through which the region has passed. However, they do not show outcrop scale complexities and heterogeneity in the distribution of bedrock. They are, therefore insignificant for many engineering operations which require very high scale maps (1 cm = 10 m).

Each geological map carries a legend or explanation of maps used in the compilation (Fig. 4.1).

Subsurface rock structures, being three dimensional, cannot be competently shown on a two-dimensional surface maps which essentially is nothing more than a horizontal projection. Therefore, to complete the information given by the surface geologic map, geological cross section or columnar information is usually added on geological map. The geological section presents the strata as they would appear on a vertical plane, if the locality was divided by such a plane. Geological sections are usually, highly interpretative if accurately constructed. In preparing a geological section, the geologist is aided by the information obtained from bore holes, well logs, road cuts, abondoned mines/quarries geophysical surveys or some type of excavation at the site. The geological section will have a uniform vertical and horizontal scale. However, it is often necessary to exaggerate the vertical scale i.e. to make the vertical scale several times larger than the horizontal scale. When, such distorted geological sections are used, correct interpretation should be given to any slopes below.

Bedrock lithology

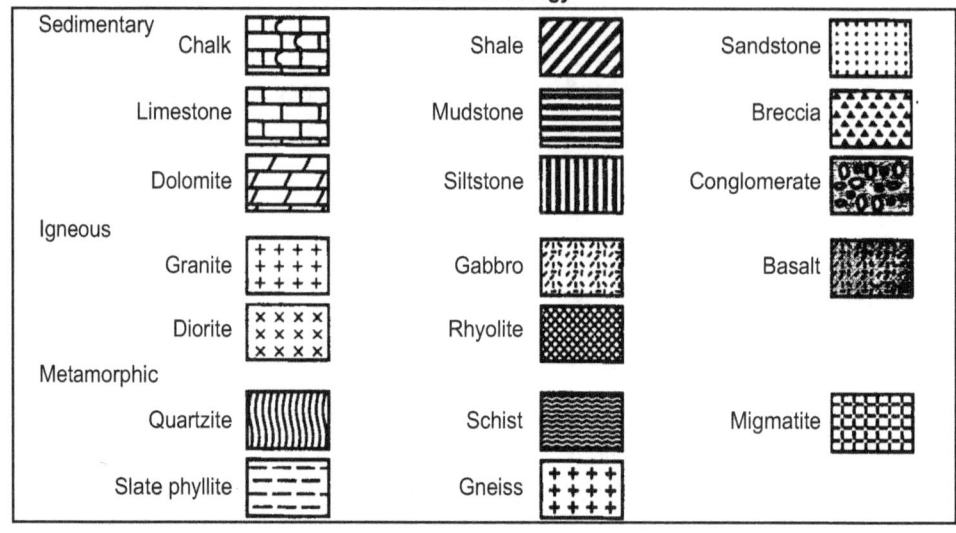

Geological structures

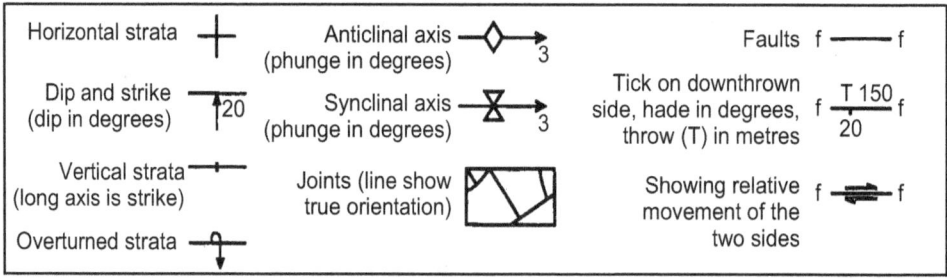

Features resulting from bedrock structure

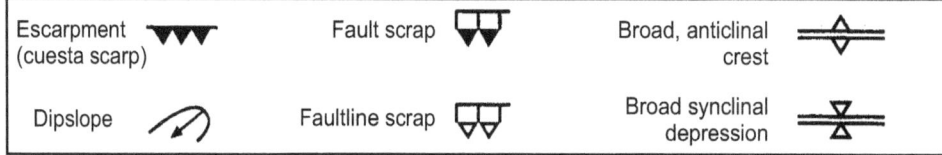

Unconsolidated materials

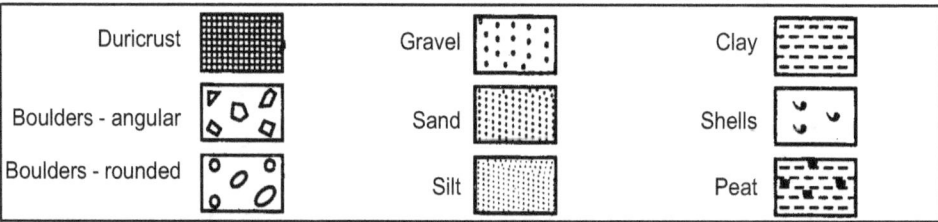

Unconsolidated materials

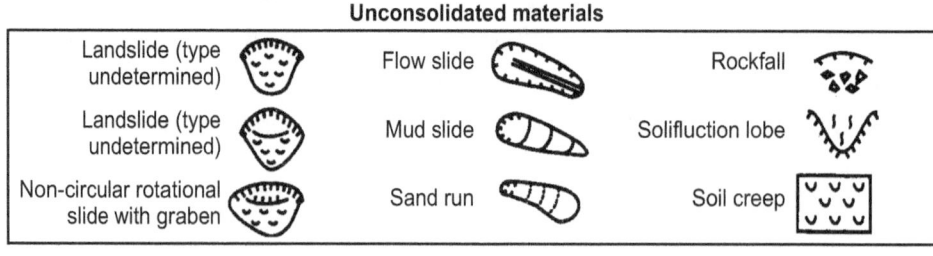

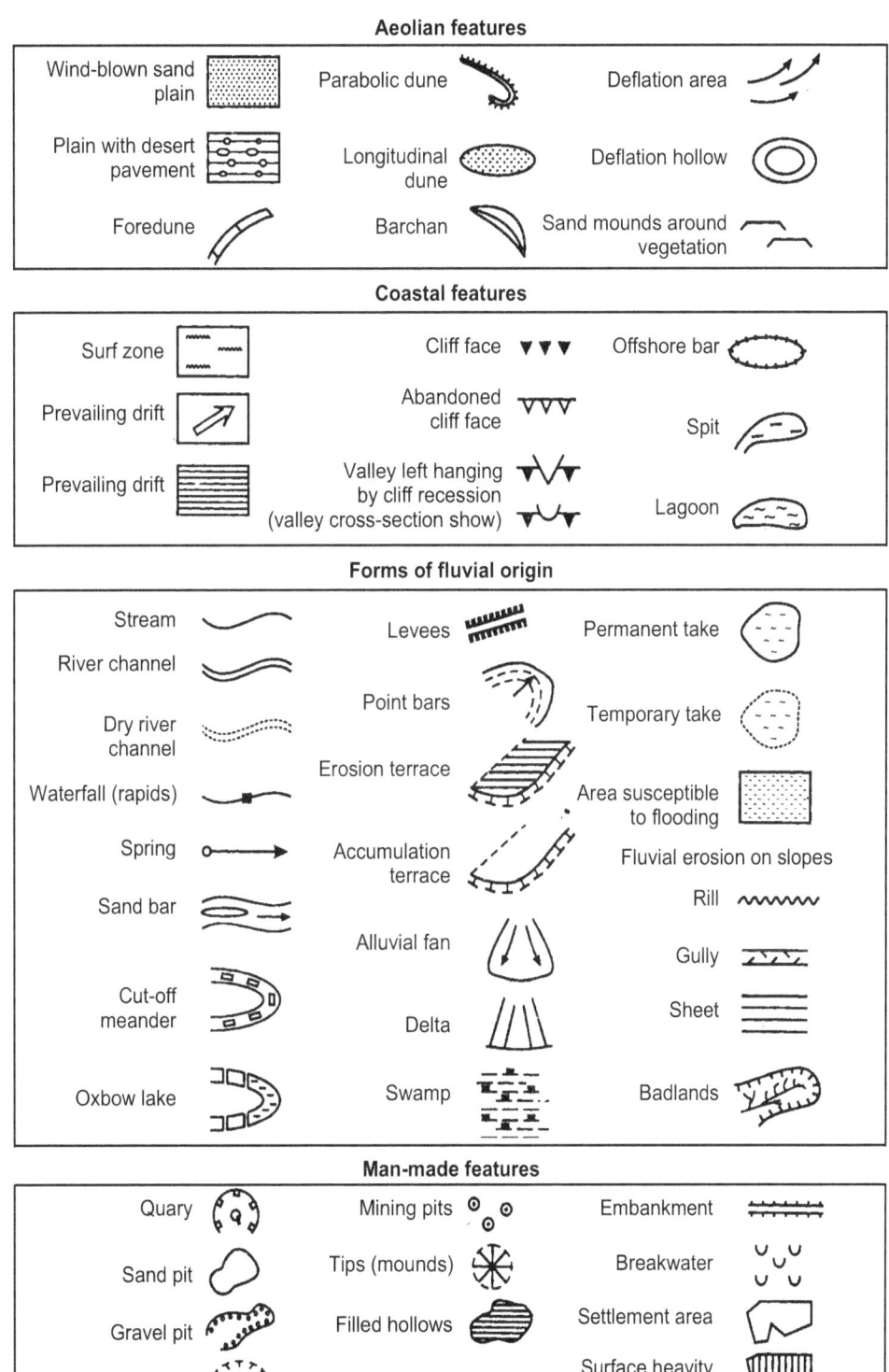

Fig. 4.1 : Conventional symbols used in the geological mapos

Sometimes surface maps and geologic sections cannot competently depict an existing complex geological condition. In such cases, block diagrams may be prepared.

(c) Engineering Geological Map :

Engineering geological maps vary in information from conventional geologic maps. The purpose for which engineering geological maps are prepared decides the scale as well as contents of the map. The information required is for evaluating the feasibility of the proposed land use, an environmental assessment or an engineering construction. In other words, the proposed individual investigations are directed towards understanding the relationship between geological environments and engineering environment.

(1) The maps may be prepared for scales varying from 1 : 10,000 to 1 : 50,000, or even 1 : 2,50,000. Commonly there is a natural progression from general small scale maps to specific large scale maps. The engineering geological mapping is recommended to be carried out in four different stages :

(a) **Regional maps :** Regional map depicts presence of geologic structures of large magnitudes. The map has certain common lithological characteristics. The scale is smaller than 1 : 2,00,000 and thus very general engineering parameters can be defined. [Fig. 4.2 (a)]

(b) Maps prepared at the scale 1 : 10,000 to 1 : 50,000 may include a suite of rocks developed under specific environmental and tectonic conditions. Though at this scale it is not possible to describe the physical and mechanical properties of the entire sequence but it is possible to give data regarding genesis of the sequence. In these maps, structural details may be given accurately. [Fig. 4.2 (b)]

(c) As the scale of the maps becomes larger and larger, homogeneity of lithologic type in respects of mineralogical composition, texture and structure may be recognised. Typically, the scale varies from 1 : 5,000 to 1 : 10,000. [Fig. 4.2 (c)]

(d) The most useful and self-explanatory maps (precise plans) are prepared by using scales larger than 1 : 5000. In these maps, individual beds of rock or soil layers are shown along with their characteristic features. For example, a sandstone bed may be associated with shale and traversed by a fault zone. The fault zone may provide easy pathway for groundwater with the possibility of localised chemical weathering. Similarly, the degree of weathering may be different at different places. In other words, instead of the sandstone as a single rock, many categories of writing sandstones with different physical and mechanical properties, are recognised [Fig. 4.2 (d)].

The plan or map as mentioned above is a sub-division within a rock type which is uniform in its physical state. The rock unit may be discriminated on the basis of degree of weathering, network and density of discontinuities. Thus, a 'domain' will have distinctive geological and engineering properties.

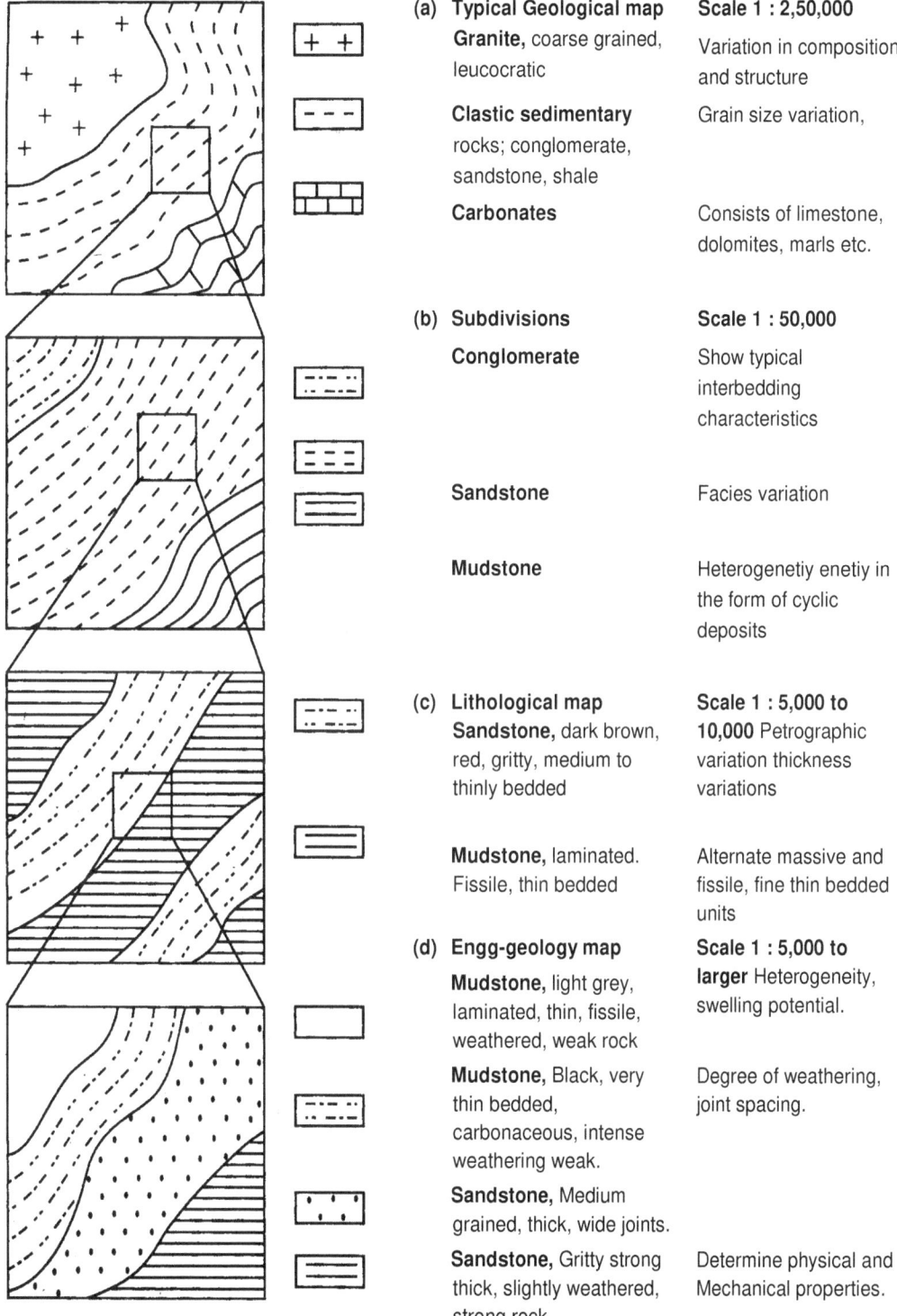

Fig. 4.2 : Typical engineering geological map and their characteristics patterns

(2) Even though, detailed analysis of rocks and soil material is important in deciding stability of engineering structures, water also plays an equally important role in this. Evaluation of hydrologic conditions, including surface hydrology, groundwater estimations etc. is therefore essential, because they have an important role to play in weathering, mass movements, solubility etc. Rock and soil properties are greatly influenced by their moisture content. Therefore, it is necessary to furnish the following information on the engineering geological maps :

- moisture content.
- movement of groundwater.
- springs and recharge zones of groundwater.
- geochemistry.
- aquifer characteristics, whether confined/unconfined and their parameters.
- biological activity.

Generally, the detailed information is provided on a separate map or on a separate plan.

(3) Geomorphological mapping is an essential part of engineering, geological mapping and also of conventional geological mapping. Evaluation of geomorphic conditions provide the basis for an explanation of :

- the relation between surface condition and geology.
- the origin, age and development of individual geomorphological elements.
- the influence of geomorphological condition on internal and external process of the Earth.
- the slow but continuous development of geomorphological features such as the erosion of river and lake banks, movement of dunes, collapses in underground mines, sea level changes.

Surface geological processes that may be active today or the legacy to formerly active processes include :

- those due to erosion and deposition.
- aeolian processes.
- slope movements.
- glacial processes.
- formation of karstic topography.
- volume changes in the soil.

Details of all these are given in Unit 2 and Unit 5. All these features can be shown on the comprehensive maps, however amount of detail depends on the scale of the map.

(4) Internal processes of the Earth, seismic and volcanic activity, may be associated with recent crustal movements resulting into uplift or depression of the surface.

Seismic activity may be mapped in terms of intensity of the event, using isoseismal lines or surface expression of present day and historic events. Mappable features include : Offset springs, faulted ferraces and man-made structures, sag ponds, hries of hot springs, linear trenches and fault scarps.

4.2 REMOTE SENSING

Definition : "Remote sensing is the science and art of obtaining information about an object, area or phenomenon through the analysis of data acquired by a device that is not in contact with the object, area or phenomenon under investigation".

- Thomas Lillesand / Ralph Kiefer

"Remote sensing is defined as the science of acquiring, processing and interpreting images and related data, obtained from aircraft and satelltes that record the interaction between matter and electromagnetic radiation".

– Floyd F. Sabins

- Acquiring images refers to the technology employed, such as an electro-optical scanning system.

- Processing refers to producers that convert the raw data into images.

- Interpreting the images is the most important step because it converts an image into information that is meaningful and valuable for a wide range of users.

- The interaction between matter and electromagnetic energy is determined by
  - the physical properties of the matter and
  - the wavelength of electromagnetic energy that is remotely sensed.

The science of remote sensing excludes geophysical methods such as electrical, magnetic, gravity surveys that measure force fields than electromagnetic radiation.

Remote sensing devices are developed to exploit a variety of physical phenomenon, including acoustical energy (sound wave), electromagnetic energy, the force fields of gravity and magnetism. (Table 4.1). For our purpose, we would concentrate only on electromagnetic energy.

Table 4.1

Method	Wavelength	Technique
Photography		
(1) Conventional Film (B and W, colour)	0.4 – 0.7 µm	Wide band recording on emulsions, convert small colour difference to large ones.
(2) Infra-red film (B and W, colour)	0.6 – 0.9 µm	Records absorption/reflection patterns on films.
(3) Multispectral Bands	0.3 – 0.9 µm	Narrow band recording on emulsion.
(4) Lasers	0.4 – 0.9 µm	Records back scattered radiation on photographic film and other media.
(5) Photometers	0.4 – 0.7 µm	Narrow and wide band recording on emulsions and other media.
(6) Thermal Infra-red	3.0 – 6 µm 8 – 14 µm	Record emitted thermal radiation by looking at elements in sequence.
Radars :		
(1) Radio frequency receivers in scanners and radiometers.	1 mm – 0.8 m	Record back scattered radiation.
(2) Electromagnetic pulse sonic waves	$0.8 - 3 \times 10^6$ mm	Measures pressure waves reflected from terrain or objects.
Geophysical :		
(1) Gravimeters	Gravity filed	Measures acceleration of gravity.
(2) Magnetometers	Magnetic field	Measures local magnetic induction.
(3) Seismographs	Sound waves	Measures elastic waves in earth.
(4) Electric logs	Electric field	Measures electric properties of substance rocks.
(5) Geochemical	Chemical reactions	Measures elements in the earth.

4.2.1 Remote Sensing Sensors and Platforms

(1) Remote sensors can be grouped into five major headings, which are as follows:

(a) **Photographic cameras :** These record objects usually in the visible and near infrared, through photo chemical emulsions when images are focussed on them. Numerous types of cameras are in use in case of aerial surveys, including panoramic, strip, multispectral cameras.

(b) **Vidicon cameras :** Such systems were commonly used in early environmental satellites. In this type of cameras, optical images are focussed and retained temporarily on photo conductive surfaces. They are then scanned temporarily for recording and/or transmission as a continuously variable electrical signals.

(c) **Scanners :** In this, a single detector is used to provide an analog signal of radiation which is incident on it, while a revolving mirror scans the object.

(d) **Spectrometers :** In these, incoming radiation is selected and dispersed by means of prisms, mirrors or filters to provide multispectral data for detailed spectral signature analysis.

(e) **Microwave radars :** These are active radiation sensor systems. The radars are useful in cloudy areas because range of wavelengths of microwave radiation is not attenuated by water droplets in the atmosphere. These may be air-borne (for terrain evaluation) or ground - based (for rainfall and storm monitoring).

(2) Following are the remote sensing platforms :

(a) Ground observation platforms are commonly used for very detailed local work. The technique is vital in deciding spectral signatures of various objects as atmospheric effects can be essentially eliminated.

(b) Balloons are either controlled or free flying and are used upto an elevation of 30 kilometres.

(c) **Aircrafts and remotely piloted vehicles :** These are used in topographic surveys, hazard monitoring, disaster assessments etc.

(d) Rockets are used upto an altitude of 400 kilometres, but their value is restricted by pseudo geometrical properties of their images.

(e) **Satellites :** Satellites are used for various purposes. Two major categories are recognised for Earth Observation operations; the polar-orbiters and the geostationary satellites.

(1) The polar-orbiters or low orbiting satellites are injected into a quasi-polar sunsynchronous orbit, thereby providing observations always at the same time from an altitude of few hundred kilometres (700 - 900 km). The polar orbiters observe the earth surface and the atmosphere along ascending (south-north) or descending (north-south) strips. Whereby two consecutive orbits (ascending or descending) overlap over the polar

regions and are either adjacent or separated by gaps over the equatorial area as a function of orbital drift. Due to relatively low attitude, very high resolution (80 metres on the multispectral scanner, 30 metres on the Thematic mapper) is attained and the same area is covered with repetition cycles from 24 hours to 16 - 18 days (Landsat).

(2) The geo-stationary or environmental satellites are rotating over the same geographic area because their angular velocity is the same as that of the Earth and their orbit lies on the equitorial plane. Due to high flight height (35800 kilometres), a large area around the sub-satellite point (upto 70-75°) is sensed by the spacecraft instrumentation. As a result, the environmental satellite cannot see the polar regions and resolution is of the order of 1 (one) kilometre.

4.2.2 The Physics of Remote Sensing

Eventhough electromagnetic radiation covers a great spectrum of wavelengths (Fig. 4.3), the most useful wavelength range used in remote sensing is the visible (0.4 to 0.7 µm) the near infrared (0.7 to 3.0 µm), the thermal infrared (3.0 to 5.0 µm and 8.0 to 14.0 µm) and the microwave (0.3 to 300 cm). The sun is obviously the most important source of electromagnetic radiation used in passive remote sensing; which covers ultraviolet, visible, infrared and radio frequency regions (Fig. 4.3).

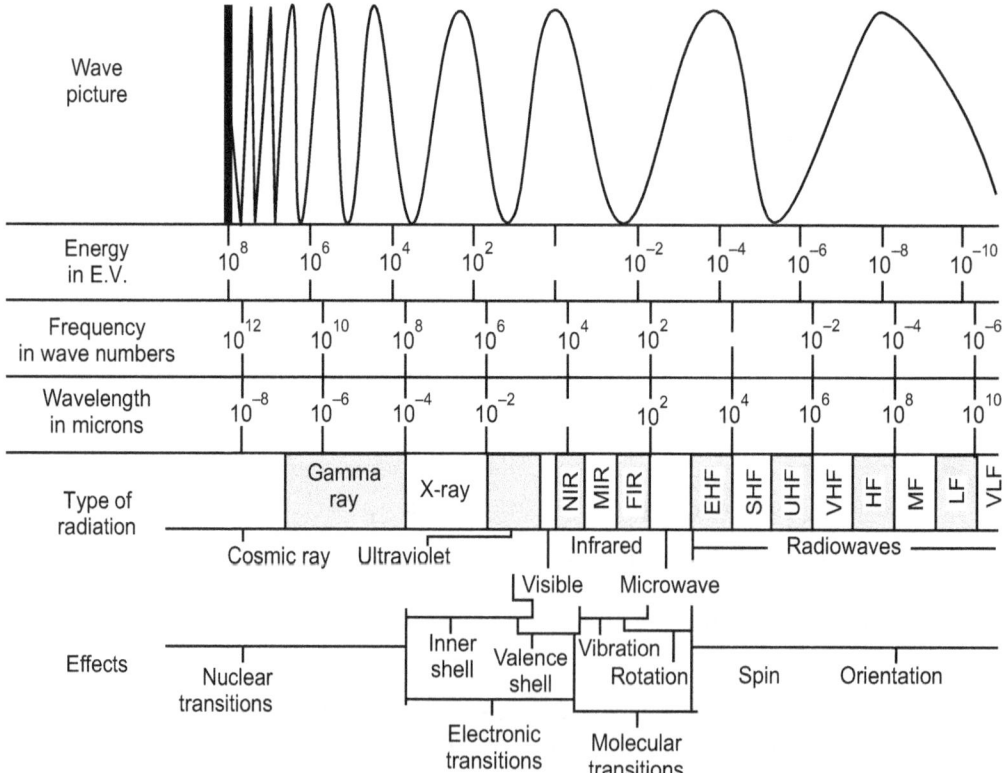

Fig. 4.3 : Electromagnetic spectrum

While passing through the atmosphere, electromagnetic radiation is scattered and absorbed by atmospheric gases. The maximum absorption takes place at wavelengths smaller than 0.3 μm due to ozone layer. On the other hand certain spectral regions (0.4 to 1.3, 1.5 to 1.8, 2.2 to 2.6, 3.0 to 3.6, 4.2 to 5.0, 7.0 to 15.0 μm, 10 mm to 100 mm) of the electromagnetic radiation travel through the atmosphere without much attenuation known as *atmospheric windows*. These spectrums are used in remote sensing techniques.

In atmospheric window, three major scattering mechanisms are recognised.

(a) **Rayleigh scatter :** Diameter of the scattering particle is less than the wavelength of radiation and as a result, information in blue band is most affected.

(b) **Mie scatter :** Diameter of the scattering particle is equal to the wavelength of radiation. Thus, it is a function of wavelength and it leads to devaluate the quality of multispectral images under heavy atmospheric haze.

(c) **Non-selective scatter :** In this, the particle size is greater than the wavelength, e.g. presence of large water bubbles.

These factors are always taken into consideration before applying appropriate correction methods, but as this is not the topic of discussion in his book, it is not discussed further.

The atmosphere is comparatively transparent to microwave than to visible and infrared regions. Thus, the radars have an all weather capacity.

The electromagnetic energy, when received by the object on the earth, gets reflected, absorbed, reradiated or transmitted from the object and is controlled by wavelength. If the surface is smooth, the energy is reflected in the forward direction known as **specular reflection** while if the surface is rough the energy is reflected in all directions called as **diffused reflection**. These are the characteristics useful in the identification of the objects also called as *signatures*. Three kinds of signature are recognised :

(a) **Spectral signatures** are the changes in the reflectance received from the object as an influence of wavelength. This may be seen in the form of change in the colour of object.

(b) **Temporal signatures** are the variations in reflectance shown by the object due to seasonal changes. For example, growth cycle of a crop can be checked by using this signature.

(c) **Spatial signature :** Geometrical variations including shape, size and texture of the object.

4.2.3 The Remote Sensing Approach

The resolution (spatial, temporal and radiometric) of a satellite data is a function of the satellite platform, its instrumentation, the detectors, processing etc. of the whole electromagnetic spectrum, only a few are of a particular interest for Earth observations;

- Visible (0.4 - 0.8 μm) : where the source of information is sunlight reflected by the objects.

- Infrared (1.0 – 3.0 μm) : where the source of the radiation is emitted by the objects due to their temperature.
- Microwaves (cm to m) : where the source in the electromagnetic energy is emitted or reflected by the objects in that range, particularly important for all weather observations; since cloud cover is transparent to microwave.

4.2.4 Integration of Satellite Data

The remote sensing provides information about colour, shape, texture, components, roughness, thermal properties, dielectric properties of the object which is useful in deciphering the recognition of features and patterns (clustering), classification of the object etc.

However, the intensity of absorption and reflection of the electromagnetic spectrum depends on the wavelength and reflection properties of the earth surface objects. From Fig. 4.4 it can be said that the dependence of the spectral signatures(s) on the wavelength of the vegetation, soil and water radiation is recognised. Water and humid environments absorb radiation in the near infrared part of the spectrum (Fig. 4.4). They result in excessive dark tones when imposed on positive copies of infrared photographs. Similarly, pure water absorbs the radiation of the 0.48 to 0.60 μm wavelength range. (Fig. 4.4). Turbidity in water leads to an increase in spectral signature and its reflectance peak migrates towards longer wavelength.

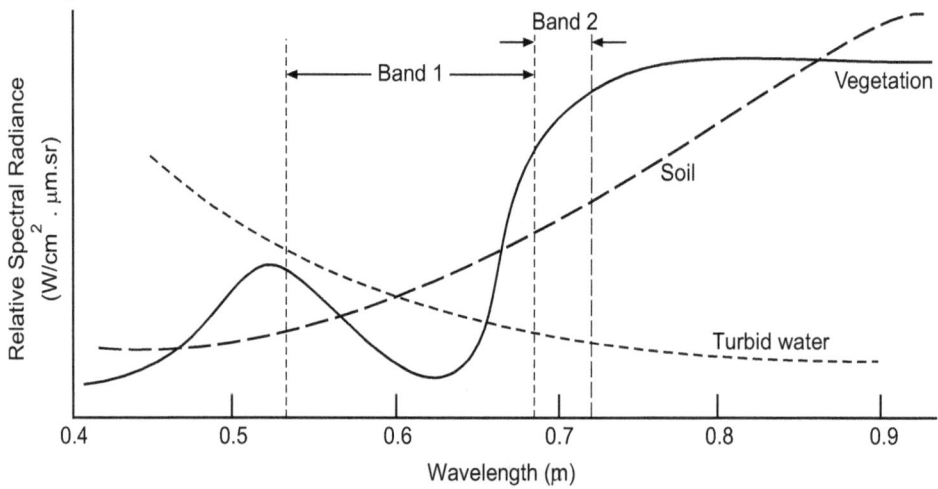

Fig. 4.4 : Dependence of the reflection coefficient on the wavelength

Similar observations can be made in the case of soil materials (Fig. 4.4). The parameters that influence soil structures are the moisture content, humus content, compositional variations, surface roughness etc. At longer wavelength (infrared), moist soils appear darker as compared to the dry soils.

4.2.5 Aerial Photography

Aerial photography is the most economic and useful of the available remote sensing techniques. In India aerial photographs of the scale 1 : 20,000 to 1 : 60,000 are available in black and white prints. Small scale photographs are commonly used in the preparation of preliminary geological maps while detailed geological maps require more detailed data and thus aerial photographs of the scale 1 : 20,000 are used.

4.2.6 Image Interpretation of Satellite Data and Aerial Photography

Image Interpretation :

Definition : It is defined as *the art of examining images to identify objects and judge their significance.*

An interpreter studies remotely sensed data and attempts through logical processes and detect, identify, measure and evaluate the significance of environmental and cultural objects, patterns and spatial relationships. It is an **information extraction process**.

Basic Principles :

(1) An image taken from air or space is a pictorial representation of the pattern of a landscape.
(2) The pattern is composed of indicator of objects and events that relate to the physical, biological and cultural components of the landscape.
(3) Similar condition in similar circumstances reflect similar patterns and unlike different conditions reflect unlike different patterns.
(4) The types and amount of information extracted is proportional to the knowledge, skill and experience of the analyst and methods used for interpretation.

Factors Governing Image Interpretation :

1. Sensor characteristics.
2. Season of the year and time of day.
3. Resolution of the imaging system and scale.
4. Atmospheric effects.
5. Visual and mental acquity of the interpreter.
6. Equipment and technique of interpretation.
7. Interpretation keys, guides and manuals.
8. Exposure and processing.

Activities of Image Interpretation :

Image interpretation is a complex process compressing physical as well as mental activities. In general, there are two techniques :

1. **Fishing Expedition :** An examination of each and every object so as not to miss anything.
2. **Logical Search :** Quick scanning and logical intensive study.

Normally, the activities in an "image interpretation" sequence include the following:

(i) **Detection** : Detection means selectively finding out an object or element of importance for the particular kind of interpretation in hand.

(ii) **Recognition and Identification** : Recognition and identification are together sometimes termed as "photo-reading". However, fundamentally they mean the same and refer to the process of classification of an object by means of specific/local knowledge within a linear category.

(iii) **Analysis** : Analysis is the process of separating/delimiting a set of similar objects by using the concept of boundary lines.

(iv) **Deduction** : Deduction is the process of separation of different groups of objects or, elements and the deduction of their significance based on converging evidence.

(v) **Classification** : It includes modification of the surface into a pertinent system for use in field investigation.

(vi) **Idealization** : It refers to the process of drawing or, standardised representation of what is actually seen in the photo-image.

(vii) **Convergence of Evidence** : The process, by which related miscible conditions are established by inference is termed as convergence of evidence.

Photointerpretation :

The ability to interpret aerial photographs for site investigations depends primarily on understanding the concepts of geology, geomorphology and geotechnology. It involves systematic examination of each stereopair of aerial photographs and satellite images. There are certain observations which helps in the interpretation of aerial photographs. These may be termed collectively as image characteristics and physical characteristics.

Image characteristics	Physical characteristics
Shape	Landforms
Size	Vegetation
Pattern	Land use
Shadow	Drainage and Erosion
Tone	
Texture	Lineaments (natural and man-made)
Site	

Image Characteristics :

Shape refers to the shape of the feature seen from the air. Manmade features are characterised by straight lines or regular curves and often recognisable by shape alone. Many natural features have distinctive shapes e.g. sink holes are commonly circular. However, many natural features may be difficult to identify on the basis of shape alone and thus require other physical characteristics to taken into account.

Size of the object can often help in identification. However it must be considered in relation to the scale of the photograph.

Shadow : The shape of objects and relied shown on aerial photographs are enhanced by shadow. Shadow affords a profile view of objects and can aid interpretation considerably. In some cases shadow can provide interpretation by observing important detail.

Pattern : The spatial arrangement of features on the ground often gives rise to patterns. For example, drainage patterns related to geological structures and lithology pattern of agricultural fields.

Tone and colour : Photo tone and colour are associated with black and white, and colour photography respectively. Tonal difference are seen in shades of grey and appear on black and white photos as a result of spectral signature of the surface objects. It is seen that the dry soil is lighter than wet soil (Fig. 4.4). Similarly, a light colour rock like granite commonly exhibits light grey colour as compared to dark coloured basalt. Significance of tone is different in conventional black and white photographs from that in infrared photography, infrared thermal imagery and radar imagery.

(1) **Black and white photographs :** As mentioned earlier, the tonal difference in this is a measure of relative brightness or spectral signature of the object. Uniformity in tone over large areas is indicative of uniform ground and geological conditions.

(2) **Infrared photographs :** Black and white infrared photos may be taken on infrared film that is sensitive to red wavelengths slightly longer than the visible red (near infrared).

Tone in this is a function of infrared radiation than of brightness. Infrared has an ability to penetrate light haze; as a result, clarity of these photos is better compared with conventional black and white photos.

In Infrared photos, water bodies appear dark (Fig. 4.4) and thus their boundaries may be marked accurately. Similarly, moist soil appears dark compared to dry soil.

(3) **Colour and false colour photos :** True variations in the colours of soil and rock variations in soil moisture etc. can be easily marked on colour photos. Furthermore, it has the advantage of evaluating underwater topography upto a depth of 30 metres.

False colour photography is also called colour infrared photography. Its spectral range is different from that of the normal colour photography. Colour IR photography responds to green, red and near infrared (Fig. 4.3) rather than the natural colours (blue, green and red) used in colour photography. Thus, green sensitive layer develops a yellow image, red produces magneta etc. as a result, vegetation appears as various shades of red, water and wet areas appear as blue and blue-grey. Similarly, differences in soil moisture are easily seen on colour IR photos than on natural colour photos.

(4) **Thermal or far-infrared imagery :** The thermal infrared spectral wavelength varies from 3 to 14 µm (Fig. 4.3) which is best for geological and environmental purposes. The wavelength range contains energy radiated from the earth, which previously has stored energy from the sun. **Emissivity** is a measure of radiating efficiency of a surface. The habit of

transfer as well as retention of heat is controlled by thermal properties (conductivity, specific heat and density). These may be used to derive thermal properties like thermal inertia and thermal diffusivity.

The thermal IR imagery are used for mapping changes in rock composition, soil, groundwater contamination etc. In this imagery, warmer areas are recorded in light tone and cooler in dark tone.

(5) Radar (microwave) imagery : Microwave imaging includes active and passive systems. In active microwave system, short pulses of electromagnetic energy are transmitted to the surface and reflected energy is measured. The system is referred to as **radar**. In this, due to longer wavelength energy required is very less (Fig. 4.3). Thus, the radar system is transparent to cloud cover.

The most popular system is **Side Looking Airborne Radar (SLAR)**.

Texture : The frequency of tonal change on a photograph can give rise to distinctive textures which can help photointerpretation. Generally, texture as seen on the aerial photographs is produced by features that are too small to be identified on aerial photographs. Texture is thus a function of tone, texture and size of the object together with pattern of shadows produced by them. A texture may be smooth or fine and coarse or rugged depending on the nature of bedrock.

Physical Characteristics :

Landforms : Landforms may be classified as constructional, destructional and a combination of both. Landforms of constructional class may be divided into the following major groups based on agency which formed them : glacial, fluvial, fluvioglacial, alluvial, colluvial, lacustrine, eolien, volcanic and tectonic. Many of them are discussed in Unit 2. Landforms resulting from erosion are numerous and varied. The erosional agencies involved may be streams, waves, glaciers, wind, gravity or combination of any of these. Those caused by streams are most widespread and important. It should be remembered that the configuration of landform is a function of many factors including composition of rock, geological structure along with length of time during which erosion was active. Details of landforms are further given in Unit 2.

Vegetation and Land-Use :

The frequent association of certain types of vegetation with specific soil type is fairly well known vegetation in a few cases which offer clue to valuable mineral deposits. The vegetation of ore bearing regions generally shows larger concentration of the elements found in the ore than of surrounding areas and this difference in concentration may produce variations in the light reflected from trees and bushes.

Land use pattern may be divided into several major categories (Table 4.2). This system has been developed by National Remote sensing agency to suit the Indian conditions.

Table 4.2 : Land-use classification system

Broad Category	Subclass
1. Built-up land	Built-up land
2. Agricultural land	Crop lands, Fallows or dry lands, Plantations.
3. Forest	Evergreen/semi-evergreen forest, Deciduous forest, Scrub land, Forest plantation, Mangrove.
4. Wastelands	Water logged land, Salt affected land Marshy/swampy land, Gullied/ravinous land, Land with scrub, Sandy area (desertic and coastal), Barren land.
5. Water bodies	River/lake/reservoir/tank/canal.
6. Others	Shifting cultivation, Grassland / grazing land, Glacial area.

Drainage : Drainage patterns may easily be recognised on aerial photos or imageries. It is primarily a function of stream energy, geometry and composition of rocks, pre-existing topography etc. Six major drainage patterns are recognised (Fig. 4.5).

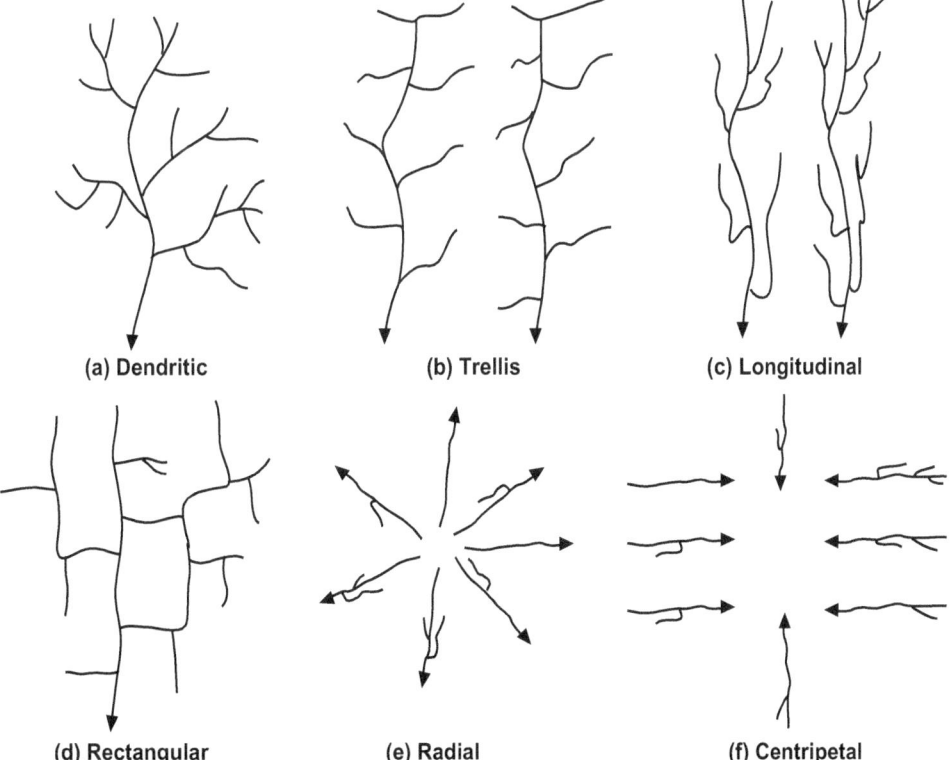

(a) Dendritic   (b) Trellis   (c) Longitudinal

(d) Rectangular   (e) Radial   (f) Centripetal

Fig. 4.5 : Basic drainage pattern depicting the geometry of different stream pattern

It must be mentioned that regional drainage pattern may be distinctly different from individual stream pattern. The latter pattern is often more informative.

Dendritic, rectangular, trellis and radial patterns are controlled by underlying geologic conditions (Fig 4.5). Dendritic pattern indicates the presence of horizontal to subhorizontal hard rock e.g. Deccan Basalts. Rectangular pattern is characteristic of jointed rocks. Similarly, trellis pattern is commonly developed in dipping sedimentary sequence of non-uniform resistance. Radial pattern is seen in the case of domal structures, while centripetal drainage pattern may indicate the presence of karstitic conditions or the presence of thick permeable soil.

The density of drainage patterns provide clues about local geological conditions. Density is expressed in terms of coarse, medium and fine. It is controlled by rock composition, discontinuity orientations, spacing, persistence etc.

4.2.7 Applications of Remote Sensing in Engineering Geology

Remote sensing should be used as a tool in preliminary, geologic investigations. It must be remembered that study of aerial photos/imageries should be followed by detailed and careful ground checks/investigations. Remote sensing gives us an idea about the area before actually visiting the area. Thus, based on remote sensing data in the form of preliminary base maps, initial traverses and critical areas should first be defined, these patches must always be checked and substantial quantitative data must be collected to get appreciable or satisfactory results.

(a) Hydrology : Data acquired by remote sensing techniques provide valuable information in various fields of hydrological projects; including measurements associated with floods, rainfall monitoring, watershed definition and planning, identification of sources of pollution, sedimentation in reservoir, water quality, groundwater investigations etc. Some of the applications are as below :

(1) Pollution studies : Variation in spectral signature in areas of homogeneous land use or on water may be due to heterogeneity in soil moisture, composition or also due to pollution. The studies are best possibly carried out by using thermal imageries. Recently, oil spills and algae populations have been identified with the help of thermal imageries.

Increase in water temperature increases the thermal radiation of the water surface. Scanner can identify their source. When the area covered by polluted water is small, an airborne survey is preferred to satellite imagery in order to achieve the spatial resolution. Similarly, turbidity changes in rivers, indicating increases or decreases in sediment load are easily seen in normal photography or imagery.

(2) Groundwater : Remote sensing is applied to :

- find likely areas for the existence of groundwater.
- find indicators of the presence of groundwater.
- indicate quality of groundwater existing near the surface or at the points of natural discharge.
- indicate regions of groundwater recharge and discharge.
- suggest areas where wells might be drilled.
- monitor aquifer changes as groundwater development proceed.
- identification of coastal springs.

(b) Mass Wasting : Surface mass wasting patterns not detectable from field observations may be evidenced on imagery or aerial photographs. Specific indicative structures such as deranged surface water flow, springs or distressed vegetation may also be inferred from remotely sensed data.

Colour infrared images are particularly useful in detecting the heterogenity in drainage, soil moisture and vegetation patterns. This help in the recognition of mass wasting processes which can be mapped, described and specified during later field investigations.

Thermal infrared images are useful in determining apparent ground temperature and moisture content of the surface from which ground water conditions can be inferred. The base maps prepared from remotely sensed data often provide sufficient clues about the terrain.

(3) Construction Material, Location and Inventory :

High altitude SLAR imagery or satellite imagery and aerial photos can be useful in the preparation of regional landform maps. Areas likely to contain economical construction deposits may be identified easily on aerial photographs. The evidence of surface or near surface construction material as seen on aerial photographs include landform shape, drainage pattern, soil moisture variation, type of vegetation cover, relationship with other landforms and discontinuities.

(4) Coastal zones : Remote sensing is useful in monitoring coastal conditions as well as establishing the historical development of coastal features. In such cases, photographs or imageries of different seasons are very useful applications of remote sensing in different aspects of engineering geology is given in Table 4.3.

Table 4.3 : Potential applications of remote sensing in different fields

Category	Applications
1. Land – use planning	– Create and update cartographic maps. – Assess suitability of land for different purposes. – Monitor the growth of cities, plan recreation area.
2. Water Management	– Estimate water supplies. – Map flood plains; inventory lakes and wetlands. – Assess regional water demands and supplies. – Develop plans for more effective use of surface and ground water resources. – Investigate sources of water contamination and develop appropriate prevention mechanisms.
3. Coastal zone management	– Monitor shore-line changes. – Map ocean surface temperatures. – Inventory types and status of land cover in fragile environments (mangrove, tidal wet lands, estuaries)
4. Environmental protection	– Assess environmental quality. – Develop regional environmental regulations.
5. Natural disaster reduction	– Prepare hazard maps. – Identify population at risk from disasters. – Identify optimal sites for human settlements, schools, health facilities, waste disposal systems.

4.3 GEOGRAPHICAL INFORMATION SYSTEM (GIS)

GIS is defined as *a system of computer hardware and software designed to allow users to collect, manage, analyze and retrieve large volume of spatially referenced data collected from a variety of sources at different scales and resolutions.*

GIS is rapidly becoming a useful tool for management of resources. GIS is a **database system** for manipulating data.

The major advantage of GIS is that it is an **information system**, digital database which can be developed at any stage can be used in future and related information can be extracted conveniently and efficiently.

4.3.1 Advantages of GIS

Powerful tool for handling spatial data collected from a variety of sources. **Large quantity of data** can be stored, maintained and retrieved at greater speed and low cost. Extremely helpful in planning scenarios, decision models and interactive processes can perform complex spatial analysis providing both qualitative and quantitative results. Able to manipulate and integrate different types of data in a single analysis which is otherwise an impossible task.

4.3.2 GIS Packages

(1) Win GIS – Windows/NI – 1990.

(2) Micro Station GIS – Integraph / UNIX – 1989.

(3) STRINGS – PCs/DOS – 1979.

(4) SPANS – PCs/DOS – 1985.

(5) Arc GIS.

(6) Gram^{++} etc.

Essential Elements of GIS :

A GIS consists of twp major elements namely hardware and software.

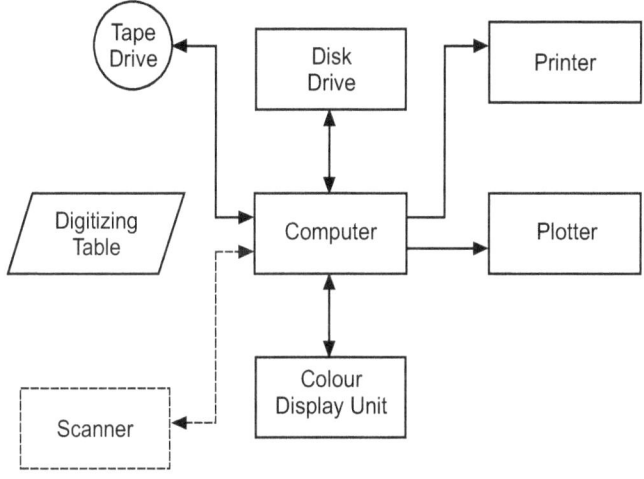

(a) Major hardware components

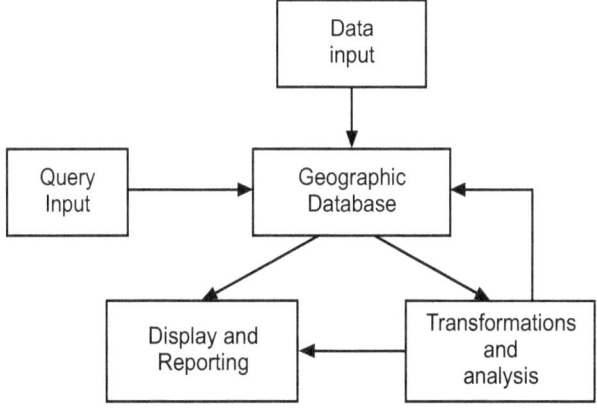

(b) Major software components

Fig. 4.6

Geographical Information System as a Management Tool :

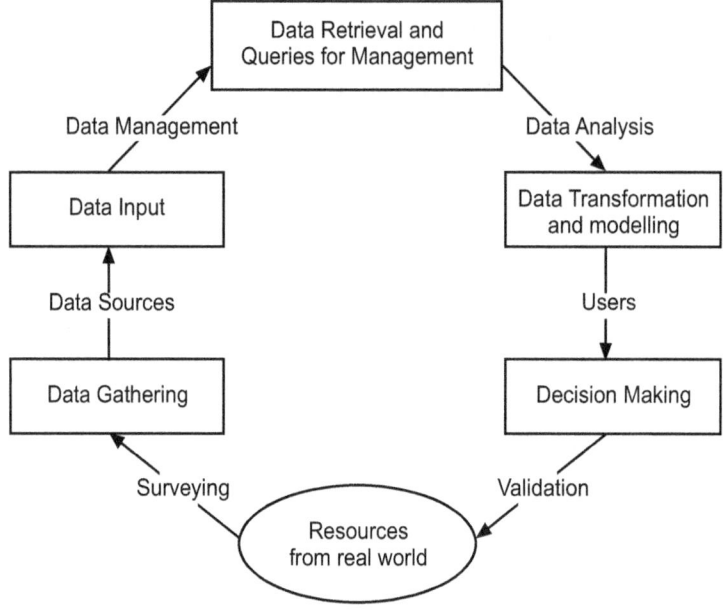

Fig. 4.7

4.3.3 Uses of GIS in Resource Mapping

(1) The area inundated by flood can be mapped and monitored effectively.
(2) GIS technique is used in ground water studies as it facilitates handling of diverse types of spatial information – topographic maps, geological maps, contour maps of W.T. and water quality.
(3) Watershed monitoring and management has been found to be economical and faster (Erosion and Sediment w.r.t. yield from the water shed) can be assessed.
(4) GIS is of great value in providing latest information on urbanisation and industrialisation and helping in the study of urban growth trends and urban landuse zonning.
(5) GIS is extremely useful in monitoring the land use and land cover changes, as well as to update the existing land use maps.
(6) GIS is extensively used for the study of forest area, changes in forest covers, strategy for forest resource protection and conservation, forest eco-system studies.
(7) GIS acts as a means to compute spatially referenced reservoir volumes, including loss of storage capacity due to sedimentation.
(8) GIS is utilized to forecast "snowmelt run-off" from river basins.
(9) GIS is useful in "wetland management" involving study of extent of dudging, lagoons, drainage and other manmade induced changes that have an impact on natural environment.
(10) GIS is used for land suitability analysis.

Geographic information system, known as GIS, is a type of art tool capable of capturing, storing, retrieving, editing, analysing, comparing and displaying spatial environmental information. A computerised GIS allows technicians to perform complex analysis by 'overlaying' and 'displaying' large volumes of spatial and non-spatial data. Spatial data pinpoint the location of features on the Earth's surface like a river, a lake or a district. Non-spatial data describes features such as, the pH and temperature of the river at the monitoring station and name of the district.

A GIS can help perform many routine and complex tasks. It can develop the following systems.

(a) **Mapping Systems** : Generates topographic base maps for planning infrastructure using photogrammetric or geologic data.

(b) **Land Information Systems** : Manages cadastral survey data, parcel data, urban growth data and property records.

(c) **Spatial Analysis Systems** : Integrates data is used in natural resource exploration, inventory and management, as well as in regional planning, site selection and impact assessment exercises related to sustainable economic development.

(d) **Network Analysis Systems** : Integrates data needed to plan and locate transportation routes and analyse natural systems, such as hydrographic networks.

(e) **Image Analysis Systems** : Displays remote sensing data and integrate these data with other types of data to update maps and for visual assessment.

In other words, GIS software is designed to manipulate spatial data in order to produce maps, tabular reports or data files. Data can be obtained from satellite images, aerial photographs, field measurements, gravimetry, aeromagnetometry and various types of maps. Analyses conducted with a GIS can provide decision makers with information in a more easy format acceptable to their needs. GIS maps can be easier to work with and more readily updated than conventional maps. A GIS can be used to pinpoint areas on map where actions are required or data are doubtful. It can also be used to visualise alternate scenarios so that they can be easily compared. It can be used to combine different types of maps and display them in a three dimensional form and the scale and features highlighted can be modified quickly. In short, GIS is a very important decision supporting tool which can be used to

- facilitate analysis that require both statistical and mapped data.
- provide regular update of maps based on data from multiple sources including remote sensing data.
- improve accuracy of analysis involving large amount of data.
- present information in a much efficient/easy form than possible with manual methods.
- simulate the range of potential impacts of policy decisions.

GIS can be of great utility in the analysis of geological hazards and vulnerability assessment. These are especially in relation to the assessment of landslide, seismic and fluvial hazards. This is a very useful exercise in urban planning by analysing, organising and evaluating existing spatial data for land use planning. An appreciation of the physical (e.g. landslip, subsidence) and chemical (e.g. heavy metals, contaminations, toxic components) hazards affecting urban area may also be possible with the aid of GIS technology.

However, there is a danger in placing too much emphasis on data analysis at the expense of data collection. This should be avoided.

PART (B)

4.4 SUBSURFACE EXPLORATION

Surface investigations often indicate the places where subsurface investigations should be carried out. This exploration defines subsurface conditions that influence stability of the siting and also performance of a project. Identification of fault zone, shear zone, expansive soil, intensely weathered rock, karstitic terrain, lack of exposures permitting identification of underlying bedrock. Uncertainty of springs and seeps to the hydrogeological conditions are typical conditions arising during surface investigation that defines the need of subsurface investigation.

Subsurface exploration gives an idea about underground features, their physical characteristics, geometry and their vertical and lateral extent. The methods used are :

(1) Excavation; (2) Drilling; (3) Geophysical methods.

4.4.1 Excavation

Excavation is a useful subsurface method for shallow depth exploration work. It includes construction of pits, shafts, adits, drilled shafts, trenches for fault investigation and elucidation of weathering grade. The method provides useful results upto depth of 10 metres, otherwise it is economically not recommended.

However, main application of this type of exploration is to check the overburden conditions. Trial pits and trenches should be taken at an appropriate interval (interval is to be decided by local geological conditions) to carry out the programme of selective sampling.

The estimated depth and amount of unsuitable foundation material necessary for the removal should be based on the trial pit information. Similarly, underlying previous/impervious bed rock should be exposed and its foundation strength must be checked.

Test trenches serve the same purpose as the test pit but have an added advantage of exposing the continuity of the formation. The method also exposes if any vertical fault is hidden below shallow overburden in the rocks, so that the proper treatment may be decided in the pre-construction phase.

4.4.2 Exploratory Drilling

The most widely used and important method, in subsurface exploration is to drill holes on the selected site. An accurate information may be available not only from the samples but also from careful observations on the rate of advancement of the drill hole.

Drill holes may be vertical, oblique or horizontal. Drilling procedure for soil and rock is different. In the case of unconsolidated or soil material, auger drilling or rotary drilling is used. After the rocks are encountered, the rotary drilling is replaced by diamond core drilling.

(a) Drilling in soft ground :

As mentioned earlier, drilling in soft ground is carried out either with the help of a drilling bit or by an auger action. The earth material removed from a bore hole is called "cutting". However, in this process, caving increases with increase in depth and diameter of bore hole, presence of cohesionless material and the presence of ground water.

In soft ground, boreholes may be stabilized by filling them with drilling fluids. It is a slurry prepared by mixing clay (bentonite) and water. Baryte is also often used. The mud stabilizes the walls of the bore by coating them with an impervious layer and by exerting a hydrostatic pressure. However, the most suitable process of stabilizing the walls of a bore hole is by the use of casing. Commonly, casing is done for the first five to ten metres. The lower end of the casing is provided with a shoe of hardened steel especially if the casing is to be driven through a harder material. However, if the ground is fairly cohesive, drilling is carried out without casing.

(b) Drilling in hard ground :

Main purpose of exploratory drilling is to get a cylindrical cone. It is usually required that core drilling should penetrate the overburden and continue into the underlying rock. For this purpose, the two types of drill in use are Diamond drills and Calyx or shot drills.

(1) Diamond drills : Two common types of diamond are used for drilling namely natural or **black diamond and industrial artificial diamond**. Obviously, the natural diamond is much harder and durable compared to industrial diamond. The cutting bit of the diamond drill is a hard steel cylinder with diamond teeth's set in and projecting partially beyond its face. The double tube barrel is made of an outer tube and an inner floating tube next to the core is suspended on ball bearing in such a way that the outer tube can move freely without the inner core. The drilled water pumped inside to cool the drill bit passes through the annular space between the two barrels. Due to free rotation of each tube, the core wedges itself so firmly that the inner tube remains stationary except for the slow downward movement of the rod. A core lifter is attached to core barrel. Generally, cores upto 90 metres can be drilled, and deep drills upto 1000 metres may be drilled. Being the hardest known abrasive, diamond drills can penetrate through the hard rocks. Similarly, smaller dimension holes may also be drilled.

Another major advantage of using diamond drills is that holes of any angle may be readily drilled and hole sides are smooth and clean. However, flexibility of rods causes deep holes to deviate from the vertical.

(2) Calyx or shot drills : In this type of drilling, single tube barrels are used. Large diameter holes can be drilled (75 millimetres to 1600 millimetre in diameter). While drilling the hole, a small stream of water is made to flow along the edge of the bit. Shot is fed to the bit by pouring it around the outside of the shell. The action of the drill is a combination of abrasion, wear and actual cutting. Cores may be separated by explosives or wedging.

The small diameter calyx drill holes are less expensive in loose rocks and boulders. However, they have many disadvantages compared to diamond drills. Generally, calyx drills are not useful in soft material. The cores are rough and as a result difficult to examine. Similarly, it is difficult to drill angle holes (more than 35 degrees to vertical).

The large diameter calyx drill holes are large enough to use as shafts but in this heavy machinery is required and thus mobility is very difficult.

(3) Core size and core recovery : Rock cores can be collected in different sizes based on requirement. They vary from 20 millimetres to 75 millimetres. The cores are to be preserved in special core boxes in the order of their extraction from the drill hole. Normally, a core run is the amount of core recovered in a single drilling. It is normally 3 metres in length. The ratio of the length of the actually recovered core to the length drilled is called core recovery which is commonly expressed as per cent loss or per cent recovered. However, if the ratio is not uniform along the entire drill hole, it is required to be recorded carefully during each run.

If the core recovery is 1.8 metres out of 3 metres run, then core recovery is 60 per cent and core loss is 40 per cent. In the case of soft material, no core is obtained and thus due to pulvarising effects, the returning drilling water is turbid. Harder rocks on the other hand produce high per cent core recovery. In other words approximate estimation of strength of the rocks may be obtained based on the observations of core recovery.

Another major criteria in the approximation of strength of the rocks is to check the rate of drilling. Rocks are softer in nature if rate of drilling is rapid, while rocks are harder if rate of penetration is slow.

(4) Angle or oblique holes : When rocks are vertical or steeply inclined, it is advisable to take angle or oblique drills which is of great significance in deciding their bearing capacity. Angle drilling is possible on rotary drilling rigs if they have a swinging or rotating drill head. These can be drilled in any direction from vertical. However, angle drills are not advisable if the overburden requires casing. Similarly, the initial inclination or direction of an angle hole seldom remains the same due to centrifugal forces and the force of gravity acting on the drilling rods.

If the angle holes are drilled in sedimentary rocks, the observer should be very careful while interpreting the recovered cores. For example, if the core shows the presence of bedding, the interpreter, should realise that the bedding is not true. Similarly, when an angle hole is logged, the log should mention whether the thickness of beds is measured along the axis of the hole or calculated depths are projected along a vertical line. Furthermore, the log should also mention whether the axis of the hole is normal or at an angle to the strike/foliation of the beds.

Angle holes are most useful in deciphering existence of vertical features like dykes, fault zones, fractures, zone of intense weathering caverns etc. Thus, it is necessary in case of investigating dams to take minimum two angle holes normal to each other from both banks of the river.

(c) Description of drill cores and borehole logging : (Fig. 4.8)

A major part of any subsurface exploration is the continuous creation of an accurate bore hole description, called **borehole log**. It furnishes very reliable information on the soil and rocks encountered during drilling. The log should also provide accurate information about geological structures and any relevant features obtained during drilling.

There should be a separate log on a separate sheet for every borehole drilled. The sheet should also include dates of drilling and elevation of ground surface on every log sheet.

Commonly during the initial phase of drilling overburden or soil material is encountered. Though it is necessary to make a cursory note of these layers, precise record should be made of the prominent constituents e.g. problematic soil.

Dirty rock core should in general be washed clean prior to making observations. Before making detailed observations the core as a whole should be examined to determine the structural boundaries and geological features to be measured. The markers indicating depths of geological horizons and start and end of each run should be carefully checked.

Drill core, commonly, is described by means of the following parameters : total core recovery (R), discontinuity frequency (F) and rock quality designation.

Total core recovery (R), as discussed earlier, is the summed length of all pieces of recovered core expressed as a percentage of length drilled. When the core is fragmented the length of such portions is calculated by assembling the fragments and estimating the length of core that the fragments appear to represent.

Frequency (F) is the number of natural discontinuities intersecting a unit length of recovered core.

Rock Quality Designation (RQD) is a modified core recovery percentage in which all the pieces of unbroken core over 10 cm in size are treated as recovered cores. The smaller cores resulting from close jointing, faulting or weathered are omitted. RQD is calculated by using an equation.

$$RQD = \frac{\text{Sum length of cores more than 10 cm in length}}{\text{Total length of the cores}} \times 100$$

A qualitative estimation on the strength of rock is attempted after determining RQD (Table 4.4).

Table 4.4 : Rock quality designation

RQD	Fracture frequency per metre	Description
0 – 25%	Over 15	Very poor
25 – 50%	8 – 15	Poor
50 – 75%	5 – 8	Fair
75 – 90%	1– 5	Good
> 90%	< 1	Excellent

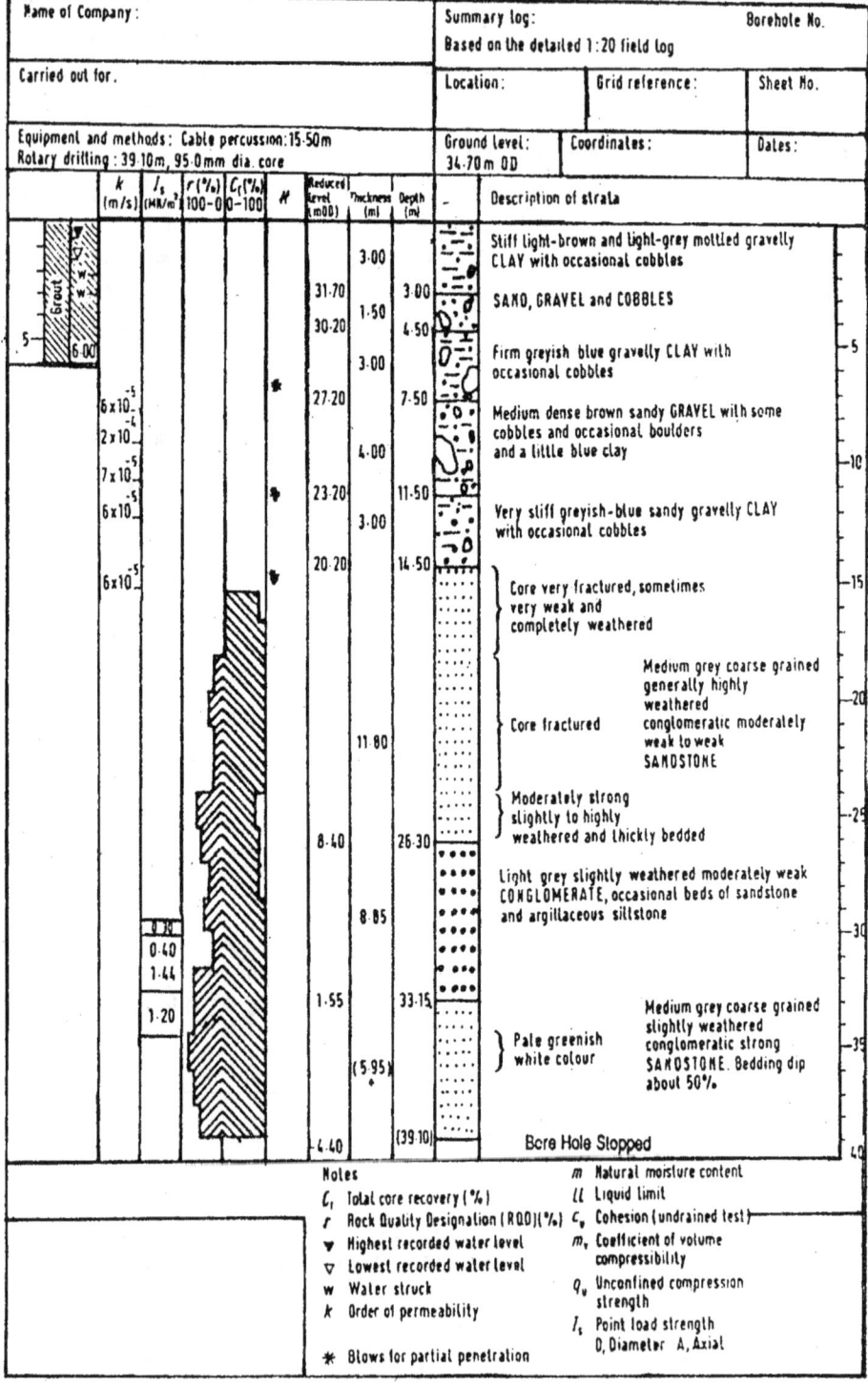

Fig. 4.8 : Typical summery log

RQD has certain drawbacks. It does not take into account composition of geological material. A further disadvantage is that if fracture spacing is more than 10 cm, the quality is excellent irrespective of the actual spacing.

While calculating frequency or RQD from drill core it is necessary to distinguish between naturally broken surfaces and artificial breaks. Generally, a rough brittle surface with fresh cleavage planes in individual mineral suggests an artificial fracture.

A smooth or somewhat weathered surface with soft coating of talc, gypsum, mica or calcite indicates a natural discontinuity.

It is necessary to maintain a separate record of frequency of artificial or mechanical fractures and associated low RQD.

In addition, the rocks encountered during drilling should be described using the following :

- colour
- texture
- grain size
- discontinuities within mass
- weathered state
- alteration
- minor lithological characteristics including cementation
- estimated strength
- hydrogeological properties.

Special attention must be given to the grade of weathering (see, Unit 2) and the discontinuities (Unit 3) within the rock. If core loss is large then justification for coreloss should be given in very precise terms.

(d) Precautions to be taken while interpreting the drilling data :

(1) It is often necessary to distinguish between an artificially broken core and naturally broken core. Due to mechanical disturbances, core may often break along a surface where joints are absent. Such mechanical fractures should not be described as jointed cores. Normally, cores that are broken along planer surface exhibit presence of naturally occurring joints. Furthermore, along joint planes, decomposition or alteration effects may be prominently seen. These effects are not observed along mechanical fractures.

(2) It is very important to note the depth at which core loss or loss of drilling fluids is maximum. This may be an indication of a fault plane, fault zone, a cavern etc.

(3) If the cores obtained are fragmentary and exhibit the presence of systematically oriented planar surfaces, it then means that the drill hole has certainly encountered a fracture zone. Spacing between discontinuities may often be measured quantitatively by measuring individual fragmentary core piece.

(4) If in the boreholes identical bed is encountered at different structural levels, it is possible to find out attitude of such beds and the bed may also be used as a marker horizon in correlation.

(e) Limitations of drilling :

Drilling is a method of exploration and thus its reliability and validity depends primarily upon spacing between two successive bore holes. In case beds are homoclines and gently dipping, it is advisable that spacing should be more. On the other hand, if the beds are steeply inclined, spacing should be less.

Drilling programme should not be started unless surface investigations are completely carried out. It is advisable to decide location and depth of drill holes with reference to surface geological structures. Similarly, vertical features will be missed if angle drill holes are not carried out.

4.5 ROCK MASS CHARACTERISATION

Rock mass characterisation or quantitative description of rock mass is most crucial and demanding element in engineering geology. Broadly speaking the term rock mass includes the rock fabric and discontinuities. The emphasis is generally the mechanical behaviour of the rock and characteristics of the discontinuities. The assessment of rock properties may range from highly subjective characterisation such as "weak, moderately strong and strong rock" to specific assignment of numerical values to properties like compressive strength, geometry and resistance of discontinuities and deformation modules. Details of the analysis of discontinuities and mechanical properties of rock are discussed elsewhere in the book. Hence an overview of rock mass classification is taken here.

Rock mass classification schemes are given by several workers and generally the classification approach varies depending on the application for which the investigations are carried out.

Following are the major schemes of classification :

 (a) **Terzhagi (1946) :** Rock load classification. The classification is used for rocks encountered in tunneling and is based on rock load factor and RQD. Nine categories of rocks are recognised from hard and intact rock from class 1 to swelling rock, class 9.

 (b) **Rock Structure Rating (RSR) system given by Wickham, Tiedemann and Skinner (1972, 1974) :**

The RSR system uses weighted values of selected rock mass parameters taken from case histories and published materials. Three parameters are recognised.

General geology : Based on rock type, hardness and geometry of structures a rating of 6 – 30 is assigned to this parameter.

Discontinuities : Parameter b is based on the behaviour of discontinuities and a rating of 7 to 45 is assigned accordingly.

Groundwater : Based on the interrelationship between groundwater and mechanical condition of discontinuities, a rating of 6 – 25 is assigned to this parameter.

The classification is particularly useful in tunnelling application particularly in the selection of steel-rib support. The classification is given in Table 4.5.

Table 4.5 (a) : Rock structure rating, Parameter
A : General Area Geology (after Wickham et al. 1974)

Basic Rock Type					Geological structure			
	Hard	Med.	Soft.	Decomp.	Massive	Slightly faulted or folded	Moderately faulted or folded	Intensely faulted or folded
Igneous	1	2	3	4				
Metamorphic	1	2	3	4				
Sedimentary	2	3	4	4				
Type 1					30*	22	15	9
Type 2					27	20	13	8
Type 3					24	18	12	7
Type 4					19	15	10	6

* Maximum value

Table 4.5 (b) : Rock structure rating, parameter
B : Joint pattern, Direction of drive (after Wickham et al. 1974)

		Strike perpendicular to axis					Strike parallel to axis		
		Direction of drive					Direction of drive		
		both	with dip		against dip		both		
			dip of prominent joints				dip of prominent joints		
		flat	dipping	vert.	dipping	vert.	flat	dipping	vert.
1. Very closely jointed		9	11	13	10	12	9	9	7
2. Closely jointed		13	16	19	15	17	14	14	11
3. Moderately jointed		23	24	28	19	22	23	23	19
4. Moderate to blocky		30	32	36	25	28	30	28	24
5. Blocky to massive		36	38	40	33	35	36	34	28
6. Massive		40	43	45*	37	40	40	38	34

Notes : Flat = 0 – 20°, Dipping = 20° – 50°; Vertical = 50° – 90°, * maximum value.

Table 4.5 (c) : Rock structure rating, parameter
C : Groundwater, joint condition (after Wickham et al. 1974)

Anticipated Water Inflow (gpm 100 ft)	Sum of Parameters A + B					
	13 – 44			45 – 75		
	Joint Condition*					
	Good	Fair	Poor	Good	Fair	Poor
None 22	18	22	25**	22	18	
Slight (< 200 gpm)	19	15	9	23	19	14
Moderate (200 – 100 gpm)	15	11	7	21	16	12
Heavy (> 1000 gpm)	10	8	6	18	14	10

* Joint condition : good = tight or cemented; fair slightly weathered or altered; poor = severely weathered, altered, or open.

** Maximum value

(c) Rock Mass Rating (RMR) System given by Bieniawski (1979) :

The RMR system is one of the most commonly used systems for rock mass characterization.

It is based on six parameters (field properties) including rock strength (unconfined compressive strength or point load index), RQD, joint spacing, joint condition ground-water condition and orientation of discontinuities. Though it is particularly applicable for classifying rock mass for support of tunnels, it is popularly used in other applications also.

The total rating 0-100 divides the rock mass into 5 classes at intervals of 20. The classification also discusses significance of each class with stand up time, angle of friction and cohesion.

Bieniawski recognised that each of the parameters used in the classification does not necessarily contribute equally to the behaviour of the rock mass. For example, an RQD of 90 or a high uniaxial compressive strength indicate that the rock is of excellent quality. But heavy inflow of water into the same rock mass could alter this assessment appreciably. Therefore, he developed a concept of rating to each parameter and an overall rating for the rock mass is calculated by adding the rating for each of the parameters. The overall rating is to be adjusted for joint orientation by applying the corrections given in part (b) of the Table 4.6. An explanation of the descriptive terms given for this purpose is provided in Table 4.6. Part (c) of Table 4.6 shows the class and description given to rock masses with various total ratings. The interpretation of these ratings in terms of stand up times for rock mass strength parameters is given in part (d) of Table 4.6.

Table 4.6 : Geomechanics classification of jointed rock masses (after Bieniawski, 1979)

(a) Classification of parameters and their ratings :

Parameter			Ranges of values					
1. Strength of intact rock material	IS MPa	> 10	4-10	2-4	1-2	For this low range uniaxial compressive test is preferred		
		> 250	100-250	50-100	25-50	5-25	1-5	<1
Rating		15	12	7	4	2	1	0
2. Drill core quality RQD		90%-100%	75%-90%	50%-75%	25%-50%	< 25%		
3. Rating		20	17	13	8	3		
Spacing of discon.		> 2 m	0.6-2 m	200-600 mm	60-200 mm	< 60 mm		
Rating		20	15	10	8	5		
4. Condition of discontinuities		Very rough surfaces; Not continuous; No separation Unweathered wall rock	Slightly surfaces; Separation < 1 mm Slightly Weathered Walls	Slightly rough surfaces; Separation < 1 mm; Highly Weathered Walls	Slickensided surfaces; or gouge or Separation 1-5 mm; Continuous	Soft gouge > 5 mm thick; Separation > 5 mm Continuous		
Rating		30	25	20	10	0		
5. Ground Water	Inflow per 10 m tunnel length	None	< 10 l/m	10-25 l/m	25-125 l/m	> 125 l/m		
	Joint H₂O press Major Principle σ	OR 0	OR 0.0-0.1	OR 0.1-0.2	OR 0.2-0.5	OR > 0.5		
	General conditions	OR Completely dry	OR Damp	OR Wet	OR Dripping	OR Flowing		
Rating		15	10	7	4	0		

(b) Rating adjustment for joint orientation :

Strike and dip orientations of joints		Very favourable	Favourable	Fair	Unfavourable	Very unfaourable
Ratings	Tunnels	0	– 2	– 5	– 10	– 12
	Foundations	0	– 2	– 7	– 15	– 25
	Slopes	0	– 5	– 25	– 50	– 60

(c) Rock mass classes determined from total ratings :

Rating	81 – 100	61 – 80	41 – 60	21 – 40	< 20
Class No.	I	II	III	IV	V
Description	Very good rock	Good rock	Fair rock	Poor rock	Very poor rock

(d) Meaning of rock mass classes :

Class No.	I	II	III	IV	V
Average stand-up time	10 years for 15 m span	6 months for 8 m span	1 week for 5 m span	10 hrs. for 2.5 m span	30 min. for 1 m span
Cohesion of the rock mass	> 400 kPa	300 – 400 kPa	200 – 300 kPa	100 – 200 kPa	< 100 kPa
Friction angle of the rockmass	> 45	35° – 45°	25° – 35°	15° – 25°	< 15°

Table 4.7 : The effect of discontinuity, strike and dip in tunnelling (after Bieniawski, 1979)

Strike perpendicular to tunnel axis				Strike parallel to tunnel axis		Dip 0°-20° irresp. of strike
Drive with dip		Drive against dip				
Dip 45°-90°	Dip 20°-45°	Dip 45°-90°	Dip 20°-45°	Dip 45°-90°	Dip 20°-45°	
Very favourable	Favourable	Fair	Unfavourable	Very unfavourable	Fair	Unfavourable

(d) Q System developed by Barton, Lien and Lunde (1974) :

Barton et al (1974) of Norwegian Geotechnical Institute (NGI) proposed an index of the evaluation of tunneling quality of a rock mass, called as Q system.

$$Q = \left(\frac{RQD}{J_n}\right) \times \left(\frac{J_r}{J_a}\right) \times \left(\frac{J_w}{SRF}\right)$$

where,
- RQD = Rock Quality Designation
- J_n = Number of joint set
- J_r = Joint roughness number
- J_a = Joint alteration number
- J_w = Joint water reduction factor
- SRF = Stress Reduction Factor

Barton et al (1974) has offered the following explanation for the three quotients used in the equation –

- $\dfrac{RQD}{J_n}$ represents structure of the rock mass which is a crude measure of block size with the two extreme values (100/0.5 and 10/20) differing by factor of 400.

- $\dfrac{J_r}{J_a}$ represents the roughness and frictional characteristics of the joint walls or filling material. When joints are filled by clayey material, the strength of rock mass reduces significantly. The clayey bands may be of swelling nature which further complicates the conditions.

- $\left(\dfrac{J_w}{SRF}\right)$ consists of two stress parameters. SRF is a measure of (a) loosening load in the SRF case of excavation through shear zone and clay bearing rocks, (b) rock stress in competent rocks and (c) squeezing load in incompetent plastic rocks. It may be considered as a total stress parameter. J_w is a measure of water pressure which appreciably changes shear strength of rock.

It may be summarised that Q can now be considered as a function of

- Block size $\dfrac{RQD}{J_n}$

- Inter-block shear strength $\dfrac{J_r}{J_a}$.

- Active stress $\dfrac{J_w}{SRF}$.

Barton et al (1974) recognised 38 support categories (Fig. 4.9) and provided tables for estimating permanent support.

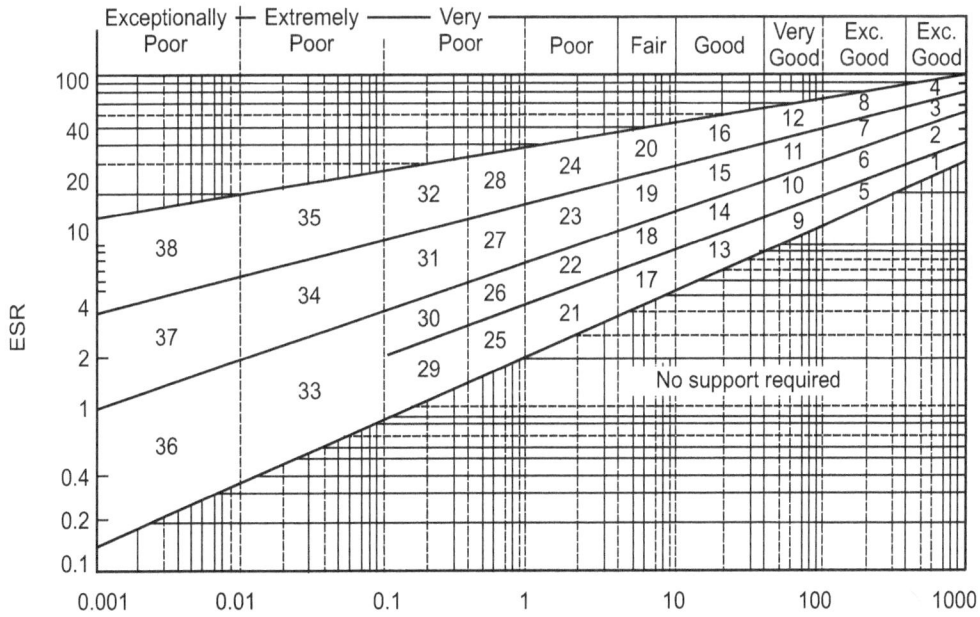

Fig. 4.9 : Equivalent dimension of tunnel versus rock mass quality, Q (after Barton et al. 1974)

It is observed that the classification based on RMR rating system and Q system are widely used. Both classifications suggest that distinction between favourable and unfavourable is adequate in case of discontinuities for most practical purposes. However in complicated geological conditions where discontinuities will tend to dominate the behaviour of rock mass (e.g. slate) or in some cases, large blocks may be isolated by a small number of individual discontinuities and become unstable when artificial openings are created. Under such circumstances, the classifications discussed here may not be adequate and special considerations may have to be given to the relationship between the geometry of rock mass and artificial openings.

4.6 GEOPHYSICAL METHODS

Geophysical methods allow subsurface conditions to be examined indirectly providing information of a more or less continuous nature over a transverse line or a grid of measuring points. Geophysical methods can be carried out on land, sea or from the air depending on the physical properties being measured. Such indirect methods have the advantage of being capable of providing detailed subsurface information very rapidly. They should be used in appreciation with geologic methods.

Geophysical methods may be used to :
(a) determine geological structure.
(b) profile geological boundaries in two or three dimensions (both quantitatively and qualitatively)
(c) locate localised subsurface features such as cavities, abondoned mine shafts, buried channels.
(d) determine the depth of groundwater and sea water invasion.
(e) prospect for economic deposits of construction materials such as sand and gravel.
It should be noted that the choice of geophysical method will depend upon the application, the expected subsurface conditions and the amount of noise.

All geophysical methods require measurement of physical properties of rock (density, magnetic susceptibility, elasticity, electrical conductivity and sometimes radioactivity). They may be divided into two major groups : (I) measurement of variations in the Earth's natural force fields (magnetic and gravitational fields), and (II) measurement of variations in the reaction of rocks and soils to artificially induced force fields (seismic, electrical). Group (I) methods are commonly used to find localised features of engineering interest whereas group II methods are usually recommended for profiling features (vertical and horizontal) such as the bedrock / overburden interface.

Accuracy of any geophysical method depends upon the contrast in one or more physical properties between different materials. Greater the contrast better is the chance for success. If contrast is low, the feature may be virtually undetectable. It is thus, necessary, to have some knowledge of the subsurface conditions of a site before using any geophysical technique. In general, reliability of any geophysical method is seriously hidered by one or more of following conditions.

(a) Complex geological structures.
(b) Heterogeneous ground.
(c) Extraneous noise.

(d) Lack of contrast of physical properties between different media.
(e) Depth of feature exceeding feature dimensions.

4.6.1 Seismic Method

The seismic methods utilize the fact that elastic waves travel with different velocities in different rocks. It is seen that waves are propagated through the earth and along the surface of the earth as body waves and surface waves respectively.

Body waves are propagated at different velocities by two different kinds of particle motions (see Unit - 5). The compressional waves travel in the direction of propagation through solid, liquid or gas. Shear waves can travel only through a solid medium by particle motion at a right angle to their direction of propagation. In seismic method, body waves (mainly compressional) are generated by the use of explosives in a shallow drill hole, by hammer blows etc.

In rocks, velocity of waves is influenced by texture and porosity. Rocks with crystalline texture and low porosity have greater sound wave velocities. Similarly, a well sorted rock will have higher velocity than a poorly sorted sedimentary rock. Mineral composition often plays a great role in deciding velocity. The presence of clay minerals in limestone will reduce shock wave velocity compared to a pure limestone. Similarly, another important factor which influences velocity in rocks is the presence of a network of discontinuities, degree of weathering of the rock mass etc. It can also be said that comparison in velocities of compressional and shear wave may indicate changes in the degree of saturation. Approximate velocities of body waves in different rocks is given in Fig. 4.10.

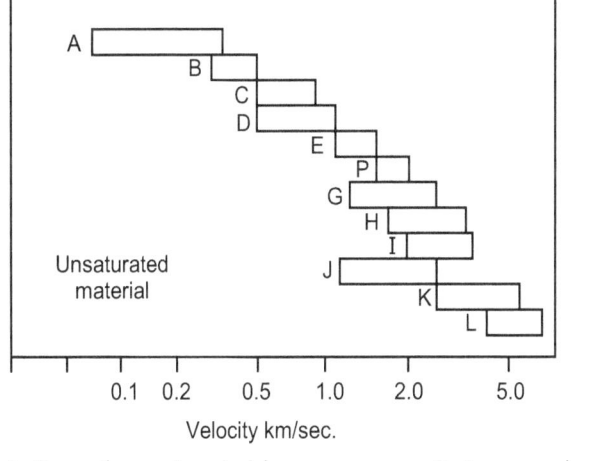
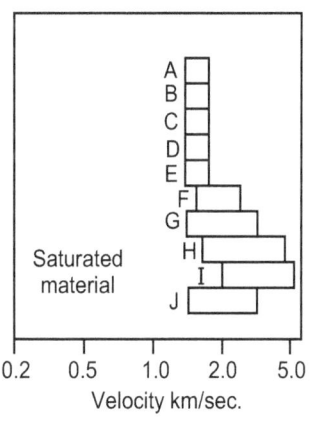

A - Top soil, organic material
C - Silt
E - Clay, till
G - Sandstone, conglomerate
I - Limestone, dolomite
K - Metasedimentary, igneous rocks

B - Loose sand
D - Gravel
F - Compact clay
H - Shale
I - Weathered and fractured rocks
L - Gneiss, Basic igneous and volcanic rocks

Fig. 4.10 : Characteristic variation in seismic velocities for rocks and soils

In seismic method, two major principles of optics are used; Refraction and Reflection.

(a) The Reflection method :

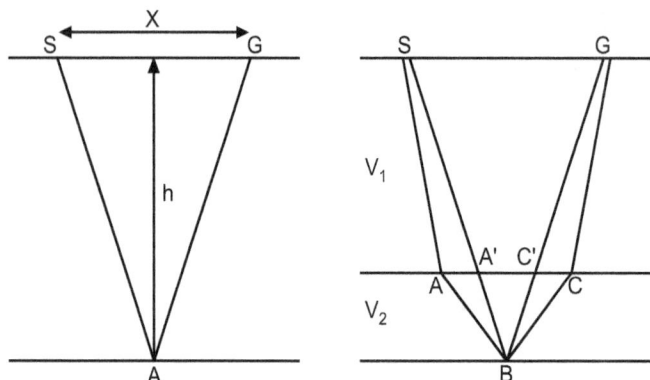

Fig. 4.11 : Seismic reflection method

Fig. 4.11 explains the pattern for reflection method in case of two layered model. In this, average velocities may be evaluated by measuring travel time from surface energy source to receiving stations below the surface in a drill. Two kinds of plots are used to find average velocity. In the first plot, reflection time from the source to receiving stations (geophones) are plotted against distance between source and receiving stations. The plotted curve is hyperbola and thus not useful to find average velocity. In the second plot, time and distances are squared and plotted. The slope of the linear plot provides the average velocity of the medium. In other words, the average velocity is obtained from the equation $1/V^2$.

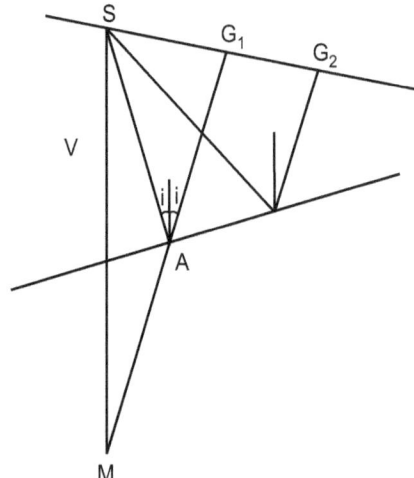

Fig. 4.12 : Reflection at a dipping horizon

From the Fig. 4.11, it can be said that where the reflecting interface is parallel to the surface, recording time for either side of the centre will be equal. The increase in recording time to the surface outward from the centre is known as move out time. Thus, in the case of dipping interface (Fig. 4.12), the move out time will no longer remain uniform or symmetrical with respect to centre; instead the down-dip time being more than normal move out time and the up dipping time being less than normal move out time. The amount of dip, thus, may be calculated by comparing actual move out time with normal move out time.

(b) The Refraction method :

This is the most important and widely used method in engineering applications. It has several advantages over the other methods, including surface measurement of wave velocity in concealed units. Evaluation of dip interface and irregularities, low cost involved, rapid data computation etc.

In this method, it is assumed that elastic waves created from source will travel at a definite velocity, V_2, in the second medium [Fig. 4.13 (a)].

Following Snell's law, it can be said that,

$$\frac{V_1}{V_2} = \frac{\sin l_1}{\sin l_2}$$

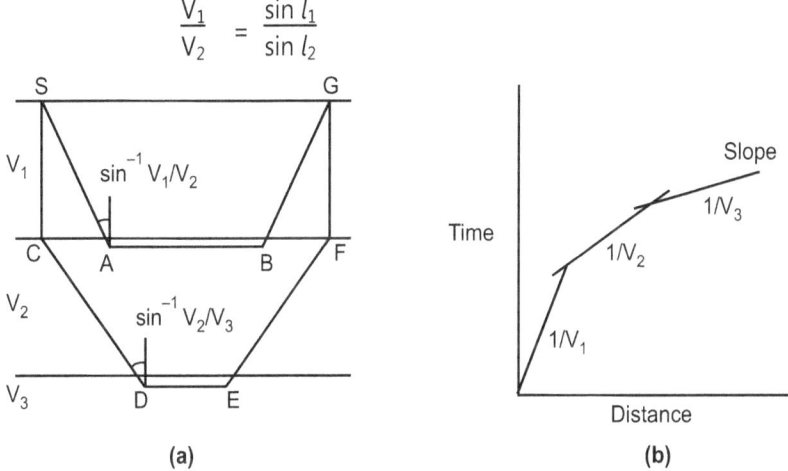

Fig. 4.13 : (a) Seismic refraction method, (b) Time - distance graph

where l_1 and l_2 are the angle of incidence and refraction for the ray. The ray SA is refracted, as a result $l_2 = 90°$ and travels along the boundary between V_1 and V_2 [Fig. 4.13 (b)]. Due to this, secondary waves are developed and ray BG is formed on the top layer with an angle l_3 to reach the receiving station. The travel time for the direct waves and other waves is different. However both plot on the straight line from the origin with the slope $1/V_1$ and $1/V_2$ respectively. If a velocity interface at depth is converging to the surface, the velocities recorded at the surface are apparent. As a result these velocities are greater or less than the true velocities.

In case V_1 has a lower velocity than V_2, then l_1 will always be less than l_2. As a result no energy can be transported along such medium and only one segment in the curve may be obtained (Fig. 4.14).

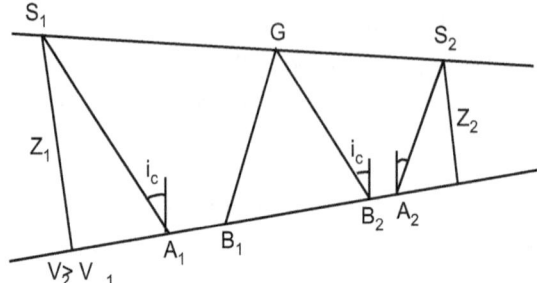

Fig. 4.14 : Dipping interface

Now-a-days, reflection method is widely used for oil prospecting, while refraction method is prominently used in major civil engineering projects for subsurface rock investigations in connection with studies of dam site investigations and hydro-electric power stations.

(c) Engineering applications :

Following are the major applications of seismic method in engineering works :

(1) Calculation of depth and dip interface of bedrock with the use of refraction method. However, reflection method provides accurate information regarding depths of bed rock.

(2) Seismic refraction method is also useful in determining thickness for landslide volume and slip surface geometry.

(3) Evaluation of rock mass quality (RQD) by using compressional wave velocities recorded from reflected and refraction surveys. Decrease in velocities of waves may be a combined effect of high discontinuity density, high weathering and compositional anisotropy. It can be said that RQD and velocity values are directly proportional.

4.6.2 Electrical Method

The electrical properties of subsurface can be measured either by using electrical methods or electromagnetic methods.

The electrical methods make use of three important parameters of rocks : resistivity, electrochemical activity (self potential method) and electrical storage capacity (inductive prospecting method). However, only the first method is described here.

Electrical Resistivity Method : In the electrical resistivity method, current is introduced into the ground by using two electrodes. The resistance of the material to current flow is collected from Ohms' law by measuring the drop in potential between two electrodes that are symmetrically positioned within the field of current electrode [Fig. 4.15 (a)].

Thus, a change in specific resistance indicates an increase or decrease in electrical potential. The conversion of resistance to resistivity is a function of position and spacing of the potential electrodes relative to the current electrode. It can also be said that resistivity is a function of the electrolyte contained in the pore spaces of the material and is inversely proportional to the porosity.

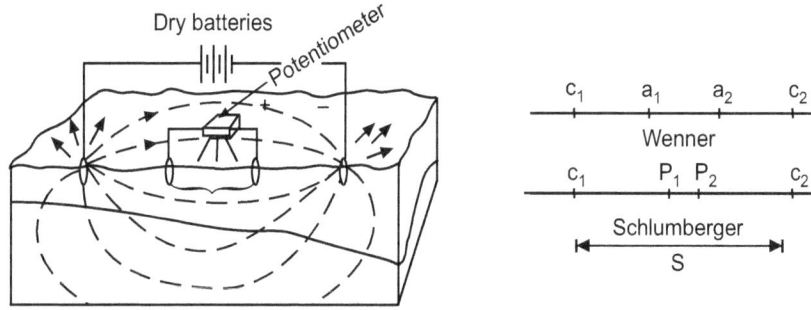

(a) Position of current used and equipotential electrode

(b) Two types of configurations used

Fig. 4.15 : Principles of electrical resistivity method

The penetration of investigation of a resistivity survey is controlled by the distance of current electrodes. Depth of investigation increases with increased electrodes spacing.

The resistivity values recorded are apparent rather than true. This is due to anisotropism of layers below the surface.

To find the resistivity, two basic types of configurations are used : Wenner [Fig. 4.15 (a)] and Schlumberger [Fig. 4.15 (b)]. In the case of Wenner configuration, the electrode spacing 'a' is kept constant and the resistivity is calculated by using the equation,

$$\rho = 2\pi a R$$

where, $R \text{ (Ohms)} = \dfrac{V \text{ (voltage)}}{I \text{ (current)}}$

In the case of Schlumberger configuration, the distance 'S' varies while 'l' remains constant. Resistivity in this is calculated by the equation,

$$\rho = \pi \left(\dfrac{S^2}{2l}\right) R$$

The a and S spacing determines depth of investigation for Wenner and Schlumberger configuration respectively.

Resistivity surveys may be carried out by vertical and horizontal profiling. In vertical profiling (also called as electric sounding/drilling) the centre of the electrode is kept constant and the electrode spacings 'a' and 'S' are increased. The resistivity data are plotted on the ordinate relative to the increasing electrode spacing on the absissa. In the case of horizontal profiling (also called electric mapping/trenching) electrode spacing is kept constant and data stations are rotated. As a result, differing resistivity values for a chosen depth of investigation or precisely at a specific electrode spacing are obtained. From the data, contour map may be prepared which could give information on local subsurface conditions. However, spacing used in horizontal profiling is often decided after conducting vertical profiling.

Interpretation of resistivity maps is based on the assumption that the resistance of a bed is uniform over the area investigated. The chief engineering applications are estimating the depth of overburden, physical characters of rocks, location of construction material, possible presence of water bearing horizons and faults.

4.6.3 Magnetic Method

The method depends upon measuring accurately the anomalies of the local geomagnetic field created by the variations in the intensity of magnetization in different rocks. Magnetization in rocks is an combined effect of magneting force associated with the earth's field and their remnant magnetization. The most important properties are susceptibility of rocks and permanent magnetization.

Generally rocks falls into three categories, diamagnetic, paramagnetic and ferromagnetic. The rocks and minerals which show net diamagnetizm are quartz, marble, graphite, rock salt and anhydrite (gypsum). Typical ferromagnetic minerals are magnetite, limenite and titanomagnetic, namely, gneisses, pegmatites, diolomites, syenites etc.

The susceptibility of rocks is controlled by the amount of ferromagnesium minerals in them, their grain size, mode of distribution etc.

It is now well understood that both igneous and sedimentary rocks possess permanent magnetization in varying degrees. Similarly, igneous and sedimentary rocks of different geologic age possess strong magnetizm but have different directions at times, opposite to the present direction of the geomagnetic field.

Magnetic measurements are carried out using different types of magnetometers. When the area for magnetic investigation is selected, a base line is drawn parallel to the geological strike and measurements are made at regular intervals along lines normal to the base. A reference point is chosen, (The point should be far from power lines, railways etc. and at this point the magnetic field is known to be approximately the normal field); and the magnetic intensity is measured as positive and negative differences with respect to the reference point.

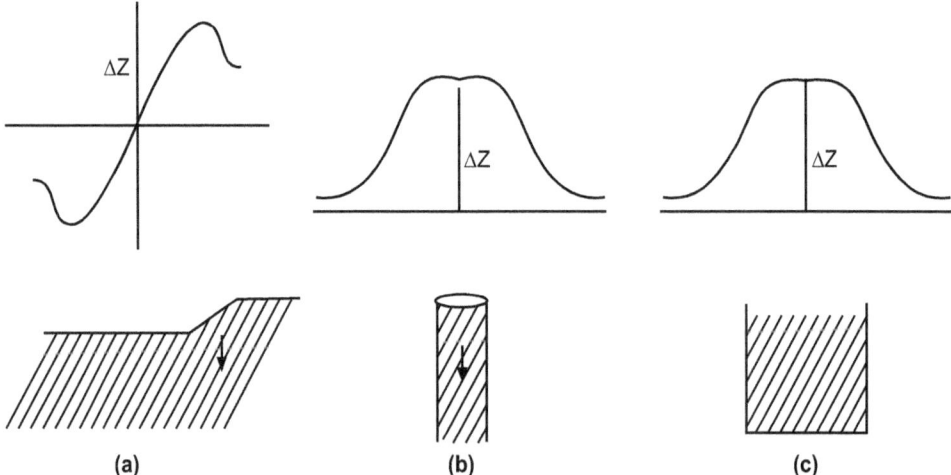

Fig. 4.16 : Miscellaneous geological features

Several corrections should be applied before interpreting the collected data including diurnal variations of the earth's field, temperature dependence of instrument and terrain correction.

Some simple features are given in Fig. 4.16. The structure in Fig. 4.16 (a) is persistent normal to the plane of the paper is encountered as a fault plane or the undulations of the bedrock below the overburden. The cylinder in Fig. 4.16 (b) may be an intrusive igneous rock. Similarly Fig. 4.16 (c) may indicates presence of a dyke or horizontal beds. It can be said that the more general application of this method is to locate boundaries where igneous rocks lie on one side.

4.6.4 Gravity Method

In this method, similar to magnetic method, a knowledge of relative measurements of gravity is required, which gives the gravitational difference between an observation point and a base point. Appropriate corrections should be applied to the differences measured at any station to reduce them to some standard conditions. The corrected values are called *anomalies*. These yield information about variation in density within the earth; and also about surfaces that bound areas of differing density.

The relative gravity measurements are carried out using different types of gravimeter. Two types are recognised, the stable and the unstable types. The stable gravimeter is a very sensitive balance that includes Askania type, Gulf (Hoyt) type, and Norgard type. The unstable gravimeter includes Lacoste - Ramberg type and Warden type.

Gravimeter observations are made at the corners of a square grid. The length of the square is controlled by the size of the object. In oil prospecting, the grid side may be 500 metres or 1000 metres, while in mineral exploration, the grid side is not more than 50 metres. Care must be taken to record the geographic position and the elevation of the station as accurately as possible. Unit for measurement of gravity is milligal (1 mgal = 10 g.u.). It is seen that the differences in density between very light rocks and dark rocks is not great enough to produce gravity differences. They are mostly in milligals. To measure such small quantities, very sensitive instruments are required.

All gravity measurements should be corrected for latitude and elevation above sea level; called as Bouger correction or Bouger anomaly. Gravity or Bouger anomalies are usually shown by contours drawn on a suitable interval through or around the observation point. An observed value of gravity greater than the compound value constitutes a positive anomaly and an observed value less than the compound value constitutes a negative anomaly which thus gives an assessment of geological structure. The data may also be plotted as curves on profiles taken at right angles to the strike. Relative gravity may be calculated from gradients.

As mentioned earlier, gravity method depend on measurements of density distributions in a gravitational field and thus no depth control is possible. A concealed denser body would show positive gravity anomaly as compared to adjacent less dense rocks. Similarly a lighter body (less dense) would give negative gravity anomaly as compared to denser rocks.

Under certain condition, gravity method is useful in civil engineering operations. Presence of subsurface, structures like fault, folds, intrusive bodies, caverns in limestone may easily be recognised using this method.

Table 4.8 : Summary of Geophysical methods used in site investigation

Method	Principle	Applications	Advantages	Limitations
1. Seismic Refraction	– Measures travel time of induced energy which has been refracted at soil/rock interfaces. – Coverage is linear at any desired horizontal spacing.	– Quantitative. Based on plotting travel time against distance between energy and detector. – Depth profiling of soil or rock strata particularly depth to 'bedrock' profiles. – Location of buried channels, faults – Throw of faults – Determination of dynamic elastic moduli of rocks and soils.	– High degree of accuracy of shallow depth. – Depth and velocities easily determined. – Field techniques relatively simple. – Equipment compact and portable.	– High background noise. – Poor velocity contrast. – Hidden layer problem – Continuous velocity increase at depth. – Water table.
2. Seismic Reflection	– Measures travel time of induced energy which has been reflected at soil or rock interfaces. – Coverage is linear at any desired horizontal spacing.	– Quantitative and quantitative – Depth profiling of soil or rock. – Location of buried channels, faults and fault zones.	– Continuous seismic reflection profiling allows shallow rock/soil interfaces to be readily identified from the seismic record.	– High noise – Continuous velocity decrease – Analysis of travel time data is complex
3. Electrical Resistivity	– Measures relative electrical resistance of soils and rocks in ohms. – Coverage is linear when depth sounding.	– Mainly qualitative. – Mapping lateral and vertical lithological variations in soils and rocks. – Determining thickness and nature of superficial deposits. – Location and mapping of buried channels, and subsurface cavities. – Groundwater mapping and investigations.	– Equipment compact and portable. – Rapid. – Interpretation is straight forward.	– Presence of underground or overhead electrical power cables. – Method suitable for simple conditions.

... Contd.

4. Magnetic	– Measures total magnetic field intensities.	– Qualitative. – Mapping clay filled sinkholes in carbonates. – Location of buried channels and cavities. – Location of faults associated with basic igneous rocks.	– Equipment compact and portable. – Large areas may be covered rapidly. – Data corrections simple and easy to apply.	– High magnetic gradients from power cables and iron objects. – Station interval larger than target dimensions. – Method not suitable for complex geologic conditions.
5. Gravity	– Measures total density variations in rocks and soils in milligals. – Coverage is spherical around point.	– Qualitative – Mapping major geological structures – Locating near surface cavities.		– Field techniques are slow. – Several corrections need to be applied. – Some corrections require accurate topographic surveys. – Station interval larger than target dimensions.

4.7 LANDSLIDES AND RELATED PHENOMENA

Mass wasting is the collective term for all gravity controlled downslope movements of weathered material. Water plays an important role in reducing the coherence and strength of loose or unconsolidated material. Mass movement may occur naturally or may be caused i.e. induced by men as well. The latter is especially true in mountainous regions.

The high intensity mass movements in tectonically active steeplands are due to combined effects of geological and climatic conditions rather than land use factors. Steep dip slopes, unstable nature of rocks due to their structural disposition (discontinuities), depth and degree of weathering, high seismicity and oversteepening of slopes due to undercutting of rivers are some of the important geological factors. Similarly, the factors of intense precipitation and the associated saturation of soils are also important. In the parts of Kosi basin, landslides were most frequent during times of both heavy rainfall and earthquake.

Irrigation canals in complex areas are frequently associated with slop failures due to the removal of toe support from slopes and also due to the saturation of the weathering mantle by seepage and overflow. Similarly, construction of large dams and subsequent overflow of valleys have substantial effects. In the reservoir area, the increased pore pressure associated with the saturation of slopes may well induce slides when the water level in the reservoir is lowered. Another important impact on slope stability is the construction of roads. However, the intensity of the problem may be reduced if proper stability analyses are carried out during the initial stages.

Table 4.9 : Factors and agents influencing the mass movements

Name of agent	Process that initiates movement	Mode of action of agent	Material prone to action	Modification
(1) Tectonic	(a) Tectonic movements	Deformation of earth's crust	Every material	Increases slope angle and shearing stresses.
	(b) Earthquakes	High frequency vibrations.	Every material	Rapid movements.
(2) Weight of slope forming material	Process that created the slope	Creep on slope	Fissured clay, shale, old slide remnants.	New joint developments, reduces cohesion.
(3) Transporting agent.	Construction operations or erosion.	Increase of elevation of rise of slope	Every material.	Increases shearing stresses and initiates swelling.
(4) Water	Rain or melting snow	(a) Displacement of air in voids.	Sand (wet)	Increases pore water pressure and decreases frictional resistnce.
		(b) Displacement of air in joints.	Jointed rock	Swelling and decreases cohesion.
		(c) Reduction in capillary pressure associated with swelling.	Argillaceous rocks	Swelling and decreases cohesion
		(d) Chemical weathering	Any rock	Intergranular
	Frost	Crystal growth	Jointed rock	Bonding decreaes. Volume expansion.
	Dry spell	Shrinkage	Clay	Volume contraction.
	Changes in water-table elevations Rapid draw-down	Rearrangement of grains.	Saturated sedimentation	Increases in pore-water pressure and liquefaction.
	Seepage from reservoir	Seepage	Fine material	Changes in pore water pressure.
		Seepage and erosion	Sand and slit	Changes in pressure.

Landsliding takes place when slope materials are no longer able to resist the force of gravity. This decrease in resistance (shear) may result from internal or external causes. Internal causes usually involve some change in either the physical or the chemical properties of the bedrock soil or its water content.

External factors that lead to an increase in shear stress on slope usually involve a form of disturbance that may be natural or induced by man. (Table 4.10)

Table 4.10 : Factors leading to an increase in shear stress

1. Removal of lateral or underlying support.
   - Undercutting by water or glacier ice.
   - Washing out of granular material by seepage.
   - Erosion
   - Manmade cuts and excavations.
   - Drainage of lakes or reservoirs.
2. Increased loading (overburden)
   - Natural accumulation of water snow, talus.
   - Manmade structures.
3. Transitory earth stresses
   - Earthquakes
   - Continual passing of heavy traffic.

It is necessary to understand two aspects : (a) those conditions that prepare the slope material for failure, and (b) those forces that actual cause it to fail. For example, tropical weathering may produce a deep mantle of soil that remains in place on a slope until the slope is undercut by a river (or human activity) and the soil is no more in stable condition.

The mass movements are also initiated by change in hydrological regime. Hydrological conditions are often modified due to construction of dams. The presence of a lake may change a previously stable slope into unstable, if factors like rainfall, runoff, infiltration etc. are unfavourable.

Surplus loading by embankment, fills etc. increases the shear stress and also pore water pressure in clayey soils that decreases their shear strength.

Slope modifications may also be due to large scale vibrations, machine vibrations, traffic vibration, earthquakes etc. which may cause a temporary change of stress due to oscillations of different frequencies.

Rain water and melt water penetrate into joints producing hydrostatic pressure. In soils, the pore water pressure increases and subsequently decreases the shear resistance. In case of abnormally high rainfalls, the recurrent movements along the slopes may be observed. Similarly presence of a heavy rain after a prolonged dry period enhances instability in clayey slopes.

Free moving groundwater exerts pressure on soil particles. Similarly, seepage of water from reservoirs, unlined canals etc. cause an increase in the pore water pressure in the slopes. The process lowers cohesion and proportionally reduces shear strength.

4.8 CLASSIFICATION SCHEMES

Mass movements have been classified on the basis of a wide variety of factors including process, product, climate, type of material moved, local geology and triggering mechanisms.

Mass wasting bridges the gap between weathering and erosion. It is considered as a transitional phenomenon. Two important factors of mass wasting are (1) the nature of movement, whether sliding or falling as a coherent mass or flowing by internal deform at ion and (2) the velocity of the movement, variable from very slow to very rapid. Landslide is a non-specific term for rapid mass movement in rocks. Movement can take place in a fall, a free falling action during which the material is not in contact with ground surface. It may occur as a slide, in which a fairly coherent material slips down along a well defined slope or it may occur as a flow where material is not coherent but it flows with a distinct chaotic and disorganised manner along with mixed material. The tabular classification of mass movements is given in Table 4.10. Another point in the discussion is the velocity at which a slide is developed and is moved under the influence of gravity. The velocity of a landslide is influenced and controlled by the material, behaviour and mechanism of its occurrence. It may be due to rapid erosion of toe surface of river erosion or destructive sea waves.

Table 4.11 : Tabular classification of mass movements

Type of movement		Type of material
Falls		Bedrock ────────────────────────────→ Soil
		Rockfall Soilfall
Slides	No. of Units: Few ↓ Many	Rotational ─────→ Planar ←───── Rotational
		Slump Block glide Block slump
		RockslideDebris slideLateral spread
Flows	Moisture content: Dry ↓ Wet	ALL UNCONSOLIDATED
		Rock Fragments ──→ Sand or Silt ──→ Mixed ──→ Plastic
		Rock Fragment Flow
		Sand run Loess flow
		Rapid earth flow Debris avalanche Slow earth flow Creep
		Debris flow: sand or silt Rubber flow: dirty snow avalanche Solifluction Mud flow

(a) Falls : The term falls refers to downslope movement of solitary grains or relatively loose assemblages of grains where each particle moves more or less independently of others. It may be in the form of rock falls or debris falls.

Rock fall occurs when slabs or pieces of bedrock undergo disintegration and fall downslopes or mountain sides.

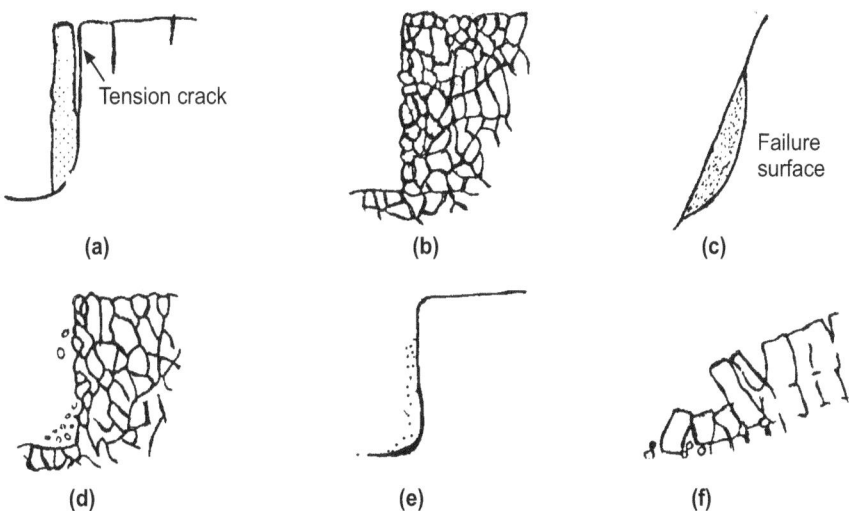

Fig. 4.17 : Types of rock fall, depedent on size and number of falling fragments. Type (a) is characterized by a large fragment bounded by a well-defined, vertical fracture. Type (b) is characterized by numerous smaller fragments, also bounded below by a relatively well-defined surface. Type (c) is characterized by sliding rock mass above a well-defined, inclined but non-vertical basal shear surface. It generally compared with (b), but contrasts with (a) in the nature of the basal contact and with (b) in the number of fragments involved. (e) is similar to (d), but only very small fragments are involved. Type (f) is termed 'toppling failure', where the fragments are large and only move a short distance, with the maximum movement occuring of the fragment. It has some resemblance to (a) and (d)

The volume of the rock fall vary from single pieces of rock to cascades of solid rock which causes extensive damage. Important factors for the formation of falls are bedrock type climate, structural geometry and steep slopes.

Massive homogeneous rocks, like igneous rocks, are less prone to falls than layered sedimentary and metamorphic rocks. Fine grained rocks will tend to produce rock falls with smaller fragments than more massive varieties, whereas massive rocks generate more voluminous rock falls.

Temperate and humid climates are ideal conditions for rock fall formation. Rain water percolating continuously in cracks and advancing weathering, reduces shearing strength of rock and subsequently diminishes the frictional resistance to slippage. Repeated freezing and thawing of circulating water also causes rapid volume changes in cracks and joints.

Presence of discontinuities will enhance rock fall generation particularly if the dip of fractures being gentler than that of rock wall.

Debris falls are downslope movements of dispersed debris under the influence of gravity. They are transitional to cohesionless debris flows. Debris falls may form if slope oversteepening occurs due to rapid sedimentation, slumping or wave undercutting.

(b) Flows : Incoherent material may be appreciably mobilized, as a result it flows like a viscous fluid with a distinct chaotic and disorganised manner. Subdivision of flow can be based either on the kind of material, the degree of saturation, or the velocity of material (Fig. 4.17). From the Fig., it can be said that the velocity of movement is greater than creep.

Three major divisions viz. debris flow, earth flow and mud flow may be recognised.

Debris flow : Debris flows have 20 to 80 per cent coarse aggregate. These move with slow and fast rate depending on flowing surface. In this, large amount of water is incorporated into the earth material so that the lowered viscosity permits much longer travel.

Earth flow : Earth flow always result from excessive rainfall. They often develop at the heads of small gullies where surface run-off concentrates to initiate streams. They may also form on planar hillsides or at the toe of large slumps. Earth flows consist 80 per cent or more of sand and mud.

Mud flow : Mud flow is the most liquid end member of the flow series. These occur in stream channels and are hybrid of water and sediment. Mud flows are generally caused by abnormal sheetwash on hill slopes where the accumulated debris is moved into a more restricted flow regime at the bottom of the slope.

Liquefaction : Liquefaction is a process of increase in pore water pressure and is best possibly seen in clay, slit and sandy soil. It can be induced by earthquakes generated shear or compressional waves. Shear waves deform the granular structure of soil resulting collapse of some voids. These collapse transfer the bearing load of the sediment from grain to grain contact to pore water. On the other hand, compressional waves increase pore water pressure during every passage of a shock wave. Due to successive waves, pore water pressure proportionally increase with the passage of each wave (Fig. 4.18). However, pore water pressure can return to normal, only if the soil is permeable.

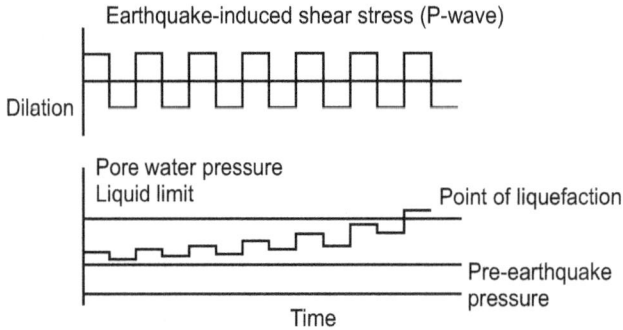

Fig. 4.18 : Effects of earthquake waves on liquefaction

If pore water pressure approaches the weight of overlying soil, then soil at depth behaves like a fluid. As a result, bearing capacity of subsoil virtually reduces to minimum.

In unconsolidated material, the finer the grain size, more the water movement is inhibited due to capillary cohesion, while in the case of consolidated material, depending on degree of consolidation, grade of weathering and depth etc., cohesion in these material exceed the increase in pore water pressure during the passage of earthquake waves.

In general, it can be said that liquefaction causes three types of failures viz. lateral spread, flow failure and loss of bearing strength.

(c) Slides : Slides are downslope displacement of sediments above a distinct planar surface where there is no internal deformation of the transported material.

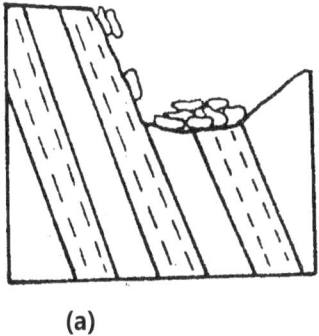   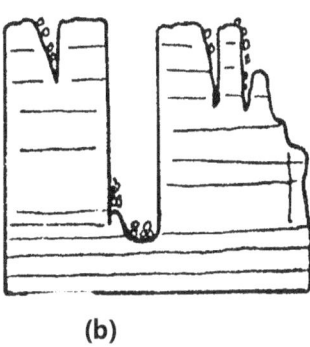

(a)   (b)

Fig. 4.19 : Translational slides

Here sliding takes place along planes of discontinuities [Fig. 4.19 (a)] or along bedding planes [Fig. 4.19 (b)]. Thus, a translational movement takes place in a downstream direction. In this, the slide material has large lateral and longitudinal dimensions in comparison with the thickness.

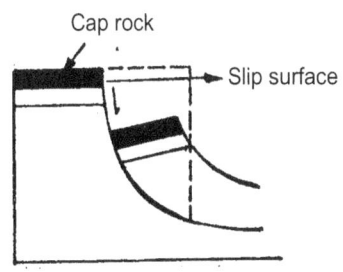   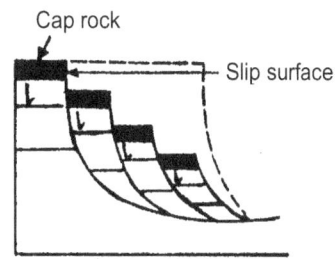

(a) Surface rotational slip   **(b) Multiple rotational slip**

Fig. 4.20 : Rotational slides

Here the surface is cylindrical or spherical so that the sliding mass is rotated during failure. The rotation of the moving mass is due to complex system of discontinuities or due to anisotropic surfaces.

(d) Slump : A slump is a rotational slip along a concave up surface or rupture passed downhill into an earthflow. It is the most common form of mass wasting.

Slumping is observed in thick, homogeneous cohesive clay material. It may be due to the undercutting action of water at the foothills. Slumps may also be initiated due to engineering constructions.

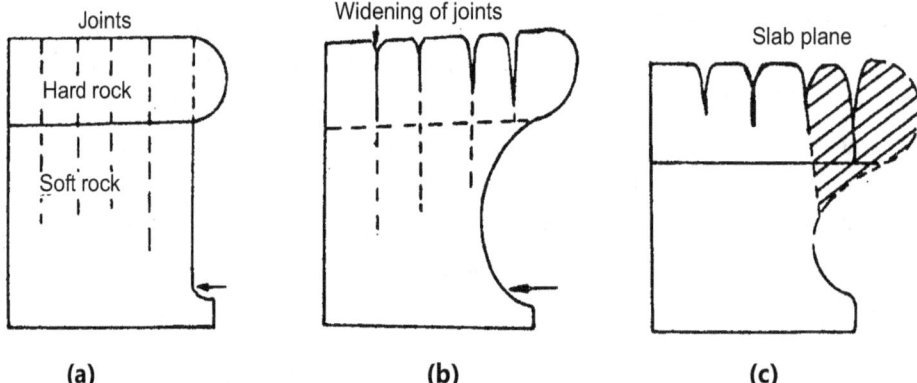

Fig. 4.21 : Development of a slab slide in an alternate hard and soft rock sequence

In the alternate competent and incompetent rock sequence, continuous undercutting of incompetent bed makes the upper surface unstable [Fig. 4.21 (a) & (b)]. As a result, tensional cracks or fractures are developed which produce potential site for rockfall [Fig. 4.21 (c)].

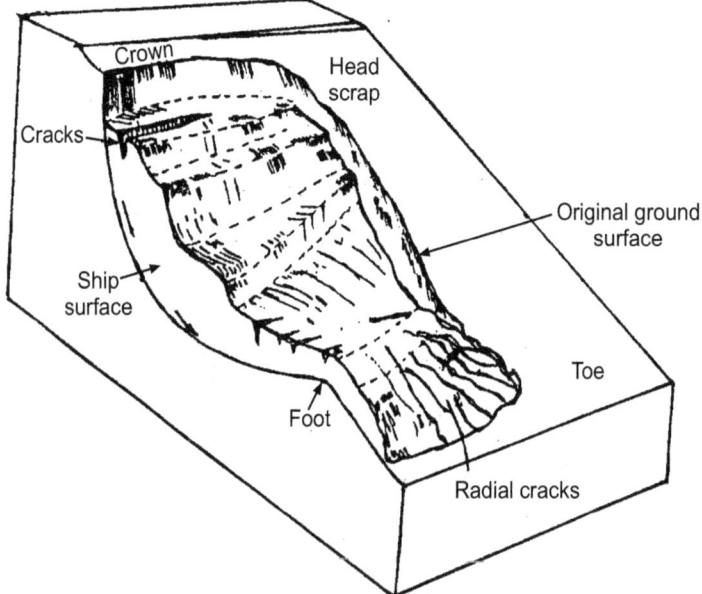

Fig. 4.22 : Forms of a typical landslide

In their most simple form, slides are spoon shaped features with a three part morphology of upslope head region, middle 'rigid' zone and downslope toe zone (Fig. 6.18). The upslope head region is concave downslope, whereas the middle region is mainly translational. The downslope toe region has a convex downslope and characteristically lobate form.

The 'head' region is dominated by a group of curved (listric) faults which tend to sole out at common level. The control part of the slide generally shows little evidence of sliding itself and thus the basal shear zone can be extremely difficult to identify particularly in fine grained sediments. In some cases, there may be evidence for internal slip between beds in the form of tiny faults of distorted bedding. These structures are important to detect and provide valuable information on the translated nature of the sediments. The margins of the slides are dominated by strike-slip deformation. Any indicative structure in favour of this thus helps to distinguish between lateral margin and toe or head particularly in areas of ancient landslides.

Contractional deformation features expressed by thrust faults and imbricate zone geometries dominate the toe region. In plan view, the morphological expression of the contractional toe zone is sometimes that of downslope lobate ridges or 'pressure' ridges.

In some cases, slides are 'open-ended' and thus do not exhibit clearly defined toe zones. This is possibly due to a high degree of lateral compaction so that strain is taken up by porosity reduction rather than thrust zones.

(e) Creep : Creep is the slowest moving mass movement and involves slow translation of sediment or soil down a slope. Creep takes place at a rate that cannot be observed directly with naked eye (few cm/year). It is an important process because it can lead to substantial land waste and in a few instances, creep often triggers other and most violent mass movement, such as landslides.

Evidence of creep of the soil mantle is found on almost every soil covered slope. Curved tree trunks, titted fence posts, telegraph posts and monuments, broken and displaced retaining walls and foundations are only a few of the signs of its presence (Fig. 4.23). A common experience of creep is detached fragments of bedrock forming imperfect bands or drawn out into an irregular downhill pattern.

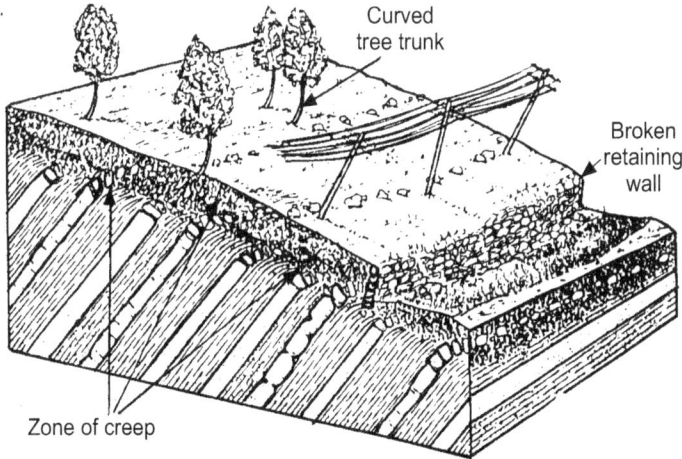

Fig. 4.23 : Diagram of creep showing associated features, tops of beds being turned downslope, trees and telegraph poles being tilted downslope, stones orientated downslope and soil pilling against retaining wall

The rate of creep of a hillslope depends not only on climatic conditions and angle of slope but also on the type of soil, parent material and other factors.

A talus is an accumulation of rock waste at the foot of a cliff. Talus materials consist of moderately coarse to very large irregular blocks. Creep can locally increase the slope inclination, causing mudslides and debris flows to be generated. The creep tonque (talus) lack sorting. They are generally less than 1 m thick, but on flatter areas they may attain greater thickness particularly where several tonques are superimposed. The tonques are smooth especially where the soil is relatively permeable, allowing downward percolation of rainwater and prevention of tonque destruction from rainfall run-off.

4.9 ROCKS AND LANDSLIDES

Rocks are generally not prone to landsliding in the same way as less cohesive beds and regolith. The presence of weak zones such as discontinuities are critical in evaluating the overall ability of the bedrock to resist landsliding.

One of the important controls of bedrock instability is the angle at which major joints intersect the ground surface. Some examples are shown in Fig. 4.24.

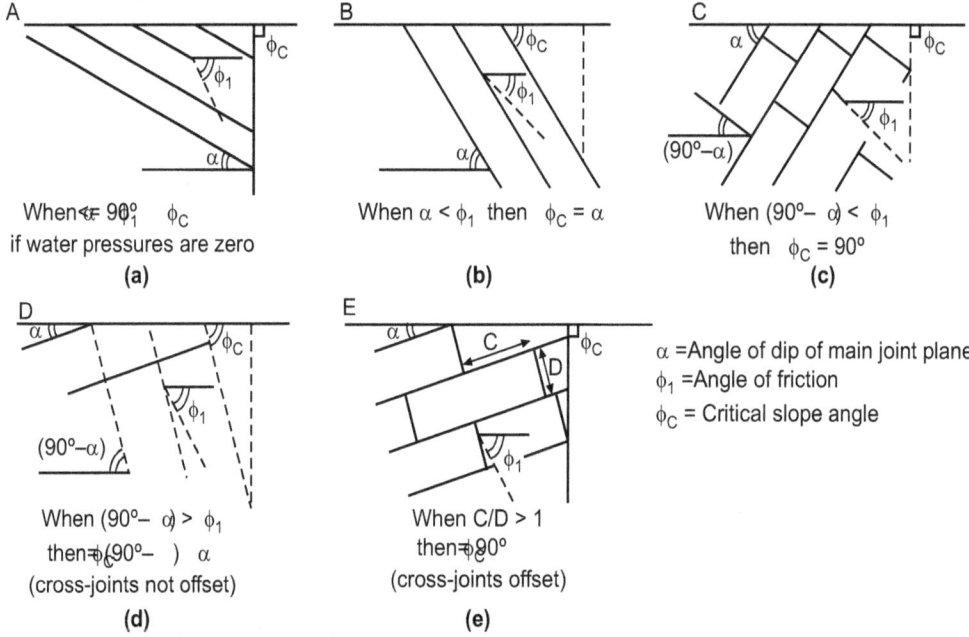

Fig. 4.24 : Some possible relationships between joints, planes in bedrock and slope stability

The Fig. illustrates the importance of the relation between the angle of friction (at which sliding would occur under gravity) along the joint plane (ϕ_f) and dip of joints (α). If $\alpha < \phi_f$, the slope could stand at any angle upto 90° [Fig. 4.24 (a)], but if $\alpha > \phi_f$, then gravity would induce movement along the joint plane [Fig. 4.24 (b)]. However, bedrock generally shows presence of many joint sets. Examples given in Fig. 4.24 (c) to (e) illustrate the relations between. ϕ_f, α and ϕ_c (secondary joint set).

The angle of friction is determined by a number of characteristics of discontinuities (persistence, surface roughness, spacing and aperture), degree of weathering and filling material. Particular reference is made of availability of gauge as filling material. The gauge may have lower shearing strength than the bedrock and the gauge-bedrock interface may have even lower shearing strength than the gauge itself.

Thus, four possibilities may arise –

1. Sliding plane passes through gauge only.
2. Sliding is partly through gauge and bedrock, as a result shear strength is dependent upon both.
3. Gauge is very thin and partially increases the shear resistance of the joint plane, and
4. No gauge and shear strength is entirely that of the joint plane.

The orientation of joints, movement of water and water pressure are also important in deciding stability of slopes. As bedrock commonly shows presence of joints of different orientations, providing several pathways for water. This is in contrast with soil where hydraulic conductivity is less. Presence of clay minerals like montmorillonite and soluble minerals like gypsum may undergo swelling and dissolution respectively which causes a decrease in shear resistance in time.

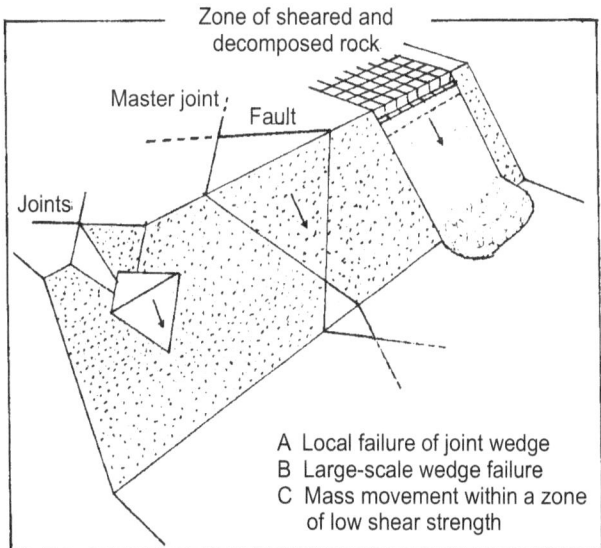

Fig. 4.25 : Possible modes of bedrock failure (a) local failure by joint wedge, (b) large scale wedge failure due to intersection of master joint and fault (c) mass movement within a zone of low shear strength

Three categories of rock slope failure are shown in Fig. 4.25 (a) local failure of joint wedge, (b) large scale wedge failure and (c) mass movement within a zone of low shear strength. The final condition allows deep weathering of bedrock, altering the strength, permeability and deformability characteristics of bedrock and producing a complicated zone of residual soil, weathered rock and unweathered rock. Localised changes in pure water pressure may lead to instability (Fig. 6.21). Once movement is initiated in any type of bedrock, the residual strength will be much lower than initial resistance of shearing and subsequent movements may occur with less efforts.

4.10 MAN-INDUCED MASS MOVEMENTS

All over the globe there has been a sharp increase in the number of man-induced landslides during the last 50 years. This is possibly due to excessive population, required urbanization and careless construction activities. Mass movements are caused by changes in the slope geometry, some of which are as follows :

(a) Highway construction : Construction of major long route roads is one of the most important ways that have directly caused landsliding. The major landslides have occurred in areas of complex geology and topography. For example, Himalayan belt.

The mass movements initiate when the groundwater regime is changed and subsequently the shear resistance of material is substantially modified (Fig. 4.26).

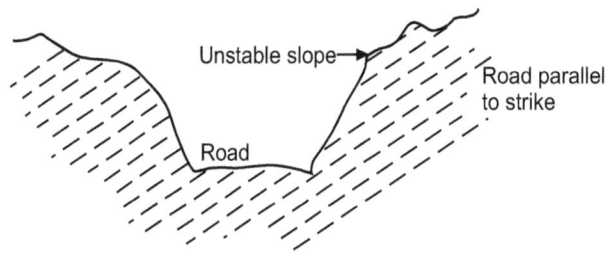

Fig. 4.26 : Sketch illustrating relationship between road cut stability and orientation of beds

(b) Urbanization : Building on hill slopes can be risky if they are poorly located (Fig. 4.27).

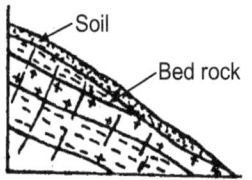 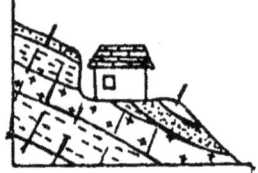 

(a) Original slope   (b) Excavation and fill   (c) Slip failure

Fig. 4.27 : Slope instability due to urbanization

(c) Impoundment of water : The construction of dams and the creation of reservoirs initiate a set of movements due to artificially induced changes in water level (Fig. 4.28), for example, Vaiont dam, Italy. On October 9, 1963, a landslide mass of 260 million m³ violently plunged into the reservoir and created giant waves of the amplitude of more than 100 m. Careful investigations revealed that a combined effect of man controlled changes in reservoir level and the presence of a peculiar geological structure of beds dipping in the adjoining valley were responsible for a occurrence of this landslide.

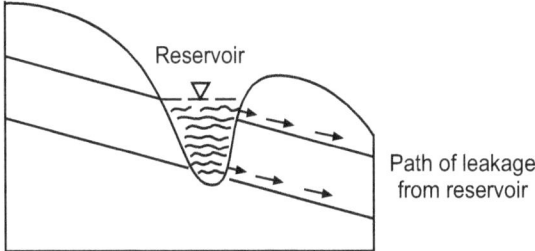

Fig. 4.28 : Slope failure due to fluctuations in water level

(d) **Earthquake :** Landslides and other types of mass movements commonly accompany earthquake. An earthquake occurred in Arunachal Pradesh in 1950 saw many landslides of great volume. In the Tidding valley a block of 6.5 km × 0.5 km slid down into the valley forming a new dam. Similarly, a number of dams were formed which brought disastrous floods in Assam. Similarly, the landslide that destroyed Ancash, Peru, averaged 320 km per hour for the 11 km it travelled.

The other earthquake induced mass movements are due to liquefaction of weak saturated sediments. The residential destruction during the Alasks earthquake of 1964 was due to lateral flowage of saturated soils. Similarly, mass movements during China earthquake were caused due to mobilization of the less deposits of the region.

Many earthquake generated ground movements result in vertical subsidence, known as *scarps*.

(e) **Other man-induced landslides :** Mass movements may initiate due to mining operations. Similarly there are other ways in which human activities create landsliding, for example, when streams are diverted and undercut, a hillside becomes over steepened and fails.

4.11 LANDSLIDE HAZARD, INVESTIGATION AND MAPPING

Landslide hazard refers to the probability of a landslide of a given size occurring within a specified period of time within particular area. The associated risk is in the form of loss of lives or damage to properties. Therefore, landslide hazard must be assessed before landslide risk can be estimated.

Slope stability analysis require the selection of specific criteria upon which the stability assessment is to be based. If large area is involved, field investigations are to be divided into several units.

Under normal circumstances, study for the stability of slopes are not carried out, unless some form of engineering structure is aimed. A detailed interdisciplinary investigation is necessary to study the stability of slopes under modifying conditions.

(1) Initial surveys are carried out by examination of aerial photographs of the area. History of the area may indicate sites of past slides. However, a geologist experienced in aerial photo interpretation can depict existence of many ancient landslides. If the site is altered by erosion, then by studying the topography, a potential slide may be recognised. Sometimes, slope maps are of immense help. Information given in Table 4.12 is useful in recognising potential.

Table 4.12 : Features indicating active and inactive landslide

Active	Inactive
• Scarps, terraces and crevices with sharp edges.	• Scarps, terraces and crevices with rounded edges.
• Crevices and depressions without secondary filling.	• Crevices and depressions filled with secondary deposits.
• Secondary mass movements on scrap faces.	• No secondary movement.
• Surface of rupture and marginal shear planes show fresh striations and slickensides.	• No new slickenslides or striations developed.
• Fresh fractured surfaces on blocks.	• Weathered fractured surfaces.
• Disarranged drainage pattern, many ponds and undrained depressions.	• Integrated drainage system.
• No soil development on exposed surface of rupture.	• Soil development on exposed surface of rupture.
• Pressure ridges in contact with slide margin.	• Marginal fissures and abandoned levees.
• Presence of fast growing vegetation.	• Presence of slow growing vegetation.
• Tilted trees with no new vertical growth.	• Tilted trees with new vertical growth above inclined trunks.

(2) Once the site is selected for construction, a detailed geological investigation is necessary. This should include description of exposed rock types supported by discussion on discontinuities. For example, orientation of bedding plans, flood geometry, fault displacement, joints etc. Bedding planes of discontinuities parallel to major slope must be studied carefully. Furthermore, in such cases, hydrology of the area must also be examined to elucidate the position of groundwater, quantity of infiltration or seepage through the discontinuities, surface run-off etc.

(3) Sometimes, climatic data are also useful and needed for the assessment of the influence for case histories and probabilistic predications.

(4) Another important factor in the investigation is the behaviour of soil and rocks, which include the information on thickness and subsurface continuation of the rock units, shearing strength of soil, swelling capacity, water bearing capacity of rocks, resistance to weathering, chemical alterations due to various geochemical interactions etc. The sub-surface information can be interpreted by means of bore holes and by geophysical methods.

(5) In case, the area is susceptiable to earthquakes and has evidenced many shocks in geological past, detailed investigation is necessary to pinpoint the "locked segments".

(6) The detailed geological history of the area with adequate information on past landslides and earthquake must be maintained. Information on probable slip planes should also be prepared. The geological information must be supported with vegetation map, and land-use map to aviod future damages. This data must be stored and manipulated to check for seismicity of different map parameters and to superimpose large sets in different ways.

(7) **Slope analysis :** In this, relationship of ground slope with rock inclination (dip) must be checked. In terms of assessment of stability, the frequency with a slope fails and the potential for failure alongwith magnitude, rate and type of movement are fundamental criterias in the analysis of slope. Based on these investigations, six stability classes are recognised (Table 4.13).

Table 4.13 : Slope stability classification : Frequency and potential criteria

Case I	Slope with active landslides. Material is continually moving and landslide forms are fresh and well defined. Movement may be seasonal or continual.
Case II	Slope frequently subject to new or renewed landslide activity. Triggering of landslides result from events with reactivation intervals of upto 5 years.
Case III	Slopes frequently subject to new or renewed landslide activity. Triggering of landslides result from events with reactivation interval more than 5 years.
Case IV	Slopes with evidence of previous landslide activity, but no movement in last 100 years.
Case V	Slopes which show no evidence of previous activity but likely to be of dormant nature. Landslide potential indicated by stress analysis or analogy with other slopes.
Case VI	Slopes which show no evidence of previous activity and is by any standard considered to be stable.

The collective information may be compiled to produce the landslide hazard zonation maps. Purpose of these maps is to locate problem areas and to help to understand why, when and where landslides are likely to occur.

4.12 PREVENTION MEASURE AGAINST LANDSLIDES

The most essential and basic requirement for landslide prevention is the reliable knowledge of geological structures. Many solutions based on the action of agent are available. Some of them are as follows:

(a) Slope reduction :

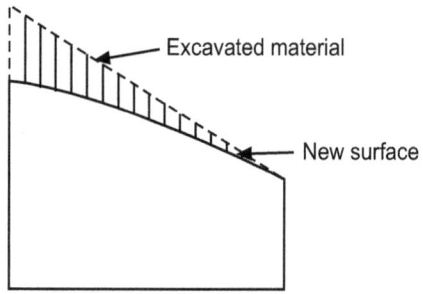

Fig. 4.29 : Slope modification

Slope is reduced by removing the top of hill. If a slope is too steep to be stable under the load it carries, the following measures can be taken :

(1) Reduce the slope angle.

(2) Reduce the overweight by removing some of the rock or soil on the slope.

(3) Place additional supporting material at the foot of slope.

(b) Removing fluid : Sometimes, a major strategy in reducing the landslide hazards is to reduce the water content or pore pressure of the rock. This is possible by covering the surface by impermeable layer and thus diverting the surface drainage.

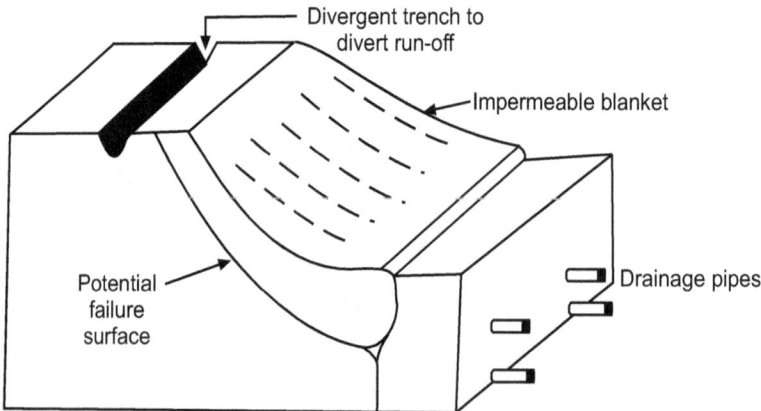

Fig. 4.30 : Removing fluid from potential failure zones

In the initial stages, any old water can be pumped out. Additional drill holes can also be constructed to increase drainage and pipelines are installed to carry out the slide area. The effect of moisture reduction is to reduce pore pressure and increase frictional resistance to sliding.

(c) The rock slope can further be stabilized with the use of rock bolts.

(d) Hardening of loose, unconsolidated soil and baking it with heat or by treating with Portland cement, may be undertaken.

(e) **Excavation and filling :** The proper unstable slope is removed and can be replaced by the same material in compacted state with better provision for drainage.

(f) **Lime column method :** The method is used to stabilize the clayey horizon upto a depth of 10 m. These are prepared and installed in-situ by combining soft clay with unslacked material. The thickness of the clay width must be checked to install the column at required depth. Sometimes, high pore water pressure in sand and silt reduces the stability of a slope due to drainage through the previously installed columns. The addition of lime column increases the shear strength promoting better stability to slope.

(g) **Erosion control :**

(1) Control the surface erosion due to run-off by use of surface drains, vegetation cover etc.

(2) Control the toe and erosional surface (in the area where the slope is under the action of sea, river etc.) by the use of concreate walls, grains etc.

(3) The slope can also be stabilized by removing the slip zones and by improving drainage.

EXERCISE

1. Discuss in detail drilling as method of sub-surface geological exploration. Give limitations also.
2. Give detailed account of preliminary geological investigations to be carried out at a project site.
3. Write notes on : (i) Elements of aerial photointerpretations, (ii) Applications of remote sensing in engineering geology, (iii) Excavation, (iv) Drilling in soft ground, (v) Core size and recovery, (vi) Angle holes, (vii) Bore hole logging, (viii) Rock quality designation, (ix) Geophysical methods, (x) Fracture surface of drill holes.)
4. Utility of remote sensing techniques in Civil Engineering.
5. Write short note on remote sensing technique.
6. Explain methods of surface and subsurface survey as a part of geological investigation at a project site.

7. Write notes on :
   (a) Fracture surfaces of drill core.
   (b) Quality and quantity of returning drill water.
   (c) Preservation of cores of Tachylytic basalt.
   (c) Loss of water.
   (d) Importance of angle holes.
   (f) G.I.S. (Geographical Information System)

8. Will you align a road along the slope of a hill where dip and slope are in the same direction ? Also add a note on preventive measuers against landslides.

9. Write a note on preventive measures against landslide.

10. Describe various causes leading to landslides and give preventive measures against landslide.

Unit 5

ROLE OF ENGINEERING GEOLOGY IN DAMS AND TUNNELLING

PART (A) : GEOLOGY OF DAM SITE

INTRODUCTION

Barier constructed across the river is called as dams. Geology of dam site on upstream side and downstream side play vital and important role in the proper functioning of hydraulic structures i.e. dam.

5.1 CLASSIFICATION OF DAMS

Dams are constructed for water storage useful for community industry, irrigation, flood control, river channelization, development of hydroelectric power etc. A multipurpose dam is the one that serves more than one purpose. Similarly, a diversion dam is one which is constructed primarily for diverting water from the river. Dams are classified into three types according to the material from which they are constructed. They are masonry, earth and rock fill dams.

The type of a dam to be constructed in given localities is decided by considering its safety, economics and the cost of annual maintenance.

(1) Masonry Dam :

(a) Gravity dam : A gravity dam is suitable if the foundation is thin and the valley is wide or broad, so that the length of the crest of the dam would be five times or more the height from the foundation. It is triangular in cross-section, the width of the base being at least two thirds of the crest height. A gravity dam relies on its own weight to resist the sliding and overturning forces imposed by the water. Often the axis of a dam is partially curved, because of which stability of the structure increases. Similarly, as the vast quantities of concrete are involved in the construction, the area of investigation must possess sufficient or adequate supplies of suitable sand or gravel or crushed aggregate.

(b) Butress dam : In this type, foundation must be very strong and capable of sustaining high pressure. If the rock is weak, the buttresses could punch into the ground and cause heave in the intervening ground. Dam sites are underlain by granite, gabbro etc. support the buttress loading quite readily. However, granites showing evidence of feldspar decomposition must be investigated carefully. In the case of bedded sedimentary rocks, sliding possibilities along bedding planes must be analysed.

(c) Arch dam : The dam is arched or curved upstream in plan; and resist the water load by arch action in addition to resisting a part of water load by its own weight. Through arch action the load is transmitted to the abutments or canyon walls.

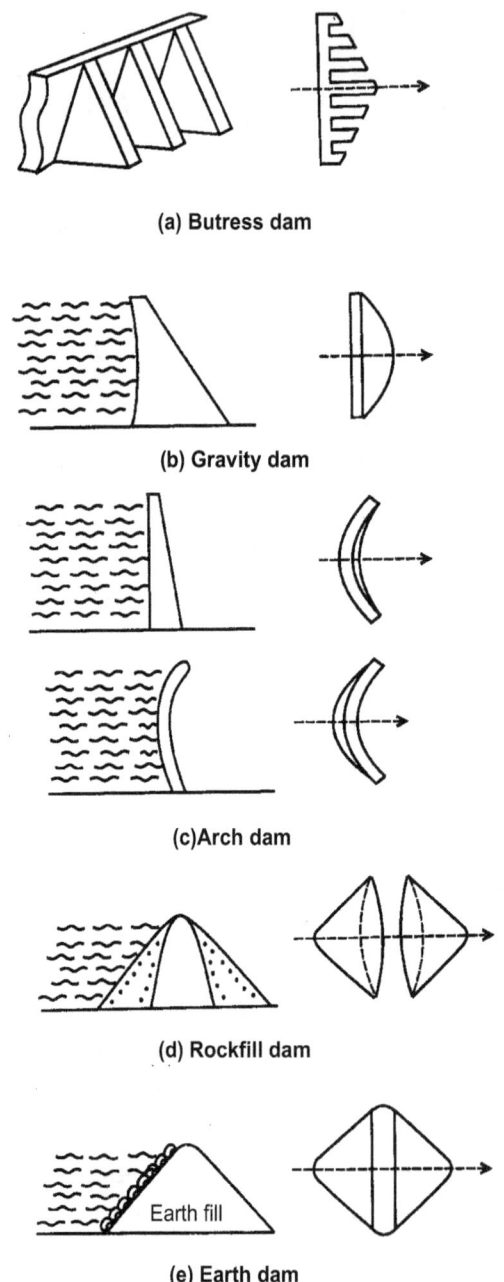

(a) Butress dam

(b) Gravity dam

(c) Arch dam

(d) Rockfill dam

(e) Earth dam

Fig. 5.1 : Types of dam

Arch dams may be of two types :

(i) **Massive Arch :** In this, a single curved vertical of steeply inclined wall covers the entire width between the abutments.

(ii) **Multiple Arch :** In this, a number of smaller inclined arch supported on butresses are constructed.

(2) Earth Dams :

This is the most common type of gravity dam constructed between wide valleys having soft floors. Earthern dams are built out of gravel, sand, silt or clay in various combinations by rolling and tempering or hydraulic puddling. These are normally least expansive and best suitable on earthern foundation and seldom on rock foundations. However, each site should be carefully investigated to determine the most suitable design considering all aspects. The value of earthern dam is often limited by the necessity of providing a more suitable spillway for the passage of floods.

Based on the method of construction, earth dams are classified as :

(a) Rolled fill earth dams

(b) Hydraulic fill dams

(c) Semi-Hydraulic fill dams.

Based on the components of the sections, earth dams can be classified as :

(a) Simple embankment

(b) Core type

(c) Diaphragm type.

(3) Rock Fill Dams :

Rock fill dams are constructed with fragmentary rock to form an embankment support necessary to withstand reservoir water pressure and other forces exerted against or within the structure. A special treatment is normally given to these dams to become water tight through the medium of an impervious material generally on the upstream face of the dam connected to a cut-off wall extending into the foundation material. Cross-sections of rock-fill dams lie between gravity dams and earthern dams.

5.2 SPILLWAYS

The spillway is a concrete structure that transmits floodwater from the valley upstream from the dam to the valley downstream without damaging either the dam or eroding the foundation. In the simplest type of spillways, the water is permitted to flow over the crest of the dam. Commonly, function of a spillway is initiated when water in the reservoir rises over the maximum water surface.

In the case of normal spillway flow, the reservoir of water is directly transmitted to the downstream valley. Often, the flow of water is passed over a weir that is normal or at an acute angle to the dam axis and is further carried by an open channel or a tunnel which is also constructed normal to the axis of the dam. The structure is known as side-channel spillways. In a shaft spillway, the excess water is transmitted vertically or obliquely below and is carried downstream in a sub-horizontal concrete pipe.

5.3 INFLUENCE OF GEOLOGICAL CONDITIONS

The stability of dams depends on bearing capacity of foundation material. Further more, selection of the type of dam depends largely on local geological conditions and also on the availability of construction material. Commonly, any massive rock foundation is suitable for any type of dam provided no other unfavorable features are noticed.

If the abutments are sound and area of hard rocks like Granite or amygdaloidal basalt and if the valley is narrow and the slopes are steep; then an arch dam is preferred. In case good quality of aggregate is not available and if the foundation material is impervious, then an earthern dam may be constructed. Similarly masonry and concrete gravity dams can only be constructed on rock foundations.

(1) Dams on bedded rocks : A large number of dams are built on bedded, stratified or foliated rocks. The trace of bedding or foliation may be parallel or across the length of the dam. The beds may be inclined or folded. The sequence may consist permeable and impermeable beds. Thus, each site requires careful examination. Commonly, it is safer to align the dam parallel to the strike foliation of the bed (Fig. 5.2), if the dam is constructed oblique to strike or foliation planes, it may cause problems of seepage or differential settlement and also it may bring in rocks of different physical characters or bearing capacity into the foundation (Fig. 5.2).

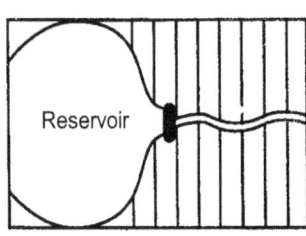
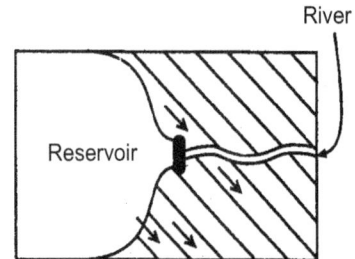

(a) Discontinuities parallel to dam axis (b) Discontinuities oblique to dam axis

Fig. 5.2 : Influence of discontinuities on reservoir and dam

(a) In complex geological areas, geomorphic expressions are invariably controlled by the geological structures. Therefore, careful evaluation of erosional valleys is often a critical step in site investigations. From Fig. 5.3 it is seen that a dam built in this valley will be water-tight up to the elevation of impervious layers, above that leakage will take place through the permeable bed, round the abutment of the dam.

On the other hand in Fig. 5.2 (b), permeable bed is seen in the stream bed and it is folded into an anticlinal bend which is enevitably heavily fractured. Here a costly foundation treatment will be required to make the site water-tight. Similarly at upper levels also, a previous bed is seen due to which the site may again be considered as a problematic. However, stability of the dam site in this case will depend on the thickness of the permeable beds, on their attitude, intensity of their folding etc.

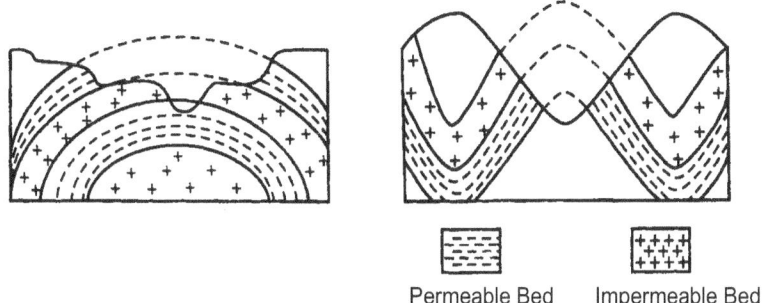

Fig. 5.3 : Erosion valleys

(b) It is advisable that the axis of a dam should be parallel to the strike of the bedding and it should be located in a manner that the impermeable beds form aprons on the edges of the dam. The most favourable condition for the dam to be water-tight is a suite of rocks dipping steeply upstream (Fig. 5.4). In this, the impermeable layer is forming an apron on the upstream side. Similarly, when beds dip steeply downstream and are not tectonically disturbed, they provide a comparatively stable dam site [Fig. 5.4 (b)]. On the other hand, the site may not be as stable if beds dip gently downstream [Fig. 5.4 (c)] provided the impermeable layer is seen on the inner side of the dam.

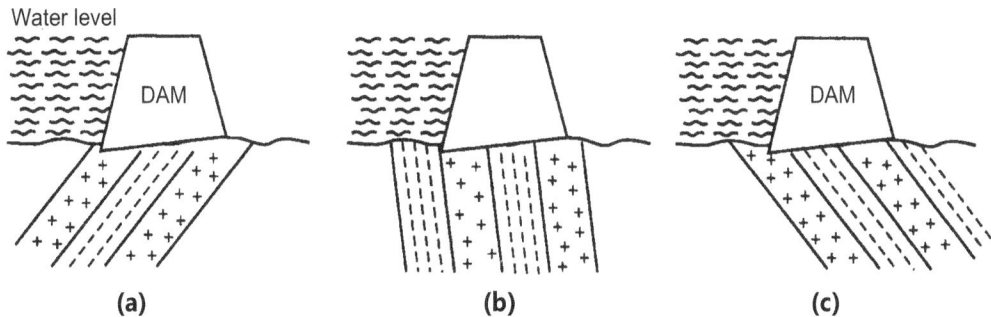

(a) Dam located on beds, dipping in upstream, direction
(b) Dam on beds, dipping steeply in downstream direction
(c) Dam on beds dipping gently in downstream direction.

Fig. 5.4 : Dam axis parallel to strike of beds

(c) In case folded structures are recorded in the area of investigation, it is always safer to locate a dam in the anticlinal limb dipping upstream [Fig. 5.5 (a)] so as to attain the ideal structure [Fig. 5.4 (a)]. If a dam is to be constructed on the limb of a syncline with a downstream dip, a heavy loss of water by percolation through the permeable bed exposed below the dam is most likely to be seen [Fig. 5.5 (b)]. However, the dam may be constructed further downstream so as to expose the permeable bed on the inner side. As a result, the problem of percolation would be solved and a structure similar to [Fig. 5.4 (a)] would be obtained.

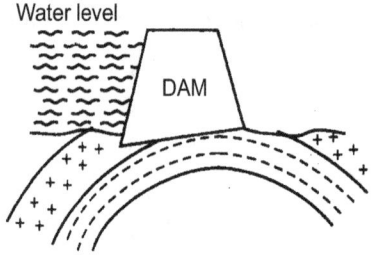
(a) Dam located on upstream dipping limb of an anticline

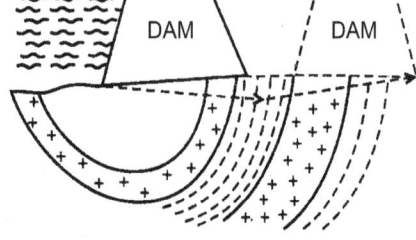
(b) Dam site is to be shifted towards downstream so that the case is similar to 5.4 (a)

Fig. 5.5 : Dams located on folded structure

(d) The fault zones exhibit presence of intensely crushed, disintegrated or decomposed, fractured rock of very low apparent bearing strength and may locally provide easy passage to running water (Fig 5.6). It is very dangerous to construct a dam on the fault plane or fault zone. Further beds on opposite sides of a fault plane are likely to displace during an earthquake and such movement, besides reopening the fissures, involve the repture of the dam. Dams may be constructed on the upstream side of a fault which crosses a valley parallel to the length of the proposed dam.

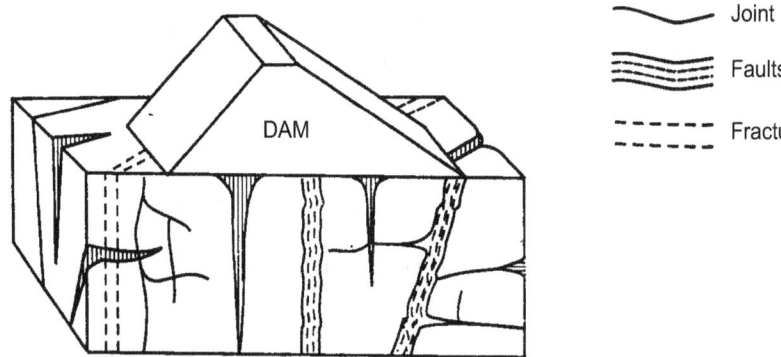

Fig. 5.6 : Schematic diagram showing relation between dam and geological structures

(e) **Carbonate Rocks :** Carbonate Rocks include crystalline limestone, marble, pure limestone, dolomite limestone, marl etc.

Carbonates may provide a good foundation bed provided their bearing capacity is impaired by hidden sub-surface cavities. Commonly, these are soluble rocks and may show the presence of solutional structures, known as *karst*. It is necessary in engineering geological investigations to understand the behaviour of carbonate rocks.

Though solution of limestone is a relatively rapid process in a geological sense, it is very slow with respect to the durability or life of the engineering structure. However, in order to prevent leakage, in most cases grout curtains are constructed before the fill of the reservoir.

In pure limestone, if fractures are open and are further widened into galleries and caverns, (Fig. 5.7). Very careful measures should be taken prior to the construction of the dam (Fig. 5.7).

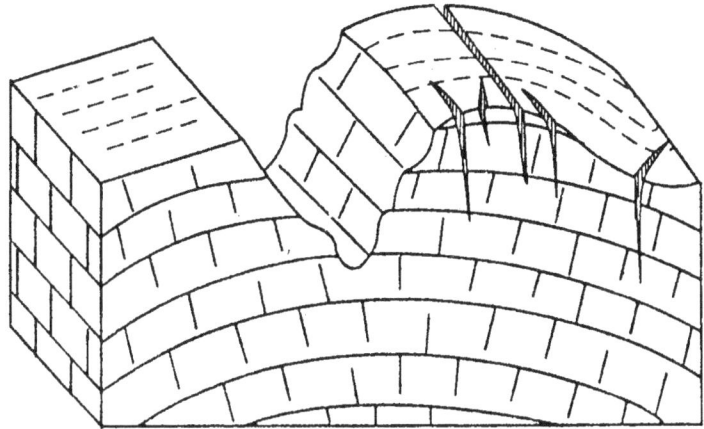

Fig. 5.7 : Schematic diagram showing fracture enhanced permeability in limestones

The karst terrains often develop subsurface features like caves, caverns, underground channels etc. but surface indications of these features may not be observed. In such cases, detailed subsurface investigations should be aimed.

(f) Argillaceous Rocks : The study of argillaceous rocks, especially shales, is often a very decisive step in deciding the stability of the structure. The argillaceous rocks exist in nature in various degrees of compaction which is controlled by composition, size and properties of clays, thickness of over burden, time of loading, presence of ingredients of other sizes etc.

In general, from engineering point of view, shales may be classified into two groups. Swelling and non-swelling. In the first group, the bearing capacity of shales is influenced by their water content. Swelling of shales create problems in the form of terminal breakdown and also in the form of heave on structural foundation. Shales of the second group are of greater strength and bearing capacity. Normally, these do not show plastic behaviour under the load that may be imposed from a dam. But the rock may develop new fissures due to release of residual stresses by deep excavation for a dam foundation.

The important factor in the discussion of shale is their shear strength, which is minimum or appreciably smaller along bedding or schistosity (in case of indurated argillites) than across the beds. Shales are considered as almost impermeable provided they are not associated with permeable beds like sandstones.

5.4 IGNEOUS AND NON-FOLIATED METAMORPHIC ROCKS

Dam constructed on coarse grained, equigranular igneous rocks, non-foliated metamorphic rocks like quartzite are always stable; provided these do not show presence of unfavourable discontinuities. In case of massive rocks like granites, presence of sheet jointing may be troublesome.

PART (B) : GEOLOGY OF RESERVOIR SITES

5.5 GEOLOGY OF RESERVOIR SITES

(1) The major geological criteria in selecting the reservoir site is that the reservoir site should be water-tight and in a deep basin shaped valley. For evaluating susceptibility to leakage, not only should the lithology of the rocks be examined but also their hydrological and chemical properties should be checked.

(2) Sedimentary rocks show presence of fractures, faults and also folds, and thus they are leaky. However, commonly discontinuities are tighten up at depth so that leakage through the reservoir may not be problematic. Often erosional valleys are formed due to removal of anticlinal closure, while the adjacent ridges generally show synclinal folds. (Fig. 5.8). In this, previous beds may occur in the floor or in the bank of the reservoir.

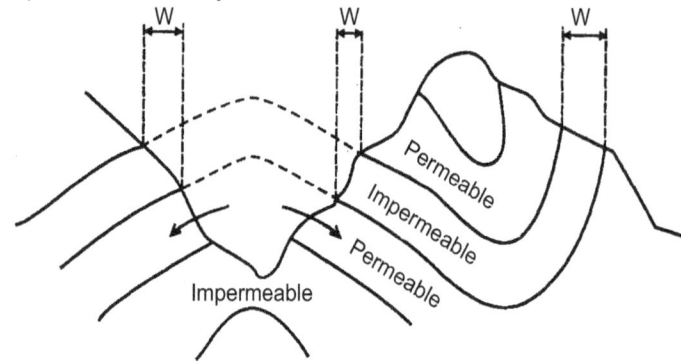

Fig. 5.8 : Erosional valley and corresponding ridge

(3) In case, the reservoir site shows presence of dip and escarpment slope, careful investigations must be carried out in the adjoining valley of the escarpment slope. Often an obvious source of leakage is through a previous bed dipping away from the reservoir and into the adjacent valley (Fig. 5.9). The neighbouring valley may be saturated with water.

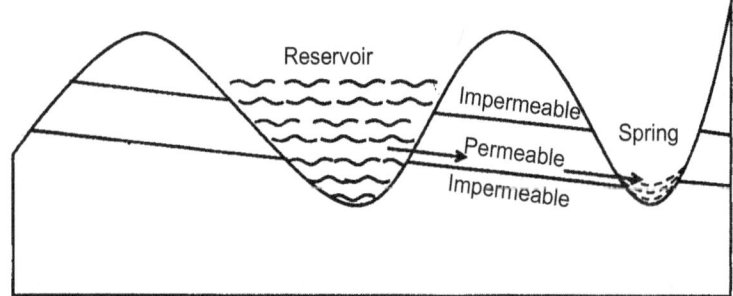

Fig. 5.9 : Occurrence of a contact spring in the neighbouring valley of reservoir

(4) If the reservoir rock is granite, there must be an investigation on decomposition of feldspar. Similarly, if quartz, pegmatitic veins are seen in granite, the quartz, pegmatite may be leaky along fractures and joints.

(5) Soft rocks, due to their high solubility, easily undergo disintegration or decomposition under prolong weathering conditions. If the weathered material is open textured, it may yield permeable soil.

(6) Limestones may be unsuitable because of possible presence of solution channels and cavern; as easy passage of water is most likely along solution channels and caverns may hold substantial quantities of water. Furthermore, quality of reservoir water is likely to change if the reservoir water is in contact with limestone.

(7) Fault zones with pervious breccia and open joints may serve as path for leakage.

(8) A river valley may always be suspected for concealing a fault. If the rock type from one side of the valley is different from the other side; it is possibly due to the presence of fault at the centre of the valley [Fig. 5.10 (a)]. Similarly, changes in the dip of beds from one side of the valley to the other side may also indicate faulting [Fig. 5.10 (b)]. Such faults may be delineated by taking oblique drill holes. On the other hand, seepage losses through joints and fissure may decrease with time as the inflow of silt and clay reduce the permeability.

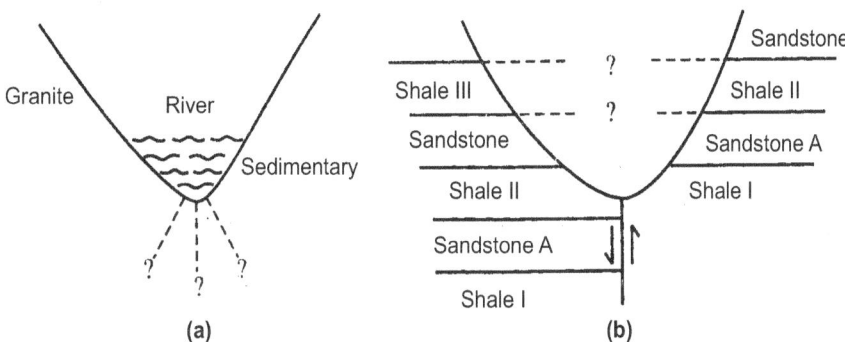

Fig. 5.10 : Fault evidence at reservoir site

(9) Hydrogeological investigations must be carried out and possible impacts of reservoir on groundwater regime must be evaluated. After impounding, the water table would be raised and could provide a leakage path along more permeable material downstream of the dam. Thus, within the reservoir area, such changes which produce change in pore water pressure and bank storage shifts may become sites for mass movements, for example, Vaiont Dam, Italy. In arid regions, large fluctuations in the water table can accelerate direct evaporation of soil water and lead to an increase in soils alinity. This in turn affects water quality and disqualifies its use for irrigation and other purposes.

(10) Slope stability analysis should be carried out in the reservoir and dam area.

(11) An adequate or sufficient amount of construction material must be available near the dam-site.

5.6 HYDROGEOLOGY AND DAMS

(1) If another valley in the neighbourhood of the reservoir area is seen, it could drain off water from the reservoir if there is any permeable rock horizon in between functioning as a hydraulic connection or if the groundwater table is below the intended reservoir level.

(2) It is also necessary to find out whether the groundwater table beneath the slopes adjacent to the dam site rises steeply or proceeds into the abutments on the level of the river.

(3) The most important aspect of hydro-geology is to find out whether a change exists between more and less permeable zones across the area of the dam.

(a) A zone of minor permeability may form a compact barrier due to a thickness of many tons of metres.

(b) A sequence of alternate bedding layers of different permeabilities exists, it becomes problematic whether results of permeability tests reflect the overall permeability.

(4) The formation of water carrying openings along joints and other types of discontinuities is a critical factor.

(5) In case of a relatively deep groundwater table beneath the surrounding slope, the impounded water effects a counter pressure and hinders the natural groundwater from maintaining its original direction and flow into the valley. The natural groundwater is forced to deviate. Normally, it will flow downstream and may appear in springs at the foot of the slope immediately below the dam. Such springs might indicate the beginning of the regressive erosion.

5.7 GROUTING

Grouting is a procedure to improve the strength properties of foundation material to diminish its permeability.

On account of the essentially different nature of the voids in soils from those in rocks, various techniques are adapted to meet specific requirements. Porosity in soil varies from 20% to 45% which differs from soil to soil. However, this is completely different in rocks, where porosity is secondary and is attributed to discontinuities. The voids, if present are caused by a partial or total openings of the various types of bedding plane. They differ extremely in size, shape and extension, ranging between widely extended fissures.

The basic aim of soil grouting is to cement the connected pores. In this unit, grouting is understood as chemical grouting.

In rock grouting, it is impossible to fill all the voids because the discontinuity network is very complex. Thus, the special difficulty of rock grouting is not only to fill the voids but to detect them and gain access. Rock grouting is pre-dominantly carried out (1) to improve the strength properties (consolidation grouting) and (2) to decrease the permeability of the rock (curtain grouting).

In the previous case, grouting normally treats widely extended three dimensional sections of the rocks (examples : foundations below large buildings or similar structures, stabilization of roof and walls around tunnels etc.). For normal consolidation grouting, a square pattern is chosen. The spacing ranges between 1 and 3 metres and depth varies between 5 and 15 metres. The short holes drilled for grouting are sealed near the top and then grouted in one section. But in general, the depth and inclination of the holes varies from project to project and depends upon the geological setting, type of structure and purpose of the grouting measure.

In the second method, curtain grouting tries to tighten the rock along theoretically assumed planes. In this, the bore holes are normally placed along a line forming the axis of the curtain. The distance between adjacent holes is controlled by local geological conditions. Curtain grouting may be carried out for a measurable depth (upto 100 m).

In general, it can be said that sufficient data from the following sub-areas are required for analysing a completed grouting programme.

5.8 EFFECTS OF DAM

Eventhough dams can produce many benefits and are inevitably essential to the society, there are a number of impacts that may result from water impoundments (Fig. 5.11).

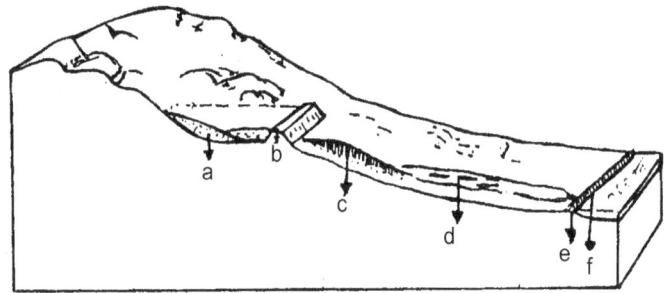

Fig. 5.11 : Environmental impact of dams

(1) Sedimentation in Reservoir : The first effect of a dam is change in the fluvial environment in the upstream into a lacustrine or a deltaic environment. Furthermore, the rate of upstream sedimentation during floods is always abnormal. As a result, the life span of reservoirs is greatly reduced.

(2) Down Erosion : The hydrologic and physiographic equilibrium of the fluvial system is greatly modified due to the character of water released from the dam. It is devoid of sediment load. As a result, the stream may again initiate the process of vertical downcutting (Fig. 5.11). In addition, chemistry of water and its temperature are also substantially changed.

(3) Catchment characteristics : Hydrologic processes like run-off formation, infiltration, evapotranspiration etc. depend on catchment characteristics e.g. soil type, soil cover, vegetation, drainage density, land use, hill slop angle etc. These parameters are conventionally estimated from maps, air photography or satellite imagery etc.

The identification of the potential location of dams in river valleys can be supported by remote sensing data as well as the detection of potential material for dam construction. Thermal infrared images may be useful in the detection of risk points in earth or rock fill darns or even in concrete dams due to temperature differences between water and the construction materials.

(4) Induced Seismicity : It is now recognised that earthquakes can occur in intraplate areas and the so called 'stable' blocks are not free from seismic activity. Unesco in 1976, has recommended the consideration of induced seismicity for 'large reservoirs and dams' defined as having either impounded water volumes greater than 10^9 m^3 and/or a depth of water of 100 m or more. However, it must be mentioned that only 0.7% dams have shown indications of induced seismicity. This, thus, can not be considered as a universally accepted concept. One must always be careful while assigning this term to any intraplate earthquake. Following are the observations related to induced seismicity.

(a) Most of the earthquakes have focal depth less than 15 km. These are, thus, shallow earthquakes.

(b) The amount of energy released is normally episodic, and prior to construction of major engineering structure, the area was aseismic or the one of low seismicity.

(c) Excepting an example from western Australia, there is no case of development of new fault/fractures. Most of the earthquakes have occured along older planes of weakness.

(d) Induced seismicity is not restricted to rocks of a particular geological age. It is related to rock of vide ages from pre Cambrian to Cenozoic.

(e) Induced seismicity is not related to any particular geological condition but these are the sites of high crustal stress, including known tectonic force fields, high topographic relief, steep gradients of gravitational anomaly, hot springs, water pathways to deeper faults, rocks susceptide to strength deterioration or volume change, and evidence of neotectonic features at surface.

The above observations stress the importance of study of older weak planes in locating current seismicity. Consideration of episodes older than Quaternary is therefore, necessary for general understanding of intraplate conditions. Following is the procedure that may be followed in paleoseismic studies.

(1) Literature study on paleotectonics and structural geology.

(2) Study of satellite imageries and aerial photos.

(3) Acquisition of geophysical data.

(4) Acquisition of focal slip solutions of earthquake giving origin.

(5) Field geological studies to establish ground truth for remote sensing to locate and describe faulting near the historic site.

PART (C) : TUNNELLING

A tunnel is an underground route or passage excavated through rocks, soil or soft ground without disturbing the overburden. Tunnels are constructed for two major purposes.

(1) Traffic tunnels used for railways, highways, subways, transportation etc.
(2) Conveyance tunnels used for hydro-electric projects, irrigation, sewer conveyance etc.

5.9 ARCHING ACTION IN TUNNELS

The rocks at great depth are under great lithostatic pressure conditions. The greater the depth, the greater is the pressure. It is believed that the rocks are always subjected to differential stress. In other words, the rock mass store the stress, called as **residual stress**. Accumulated stress is relieved if the exerted lithostatic pressure is decreased. As a result, cracks are developed normal to the direction of pressure relief.

Though, the rock mass is not under lithostatic condition, openings created due to construction activities (tunnelling) allow the rock to flow. That is to say excavation for tunnelling disturbs the natural equilibrium. The equilibrium may be restored by developing self balance system of shearing stress in the form of arching around the tunnel. The arching action involves radial stresses acting normal to the wall of the tunnel and the circumference stress is parallel to the circumference. Hence, the examination of the rock in the vicinity of the tunnel for evaluating its capability for forming arches during excavation work, constitutes an important factor of the geological investigation of the site. The tunnel remains stable till the boundary stress balances the compressive strength of the rock.

5.10 RELATED TERMS

(a) A shaft is an opening in the ground or in the hill, driven vertically or at an angle and is constructed for various purposes.
(b) An adit is either horizontal or gently inclined excavation driven to connect two major tunnels or shafts.
(c) Drives are tunnels that are used in underground work in mines.

5.11 GEOLOGICAL CONSIDERATIONS IN TUNNELLING

The geological conditions can be evaluated in three phases:
(a) Preliminary geological investigations.
(b) Detailed quantitative analysis and risk evaluation.
(c) Exploration to confirm geological conditions.
Detailed of these individual factors are dealt with in appropriate sections.
The important geological factors considered in tunnelling projects are as follows:
(1) Composition, attitude and thickness of geologic formations,
(2) Hydrogeological regimes,
(3) Geomorphic expressions,
(4) The temperature in very deep tunnels and the need for ventilation.

5.11.1 Geological Conditions

The influence of geological conditions varies depending on the composition, attitude and thickness of available rock material. Tunnelling conditions through an igneous, sedimentary and metamorphic rocks are altogether different. In igneous rocks, weak planes are available in the form of joints, dykes or fractures etc. In sedimentary rocks, stratification is most important. Furthermore, sedimentary rocks due to their layered appearance, are prone to deformation, and therefore structural features such as folding, faulting and jointing are easily observed in them. Metamorphic rocks exhibit structures like schistose, gneissose, granulose etc. This study is further supported by hydrological investigations, as water bearing capacity of rocks varies according to their composition and presence of weak planes. It is observed that massive igneous rocks generally propose favorable tunnelling conditions.

(a) Tunnelling Through Stratified Rocks :

In some, stratification i.e. layered appearance of the rocks is the most common structure. Thus, the relation of strike and dip of rock i.e. attitude of rock, with the axis of the tunnel must be discussed. In stratified rocks, two conditions are established to be favourable, they are :

(1) Horizontal or gently dipping beds with their strike parallel to the axis of the tunnel [Fig. 5.13 (a) and (b)].

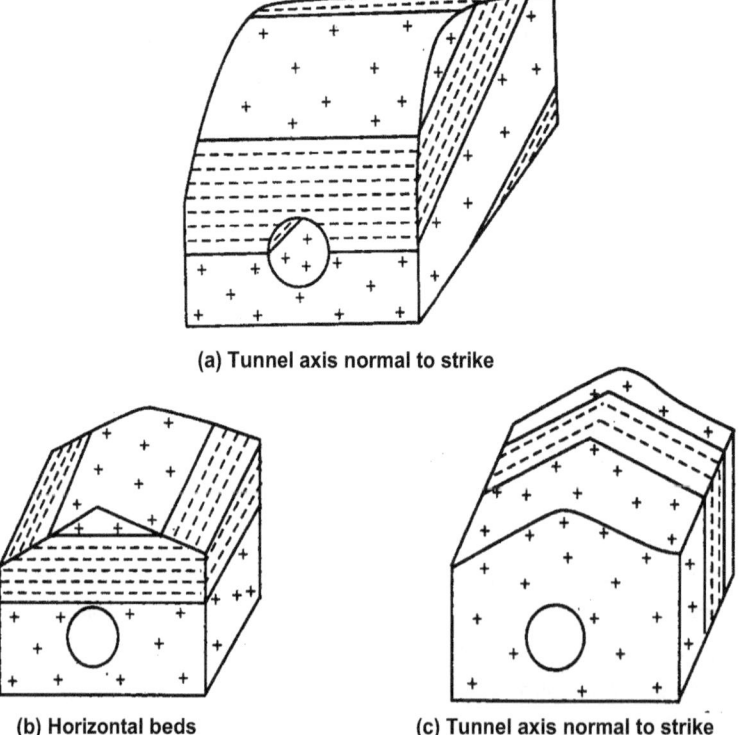

(a) Tunnel axis normal to strike

(b) Horizontal beds   (c) Tunnel axis normal to strike

Fig. 5.12 : Relation between tunnel axis and attitude of beds

(2) Gently dipping or vertical beds with their strike perpendicular to the axis of the tunnel [Fig. 5.12 (a) and (c)].

The above Fig. shows a uniform vertical pressure on the tunnel. However, in the first and third case, the problem of seepage would arise. If the beds are vertical and beds are thick enough, then these rocks would act as a girdle to provide further stability to the tunnel.

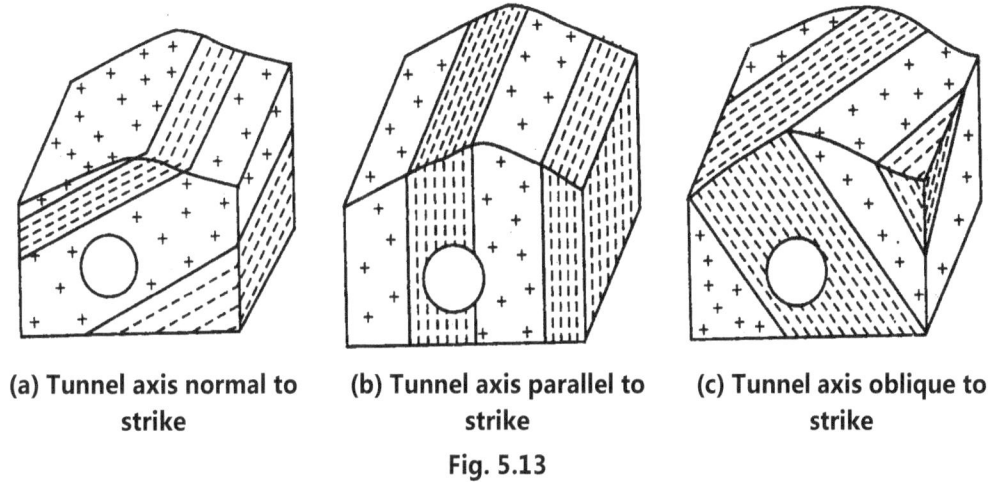

(a) Tunnel axis normal to strike

(b) Tunnel axis parallel to strike

(c) Tunnel axis oblique to strike

Fig. 5.13

In the cases (a) and (b) of Fig. 5.13, beds are parallel to tunnel axis and in Fig. 5.13 (c) the strata is oblique.

The Fig. above shows that as the pressure exerted on tunnel being uneven or asymmetrical, it would create major problems. The danger of the collapsing roof collapse is most likely due to the disturbance in the equilibrium conditions.

Furthermore, if the succession consists of alternate hard and soft or competent and incompetent rocks and is exposed in the area of interest, many more problems like seepage of water, swelling of material, roof collapse etc. due to softer and permeable strata would arise, depending on conditions prevailed.

(b) Anticlines and Synclines :

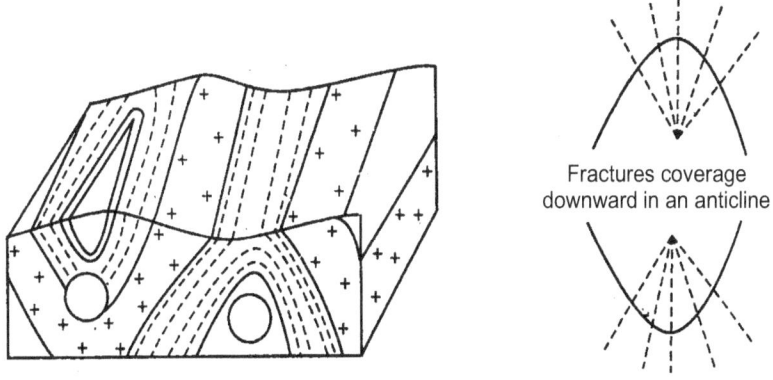

(a) Tunnel axis parallel

(b) Fracture diverge downward in a syncline

Fractures coverage downward in an anticline

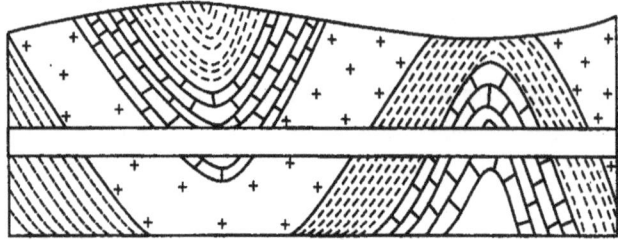

(c) Tunnel route located normal to fold axis

Fig. 5.14 : Schematic diagrams showing relation of tunnel axis and fold axis

Tunnelling through folded rocks need very careful observations since strain concentration is maximum in the zone of maximum curvature. If a tunnel is constructed through the core of an anticline (a), the undulatory strata would provide natural arch action, thus pressure is less. But by considering the pattern of fracturing in the core and surface of anticline, it is advisable to locate the tunnel at a depth where fracturing is minimum. In an anticline, upper strata are more bent and more fissured due to tensional forces than the lower strata. Further more, points always converge downward indicating less change, or fall [Fig. 5.14 (b)]. If the strata is water bearing, the anticlinal tunnel will have water flow away from it. But if tunnel is constructed perpendicular to the axial surface of folds, then it would create many problems by wedgeing and fracturing of strata [Fig. 5.14 (c)]. However, the only asset in this is lateral pressure on the tunnel is greater towards entrances than at the middle.

In the case of syncline, pressure exerted on tunnel will be tremendous. Joint patterns typical of synclines always converge upwards. Thus [Fig. 5.14 (b)] block-gliding may be possible. Furthermore, if the strata is water bearing, due to typical downward closure, water may rush inside the tunnel and in certain cases the tunnel will be water bearing. If a tunnel is constructed across asyncline, lateral pressure will be greater at the centre than at the entrances [Fig. 5.14 (c)].

(c) Influence of Joints :

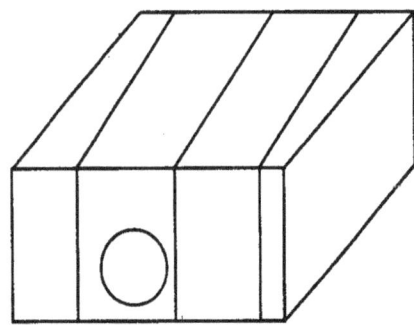 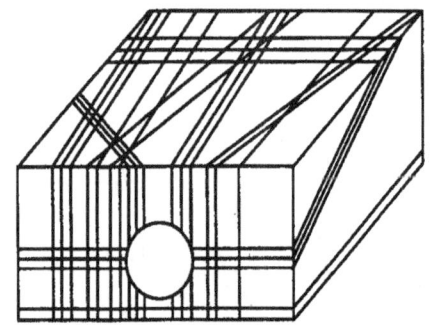

(a) Joints are extremely widely spaced and density is too low

(b) Joints are close spaced and density is high

Fig. 5.15 : Influence of joint spacing and joint density on the stability of a tunnel

Joints parallel to the tunnel axis are very dangerous, if they are steeper than 45°. This condition favour roofs-collapse or fall out. If the joints are evenly spaced with their width more than that of the tunnel, the block would act as a girdle [Fig. 5.15 (a)]. On the contrary, if the joints are closely spaced and irregular in orientation, the tunnel would experience fallout and overbreak, [Fig. 5.15 (b)]. Furthermore, the joints favour easy movement of water. Thus, the information necessary to study the joints can be broadly divided into two categories : (1) the orientation of joints with respect to major structures; (2) their spacing and continuity.

Heavily jointed rock may cause serious problem.

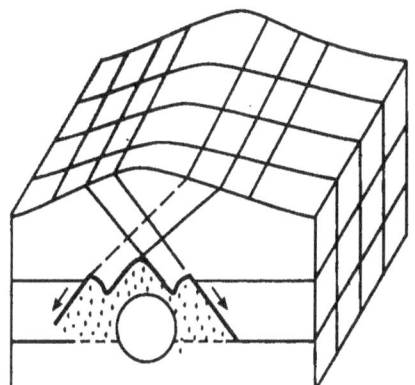 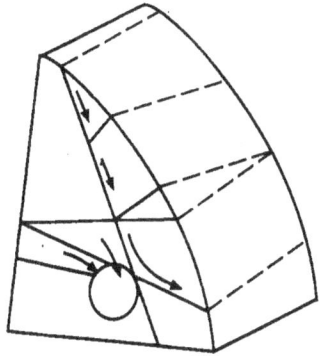

Fig. 5.16 : Relation between attitude and density of joints with the stability of a tunnel

If the pressure exerted is high and/or stress distribution is uneven, the joint opening would propagate and become unstable. In the case of vertical joints, or joint normal to valley site a seepage path from the tunnel to the ground surface may be formed when the cover is thin. A similar condition can be visualised in [Fig 5.16 (a)] where horizontal joints may provide a seepage path by intersection with other joints connecting to the surface. If an inclined joint parallel to ground slope intersects another inclined joint dipping in opposite direction towards the tunnel, a landslide in the adjoining area may occur [Fig. 5.16 (a) and (b)].

When the joints are filled with secondary material which are prone to erosion, the action of seepage water will erode the material, thus causing a significant decrease in the strength and increase in permeability index, leading to a major fall.

(d) Fault and Shear Zones :

It is always essential to elucidate relation between fault and tunnel axis.

Space between the fault walls may be filled up with gouge material (very fine material) which when mixed with water, possess a tendency to swell. Many a times, the fault walls may be filled up with loose material which may flow into the tunnel. If we consider Fig. 5.17 (a), tunnel is constructed in the hanging wall. Effects of fault are concentrated towards only one side of the tunnel. In the Fig. 5.17 (b) and (c), tunnel is constructed across the fault plane, thus weaker zone is restricted to a certain region which can be minimised by special treatment. However, in the Fig. 5.17 (b) faulting causes unequal stress distribution on the tunnel. In the Fig. 5.17 (d) tunnel is essentially constructed through granite and fault is not recorded in the tunnel.

Another important aspect in case of a fault is whether it is active or passive. Thus, a detailed geological history must be carried out with the help of reported literature or field observations etc. The rail-road tunnel near wright station, Santa Cruz Mountains, California was disturbed by movement along San Anereas fault in 1906. In this tunnel, a new fracture was formed at an angle of 80° with the axis of the tunnel. In a certain zone, the tunnel was displaced by 1.6 metres. Thus, in such regions, it is always safe to shift the alignment of a tunnel.

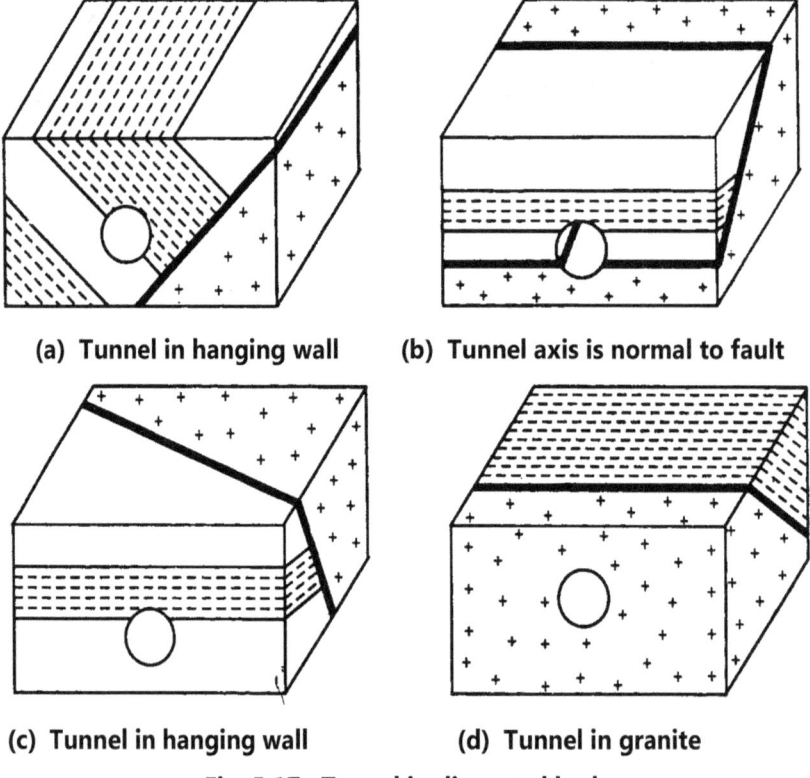

(a) Tunnel in hanging wall   (b) Tunnel axis is normal to fault

(c) Tunnel in hanging wall   (d) Tunnel in granite

Fig. 5.17 : Tunnel in disrupted beds

Precautionary measures must be taken, if the area is considered as seismically 'locked segment'. In such areas, stresses are accumulated under favourable conditions in rock masses. These rocks thus store strain energy which can be released by means of artificial opening in the form of tunnelling. Therefore, provision must be made in the tunnel to accommodate the movement that may take place.

The effects of faulting are prominently influenced by its thickness. In the case of a shear zone, where rocks are completely crushed, the region is very hazardous. Furthermore, Rock falls may initiate along these weak planes particularly when two zones intersect each other. A similar condition was observed in *Jaldhalea* hydel project, Darjeeling. In the *Malprabha* tunnel, a fault zone of 12 metres in length was located. The quantity of water pumped out from this zone and weathered rock was approximately 75,000 gallons per day.

(e) Metamorphic rocks : Metamorphism brings a change in the strength of the rock. The massive quartzite, schist and gneiss are considered as a favourable rocks for tunnelling due to their better strength. In marble, care must be taken to check the cavities in the rocks which may cause groundwater leakage and seepage.

Metamorphic rocks are the altered products of sedimentaty and igneous rocks. The original texture and primary bedding may be obliterated due to metamorphism. In certain cases, the rocks develop easy planes or separations called foliation along which rock is weak, thus providing easy passage for water. Therefore, similar to stratified sedimentary rocks, the tunnel should be aligned perpendicular to foliation plane.

(f) Tunnelling through igneous rocks : The strength of any igneous rock is largely influenced by cooling rate and composition of material. However, it is observed that the igneous rocks are generally homogeneous in composition, granular in texture, massive in structure and therefore, considered as the most favourable rocks for tunnelling, especially basalts and granites.

5.11.2 Influence of Topography

In certain cases, topography along with rock stratification plays an important role in the selection of tunnel site. It is suggested that tunnels should be located as close as possible to the steeper rock slope to reduce the cost of the line.

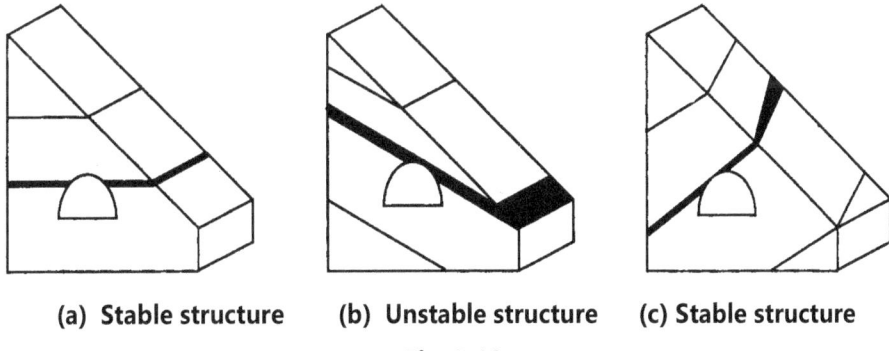

(a) Stable structure   (b) Unstable structure   (c) Stable structure

Fig. 5.18

Fig. 5.18 (a) and (c) are considered as a stable tunnels, whereas Fig. 5.18 (b) detailed geologic investigations should be aimed, since rock slope is gentle than hill slope. Furthermore, the factor of water pressure must be taken into consideration. In case (a) and (c) hill slope is steeper than rock slope, and they dip in opposite direction, the water would essentially flow along the steeper hills. Therefore, the problem of leakage would be less compared to that in Fig. 5.18 (b).

5.11.3 Water in Tunnels

Construction of a tunnel may locally change the flow of water due to change in local stress regime. Tunnel is considered as a underground drain for water regime. The problems of water seepage are severe if the strata is fissured or show folds or exhibit many weak planes like fault and shear zone as e.g. In Malaprabha tunnel, during tunnelling there was a severe seepage through the fault zones and shear. It was

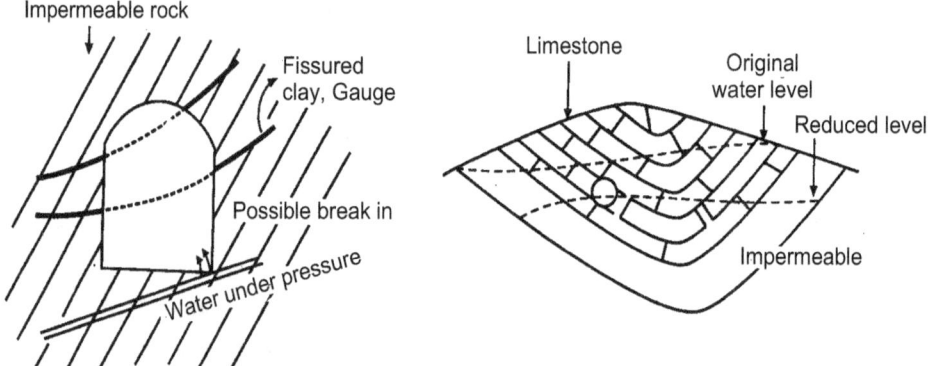

(a) Presence of a fracture zone may alter water channel in an otherwise impermeable rock

(b) Changes in water regime as caused by a tunnel

Fig. 5.19 : Water in tunnel

estimated that the water pumped out was nearly 75,000 gallons/day and during monsoon season it was nearly 2,00,000 gallons/day. The problem was partially solved by grouting the jointed rock. Similar was the case of Kundan tunnel, Tamil Nadu. Therefore, when tunnel strikes a permeable zone, the problems of seepage are always severe. This is essentially due to primary porosity and permeability, and secondary, permeability (fault, joints etc.) However, due to continuous pumping the groundwater level in the local area may be considerably reduced. To avoid this, it is suggested that a tunnel constructed above the water table is safer. If such location is not appropriate for other geologic reason, the problem of seepage can be reduced by grouting method i.e. by sealing the opening.

5.12 TUNNELLING IN UNCONSOLIDATED SEDIMENTS

Tunnelling in unconsolidated or softer rocks is easier than in competent, harder rock due to easy response and fast progress. However, problems due to their softness would be tremendous. Therefore, for these tunnels a permanent lining is necessary due to (a) softness of material, (b) low cohesion and internal friction, (c) fluctuating ground water condition, and (d) differential behaviour of clayey material.

Certain clay minerals e.g. Montomorillonite when in moist state swell 10 times (approximately) to its original volume, and cause tremendous pressure on tunnel lining support. The hearing and tensile strength of unconsolidated or soft material is essentially less than hard and compact rocks. Therefore, the stand-up time (Time during which unsupported rock remains in equilibrium) of soft material is less than compact rocks. These conditions are summarised in Table 5.1.

Table 5.1 : Classification of soft ground tunnelling condition

Classification	Behaviour	Typical material
(1) Swelling	(a) Volume expansion due to absorbing water. (b) Heave in tunnel.	(a) Montmorillonite ring soil/weak rock. (b) Clay with plasticity index more than 30.
(2) Flowing	(a) Soil and water can flow into a tunnel like a viscous fluid. (b) Possess ability to flow great distances and can fill tunnel completely in rare cases.	(a) Mud flow, earth flow material, clay content in such material may become cohesive and plastic. (b) High sensitive clay can exhibit flow properties when distributed.
(3) Squeezing	(a) Plastic deformation into tunnel without visible fracturing. (b) Ductile plastic behaviour due to exerted stress without increase in water content.	(a) Ground of low frictional properties. (b) Squeezing rate is controlled by the magnitude of exerted stress.
(4) Ravelling	(a) Flaking around tunnel especially parallel to arch action. (b) Fast ravelling can occur below water table within a few minutes.	(a) Residual soil. (b) Fissured clay.

EXERCISE

1. What are the possibilities of leakage below a dam ? Suggest some preventive measure.

2. Describe what geological studies are required for the selection of a dam-site.

3. Write notes on dams on folded and faulted rocks.

4. Write notes on :

    (i) Dams on folded rocks

    (ii) Limestones,

(iii) Surface survey,

(iv) Geological features leading to leakage below a dam,

(v) Treatment given to jointed rocks at dam-site,

(vi) Ground water studies and a dam-site,

(vii) Geology of reservoir sites,

(viii) Grouting effects of dam on ecosystem.

5. Write an account on tunnelling conditions in trap region.

6. Write notes on : Tunnel (i) Passing through a syncline, (ii) Across a fault, (iii) Along strike direction of thin bedded dipping sedimentary rocks, (iv) teep dipping beds, through limestone area, (v) Faults and shear zones, (vi) Influence of joints, (vii) Influence to topography, (viii) Water in tunnel, (ix) Tunnelling in soft ground.

7. Write short notes on : Feasibility of tunneling in tectonic areas.

8. What is the relationship between type of dam and local geology.

9. Write in detail the treatment to be given to a fracture crossing dam alignment.

10. Write short note on dams on lime stones and marbles.

11. Will you align a tunnel in E ↔ W direction of dopping sedimentary beds exhibiting true dip towards north ? Give reasons.

12. Explain geological features leading to leakage below a dam.

13. Explain in detail studies to be carried out in reservoir area of a dam.

14. List various types of dams.

15. What are the difficulties to be faced while taking a tunnel along and across the strike direction of beds.

16. Explain in brief importance of pilot cut along dam alignment.

17. What is the role of groundwater and influence of divisional planes during tunneling work ?

18. Explain in detail treatment to be given to a dyke and fracture crossing dam alignment.

❑❑❑

www.ingramcontent.com/pod-product-compliance
Lightning Source LLC
Chambersburg PA
CBHW080423230426
43662CB00015B/2193